Lion
of the South

General Thomas C. Hindman

The publication of this book
is made possible through a generous grant from
the Watson-Brown Foundation, Inc.,
Thomson, Georgia.

Lion
of the South
General Thomas C. Hindman

Diane Neal

Thomas W. Kremm

Mercer University Press
Macon, Georgia
1993

ISBN 0-86554-556-1
MUP/ P165

Lion of the South: General Thomas C. Hindman
by Dianne Neal and Thomas Kremm

© 1997 (paperback edition)
Originally published 1993 (hardback edition)

Mercer University Press
6316 Peake Road
Macon, Georgia 31210-3960

The paper used in this publication meets the minimum requirements
of American National Standard for Information Sciences—
Permanence of Paper for Printed Library Materials,
ANSI Z39.48–1984.

Library of Congress Cataloging-in-Publication Data

Neal, Diane.
Lion of the south: General Thomas C. Hindman / Diane Neal,
Thomas W. Kremm.
xii + 319 pp. 6x9" (15x23 cm.)
ISBN 0-86554-556-1
1. Hindman, Thomas Carmichael, 1826–1868. 2. Generals—Confederate
States of America—Biography. 3. Confederate States of America—
Biography. 4. Arkansas—History—Civil War, 1861–1865. I. Kremm,
Thomas W. II. Title.
E467.1.H565P47 1993
973.7' 092—dc20   93–9917
                                                            CIP

Contents

[Editor's Note: In light of the method of documentation used by the authors and to maintain the flow of the narrative, all notes are presented at the end rather than as footnotes.]

Preface

A man of action, determination, and decisiveness who possessed personal and physical courage, Thomas C. Hindman was hot-tempered, bold, and totally committed to triumphing over his enemies. A resident of Mississippi prior to moving to Arkansas, he entered politics at the height of the debate over the Compromise of 1850. Convinced that the agreement had left the South with nothing tangible and that abolitionists would not abide by terms of the Fugitive Slave Law, he became an uncompromising advocate of Southern state rights and defender of the peculiar institution.

Arriving in Arkansas in 1854, he burst on the scene like a whirlwind and became the pivotal political figure in the state. Beginning in 1855, he successively rescued the Democratic Party from the threat of Know Nothingism and wrought a revolution by destroying the organization that had dominated Arkansas politics since the territorial period. As a fire-eating member of Congress, he championed immediate secession if the South did not receive guarantees that slavery would be protected where it existed and be permitted to expand into territories acquired as a result of the Mexican War. His role in the 1859 fight to elect a Speaker of the House acceptable to state rights Southerners and his speech on Hinton Rowan Helper's *The Impending Crisis of the South* made him a national figure. Although most Arkansans favored a wait-and-see approach after Abraham Lincoln's election to the presidency, Hindman undertook a vigorous campaign for Arkansas to withdraw from the Union after the secession of South Carolina. Once Arkansas joined the Confederacy, he raised a regiment at his own expense and, although not a member of the secession convention, drafted the ordinance that established a state military board.

He rapidly advanced from colonel to major general and served as Commander of the Trans-Mississippi District from 31 May to 20 August 1862. As the most able Confederate commander to serve in the Trans-Mississippi, stepping into a vacuum of leadership, he transformed Arkansas from a state stripped of soldiers and without weapons, ammunition, and other needed items into an armed camp capable of supplying many of its own needs. He raised an army of 18,000 effective infantrymen where none had existed when he arrived, stimulated home manufacturing, employed guerrillas to operate behind enemy lines, made the cavalry useful rather than ornamental, and—at least temporarily—saved the Arkansas Valley from capture by Union forces.

Recognizing that the magnitude of the war and conditions in Arkansas required extraordinary measures, Hindman broke down any obstacles in his path. As commander of the Trans-Mississippi District, he instituted martial law, rigidly enforced conscription, and established price controls. The end result of his bold actions was a howl of protest and the assignment of Theophilus Holmes to supersede him.

Undaunted and as committed as ever to the Southern cause, Hindman convinced Holmes to preserve many of his policies and to let him launch an offensive against Union forces in northern Arkansas. The result was a stalemate at Prairie Grove and Hindman's ultimate transfer to a new command east of the Mississippi River. He subsequently fought at Chickamauga, where he received a neck wound, and participated in the Atlanta campaign until he was thrown from his horse and severely injured.

When the war ended, rather than surrender, Hindman went to Mexico, where he remained until just before the collapse of the government of Maximillian. Unpardoned and disfranchised, he returned to Arkansas in the spring of 1867 and soon became the leader of the "Young Democracy," which although opposed to the Republican Party was willing to accept the first Reconstruction Act as the basis for restoration of the Union. In September 1868, still unable to vote and hold office and under an indictment for treason, Hindman seemed to be on the verge of building a biracial political organization capable of competing with the Republican Party. Whether he would have succeeded is uncertain. On 27 September 1868, an unknown assassin shot him as he sat quietly in his living room.

Diane Neal
Thomas W. Kremm

Acknowledgments

In completing this study, we incurred many scholarly debts. Mrs. Lewis Powell and Debbie King of the Phillips County Museum provided access to the Hindman Family Collection. Sarah Doxey Tate, T. C. Hindman's great niece, supplied genealogical information. We owe special thanks to R. P. Baker of the Arkansas History Commission and Andrea Cantrell of the University of Arkansas Libraries.

We extend thanks to librarians and archivists at the following institutions: Chicago Historical Society; William R. Perkins Library of Duke University; Robert W. Woodruff Library of Emory University; Houghton Library of Harvard University; Huntington Library; Illinois State Historical Library; Mississippi Department of Archives and History; National Archives; Oklahoma Historical Society; Prairie Grove Battlefield State Park; Ripley, Mississippi, Public Library; Virginia Historical Society; Virginia State Library and Archives; and Western Reserve Historical Society.

Mary Sweeney of the Oklahoma Department of Libraries and Doylene Manning of the University of Central Oklahoma Library obtained endless rolls of newspapers on interlibrary loan. Pam Belote and James C. Ashby drew most of the maps. Ivey S. Gladin provided photographs of Hindman family members, and John Osburn photographed the battlefield maps. Finally, we extend our gratitude to Publisher Cecil Staton and Managing Editor Scott Nash of the Mercer University Press. Dr. Nash's copy editing greatly improved the manuscript.

List of Illustrations

CHAPTER 1

THE MAKING OF A SOUTHERN FIRE-EATER

On the evening of 27 September 1868, Thomas C. Hindman sat quietly reading a newspaper and smoking his pipe in the sitting room of his Helena, Arkansas, home. Suddenly, without warning, muskets shots rang out striking him in the jaw, throat, and hands. Blood spewed forth from the wounds as he gasped for breath. Death followed eight hours later bringing to an abrupt end the life of Arkansas' highest ranking Confederate military officer and one of the most notable and controversial politicians of his day.[1]

Thomas Carmichael Hindman, Jr. was born 28 January 1828 in Knoxville, Tennessee, into a family with a proud heritage of notable English and Scottish ancestors. His maternal lineage boasted of Major Robert Holt, a wealthy planter and a 1655 member of the Virginia House of Burgesses. The Holts lived in Halifax County, Virginia, before responding to the beckoning call of the West that led them to Knoxville. His paternal lineage was also distinguished. In Scotland, his Carmichael ancestors had allied themselves with the ill-starred course of Bonnie Prince Charles and fought in the disastrous battle of Culloden on 16 April 1746. After the well equipped forces of George II routed Charles's half-starved Scottish followers, the Crown banished nine hundred survivors to America and the West Indies. Descended from those Scottish exiles, Sarah Carmichael married Samuel Hindman, a prosperous Pennsylvania merchant, and in the early 1790s they moved to Knoxville, Tennessee, where their youngest son Thomas C. Hindman, Sr. was born on 10 November 1793. According to family legend, he was the first white male child born in Knoxville.[2]

During the War of 1812, Thomas C. Hindman, Sr. entered the Thirty-Ninth United States Infantry on 29 July 1813 as an ensign. The young Tennessean was successively promoted to third lieutenant (11 January 1814) and second lieutenant (20 May 1814). During the war, he served as regimental adjutant and fought in the Battle of New Orleans. He remained on active duty until 30 June 1816 when he resigned because of ill health.[3]

After leaving the army, he operated a military ferry on the Tennessee River in the Alabama Territory and served as a lieutenant colonel in the Tenth Territorial Militia Regiment. Hindman also established himself as a prosperous merchant licensed to trade with the Cherokee Indians along the Tennessee, Alabama, and Georgia border. These business dealings brought him into frequent contact with Lewis Ross, brother of John Ross who was elected chief of the Cherokee Nation in 1828. A close personal friendship quickly developed, and he became a regular visitor to the home of Lewis and Fanny Ross. As a result of his relationship with the Ross family, Hindman met Fanny's sister Sallie Holt, and after a brief courtship they were married in Knoxville on 21 January 1819.[4]

Following their marriage, the Hindmans settled in Rhea County, Tennessee, where their first daughter Frances was born in 1820. Three other children, Robert (1822), Mary (1823), and Sarah (1826) were born after the family moved to nearby Post Oak Springs. In 1827 the Hindmans returned to Knoxville where their last two children, Thomas Jr. (1828) and Mildred (1829) were born.[5]

While living in Tennessee, the elder Hindman made frequent business trips to Alabama. Impressed by the economic opportunities there, in 1831 he bought several lots in Jacksonville, a new settlement in the Cherokee lands, and announced to his family that they were moving. He immediately sold his Tennessee holdings and chartered a flatboat to transport the entire household down the Tennessee River. During the journey down river, three-year old Tom and two-year old Mildred played among the barrels of dried fruit, apple butter, marmalade, and other supplies. Traveling from Fort Gibson on the river to Jacksonville by wagon, the Hindmans camped out under the stars, which the children considered a grand adventure. The family's new home was a spacious and comfortably furnished log house. As a successful businessman, Tom Hindman was able to provide his wife and children with much more than necessities. Although perhaps somewhat of an exaggeration, Mildred later recalled that her father spared neither time nor money in indulging his family. "Everything Mother and the family wanted, we got."[6]

As a merchant, Hindman acquired a reputation for honesty and integrity among his Cherokee neighbors and associates. His testimony against "intruder[s]" selling goods without licenses and those who attempted to seize the property of widows or harm individuals in the Cherokee Nation won him approbation as a true friend of the Indian people. In recognition of his forthright business dealings and friendship, the Rosses petitioned President James Monroe to name Hindman sub-agent to the Cherokees and later urged President Andrew Jackson to appoint him to the post of United States Agent for the Cherokee Nation. His conscientious performance of his duties in these capacities earned him the continued confidence of the Cherokees.[7]

When the federal government began the wholesale forced removal of the Cherokees to the newly established Indian Territory west of the Mississippi River, Hindman was appointed quartermaster and personally accompanied them on the infamous Trail of Tears inspecting wagons, distributing supplies, and selecting campsites.[8]

Following the forced migration of the main body of Cherokees, Hindman continued to represent their interests and frequently traveled to Washington, D. C. to discuss questions relating to various treaty obligations. As a close associate and a relative of Lewis and John Ross, in 1841 Hindman was designated by Acting Secretary of War Albert M. Lea to ascertain why Cherokees in North Carolina had spurned the brothers' suggestion to join the majority of the tribe in the Indian Territory. As the government's emissary, Hindman spent two months unsuccessfully trying to persuade the eastern Cherokees to "rejoin the nation in the West."[9]

Hindman's work with the Cherokees, especially during the removal, required much travel. Since Jacksonville offered few educational opportunities, he sent all of his children away to school except Mildred, who persuaded her parents to let her attend schools locally. Young Tom was sent to New York where his Ross relatives were staying until their new home in Indian Territory was finished and later followed his older cousins John and Robert Ross to the Lawrenceville Classical Institute near Princeton, New Jersey.[10]

Following the failure of his mission to the North Carolina Cherokees, Hindman returned to Alabama in 1842 to finalize plans for moving to the northern Mississippi town of Ripley, where he had purchased a large cotton plantation the previous December. After overseeing the building of a ten room, two story house, he returned to Jacksonville to supervise the family's two hundred and fifty mile trip by wagon train. Away at school in New Jersey, Tom missed the fun of camping out and helping drive the wagons, as well as the excitement of moving into the new house.[11]

In keeping with the Southern tradition of the time, the elder Hindman planned to train his older son Robert to take over the family land holdings and to groom his younger son Tom for a career in one of the professions. The Lawrenceville Classical Institute seemed an ideal choice for Tom. Incorporated in 1808 (classes began in 1810), Lawrenceville was the oldest boarding school in New Jersey and the third oldest in the country. Only Andover (1778) and Exeter (1783) predated it. Under the leadership of Dr. Samuel Hamill, the institute enjoyed a national reputation and drew students from every part of the United States and a few foreign countries. Approximately fifty students attended Lawrenceville during Tom Hindman's tenure.[12]

Designed to prepare young men for college, the school emphasized classical languages, history, mathematics, and English grammar. The regimen was hard as boys crowded into classrooms to "learn by heart" the old-fashioned Latin and Greek grammars and mathematical formulas. As devout Presbyterians, Samuel Hamill and his brother Hugh placed almost as much emphasis on devotional activities as on studies. All students were required to attend prayer meetings "just after rising and again before retiring" and to recite a different verse of scripture each morning after breakfast. Hymn sings, followed by religious lectures, occurred two evenings per week, and on Sunday mornings, the "neat, clean, and somber-suited" boys marched two abreast down Lawrenceville's main street to the Presbyterian church. Sunday afternoon and evening Bible classes and religious lectures were theoretically optional, but students who chose not to attend were required to "read religious books" in the chapel.[13]

Boys at Lawrenceville led strictly regimented lives. The first bell awakened them at six o'clock in summer and at seven in the winter. Once dressed, they went outside to the pump room to wash their faces and brush their teeth before reporting to the dining hall for breakfast and prayers. If luck had been with young Tom, he might have lived in the one heated dormitory. Otherwise, he would have found himself in the second or third dormitory; both were unheated but not "uncomfortable."[14]

When he first arrived at Lawrenceville, Tom probably found himself the victim of hazing by older boys. Even well into the 1880s, older students took the new arrivals to a spot near the "old pond" called the "hazing place" and made them run a gauntlet while being kicked, hit with clubs, and shoved against trees. New arrivals quickly learned that they must become aggressive and learn to defend themselves in order to adapt to their surroundings.[15]

Despite hazing and the rigorous regimen of studies and piety, most students considered Lawrenceville "a happy place." In the summer months, Tom and the other boys enjoyed boating, fishing, swimming, and picnicking with girls from the nearby Lawrenceville Female Seminary. Winter brought ice skating, sleighing, and snowball fights. Other extracurricular activities included a Bible Society founded in 1822 and a temperance society formed a decade later with nearly all boys in the school listed as members.[16]

Like many preparatory schools, Lawrenceville placed great emphasis on oratory and debate. Debates were held on alternate Saturday mornings with the entire student body taking part. Students read aloud their written presentations and followed these with extemporaneous oral discussions that often became quite "animated." After he entered politics in the 1850's and emerged as a powerful orator who could almost mesmerize audiences, Tom Hindman must have fondly recalled the debating experience gained at Lawrenceville.[17]

As a rule, formal debates usually focused on philosophical topics such as the impact of wealth and knowledge on human events. Potentially divisive contemporary issues such as the abolitionist crusade against slavery were down-played since the Hamills wanted to keep enrollment "at capacity." A boycott by Southern families, as school historian S. R. Slaymaker pointed out, "would not have done at all." Still, social and political controversies of the day could not be ignored, and James Falconer of New York City later recalled "fearful fights" that involved "hot headed southern boys" and other students.[18]

After four years of diligence and hard work, on 25 September 1843 Tom Hindman graduated with high honors. As class salutatorian, he was singled out for special recognition and delivered an address entitled "The Ruins of Time." Following a brief period of visiting with relatives and studying in New York, Tom joined his family in Ripley where he began reading law under the tutelage of Orlando Davis, a highly acclaimed local attorney and Whig politician.[19]

Although the Hindmans had lived in Ripley only a short time, they had already come to enjoy the lively society it offered. All of them loved

Plate 1.1   *T. C. Hindman I*
Courtesy: Walter J. Lemke Papers, Special Collections Department,
University of Arkansas Libraries

Plate 1.2   *Sallie Holt Hindman*
Courtesy: Walter J. Lemke Papers, Special Collections Department,
University of Arkansas Libraries

dancing and regularly attended parties. On his last trip to Washington for the Cherokees, the elder Hindman stopped in Philadelphia where he purchased rich carpets, cut glass, and china for the house and elaborate dresses and shawls for his wife and daughters. He kept a fine carriage and horses. When Sallie Hindman chided her husband for extravagance, he replied, "I have plenty. I want my family to use it." The world of lavish entertaining and abundant hospitality must have seemed strange to Tom in comparison with the rigorous conditions that had prevailed at Lawrenceville.[20]

When he returned home, Tom found his father an active participant in Mississippi politics. A staunch proponent of internal improvements and other issues of significance to the West, Tom Hindman, Sr. enthusiastically championed the Whig Party. In 1844 he served as a member of the executive committee of the local Henry Clay club. The following year, his interest in internal improvements led to his selection as a delegate to the Memphis meeting of the Southwestern convention that had assembled to promote various transportation projects for the South and West.[21]

Not long after Tom arrived home and began studying law, the Mexican War began. To him, the conflict offered an opportunity to gain military laurels and punish a country he believed had transgressed against the United States. The young, prosperous planter's son, caught up in the war hysteria, had no way of knowing that the conflict would ultimately shatter the fragile Whig Party of his father and tear Mississippi's political structure asunder.

Prior to the outbreak of hostilities, Mississippians had supported the United States' attempts to purchase California and New Mexico and to secure recognition of the Rio Grande as the southern boundary of Texas. When negotiations collapsed in early 1846, an editorial in the Jackson *Mississippian* called for a "strong army . . . to thrash Mexico at once" and predicted that volunteer companies would spring up all over the state to render service against an enemy that had greeted "overtures for peace with renewed insult."[22]

On 13 May 1846, following a skirmish between Mexican forces and General Zachary Taylor's troops along the Rio Grande, Congress approved a declaration of war against Mexico and President James K. Polk called upon the states to furnish 50,000 volunteers to supplement the regular army. Mississippians welcomed the announcement, and newspaper editors across the state summoned residents to action. "To arms! To arms! Ye brave! Th' avenging sword unsheathe: March on, march on, all hearts resolved, on [to] victory or death," proclaimed the Holly Springs *Guard*. According to the editor, "any other course than the invasion of Mexico and a consequent honorable peace at the point of the bayonet" was "ridiculous." The Yazoo *Democrat* exhorted Mississippians to heed "the voice of humanity" and to "RALLY TO THE RESCUE" of the country. Caught up in the frenzy and euphoria, men from the Magnolia State rushed to answer the president's call for their services.[23]

Volunteer companies immediately began springing up and drilling on the streets of Mississippi towns. Convinced that the state would be allotted at least two regiments, Governor Albert G. Brown conditionally accepted twenty-eight infantry companies and began organizing a cavalry regiment. When the state's requisition for troops arrived on 29 May, Mississippi's quota was "one regiment of Infantry or Riflemen." Brown immediately issued a call for one regiment that would consist of the first ten companies to arrive at Vicksburg.[24]

When news of the requisition reached northern Mississippi units such as the Tippah Guards, they howled in protest since the state's quota would be filled by troops near the rendezvous site. Indeed, two Vicksburg units--the Southrons and the Volunteers—were accepted, while hundreds of bitterly resentful would-be soldiers chafed at what they perceived to be blatant discrimination.[25]

The units that made it into the First Mississippi Rifles won acclaim for their gallantry. Future governor John Quitman, who was appointed brigadier general of the Mississippi volunteers, fought in the Battle of Monterey and was later promoted to major general in the regular army. In the attack on Mexico City, his troops stormed the Belen gate and planted the first United States flag in the Mexican capital. Fame also came to Colonel Jefferson Davis, the young congressman whose troops held off a superior enemy force at Buena Vista on 22 and 23 February 1847 until American reinforcements arrived.[26]

A number of states, including Massachusetts, Connecticut, and Rhode Island—fearing that successful prosecution of the war would aid in expanding slavery—failed to fill their quotas. Totally committed to the war and still fuming over Mississippi's allotment of only one regiment, Governor Brown wrote to Secretary of War William L. Marcy and offered to fill the quotas of delinquent states. Unlike states that had balked at providing their share of soldiers, Mississippi would do whatever it could to advance the prosecution of the war.[27]

In need of additional troops, President Polk issued a second call to the states in November of 1846. Declaring his sympathy with "the patriotic soldiers who were disappointed" at being denied service in the first regiment, an elated Brown immediately called upon "the martial spirit of the freemen of Mississippi" to respond to Polk's request. Many who had been turned away when the first call was oversubscribed again rushed to offer their services to the government. For Thomas Hindman, Jr. the second call seemed a godsend. On 7 December 1846, he enlisted as a second lieutenant in company E of the Second Mississippi Infantry (Rifles). Older brother Robert joined the same unit as a private and was promoted to sergeant prior to his later discharge for a medical disability.[28]

Although the men of the Second Mississippi longed to share the glory of Buena Vista, the charge at Monterey, and the march into the Mexican capital, the triumphant excitement of battle eluded them. Adversity beset them from the beginning. Before leaving for Mexico, the regiment assembled at Camp McClung, three miles north of Vicksburg, for organization and drill. Early January 1847 was unseasonably warm, and many of the men left home without appropriate heavy attire, expecting to purchase it if necessary with their clothing allowances. Scarcely had the troops mustered when high winds and hail shredded tents and heavy rains deluged the camp covering it with mud and water. Tom Hindman and his comrades huddled in wet blankets and cold "comfortless" tents and over "smoking fires," feeling "as if the very marrow of their bones had congealed." Unprepared for the wintry blast, many soldiers fell victim to influenza, pneumonia, and "the cold plague."[29]

Still suffering the ill effects of life at Camp McClung, in late January they embarked upon steamboats for New Orleans. If they expected better weather, they were disappointed. When they reached the Crescent City, heavy rains and "blasts of cold wintry winds" greeted them. Despite the driving rain and wind, army officials refused to permit the Second Mississippi and a Pennsylvania regiment to use camp barracks reserved for the regular army, leaving them to camp in tents on the old battle ground, which quickly became saturated. Initially, even the sick were left to suffer in tents on the submerged ground. As a result, many soldiers died before the government finally provided a "cheerless building" with straw couches for use as a hospital. When the regiment departed New

Orleans, it left behind eighty men who never recovered sufficiently to rejoin their unit. Outraged at the treatment of the Second Mississippi, the Vicksburg *Sentinel* angrily lashed out at the federal government. Mississippians had been "thrust out like beasts, without clothing and denied the shelter they saw others enjoying, put to wallow in the mire and exposed to the bitter elements which they felt every moment destroying their lives."[30]

The long tedious voyage to the seat of war claimed the lives of twenty-eight more men. The dampness from still wet blankets and tents formed droplets of condensation on the ceilings of the cramped quarters, and seasickness produced an intolerable "effluvia."[31]

Still, as Colonel Reuben Davis later recalled, military glory would have been a "balm for every woe, and an answer to each detractor." However, no opportunities for glory presented themselves. The Second Mississippi reached Matamoras at the mouth of the Rio Grande on 24 February—one day after the battle of Buena Vista—and then marched for three days virtually without water for the troops and horses. At Monterey more sickness followed, and by June 167 men had died, 134 had been discharged, and 38 had deserted. Although the men who remained were "eager for a fight," their hopes "melted away with dew before the morning sun." As General Winfield Scott moved towards Mexico City, the Second Mississippi was shifted to Saltillo and from there to Buena Vista for guard duty. Captain William Barksdale wrote that the men of the regiment were "complaining dreadfully" of their "hard fate" and feared that they would have to "remain in [that] position during the whole war." It was indeed, he remarked, a "melancholy fate . . . which [he hoped would be] averted." Barksdale's fears were well founded. Except for "an occasional alarm, there was no experience of war."[32]

Confined to the role of occupation troops, the Second Mississippi watched helplessly as its ranks were decimated by small pox and diarrhea. Unlike his brother Robert, whose illness resulted in a medical discharge on 23 April 1847, Tom Hindman was able to escape the ravages of weather and disease. The laurels of a conquering soldier, however, eluded him. Except for participating in a few raids to pursue "guerillosos" when the regiment was encamped at Monterey, he remained on boring garrison duty. Taking advantage of Hindman's educational background and fine penmanship, Colonel Charles Clark assigned him to the position of acting adjutant of a detachment at Mazafil on 25 March

Plate 1.3   *Thomas C. Hindman and Robert Hindman (1843)*
Courtesy: Ivey S. Gladin, Photographer, Helena, Arkansas

1848. Evidently, he performed satisfactorily for he was made Post Adjutant on 26 April and served in that capacity through May when the war ended. Although Hindman and the other members of the Second Mississippi had not "lacked courage," the chance for glory bypassed them. Still, their friends and family at home regarded them as heroes, and accordingly, residents of Wilkinson County staged a barbecue at Fort Adams on 3 August to celebrate their homecoming.[33]

After returning to Ripley, Thomas Hindman resumed studying law under Orlando Davis and was admitted to the bar in 1851. This triumph, however, was marred by a tragedy that had occurred two years earlier. In May 1849 a quarrel erupted between Robert Hindman and William Falkner, whom Robert mistakenly believed had tried to block his membership in the Ripley Sons of Temperance. In the fight that ensued, Falkner fatally stabbed Robert after Robert's gun failed to fire. Falkner was tried for murder but was acquitted when the jury ruled that he had acted in self defense. Subsequently, Falkner killed Erasmus V. Morris, a friend of the Hindman family. He was again tried for murder and acquitted. These two homicides culminated in a gun fight between Tom Hindman and Falkner in which neither was hurt. Violence almost erupted a short time later in the form of a duel. They averted bloodshed, however, and effected a reconciliation, thanks to the efforts of Matthew C. Galloway, future editor of the Memphis *Appeal*.[34]

Although Robert Hindman's application to join the Sons of Temperance had ultimately led to his violent death, the tragedy did not deter his younger brother from affiliating with the society. Long interested in the temperance cause from his days at Lawrenceville, Tom Hindman became an active member of the Ripley chapter in the early 1850s. He faithfully attended the weekly meetings on Saturday afternoon and in 1852 became the "recording scribe." Almost every meeting found him recommending prospective members, bringing charges against existing members for violating their pledges not to buy or drink intoxicating beverages, or giving reports on the society's finances. He industriously promoted the interests of the organization and encouraged members to approve an increase in dues to finance completion of a meeting hall.[35]

Hindman urged members to write essays on temperance to be read at the meetings and solicited everyone's participation in a special procession scheduled for 4 November 1852 to promote temperance reform in Ripley. Equally enthusiastically, he recommended that the local chapter contribute thirty dollars towards the hiring of a Grand Lecturer to canvass Mississippi for the cause. Hindman also hoped to involve the Sons of Temperance in the local Christmas celebration in 1852. As a member of the special committee on arrangements, he helped organize a "procession of transparencies at night and an address" at the Presbyterian church. For the occasion, he composed a song for the society's choir:

> They who fill the mad'ning bowl,—
> Feed on tear-washed fruits of toil,—
> Mock at hapless orphans' wail
> And widows' misery. . . .
> Sons of Temperance! Let's unite
> 'Ainst the wrong and for the right;
> Dauntless, let us wage the fight
> And battle ceaselessly![36]

Hindman remained active in the Sons of Temperance through the fall of 1853 when he was often absent campaigning for a seat in the legislature. Even while the General Assembly was in session, he attended meetings whenever possible and paid his dues to the organization. On 18 March 1854, he resigned his membership prior to moving to Arkansas.[37]

Temperance and the law by no means absorbed all of Tom Hindman's energies. The turbulent world of politics presented an exhilarating challenge. In August 1846, Pennsylvania Democrat David Wilmot had attached a rider to a Mexican War appropriations bill that would have outlawed slavery in any territory acquired as a result of the conflict. Known as the Wilmot Proviso, the measure was never enacted into law. Nevertheless, it brought the issue of slavery extension to the forefront of the political scene. Northern proponents of the proviso, known as free soilers, did manage to obtain endorsements from a number of state legislatures. They also demanded that slavery be prohibited in the District of Columbia. Alarmed by the threat to the peculiar institution, a number of Southerners responded quickly.

Reaction to the proviso and the activities of free soilers was intense in Mississippi. In October 1849, opponents of the proviso met in Jackson and adopted resolutions maintaining that Congress had no constitutional authority to outlaw slavery in the territories or the District of Columbia or to obstruct the interstate slave trade. They would regard passage of the

Wilmot Proviso "as an unjust and insulting discrimination" to which slaveholding states could not "submit." The delegates established a state association and called upon the state legislature to summon a special convention if Congress passed the proviso or abolished slavery in the nation's capital.[38]

When Congress began debating the admission of California as a free state and other measures that were eventually consolidated into the omnibus Compromise of 1850, it rocked the political system in Mississippi to its foundation. During Congressional debates on the Compromise proposals, Mississippi's United States senators found themselves at opposite ends of the spectrum. Fresh from his triumph at Buena Vista, Jefferson Davis had been elected to the Senate in January 1848, where he quickly emerged as a strong champion of Southern rights and slavery. Believing that the South's growing population needed room to expand, Davis opposed any attempt to exclude the peculiar institution from territories acquired as the result of the war with Mexico. Admitting California as a free state would permanently destroy the political balance of power between North and South and could ultimately force the slave states to decide if they must use force to secure their rights. Like the admission of California as a free state, organizing the remainder of the Mexican territory according to popular sovereignty was an anathema to Davis. He vehemently argued that Congress had no right to discriminate between different types of property in the territories and denied that a territory composed of "first-comers" had the right to exclude slavery. Moreover, he protested against measures that would prevent Southern soldiers who had served in the Mexican War from settling with their slaves in the territories that had been "acquired by common blood and common treasure."[39]

Mississippi's senior senator Henry S. Foote, a little man with a "big voice and a combative nature," represented the opposite viewpoint. After initially opposing any compromise, he changed his mind and worked zealously for its passage. Regarding the Compromise of 1850 as "necessary to save the Union," Foote defied the Mississippi legislature's instructions to its United States senators to resist the "false and unjust" admission of California as a free state "by all honorable and constitutional means." Later, he bragged that the compromise was based upon bills that he had introduced.[40]

The Congressional debate spilled over into the Mississippi political arena in the fall of 1851 and soon enveloped Thomas Hindman. Both Davis and Foote undertook a state-wide canvass to influence the selection of delegates to a state convention scheduled to meet in November to decide whether or not to accept the Compromise. Fresh from his triumph in Mexico and a successful gubernatorial campaign, John Quitman emerged as the leader of the State Rights Democrats. His zeal for expanding Southern slave territory seemed to know no bounds. He had recently been indicted for violating United States neutrality laws by supporting filibustering expeditions to Cuba aimed at acquiring that island for the United States. With charges pending against him, on 3 February 1851, Quitman resigned the governor's office in order to answer the indictment. In the fall elections, however, he again sought the post as the candidate of the State Rights faction of the Democratic Party. The race pitted the uncompromising proslavery Quitman against Foote, the candidate of Union Democrats and Whigs. The September election for delegates to the state convention resulted in a Unionist triumph over the State Righters by a margin of 28,402 to 21,242. Regarding the election as an indication that Mississippi was "content with the LATE AGGRESSIVE MEASURES of Congress" and realizing that his gubernatorial chances were nil, Quitman withdrew from the race and was replaced by Davis.[41]

Mississippi was ablaze with emotion during the election. Foote vigorously defended his support of the Compromise and sought to portray his opponent as a "disunionist." Davis countered by stressing his opposition to the Compromise, which he characterized as submission to the demands of free soilers and abolitionists. To his side, Davis rallied a number of young, aspiring politicians, as well as established leaders of the State Rights party.[42]

Among the new faces in politics were Lucius Q. C. Lamar, and Thomas C. Hindman, Jr. The twenty-three year old Hindman enthusiastically plunged into the campaign, serving as a delegate to the Tippah County Democratic convention and the Mississippi Democratic Southern States Rights Convention. As a delegate to the Southern States Rights gathering, he supported a platform that affirmed a "cherished attachment to the Union." The attachment, however, carried with it a demand that the Union not become "an engine of oppression." Under the Constitution, slavery was purely a state matter and Congress had no power to interfere with it "directly or indirectly." The platform "strong[ly] and unequivocal[ly]" condemned the Compromise of 1850 and upheld "the right of a State peaceably to withdraw from the Union, without denial or obstruction from any quarter." "Under existing circumstances," Mississippi's withdrawal from the Union would be "inexpedient" and was not favored by the convention. However, secession was an "essential" right that states could use as "a last remedy" to protect their rights.[43]

Although he initially favored Quitman, Hindman transferred his support to Davis when Quitman withdrew from the race. Full of energy and ardor for state rights, he canvassed northern Mississippi, delivering rousing speeches on Davis's behalf. Foote smarted from Hindman's blistering attacks, which led him years later to brand the young orator as "a most noisy and unscrupulous advocate of Jefferson Davis and secession." In the balloting following the close of the canvass, Foote defeated Davis by less than a thousand votes. Although the Union ticket had emerged victorious, the results clearly indicated that protection of slavery and state rights were uppermost in the minds of almost half of the Mississippi electorate.[44]

Foote's triumph and that of Mississippi's Union Democrats and Whigs were short-lived. Alarmed by events in Congress and the growth of abolitionism in the North, more and more Mississippians embraced Southern rights. In the 1853 election, John J. McRae, a State Rights Democrat, was elected governor. In the same election, Tippah County voters chose Thomas C. Hindman, Jr. to represent them in the state House of Representatives. Rather than wait for McRae to be sworn into office, Foote resigned from the governorship five days before the expiration of his term. Recognizing that the climate of opinion had swung more sharply towards Southern rights and that he had little chance of regaining a seat in the United States Senate, Foote announced that he was withdrawing his name from consideration.[45]

As a first term legislator, Hindman eagerly entered the legislative frays over various reform issues amidst the sectional turmoil still swirling in the aftermath of the Compromise of 1850. Although sessions often did not adjourn until late in the evening, he requested no leaves of absence and on only one occasion did he have to be summoned by the sergeant-at-arms for roll call. As a lawyer, he welcomed appointment to the judiciary committee and used his position to promote judicial efficiency and the interests of his hometown. He served on a special committee assigned to report "a bill to establish a vice chancery court at Aberdeen and Ripley" and was acting chair when the House voted fifty-seven to eighteen to accept the committee's report to establish an inferior chancery court in every county of the state. He also voted with the majority in approving a bill to provide for updating of the Mississippi code of laws.[46]

Education, tax reform, and internal improvements also interested Hindman. He introduced a motion to instruct the committee on education "to inquire into the expediency of adopting a new and more efficient common school system." Another of his motions requested that the Ways and Means committee examine the existing laws in relation to lands "forfeited for taxes."[47]

Cognizant of the close relationship between economic growth and railroad construction, Hindman worked to promote railroads in Mississippi. He was aware that the zeal that accompanied railroad building in the 1850s, however, often led to lack of oversight on the part of state governments in insuring that the railways complied with bond requirements in their charters. Hence, he moved that the House Committee on Internal Improvements report on whether the Southern Railroad had posted bond within the specified time period. He also requested an inquiry as to whether the railroad had faithfully adhered to Congressional regulations requiring it to pass through the town of Brandon, southeast of Jackson. His initial motion was tabled by a vote of thirty-five to fifteen. At the third reading of the bill incorporating the Southern Railroad, he again unsuccessfully tried to amend it to include a report on compliance with the Congressional mandate for the route to go through Brandon.[48]

Representing the interests of his constituents, he co-sponsored a bill originating in the Senate that was designed to regulate the procedures for "selecting and empaneling" grand jurors in Tippah and other counties. As a newcomer to the House, Hindman must have been pleased when he was appointed chair of the special committee in charge of the inauguration ceremonies for Governor John J. McRae.[49]

The session gave Hindman the opportunity to involve himself in a matter that was both personal and political. When nominations were made for the position of superintendent of the penitentiary, his father was among those suggested. The elder Hindman remained in contention through six ballotings. At the start of the seventh, he withdrew and E. P. Russell of Hinds County was elected.[50]

While other matters received careful attention, the greatest excitement pervaded discussions and votes on questions relating to sectional politics.

The previous antagonisms of the early 1850s flared up on numerous occasions. For example, even though Henry S. Foote had removed himself from competition for the vacant United States Senate seat, he still received twenty-two votes on 5 January when Albert Gallatin Brown, a State Rights Democrat, was elected to the post by seventy-six votes (including Hindman's).[51]

When the legislature convened, rather than issuing a customary address, Foote used the opportunity to justify his support for the Compromise of 1850 and subsequent political actions. He was neither "an enemy of *State Rights*" nor "an opponent of the Virginia Resolutions of 1798." He was "a National Democrat of the faith of Jefferson and Madison and Jackson; true to the Constitution . . . and true to the *Compromise and the Union.*" The Compromise of 1850, "as all sensible men" knew, "*saved the Union.*" Jefferson Davis had run for governor "at the instance of a small squad of ultra secession admirers." Subsequent events clearly indicated "the *wisdom*, the *justice*, and the *constitutionality* of the Compromise enactments, . . . once so much ridiculed and scoffed at by the shallow pretenders of the hour."[52]

The measures adopted in 1850 had become popular and were "now generally acquiesced in throughout" Mississippi. The Fugitive Slave Law was being promptly and efficiently enforced and the admission of California "far from being injurious to the South" had "been greatly beneficial," especially in providing votes in Congress "against Abolition and Free Soil." It was "wonderful that the people of the South" were "altogether satisfied with the Compromise, and resolved to adhere to it, firmly and faithfully," in spite of "the meddlings of designing Demagogues and Factionists."[53] Foote's message outraged the majority of senators and representatives, who ordered the document printed with a disclaimer that repudiated "the accuracy of" both its "conclusions and averments" that attempted to "define the motives and positions of parties and of distinguished and patriotic citizens." On a related question, Hindman voted with the majority (49 to 32) to table an amendment that asserted that the resolutions passed by the 1850 legislature censuring Foote for his support of the Compromise were "premature, uncalled for and undeserved." He also voted with the majority (50 to 30) to table an amendment declaring that the Compromise measures were "constitutional, and never afforded any ground for forcible resistance or secession on the part of any state."[54]

The legislative votes on Foote's course during the Compromise crisis indicated that sentiment in Mississippi favored a strong stand in support of state rights. Like the editor of the Yazoo *Democrat*, Hindman and many other Mississippians believed the affections of a large class of Southerners had been "alienated from the Union. . . . They do not regard secession as . . . a calamity to be avoided, but as an object most desirable; not the least of two evils, but under the circumstances a positive blessing." They would abide by the Compromise of 1850 "as a permanent adjustment to the sectional controversy." But, they were adamant that they would make no further concessions to prevent slavery from expanding into the territories or to weaken it where it already existed.[55]

When the legislature adjourned in March 1854, Hindman's brief career in Mississippi politics came to an end. As a new legislator, he had conscientiously represented the views of his home county regarding internal improvements and reforms in education and taxation. More importantly for future developments, during the acrimonious battle in the state over the Compromise of 1850, he had emerged as a consistent and unwavering defender of slavery and state rights. Known for his eloquent, impassioned oratory in defense of these causes, the future looked bright for a young man with Hindman's enthusiasm and abilities.

Chapter 2

"A BRILLIANT AND GLORIOUS TRIUMPH": THE EMERGENCE OF AN ARKANSAS POLITICAL LEADER

When the Mississippi legislature adjourned in the spring of 1854, Thomas Hindman found himself in a position similar to what of his future father-in-law, Henry L. Biscoe, had occupied in 1819. Josiah Shinn described it thusly.

> His people . . . were of the most respectable kind and his education had therefore been the most liberal. His career, however, had to be made, and . . . [Mississippi in the 1850s] was crowded with well-educated, ambitious young men, who might and would win, but who would have to wait a very long time for their laurels. Elbow room is a great thing, and it is a sign of a great mind for a young man to decide that his home field is too crowded for his rapid development, and who casts aside his easier and more settled life for the greater and harder ordeal of a life in the woods.[1]

To a young man who hoped to make his mark in the world, Arkansas in the 1850s offered ideal opportunities. It was still a developing frontier with a growing population, an abundance of inexpensive fertile lands, and access to the lower South via the Mississippi River. Helena, a steamboat landing on the river, lured Tom Hindman in the spring of 1854. During the territorial period and early statehood, Helena had earned a reputation as a "sink of crime and infamy" where robbers, murderers, thieves, counterfeiters, and gamblers abounded. Anti-gambling societies and temperance organizations formed during the 1830s and 1840s, however, had drastically altered the town's image by 1850. The advent of schools, churches, and private libraries also lent respectability and the promise of active religious and educational opportunities.[2]

Phillips County, with its seat at Helena, was one of the earliest settlements in Arkansas as alluvial and western upland soils enticed farmers eager for agricultural expansion. By 1850 Phillips County was the state's third largest cotton producing area, and its agricultural wealth was exceeded only by Chicot County. The rapid economic growth saw a similar jump in population, especially in the number of slaves. Slaves outnumbered whites 8,940 to 5,931, a development that had significant political ramifications for Tom Hindman and other state rights Arkansans. Keeping pace with the county as a whole, Helena's population had climbed from a mere 250 residents in 1840 to 1551 in 1860.[3]

Despite its expansion, in the 1850s Helena was in reality little more than a village. Even so, it boasted of three newspapers: the *Southern Shield*, the *Democratic Star*, and the *State-Rights Democrat*. The town "swarmed with lawyers" attracted by the large amount of litigation over land and the usual routine of wills, mortgages, and other property related transactions. In addition, because of their familiarity with land titles, lawyers stood fortuitously to become successful speculators.[4]

As a thriving river port, Helena had the potential for even more rapid growth if transportation facilities could be improved. Navigable rivers running through and near the town gave farmers and merchants easy access to markets during normal periods of rainfall. Heavy rains brought fear of disastrous flooding, however, as well as the possibility that high waters could surround the town making it virtually inaccessible. The reverse was true when periods of drought drastically lowered river levels to the point that only shallow boats could reach the town. Many thought that if they could link up Helena with the Memphis-Little Rock Railroad, they could ameliorate these vicissitudes. The prospects for growth were almost unlimited, or so local promoters thought.[5]

To Tom Hindman, a lawyer and aspiring politician, Helena was a magnet. In addition to potential economic and political opportunities, the bustling river town provided a desirable link with his family, since steamboat and stage coach connections yielded ready access to his former home in northern Mississippi.

In June 1854, following the adjournment of the Mississippi legislature, Hindman traveled to Helena and decided it was ideal for his economic and political goals. He formed a law partnership with John Palmer, a twenty-seven year old Kentucky native, who was already known as a "distinguished member" of the Helena bar. Hindman's reputation as a political orator preceded him. Noting that he had gained prominence as a "talented and eloquent Representative" from Tippah County who had "figured prominently and creditably in the more recent exciting canvasses of our sister State," the editor of the *Democratic Star* welcomed him, predicting that his identity with Helena would not only "promote his own fortune, but those of our rising town."[6]

Hindman energetically plunged into his law practice. Recognizing that Helena was a crossroads between Tennessee and Mississippi, the advertisement for their firm declared that Palmer and Hindman would administer oaths for Tennessee and Mississippi and transact routine legal business. Conveniently, their office was opposite the courthouse.[7]

Equally enthusiastically, Hindman took an active interest in civic affairs and proposals for economic development. Independence Day 1854 festivities included a barbecue, the breaking of ground for the Arkansas Midland Railroad, and brief speeches by local notables, including Hindman who spoke on the importance of railroad development and the promotion of the Midland line.[8]

After dinner, United States Senator William K. Sebastian delivered a patriotic oration, and James L. Alcorn, a well-known Mississippi Whig, followed with an address that was distinctly partisan. In the absence of a prominent Democrat to reply, M. Butt Hewson who had heard Hindman speak in Mississippi, suggested that he respond to Alcorn. Bowing gracefully, Hindman assented, delivering remarks "so thrilling and so thrusting that the Whigs began to show a little restlessness." Encouraged by the friendly crowd, he spoke for about two hours. At the conclusion of the holiday celebration, Alcorn challenged the newcomer to Arkansas politics to continue the debate at the courthouse. Although spectators pronounced the debate a "draw," it established Hindman's reputation for political oratory in his adopted state.[9]

The debate also led Hindman into a nearly violent confrontation the following day in front of the Fadley Hotel where he resided. As a crowd of men discussed the merits of the two debaters, a local Whig lawyer, David Badham, sided with Alcorn and made provocative remarks to

Hindman, whom he addressed as "my sweet scented individual," referring to the latter's dapper personal appearance. Bystanders prevented an altercation on the spot, but Badham challenged Hindman to a duel.[10]

Accepting the challenge, Hindman selected bowie knives as his choice of weapons and specified that the antagonists would hold the knives in their right hands and have their left hands tied close to their bodies. Fortunately for both men, Patrick Cleburne, an opponent of dueling, intervened arguing that the conditions were brutal and the contest unfair because the "diminutive" Badham was physically unequal to Hindman. Cleburne arranged for Gideon Pillow, a Tennessean with extensive landholdings in Helena, to intercede. Pillow was able to cancel the match without loss of honor to either party.[11]

The Independence Day debate and subsequent altercations marked Thomas Hindman's entry into the wild, turbulent world of Arkansas politics and enhanced his image in a state where politicians were often expected to prove themselves in impromptu fisticuffs and formal duels. As his future course demonstrated, Hindman was more than ready to meet the challenges that came his way.

Hindman took his newfound role as a Democratic spokesman into the summer legislative canvass, although not as an office seeker. At the close of the candidates' speeches, he "made some highly appropriate and sensible remarks on the subject of the Midland Railroad" which led the editor of the *Southern Shield*, a Whig organ, to label him a "gentleman of talent, [and] easy, elegant manners." The *Shield* lamented that its only regret was that he was not a Whig, while the *Democratic Star* joyfully predicted that in due time it expected to see him bearing "aloft our banner to victory" since it is next to impossible for one of his talent and temperament to keep out of the political arena."[12]

During the rest of 1854, Hindman continued to promote Helena's railroad interests and build a political base of power for the future. When the legislature convened in Little Rock in December, he traveled to the capital to lobby for the Arkansas Midland Railroad. Though he looked like a mere boy with his almost beardless face, Hindman impressed legislators and spectators with his "self-confidence and intellect." He remained in the city for six weeks attending legislative sessions and working behind the scenes to further railroad development beneficial to Helena.[13]

Unfortunately for Thomas Hindman, an odd juxtaposition of events occurred. The previous winter while serving in the Mississippi legislature,

Plate 2   *Thomas C. Hindman (ca. 1854)*
Courtesy: Graphic Records Collection,
Mississippi Department of Archives and History

he met J. W. McDonald, an associate of John Quitman, and expressed a desire to participate in a rumored filibustering expedition to liberate Cuba from Spanish rule and annex it to the United States. Upon McDonald's endorsement, in June 1854 Quitman sent Hindman a "private and confidential circular" about the proposed expedition. Since Hindman, like many Southerners, hoped to see Cuba annexed as a means of acquiring additional slave territory, he welcomed the opportunity. He wrote to John S. Thrasher, another Quitman associate, and requested the "privilege of risking reputation and life in the enterprise." Holding himself in readiness for the signal to leave for Cuba, he also solicited Arkansans for the expedition. In January 1855, he proudly notified Quitman that he had enrolled ten young men from Helena and predicted that within five days, forty more would be enlisted in Phillips County. Confidently, he told Quitman that he expected one hundred "good men from Helena . . . [would soon be] ready to march at five days notice."[14]

Hindman was not to be in that number, however, as he later regretfully explained to Quitman. While engaged in railroad lobbying, he was involved in a violent confrontation with two men—Dr. Moon from Dardanelle, Arkansas, and an associate named Wilson. On the night of 18 January 1855, without "any previous difficulty" between them, Moon pointed a cocked pistol at Hindman in a Little Rock hotel barroom. Since he was unarmed, Hindman expressed his willingness to fight both Moon and Wilson when armed. Because they had threatened an unarmed man, he denounced Moon and Wilson as "cowardly and assassins." He later deduced that Moon had been persuaded to attack him by a relative, C. C. Danley, editor of the *Arkansas State Gazette*, to whom Hindman had refused an introduction on the grounds that he was not a "gentleman."[15]

The following night in the hall of the House of Representatives, the men again approached, and Wilson drew a "repeater." Responding, Hindman drew a derringer and fired at Moon; the bullet deflected off a buckle on Moon's pistol belt and shattered his arm. He then drew another pistol and leveled it at Wilson, who was hiding behind a desk. In the pandemonium that ensued, a mob advanced towards Hindman, crying "kill him." This caused him to seek refuge in the Speaker's stand, where he declared that he was ready to surrender to "lawful authority." Following the arrival of the sheriff, Hindman was taken before a judge and ultimately bound over for trial at the June session of court. He was released after posting a two thousand dollar bond and returned to Helena.

Although free, as he explained to Quitman, he could no longer depart for Cuba on short notice without disgracing himself by becoming a fugitive from justice, which he was unwilling to do.[16]

Subsequently, Hindman was cleared of the charges, and the Holly Springs (MS) *Democrat* concluded that he had acted as "prudently as any reasonable man could under the circumstances" since Moon had attacked him previously.[17]

In contrast to his stay in Little Rock, the remainder of 1855 passed rather calmly. Cognizant of the South's need to develop transportation facilities and eager to promote Helena's communications with the outside world, he continued to encourage railroad expansion and served on a committee to solicit contributions to build a plank road between the city and Tunica, Mississippi.[18]

Still striving to overcome its earlier reputation as a haven for drunks and gamblers, Helena in 1855 had an active temperance society. On 1 May 1855 Hindman spoke to temperance advocates at a local Baptist church, praising the "purely good and divinely benevolent" acts that temperance supporters had achieved within the span of a few years. He antagonized many in the audience, however, when he questioned whether temperance's "onward path" might be "beset with perils which stand like angry lions in its way." Among the obstacles to progress, he listed the tendency of temperance advocates to lose their zeal after a few victories. Tempers flared when he predicted that support for measures such as the Maine law, which prohibited the sale of intoxicating beverages, could prompt fierce resistance. He suggested that a more preferable approach was a strictly enforced license system. As a staunch Democrat, he warned his listeners against the establishment of separate temperance parties. He asserted that it would be better for men of both parties to work within their party organizations to promote temperance goals.[19]

The publication of Hindman's speech evoked strong opposition from Dr. T. M. Jacks, a local temperance activist who objected to Hindman's condemnation of the Maine law and separate temperance parties. In addition, Jacks lambasted Hindman's licensing plan. Hindman stood by his remarks and declined to reply to Jacks's open letters to local newspapers. According to Jacks, by refusing to defend his premises, Hindman had beaten a retreat.[20]

In May 1855 Tom Hindman catapulted to the forefront of Arkansas politics when he mounted a campaign to counter the growing influence of nativism in Arkansas. The influx of immigrants, many of whom were Roman Catholics, into the United States in the 1840s and 1850s had spawned hostile feelings that crystallized into the formation of the American, or Know Nothing, Party. The new party played upon the fears that the flood of immigrants would corrupt the Anglo-Saxon heritage and the structure of American government, the belief that the pope was plotting the overthrow of the United States, and the tendency of temperance advocates to associate Irish and German immigrants with the evils of grog shops. In the aftermath of the dissolution of the Whig Party that followed the passage of the Kansas-Nebraska Act in May 1854, the new party became a refuge for "stranded Whigs" and a few "disaffected Democrats." In the South, the new organization appealed to old Whigs as well as some Democrats who felt that the state rights faction of their party was becoming too extreme or who wished to challenge the dominance of the existing power structure.[21]

The establishment of the American Party in Arkansas was largely the work of former Whig Albert Pike. He played an active role at the Know Nothing convention in Philadelphia in June 1855 when he helped draft a national platform that included a plank denying congressional power to legislate on slavery and calling for the repeal of the Missouri Compromise. During the summer of 1855, Pike and other prominent ex-Whigs organized rallies and mass meetings that lured dissident Democrats who objected to the Kansas-Nebraska Act, which embraced popular sovereignty and repealed the Missouri Compromise. In addition to opponents of the Kansas-Nebraska Act such as former United States Senator Solon Borland, Know Nothings in Arkansas benefitted from dissatisfaction with Senator Robert W. Johnson and other top Democratic Party leaders. Included in the latter category was Christopher C. Danley, editor of the influential *Arkansas State Gazette*, who joined the emerging nativist coalition.[22]

Although the Know Nothing party made "less progress in Arkansas than in any other Southern state with the possible exception of South Carolina," its lightening growth ignited Democratic fears and spurred Tom Hindman into action. The preponderance of abolitionists and free soilers in the ranks of Northern Know Nothings convinced him that the American Party was as inimical to the interests of the South as the Republican Party, which had made its debut in 1854 with a commitment to opposing the spread of slavery into the territories. Hindman considered

Know Nothings "pestilent fanatics" who closed their doors to foreign born "friends of the South," while opening them to "anti-slavery fanatics and their Southern sympathizers." "The bitterest of all abolitionists" were Northern Know Nothings whose "hostility to immigration" was "as notorious" as it was "relentless." "All friends of the South" must oppose these "unscrupulous demagogues and political preachers" who had "banded together" in an anti-Catholic crusade that threatened religious liberty. Hindman determined to crush the Know Nothing monster, with its secret pass words, oaths, and hand clasps, before it could seriously imperil Democratic hegemony in Arkansas.[23]

To counter the nativist threat, in May 1855 Hindman organized a Democratic Association in Phillips County. The association's constitution, which he authored, provided for open meetings, elected officers, and the equal voice of all members. Decisions were to be made by majority vote; and secret signs, grips, pass words, and oaths were explicitly forbidden. Members would "use all honorable and lawful means to promote the principles set forth in the Democratic Platform of 1852" and work to defeat "every political organization which meets or acts in secret, or which makes religious belief and place of birth, or either, a political test, or a qualification for office."[24]

Through the summer of 1855 Hindman devoted himself almost full time to the defeat of the Know Nothings. The Phillips County Democratic Association won the endorsement of United States Senator William K. Sebastian of Helena who asserted that its constitution was "but a new declaration of fidelity to old principles, at a time when many have faltered." Hindman's efforts were staunchly supported by his law partner and close friend, John Palmer, a Catholic and former Whig, who emotionally declared that the American Party was not the heir of the Whig party. As far as he was concerned, the warfare against Democracy had ended "when the old flag which Henry Clay had borne to victory was lowered to the black and bloody standard" of Know Nothingism.[25]

Throughout the summer and fall, Hindman zealously labored across the northern part of the state for the Democratic cause. In October, he traveled to Greene County to aid in the establishment of a Democratic association and urged the "gallant democracy" not to lag behind their brothers in other counties in "meeting the invidious attacks of the enemy. They . . . [should] organize to work for the good course of civil and religious liberty." In Monroe County, he aroused Democrats who had previously "manifested but little interest in political matters" to the point that an admirer predicted a requiem for the soon to be defunct Know Nothings in the county. The result was the same in Poinsett County where his proposal and constitution for a Democratic association were unanimously adopted. His performance at Marion in November was so inspiring and eloquent that the Memphis *Appeal* exclaimed that his "brilliancy of intellect" would soon place him in the "front ranks of debaters in Arkansas. The politician, young or old, who sees fit to break a lance with him, will find a 'foeman worthy of his steel' and withal rather hard to manage."[26]

The culmination of his efforts came with a grand barbecue and rally at Helena on 22 and 23 November. Preparations were made for 10,000 Democrats from Phillips and surrounding counties who assembled to strike "one more blow for civil and religious freedom." As secretary of the arrangements committee, Hindman coordinated the grandiose plan.[27]

The festivities began with a procession featuring a brass band brought from Memphis by Patrick Cleburne and mounted horsemen each bearing the Stars and Stripes. Cannon from various steamers boomed a resounding welcome to the meeting site, symbolically named Camp Jefferson, where tables groaned with the weight of meat, breads, cakes, pickles, and beverages. Surrounded by colorful flags, John Palmer opened the assembly and presented resolutions reaffirming fealty to Democratic principles, endorsing the Kansas-Nebraska Act, and asserting that Democrats chose their political candidates on the basis of "personal merit" and "political soundness" and "without regard to nativity or religion."[28]

Miss Emily Yarborough presented the Phillips County Democratic Association with a white satin banner emblazoned with a spread eagle, half circled with bullion stars and the motto: "ARKANSAS DEMO-CRATS: The Old Guard Never Surrenders." Hindman publicly accepted the banner and promised the ladies of Phillips County that Arkansas Democrats would not "falter or retreat" or lay down their arms until Know Nothingism was "extinct and Democracy everywhere [emerged] triumphant."[29]

For keynote speakers Hindman brought in several prominent Mississippians including former Congressman Jacob Thompson, who exhorted Arkansas Know Nothings to remember that they were Southerners and that their "most vital interests were now imperiled by a fanatical majority at the North." He warned against browbeating and abusing Catholics and adopted citizens whose assistance might soon be required to maintain the South's honor and integrity.[30]

Ex-Governor Joseph W. Matthews of Mississippi delighted Democrats in the audience when, playing upon the Know Nothings' nickname of "Sam," he proclaimed,

> "Sam," stripped of his peacock's plumage, was shown up a carrion crow of the blackest feather, unworthy the association, much less the support and fellowship of the southern people. . . . "Sam's" wings are clipped, and instead of his ruling America, America has ruled him out.[31]

Excitement continued to run high the second day of the rally as local notables such as Senator William K. Sebastian and visitors such as Gideon Pillow of Tennessee and J. R. McClanahan of the Memphis *Appeal* addressed the crowd. A magnificent supper and ball at the Commercial Hotel wound up the proceedings. Recounting the "grand and glorious demonstration," the *Democratic Star* boasted of several original songs that Phillips County Democrats had composed for the occasion. Sung to the tune of "Old Virginia," a lively ditty entitled "Carry Him Back to Yankeeland" celebrated the defeat of the Know Nothings.

> O have you heard the news of late,
> How Sam got whipped all 'round
> In ev'ry true blooded Southern state,
> We've run him under ground.
> So carry him back to Yankeeland,
> He can't hide here any more;
> His tyrant code finds no demand,
> Upon our southern shore . . . .
> To prove we're not Americans,
> He turned his footsteps south;
> But we'll send him home with empty hands,
> And his fingers in his mouth.
> So carry him back to Yankeeland,
> We loved our homes before,
> The patriot's fire need not be fanned,
> Upon our Southern shore.[32]

Another song entitled "Invitation," repeated the theme of the United States as the refuge for the world's oppressed population.

> We will not spurn for this free land,
> The stranger, weak and worn.
> Who seeks like a bird with drooping wing,
> Shelter from wind, and storm;
> He flies to this, our far famed shore,
> As a home for the poor oppressed,
> We'll not thrust him back with scorn,
> To seek elsewhere for rest.
> Then come along, come long, make no delay,
> Come from every nation, come from every way;
> Our lands, they are broad enough--don't be alarmed,
> For Uncle Sam is rich enough to give us all a farm.[33]

The November rally marked the culmination of Hindman's Democratic crusade to rid Arkansas of Know Nothingism. Across the state, Democratic leaders congratulated him for "setting the ball in motion, in Phillips County, that . . . [had] since swept the state . . . rallying the party so gloriously." Although only twenty-seven years old and a resident of Arkansas for just over a year, he had already achieved a brilliant reputation.[34]

While his powerful oratory and organizational skills won Hindman accolades from all over the state, little was known outside Helena of his great personal courage in the face of human adversity and tragedy. On 5 September 1855 a Helena newsboy, William Burnett, boarded a steamer from New Orleans at the local dock unaware that several people on board were ill with yellow fever. He contracted the disease, which spread quickly throughout the town. As news of the disease traveled, "all who could get out of town fled to the country for safety, leaving only a few to take care of the sick and bury the dead." Doctors Charles E. Nash, T. M. Jacks, and Hector M. Grant remained to attend sufferers. The "complete panic" drained the town of "volunteer nurses" so that when the doctors made known the emergency, only three people came forward to offer their services—Tom Hindman, Patrick Cleburne, and a young Methodist minister John H. Rice. According to Nash, with no thought for their own safety, they made their rounds day and night, doing all the labor of women consistent with modesty and decorum. They went to the bakery and with their own means purchased bread, made tea and soups with their inexperienced hands, and performed all kinds of menial labor.[35]

When the epidemic subsided, the editor of the *Democratic Star* conveyed the sincere gratitude of the townspeople to Hindman and the other young men who had constituted the Helena Relief Committee. "They dressed and buried the dead with proper respect--they nursed and comforted the sick. . . . They have proved themselves friends to the sick and the dead, the poor and the needy, and to the widow and orphan."[36]

Their close association during the yellow fever epidemic made Hindman and Cleburne inseparable friends. As they walked the streets of Helena, they must have seemed an incongruous pair. Cleburne was nearly six feet tall with gray-blue eyes, dark brown hair, and a pleasant disposition that was slow to provocation to anger. The fiery Hindman was a dapper, well-dressed man just barely five feet tall with blue-gray eyes and light brown, almost blond, hair that curled about his ears giving him a boyish appearance. Not only were Hindman and Cleburne close friends, they became law partners for a short time and joint investors and business associates when, along with William Weatherly, they bought the *Democratic Star* in December 1855.[37]

The dawning of 1856 found Hindman at the helm of the crusade against the Know Nothings. Seeking the Democratic nomination for the state's first Congressional district, he embarked upon a tour of northern Arkansas from 24 January through 11 March that attracted attention and spawned exuberant praise throughout the state.

At Van Buren on 9 February, he employed techniques that he utilized successfully throughout the Congressional canvass. Customarily, he invited local Know Nothings to meet him in debate. Armed with documents, he traced the rise of the American Party and the sectional struggle over slavery, claiming that understanding both issues was necessary for the "proper presentation of the vital points now before the people of the south." "Upon the [Democratic] party alone the South could repose with safety, her interests and her honor." Reviewing the antislavery antecedents of the American Party, he contended that "Sam had been [completely] swallowed by the abolitionists of the North, leaving nothing but the southern Know Nothings in sight, as the tail that showed where the body had gone." He concluded by stating that the Know Nothings were "a rag tag and bobtail society, made up like an old woman's quilt of the cast off garments of twenty years." His addresses superbly combined the mingling of facts with amusing anecdotes and illustrations, leading one listener to conclude "without other laurels won on former occasions in bold advocacy of his party and his section, this effort would alone place him in the front ranks of popular orators of the South."[38]

One of his most effective techniques was to discuss the so-called Macon Resolutions adopted by the House and then expunged from the record during the previous session of the state legislature. The resolutions labeled Know Nothingism "subversive of civil and religious liberty" as well as "anti- republican and abolitionist" in sentiment. Hoping to hide their membership in nativist lodges or to diffuse the issue, a number of Know Nothing legislators voted for the resolutions. In control of the House, shortly after the resolutions were approved, nativists voted to expunge them from the House journal. On the stump, Hindman's sharp questioning frequently wrung confessions from legislators such as G. P. Nunn of Lawrence County that they had joined the Know Nothings despite their public support for the Macon resolutions. The results in other parts of northern Arkansas were the same. Countless Arkansans agreed with an open letter signed "Flinn" of Marion County that pronounced Hindman a "simon pure Jeffersonian democrat" who was true to the great principles which lie at the foundation of all free government."[39]

Despite Hindman's popularity, his Congressional candidacy had to overcome two major obstacles: first, his youth and short residency in Arkansas; and secondly, the popularity of the incumbent Alfred B. Greenwood, described as "a vigilant and faithful representative" who had "neglected no interest of this congressional district." For these reasons, his supporters believed that voters should reward his faithful service by electing him for another term. By contrast, advocates of Hindman's candidacy responded that unlike Greenwood, a young, ambitious, vigorous candidate would crush Know Nothing candidate Hugh Thomason of Fayetteville.[40]

The canvass came to an end on Monday, 5 May when the first congressional district nominating convention opened in the Batesville Methodist church. Prior to the selection of a candidate, the delegates approved a series of resolutions endorsing the repeal of the Missouri Compromise. They condemned the American Party for denouncing the repeal of the Missouri Compromise, an action which the resolutions labeled "hostile to southern rights, and unfit to be approved by any southern man," and for proscribing citizens because of their religion or place of birth.[41]

After adopting resolutions that definitely bore the stamp of Hindman's influence, the delegates proceeded to the selection of a candidate. Others under consideration in addition to Greenwood and Hindman were William W. Floyd and Thomas B. Hanly, whose names were withdrawn early in the balloting. From the third vote through the 250th Greenwood led by two votes, but failed to secure the two-thirds majority necessary to win the nomination. After the 250th vote a late arriving delegate from Izard County was seated, and the convention president was authorized to cast proxy votes for Pope County. From the 251st vote through the 276th, Greenwood led by three votes but still failed to secure the nomination. Finally, on Saturday morning, in the interest of party unity, Hindman withdrew his name and asked his supporters to vote for Greenwood. Amid "vociferous cheering" he told the delegates that "it was the duty of a genuine democrat to sacrifice his own aspirations for the good of the cause." Following Hindman's remarks, Greenwood was unanimously nominated.[42]

Hindman's withdrawal when he had the power to prevent Greenwood from receiving the two-thirds vote necessary for nomination earned him a commendation from the convention for "sacrificing" personal interests for the good of the party. The delegates eagerly accepted his "magnanimous" offer to canvass the district in Greenwood's behalf since the incumbent was absent from the state on Congressional business.[43]

Although he had dropped out of the race, Hindman would be more visible during the canvass than Greenwood and would be in position to win the nomination in 1858. For the time being, he was content to campaign vigorously for Greenwood, lead the final effort to crush the Know Nothings in northern Arkansas, and keep his name prominently before the public.

As the primary spokesman for the Democracy of northwest Arkansas, Hindman served as secretary of the convention that nominated George W. Beasley for judge of the first judicial district and penned the resolutions adopted by the Arkansas State Democratic Convention. According to the editor of the *State-Rights Democrat*, these resolutions were an eloquent statement of the Southern state rights cause "worthy [enough] to be framed and hung in the house of every constitutional man in the Union." The resolutions proclaimed as "true friends of the Union of these States those who defend their equality, faithfully execute all the stipulations of the constitution, and oppose in sentiment and action the anti-slavery party, in its efforts to destroy the equal rights of the slaveholders and slaveholding States." Other resolutions endorsed the Kansas-Nebraska Act which recognized the right of the people in territories to "form and regulate their domestic institutions . . . subject only to the Constitution of the United States" and endorsed the Fugitive Slave Act of 1850 as a "plain fulfillment of a constitutional requirement." Any attempt to impair the law would strike "a fatal blow at the existence of the Union, and should be resisted by all good citizens." Abolitionists, free soilers, and Republicans were denounced as "subversive to the principles of the government, and dangerous to the peace of the country." The American Party was condemned for its "secret meetings, its ceremonials, its oaths and mummeries, . . . [which] tended to demoralize public sentiment." According to the delegates, its religious intolerance violated the spirit of the Constitution and aimed "a deadly blow at the highest and most sacred rights of man."[44]

Hindman's crusade against the Know Nothings nearly cost him his life. In June 1855, he had incurred the wrath of W. D. (Dorsey) Rice, a legislator from Phillips County, when he insinuated that Rice was a Know Nothing. Initially Rice denied the accusation and declared that he was a Democrat "not from accident, but from choice." Ill will between the two continued to escalate, and on 18 October 1855, they engaged in a spirited debate of their political differences. Hindman boldly led off by declaring that as a member of the state House of Representatives, Rice had voted for the Macon resolutions denouncing the Know Nothings' attempts to achieve religious proscription as counter to the substance and essence of the Constitution and their alliance with antislavery forces as treasonous to Southern rights.[45]

According to Hindman, Rice, along with other members of the American Party, was bound to secrecy and had voted for the resolutions to conceal his true political allegiance. The Know Nothings rallied their forces and on 12 January 1855, W. K. Patterson of Jackson County introduced a successful motion to expunge the Macon resolutions. Still true to his secret oath, Rice voted against the Patterson motion and launched his own verbal warfare on the Know Nothings, making an open denial of his affiliation with them on 28 May 1855 in a meeting of the Phillips County Democracy. These actions, notwithstanding, Rice then presided over the grand American Party ratification meeting in Little Rock in August 1855.[46]

Hindman relentlessly pressed the point that one could not be a good Democrat and a Know Nothing at the same time. Insisting that Know Nothings were speaking with a "forked tongue," he vehemently asserted that

> if the Know Nothing doctrines should be "incorporated into the administrative policy of the country," as Arkansas Know Nothings desire, Cuba can never be a slave State, and not one foot of slave territory can ever be added to the Union.[47]

In tracing the antecedents of the American Party, Hindman found its roots in the old Federalist belief that "wealth and learning" were "necessary ingredients for American citizenship." As proof of his assertion, Hindman read a statement from Rice suggesting that votes for a Democratic gubernatorial candidate in Alabama had come from a county in which large numbers could neither read nor write. Hindman countered assertions that persons of foreign birth should be prevented from holding federal office because of divided loyalties by pointing out that many of foreign extraction had served with distinction in the United States military forces during foreign wars.[48]

Finally, Hindman equated Know Nothingism with abolitionism, noting that Southern American Party members had expressed regret when their abolitionist colleagues had been defeated in Northern political contests. He predicted that the Know Nothings were doomed to destruction for their assaults on Democratic measures such as the Kansas-Nebraska Act. For these reasons, Hindman emphatically reiterated that a man could not be a faithful Democrat and a Know Nothing simultaneously.[49]

Commenting upon the encounter, Whig Henry Mooney claimed that Hindman had "stripped every vestage [*sic*] of political clothing from Rice and left nothing but his naked deformity." The bitterness between Hindman and Rice finally flared into open violence following a sharp exchange of letters in Helena newspapers in May 1856. Stung by

Hindman's declaration that the onus of obtaining satisfaction was on him and by an editorial in the *State-Rights Democrat* that a man who considered himself aggrieved but retaliated in words only was a "fool or coward," Rice persuaded his brothers J. W. and F. H. Rice and a nephew James T. Marriott (Maryatt) to lend assistance if needed.[50]

About one o'clock on the afternoon of 24 May, a street fight ensued between Rice and his associates on the one hand and Hindman and Patrick Cleburne on the other. Obviously, each side offered conflicting testimony as to what transpired. Expecting violence, all parties were armed. By all accounts, W. D. Rice fired first; his bullet grazed Hindman's right arm, temporarily paralyzing it before settling in his right breast just below the shoulder blade. Cleburne was shot in the right side, the bullet passing through his lung before lodging near the spine. Marriott was hit twice in the abdomen and died in agony a short time later. Unhurt, W. D. Rice, still armed with a pistol and a bowie knife, ran down the street with Hindman in pursuit for approximately a hundred yards before the latter collapsed from loss of blood.[51]

Borne by friends to a nearby office of a justice of the peace, Hindman was operated on by Dr. Joseph S. Deputy, while a throng of bystanders (including some Know Nothings) watched. Fully conscious during the operation, Hindman laughed and smoked a cigar. When a friend later asked if the incision had hurt, Hindman replied, "Yes," but added that he "would not let those d——d Know Nothings" know that he was in pain.[52]

Cleburne almost died. The bullet perforated his lung and stomach before lodging near his spine, and he lingered near death for ten days with two doctors in constant attendance. When the crisis passed, Hindman and Cleburne appeared before the grand jury to answer any charges against them. Completely exonerated, after the proceedings they left for Hindman's parents' home in Mississippi to recuperate.[53]

By the time they returned to Helena in early July, the state canvass was nearly over. In keeping with his pledge at Batesville, however, Hindman resumed his speaking schedule and prepared to give Know Nothings the "heaviest grape" in the coming contest. His efforts and that of other Democratic stalwarts paid off handsomely in the August elections when the party captured the governorship, both Congressional seats, all races for judge and prosecuting attorney, twelve out of thirteen state senate seats, sixty-two house seats, and three-fourths of the various county races. Commenting on the results, the Little Rock *True Democrat* exulted that the election in Arkansas had been a "brilliant and glorious triumph." Success continued as Democrats James Buchanan and John C. Breckinridge swept to victory in the November presidential canvass. Rejoicing, Hindman boasted that "the twin brothers, Sam and Sambo . . . [were] beaten and crushed."[54]

The year finished with a note of personal as well as political triumph for Thomas Hindman. Earlier in the year he had begun courting the "beautiful, accomplished" Mary (Mollie) Watkins Biscoe, daughter of Henry L. Biscoe, a wealthy Helena planter. She delighted visitors to the Biscoe home with her voice as "sweet and natural" as a nightingale while her fingers glided lightly over piano keys. The attraction was mutual, a disturbing development for Henry Biscoe who believed that at eighteen, his daughter was too young to marry. Hoping to crush the budding romance, he sent her to the convent of St. Agnes in Memphis with strict orders to the nuns to allow no visitors except members of the family. Forewarned, Hindman convinced the convent staff that he was Mollie's uncle Peter and was thus eligible to visit her.[55]

After discovering that he had been outwitted, Henry Biscoe "stamped the floor, pulled his hair" and cursed. Equally distraught, Laura Biscoe, Mollie's stepmother, wrung her hands and cried. Realizing that they had no choice, the parents reluctantly yielded to Mollie's pleas and gave their blessing. The Reverend Thomas Welch, the local Presbyterian minister officiated at the couple's wedding at the Biscoe home on 11 November 1856. Not unexpectedly, Patrick Cleburne was the best man while Maggie Tollison, Cleburne's current sweetheart, was bride's maid.[56]

The honeymoon trip to Little Rock amply illustrated the difficulties of traveling in frontier Arkansas. Accompanied by Pat Cleburne and Maggie Tollison, the newlyweds took a steamboat down the White River to Aberdeen where they boarded a stagecoach to the capital city. At various points along the way Hindman ran into the rest stops for warm bricks for his bride's cold feet. In Little Rock they visited Mollie's relatives Dr. and Mrs. Robert Watkins and met with Democratic political leaders. Upon returning to Helena, they resided with the Biscoes until their new home was constructed. So that Mollie could be close to her family, they decided to build on a site south of the Biscoe residence. In 1860 the Hindmans happily moved into their new two-story, Palladian style brick house with an impressive view of the Mississippi River.[57]

Before their new home was ready, Tom and Mollie rejoiced over the birth of their first child. Born 18 October 1857, the little girl was christened Susan after Mollie's mother who had died in 1840. A second daughter Sallie, named for Tom's mother, followed in early 1859. As a proud father and caring husband, Hindman hoped that Mollie and the children would be able to live comfortably in the event of his death. With such an exigency in mind, on 13 February 1859 he deeded over to his wife five choice blocks in Helena and New Helena.[58]

Chapter 3

REFORMER OR "DISORGANIZER"? TOM HINDMAN AND THE DEMISE OF THE "FAMILY" IN ARKANSAS

By the fall of 1856, despite his withdrawal from the Congressional race, Tom Hindman had become the "leader of the great democratic party of Eastern Arkansas." To fellow party members he was a "beacon upon the mountain top, a light set on a hill. . . [who] was more than a match for any man the Know Nothings could bring against him." In the months following his marriage and the presidential election of 1856, while busying himself with domestic responsibilities and a thriving law practice, he continued to strengthen his political base.

In mid-summer 1857, he became interim editor of the Helena *State-Rights Democrat*, a position that offered the opportunity to display his talents as an "able and spicy writer" and to keep his name prominently before the public. In addition to its political benefits, the editorial post afforded an excellent platform from which to promote economic prospects for Helena. Along this line, in November 1857 he journeyed to Memphis "for the purpose of procuring telegraphic communications between 'Helena and the balance of the world.'" After a series of meetings, the Memphis and Ohio Railroad agreed to build a branch telegraph line between Helena and Panola, Mississippi, using an underwater cable to traverse the river at a cost of $5,000.00. Hindman returned home confident that he could raise the required funds and pave the way for Helena to emerge as the major source of news and communication for the entire state.[1]

Building on his growing popularity, in the closing months of 1857 Hindman publicly began to campaign for the nomination to Arkansas' first Congressional seat. He launched his campaign by speaking at a Democratic meeting in Jacksonport, following the conclusion of the circuit court session. In a "forcible" address, he exulted over the "utter annihilation of the American Party North and South" in the 1856 elections. Although nativists no longer threatened the country, he predicted that abolitionists would make another effort to achieve their goals in the political arena, a move which could lead to the "overthrow of our glorious Union." His remarks electrified the crowd, which rose in thunderous applause at the conclusion of his speech. Wild with enthusiasm, his listeners proclaimed their "undiminished confidence" in his "ability, patriotism and true democracy."[2]

In contrast to the heated contest two years earlier, the campaign for the 1858 Democratic congressional nomination was remarkably quiet. With no serious opponent, Hindman was a cinch to win the race. Editor Richard H. Johnson of the Little Rock *True Democrat* reminded voters that Hindman had sacrificed his own aspirations for the interests of party harmony in 1856 and praised him as a "thorough going Democrat" of "marked abilities." Across the district, Democrats echoed these sentiments and pledged support for his candidacy as meetings in county after county instructed delegates to vote for him at the nominating convention in Batesville. Ladies in Greene County presented him with a banner which proclaimed "Hindman or None," while rallies in Conway and Pope Counties labeled him their "first, last and only choice for Congress."[3]

Noting Hindman's promise to "labor assiduously" to promote the interests of his constituents and his pledge of "fidelity to State-rights democracy and unswerving loyalty to the south," supporters in Izard County expressed hope that his youthful ambition would yield "action and results," especially in the area of internal improvements, which the mountain counties desperately needed.[4]

On the first ballot at the Batesville convention, Hindman easily triumphed over A. M. Wilson and Dandridge McRae who received a total of six votes to his twenty-five. Resolutions passed at the convention, most of them aimed at the General Assembly, bore the Hindman stamp. One resolution urged that the time for electing congressmen be changed so that they would be elected in the same year that they took office, rather than fifteen months prior to taking office. As matters stood in 1858, the supporters of the resolution contended, too many issues could intervene before newly elected representatives took their seats. A new approach would insure that they would be "fresh from the people" when sworn into office. Resolutions reflected the intense interest in internal improvements: support for railroads connecting Van Buren with Springfield, Missouri, and Helena with the Iron Mountain line; an overland mail route along the Thirty-fifth parallel from Memphis to Albuquerque through Fort Smith and Van Buren; and the improvement of several Arkansas rivers. To promote Southern interests, legislators were urged to adopt measures that would encourage more citizens to become slaveholders. Moreover, some asserted that "worthless and dangerous" free blacks were becoming "too numerous and too troublesome" and must be expelled from Arkansas.[5]

Although Hindman drew only token opposition in the August general election, he vigorously campaigned on behalf of his own candidacy and for other duly nominated Democrats. With his election a foregone conclusion, Democrats all over the first district heaped praise on Hindman. An admirer claimed that his 12 July speech at Batesville was so potent that it carried his convictions "to the minds of all save a few Know Nothings, who like Ephraim of old are joined to their idols." His eloquence, supporters predicted, would soon "prove a powerful bulwark against Northern fanaticism."[6]

During the campaign he narrowly escaped death in a carriage accident. Following a speaking engagement at Burrs' Spring in late July, Hindman was forced to jump from his carriage in order to avoid being hit by a newly cut tree that fell just as his carriage approached. He landed on his side, breaking a thigh and severely injuring a hip. Unable to obtain immediate medical treatment, Hindman's injured leg was left "much shorter than its fellow, compelling him to wear a boot with a high heel . . . and [to walk] with a slight limp" for the rest of his life.[7]

Even though the injury kept him off the campaign trail for the rest of the canvass, Hindman crushed his opponent William M. Crosby, described by a Hindman supporter as "an honest mechanic . . . [who allowed] others to use his paw in the embers" of the canvass. According to results published in the *True Democrat*, Hindman outpolled Crosby 18,255 votes to 2,853![8]

By his direct appeal to voters in 1856 and 1858, Hindman set in motion a major challenge to the existing political structure in Arkansas, a system without parallel in the antebellum South. Although occasionally frightened by challenges to their hegemony from political opponents both within and outside the Democratic party, a small cadre known as the "family" (hereafter referred to as the Family) or the "dynasty" dominated Arkansas politics from the territorial period until the Civil War. Bound together by "complicated ties of kinship and friendship," the Johnsons, Conways, and Seviers, supported by their loyalists, dominated state politics. All were originally involved in federal patronage and land dealing. John Hallum has noted: "In the midst of a growing frontier democracy, these men contrived to hold an aggregate 190 years in office, nearly all of it before 1860."[9]

Hegemony "was made easy" because the "dynasty" controlled the process of selecting delegates to conventions that chose candidates for Congress and governor. Delegates were chosen at township and county meetings, and notices were distributed only a few days before the gatherings and normally given only to "a chosen few." Because of slow communications, these tactics virtually guaranteed that party leaders would have no difficulty conducting "amenable gatherings." Pre-convention caucuses selected chairmen and instructed them on how to control the meetings, picked candidates, and arranged other logistical matters. Under the careful orchestration of the "family," most Democratic state conventions "were little more than staged plays."[10]

In spite of its domination, by the mid 1850s, the power of the Family was waning. "Paradoxically," its declining fortunes were in part the result of its previous success. Over the years, potentially divisive issues relating to internal improvements, banking, and education became subordinated to the more important issue of maintaining political control. A rapidly increasing population brought with it people who expected state government to provide adequate transportation, schools, and a sound banking structure. "Old political obligations" and "masterly inactivity" were not acceptable platforms. Moreover, the final demise of the Whig Party and the rout of the Know Nothings in 1856 left the Family without its "most useful weapon, the quadrennial exhortations to the faithful to maintain party (i.e., Family-dictated) regularity."[11]

Although it was not a major issue, criticism of Family domination was present during the 1858 canvass. A Democrat in White County indicated as much in July 1858, when he noted that the discontent that Hindman's 1856 canvass had roused in northern Arkansas initially brought out three candidates for a state senate seat in his district.

Although two aspirants later withdrew and supported the party nominee, there was much truth in the assertion that by challenging the status quo, Hindman had opened the doors to political revolution.[12]

Newspaper editors critical of Family leadership took up the gauntlet. The Batesville (AR) *Independent Balance* rejoiced to see people

> repudiating the doctrine that no man has the right to aspire to office or to be a candidate without the authority of a *packed* convention. . . . The fetters of partyism . . . [were] becoming so much weakened that public men no longer fear to disregard the intrigues and *dicta* of bogus conventions and to show their independence by appealing for support in their honest aspirations, to the unfettered will of the people.[13]

An editorial in the Napoleon (AR) *Planter* in June 1858 similarly criticized the tactics of the Democratic hierarchy. The editorial charged that they manipulated political meetings and conventions so as to give the appearance of an open contest between candidates when the real choice lay only between Family favorites. The *Planter* labeled the convention system of choosing candidates a "fungus growth upon the body politic" and contended that conventions were not sanctioned by either the United States or the Arkansas state constitutions.[14]

One supporter of the independent candidacy of James Jones against Albert Rust, the Family candidate for the second district Congressional seat, wrote to the Ouchita *Herald* gloating that Richard H. Johnson, the "Ring Master of the great democratic party" had been challenged. "Unfortunately for him," he wrote, the people of Arkansas would no longer be "so easily guiled, and if they had been the dupes for a long time past of a few prominent *Whangdoodles* they have learned better, and cannot be so easily hoodwinked." A follow-up editorial asserted that one result of the campaign was that the "rotten carcass of modern democracy is consigned in this State, to its last resting place." While the editor predicted the election of the convention-nominated candidates for Congress, he still felt that the party would "hereafter never dictate to the masses for whom they shall cast their suffrages."[15]

Although certainly aware of the undercurrent of hostility directed at Family dominance, Hindman stressed Democratic unity during the 1858 canvass. He urged party members to present a united front at all levels against opposition challenges, whether from "Know Nothings, disorganizers, neutrals, independents, or what not." He spurned the support of the Smithville (AR) *Plaindealer* because its editor was backing an independent candidate for circuit court clerk who was running against the regular Democratic nominee. Not surprisingly, his actions won commendation from Richard H. Johnson of the *True Democrat*, who insisted that all good Democrats should follow Hindman's example and put aside personal preferences in order to "insure the triumph of principle" and the success of the party.[16]

Despite this ringing endorsement from the state Democratic Party's leading newspaper, within a few months Hindman found himself branded as a self-serving disorganizer who had elevated personal aggrandizement above party fealty. The roots of the rift between Hindman and many leading Arkansas Democrats lay in a caucus held in November 1858 for the purpose of nominating a candidate for the United States Senate.

According to Hindman, on the evening of 7 November 1858 supporters of incumbent William K. Sebastian held a private caucus in the Little Rock hotel room of J. C. Johnson of St. Francis County, a well-known Know Nothing. At the meeting, Dr. D. Griffin of Hempstead, a leader of the Sebastian forces, was selected to present a resolution to the Democratic legislative caucus when it convened on 9 November. The resolution called for waiving the traditional requirement that a candidate receive a two-thirds majority to be nominated. Although Sebastian was their choice, Family members knew that they would be unable to muster the votes necessary to secure his nomination under the two-thirds rule.

When the caucus assembled, Griffin dutifully offered the following motion: "Resolved, That all questions to be determined by this Convention, shall be determined by a majority of those who are present, in person, or by proxy." Hindman charged that the purpose of the resolution was to allow participation by "Know Nothings and Disorganizers" who had been admitted to the caucus in order to guarantee Sebastian's nomination. In his words, "The Democratic members were there, 'Satan came also among them.'" He alleged that the Griffin resolution was designed to "make room for him—in the 'family.'" His assertion was not without validity since thirteen former Whigs and/or Know Nothings participated in the meeting.

Determined to have their way, Sebastian's supporters brushed aside counter resolutions by Elisha Baxter of Independence County and W. H. Hammond of Hot Spring County to admit only "good and true

State-Rights Democrats" who would endorse the 1856 platform of the national Democratic party. By rejecting the Baxter and Hammond resolutions and repudiating the previous practice of requiring a two-thirds vote for making nominations, the caucus had, according to Hindman, "murdered in cold blood" the "national Democratic platform, the convention system and the majority rule." He insisted that when he learned of the "secret caucus," he had approached Richard H. Johnson and appealed to him to "come to the rescue of the Democracy" by publishing the accounts of the "disorganizing conspiracy." Johnson, stated Hindman, refused to intervene.[17]

Outraged that Family members would stoop to incorporating political enemies into Democratic leadership circles to secure Sebastian's nomination, Hindman issued a public protest. When Johnson of the *True Democrat* and other Family members responded, Hindman labeled their actions "the most concentrated wrath of the small managers of the caucus and of certain outside high-priests who manage[d] them." Disagreement soon became open warfare, and Johnson and other Family leaders threatened to block Hindman's re-election to Congress in 1860. Undaunted, the Congressman issued a passionate address in which he proclaimed,

> I know not what others may do, but for me, come weal or come woe, I will adhere to the old principles of State Rights and the ancient land-marks of Democracy—opposing fusions and coalitions and insisting, not only on the exclusion of men who do not approve our creed and abide by our usages, but on the rebuke of those who had attempted to smuggle alien enemies into our ranks. This is the path of honor and duty.

Confident of his political power, he concluded by predicting the speedy overthrow of "the fusionists" and "champions of amalgamation."[18]

Not unexpectedly, Family spokesman Richard H. Johnson used the columns of the *True Democrat* to rebut Hindman's charges. Instead of denying the allegation that nativists and other Democratic opponents were admitted into the party caucus that had nominated Senator Sebastian, Johnson asserted that the outcome of the caucus would have been the same even without the inclusion of non-Democrats. From the ranks of Family supporters came counter accusations that Hindman had denounced the caucus solely because it had selected Sebastian instead of choosing him or his dictated choice. His protest, Johnson said, was "a wail of disappointment—a cry of revenge—patriotism, or love of party has nothing to do with it." The Batesville *Sentinel*, another Family organ, claimed that Hindman's "unhallowed ambition," and not principle, had spawned the rebellion against the caucus leaders.[19]

In the ensuing warfare, accusations flew as the antagonists charged each other with using scurrilous language and undeserved, unfair personal invectives. Richard Johnson insisted that Hindman had instigated the fight. Instead of gratitude for the Family's endorsement and sympathy in the recent Congressional election, he had repaid the debt with "abuse and vilification." Hindman and not the Family would be the loser. His "over-weening vanity" and "dictatorial course" had destroyed any chance for future political advancement. Johnson charged that Hindman had won his current Congressional seat "almost by force." He had come to Arkansas as a "needy, political adventurer" who, even before he had cast a vote in the state, had announced that "he would do the benighted people . . . the distinguished honor to represent them in Congress." Seizing upon the supposed Know Nothing threat, he had "sallied forth to cut off the head of the dead Sam. By impudence, by pushing, bullying and forcing himself upon the people, he had gained the office." Then, "inflated with his undeserved honor, puffed up with the idea that he was a real giant, that all men were his vassals, he took whip and spurs and mounted the back of democracy." He had come "strutting like a turkey cock" to dictate the nomination for the senate seat. "Unscrupulous demagogue," bully, tyrant, and "disorganizer" were fitting epithets for the Helena politician.[20]

Family supporters across the state echoed Johnson's sentiments. The Fayetteville *Arkansian* published a stinging editorial asserting that the Arkansas Democratic Party had been

> united and harmonious until in an evil hour it took on Mr. Hindman as a leader. . . . No sooner had this gentleman been promoted beyond his merits and most sanguine hopes than his inordinate selfishness prompted him to aim at supreme power in Arkansas.

To achieve his selfish ambition, Hindman would "sink the party" by "cut[ting] down" and "silenc[ing]" the best men of long residence and great popularity. "An old Democrat" from Madison County wrote that in turning on the Family Hindman had cut off his head "square to his shoulders; he is not only a fratecide [*sic*] but a suicide."[21]

In response to these attacks, Hindman repeatedly insisted that he had voiced no opinion on the senate seat until he saw that Sebastian had entered into a "bargain, intrigue and coalition with Know-Nothings and disorganizers." At that time, he expressed his hope and belief that Sebastian would be defeated. Countering the charge that he desired the seat for himself, Hindman declared that his only political ambition was to retain the Congressional seat he already held. In an effort to sound more convincing, he incorrectly asserted that at the time of the senatorial caucus, he had not yet met the constitutional age requirement of thirty. In reality, he had turned thirty on 28 January 1858.[22]

The rift between Hindman and the Family widened as the 1860 state elections approached and other issues, including some legislators taking per diem payments during a recess of the General Assembly, polarized voters. According to Hindman, the House and Senate had concurred in a desire to recess between 21 December 1858 and 11 January 1859. The Senate had adopted a resolution amendment prohibiting members from taking per diem pay during the recess. When the House rejected the proposal, the motion to recess failed. A similar House resolution calling for a recess between 21 December and 10 January failed in the Senate because it was silent on the per diem question.[23]

According to Hindman, at this juncture a small coterie of Family members in the House led by James B. Johnson and Jilson P. Johnson exploited the per diem matter by forcing a recess on the legislature. In a secret caucus on 21 December, they obtained the signatures of twenty-eight legislators who agreed not to take their seats until 10 January so as to prevent the House from obtaining a quorum and force it to adjourn. The Johnsons then approached Governor Elias Conway and appealed to him to issue a proclamation adjourning the legislature. Conway agreed to do so, as long as the president of the Senate and the speaker of the House certified in writing that the two houses were unable to reach agreement on an adjournment date. Senate president Thomas B. Fletcher complied, but Speaker Oliver H. Oates refused on the grounds that the chambers had agreed on an adjournment date, but not on the per diem issue. Despite Oates's refusal to sign the requested certification, Conway issued the proclamation. Hindman criticized their action in a speech delivered in Helena.

When the last word of the proclamation fell from the lips of the [governor's] private secretary [Richard H. Johnson], at that very moment, the president of the senate and speaker of the house rapped their mallets on their respective desks and declared the two houses adjourned! Thus, by an act of . . . high-handed despotism . . . did Governor Conway force the recess on an unwilling legislature.[24]

When the legislature reconvened on 17 January, some House members asked Oates to sign certificates for per diem pay. Oates refused, "alleging that his conscience would not allow it." B. Vaughan of Madison County then offered a resolution "for the relief of the speaker's conscience" that authorized him to sign the certificates. Oates, then added the words "and hereby required" after "authorized," which would compel him to do the very thing that he had said his conscience prohibited. Even though he suggested the amendment, Oates still opposed paying per diem and announced his intention to resign as speaker. After passage of the resolution as amended by Oates, Hindman suggested that the speaker not resign because to do so would result in the selection of a new speaker who would sign the certificates. Oates resigned anyway, and Ben T. DuVal, a Hindman supporter who had publicly stated that the members were "legally and morally entitled" to per diem pay, was elected speaker. He promptly signed the certificates for many legislators, including "some of the most devoted adherents of the Johnsonian faction."[25]

When Johnson of the *True Democrat* attacked the payments, Hindman labeled his action a "humbug." He contended that the legislature was in continuous session despite the enforced recess and that legally legislators were entitled to per diem payments. He advised against accepting payment, however, because it would give the Johnson faction "a hobby about money, with which to excite the people and cover up the bargain, intrigue and corruption of Sebastian's nomination, and other misdeeds." He said, "It would be a great pity to give the faction such a handle." Moreover, he claimed that members of Congress routinely collected per diem during Sunday recesses and adjournment. Shifting attention to other congressional benefits, he claimed that senators Robert W. Johnson and William K. Sebastian had actually collected double mileage from their Arkansas homes to Washington for special sessions in 1849 and 1851, even though they had never left their Washington boarding houses! The *True Democrat* had defended those payments as the senators' legal right.

Was it right, Hindman queried, for senators to take pay for services not rendered and miles not traveled, and to deny the same to legislators?[26]

Family spokesman Richard Johnson countered by claiming that "the arch-agitator" Hindman had instigated the whole controversy by setting traps, manufacturing opinions, and scheming. Legislators who had taken the per diem pay had done so out of the sincere belief that they were entitled to it, and the Vaughan resolution that had preceded Oates's resignation would not have passed without Hindman's "persistent striving and maneuvering." Responding to Hindman's accusation that R. W. Johnson and Sebastian had collected double mileage in 1849 and 1851, the *True Democrat* dismissed the allegation as nothing but a "Mare's Nest" with "one or two addled eggs in it."[27]

A perennial topic in Arkansas politics surfaced again and became a major point of contention between Hindman and the Family. At issue was the debt left by the collapse of the Real Estate Bank, chartered in 1836. With its main facility in Little Rock, the bank maintained branches at Helena, Columbia, and Washington, all of which were major cotton-producing areas. Although owned by private stockholders, the bank was authorized to pledge the credit of the state up to two million dollars through the sale of state-backed bonds.[28]

Both the Real Estate Bank and its companion, the state-owned Bank of Arkansas, fell victim to the Panic of 1837. The combination of "bad luck, folly, and embezzlement" was too much for them, and by the end of 1839 both had suspended specie payments. Following a legislative investigation in 1843, the Real Estate Bank was assigned to private trustees, one of whom was Henry L. Biscoe, who became Hindman's father-in-law. In 1855 a court decree transferred the bank's assets to a state-appointed receiver.[29]

By 1859, when the Real Estate Bank became a point of contention between Hindman and the Family, the issue had been intertwined with a proposition to reduce taxes. Upon the realistic possibility of a surplus in the state treasury, the legislature had voted to reduce the ratio of state taxation from one sixth to one tenth of a percent. Governor Conway pocket-vetoed the bill, arguing that the surplus should be used to pay off the bank's debts, which in 1861 would amount to $3,634,000.00[30]

Hindman advocated reducing the state tax and paying off the debt by foreclosing on mortgages held by the bank. Lands obtained by foreclosure should be sold, along with the lands held in the bank's trust fund. He advocated collecting all amounts owed to the bank, suing its stockholders, and selling the property they had put up as collateral to pay the interest on the state-backed bonds. He contended that the Johnsons opposed the last proposition because they were major stockholders. Furthermore, he charged that several Family members had paid their debts to the bank with depreciated "bank paper" purchased at heavy discounts and that they should be compelled to remit the difference between par funds and the depreciated paper they had used to pay their debts.[31]

Richard Johnson of the *True Democrat* offered a strikingly different view of the bank question. Hindman, stated Johnson, was the "bank champion" and his interest in resolving the financial crisis lay in the fact that his father-in-law Henry L. Biscoe was a former trustee and still owed it money. He asserted that as a result of mismanagement by Biscoe and the other trustees the bank's deficit had increased from $64,017 in 1842 to $1,354,165 in 1855. Johnson claimed that Biscoe had paid off a $16,200 debt to the bank with 360 acres of land which he valued at forty-five dollars per acre, when in actuality the land sold for only $27.78 per acre, leaving the bank with a loss of $6,200.[32]

To most voters, the arguments presented by both sides on the bank question were baffling and the evidence complicated, confusing, and con-tradictory. While few doubted that the state should meet its responsibility, the question for most people was whether taxpayers who had no stock or loans from the bank should have to shoulder payments for its failures or whether the stockholders should have to pay off the debt. Most appar-ently felt that Hindman had derived no benefit from his father-in-law's connection to the bank and heartily endorsed his position that those who had nothing to do with contracting the debt should not be taxed to pay it.[33]

The warfare between Hindman and the Family escalated when he charged that the state was overpaying the *True Democrat* for public printing. By giving contracts to the paper instead of awarding them by competitive bidding, the government had created a costly monopoly. The *True Democrat* denied that it overcharged the state and declared that selfishness was Hindman's motive rather than concern for the public welfare. He controlled both the Helena *State-Rights Democrat* and the newly established Little Rock *Old Line Democrat* and wanted printing contracts awarded to them.[34]

Hindman's effort to change the date for electing members of

Congress from August in even-numbered years to October in odd-numbered years was defeated in 1859. Opponents charged that its only useful purpose was to enable a "political adventurer to traverse a portion of the state, and force himself among the people." When Governor Conway vetoed the bill on the grounds that it would be detrimental to the best interests of the state, Hindman denounced the action as a deliberate maneuver to insure that the 1860 canvass would be held while he was in Washington, thus giving rivals for his seat an advantage.[35]

Hoping to distract attention from other issues, Hindman's opponents charged that in his rebellion against the Family he had allied with Know Nothings, Whigs, and other enemies of the Democracy. He indignantly denied the accusations, hotly declaring that Family members had admitted Know Nothings to their caucuses in order to maintain control of the Democratic Party. In the process, they had "torn their flag from its bearer and trampled it in the dust." They had "spit upon their platform and covered it with defamation." To buttress his argument, he quoted an editorial in the *Arkansas State Gazette*, an avowed nativist newspaper, which condemned him for "his unjust, unrelenting, and bitter war against the American party" and endorsed the candidacy of Charles A. Carroll, an aspirant for the first district Congressional seat. The same editorial, Hindman gleefully noted, praised Family member Senator Robert W. Johnson for not making speeches in or out of the Senate "against Americanism." According to Hindman, this contrasted markedly with his belief that only "good and true Democrats" should be entitled to a voice in Democratic nominations from "constable up to President."[36]

So harshly did he condemn the admittance of former nativists into the Democracy that a letter to the *True Democrat* complained that old Whigs who had briefly joined the American Party had nowhere to go since Hindman and his followers had denounced them as "'pizerinetunes' or soft horns and with bell, book, and candle [had] formally excommunicate[d] . . . [them] from the church democratic."[37]

To differentiate his supporters from those of the Family, Hindman's political organization adopted the name Old-Line Democrats to signify their support of traditional party principles and christened their Little Rock campaign newspaper with the same name.

Hindman's attacks attracted support from a wide range of voters un-happy with the Family's domination of state politics. For example, Whig stalwart David Walker of Washington County applauded "every blow that Hindman struck at the party" and his face radiated smiles as "Hindman gave it to his old enemies." In northern counties that were regarded as Democratic strongholds, Hindman's revolt appealed to yeomen who were "tired" of the Johnson faction and were, to a man, ready to join with him in the attempt to dethrone the "would-be masters."[38]

Similarly, a letter signed "V" to the *Old-Line Democrat* in September 1859 stated that in the past when a man had the courage to speak out against the Family, he was "killed politically," while the editor of the *True Democrat* reclined in his easy chair and dreamed of his "influence and power." With Hindman at the helm, the people were able to see "inside of the menagerie" and "the veil between the people and their rulers" had been "drawn aside" so that they could "witness the foul corruption and wrongs inflicted upon them." Reflecting the deep-seated belief that the Family had blocked internal improvements and other measures designed to promote economic progress in order to perpetuate themselves in power, "V" exclaimed that Arkansans must replace the "reign of error and misrule" before they could achieve "anything tending to prosperity." To men such as "V," Hindman's challenge to Family domination offered hope for a change in leadership and new policies to promote progress and a strong economy.[39]

As the warfare between Hindman and the Family intensified, the *True Democrat* charged that when none of the Johnsons was present to contradict him, Hindman made vicious and unwarranted personal attacks against them. In contrast, when they were present, he refrained from indulging in "gross personalities." Hindman admitted that he had bitterly assailed the Johnsons' leadership, but he insisted that his remarks were not personal insults. To demonstrate that he was unafraid of a personal confrontation, he announced that he would come to Little Rock and denounce the Johnsons to "their faces" on 24 November 1859.[40]

The promised encounter did not occur. On 17 November the *Old-Line Democrat* published a letter from Hindman dated 12 November describing a carriage accident in which his mother, sister, and three nieces were injured. His mother suffered a broken collarbone, bruises, and a concussion. Anticipating a lengthy trip to Mississippi, he cancelled the Little Rock appointment. Claiming that he was unaware of the change in plans, Senator Robert Johnson journeyed from Pine Bluff for the occasion. When Hindman failed to appear in Little Rock as scheduled,

Johnson labeled his excuse "false in spirit and paltry in fact" and declared that he had manufactured the "whole affair," which was nothing but another "ingenious device to win for himself a name for courage and to fling on others an imputation of cowardice." Hindman was "a bully, and imposter in the ranks of honor." When the *Old-Line Democrat* reprinted a letter from Dr. Charles W. Winston, Mrs. Hindman's physician, attesting to the seriousness of her injuries, Elias Boudinot, the bitterly anti-Hindman editor of the Fayetteville *Arkansian*, claimed that Hindman had returned to Helena by 19 November in time to deliver speeches there and throughout Phillips County even though he failed to keep his Little Rock appointment on 24 November. He queried,

> Can it be that Col. Hindman's ambition so o'leaped itself as to blind him to the natural impulses of a son, and moved him to desert his aged mother in such extremity, and take the stump for the advancement of his mere political interest? Yet such appears to be the case.[41]

Hindman's attacks on the Family split the Democracy asunder, and Richard H. Johnson and his allies vowed to crush him in 1860, even "if it caused Heaven and Hell to meet." It was, indeed, war to the knife. The Helena Congressman had no thought of turning back and was prepared to confirm the assessment of a Des Arc observer that he was an "untamed tiger."[42]

In the fall of 1859, hoping that Hindman's veracity could become a viable issue, the Fayetteville *Arkansian* claimed that under the pseudonym of "Viator" Hindman had authored a series of letters to the *State-Rights Democrat* and the *Old-Line Democrat* lauding his own speeches. For six weeks after the first accusation, Hindman stood "mute," which prompted editor E. C. Boudinot to conclude that he had admitted "the justness of the charge." Subsequently, W. L. Martin of Helena, a close personal friend of Hindman and his "traveling companion" during his 1859 speaking tour, claimed authorship and asserted in a letter to the Helena *Notebook* that Hindman "had nothing whatever to do with their composition."

Hindman, himself, made no public response until the *Arkansian* presented statements from thirty-five men who claimed to have compared an original "Viator" letter dated 13 September 1859 with other letters written by Hindman and concluded that they were in the same handwriting. Boudinot gleefully noted that the evidence clearly convicted Hindman of singing his own praises, and the *True Democrat* happily printed letters attesting that Hindman was "politically dead" in northern Arkansas as a result of the "Viator" episode. In a public letter dated 21 January 1860 Hindman finally responded to the allegation. Martin had authored the letters that contained reports of his speeches, but in the interest of accuracy, had requested him to read them and make any "proper" editorial changes. He had only done what members of Congress did before their speeches were published in the *Congressional Globe*. Making editorial comments prior to the publication of their speeches was a universal practice that was "the right of every public speaker." He offered no apology and boldly asserted that he would "do the same thing again, under similar circumstances."[43]

Family supporters crowed over the "Viator" letters. Although embarrassed by the revelations that he had edited the documents, Hindman had not suffered any real political damage, and the issue was dead when the 1860 campaign began in earnest. Confident of his political power, he took his seat in Congress and plunged into the debates over choosing a new speaker of the house and quickly emerged as one of the South's most vocal critics of Republican aspirant John Sherman of Ohio. His wit and sharply worded barbs thrilled supporters, who relished the Republicans' discomfort as he pressed them to take public stands on issues such as admitting new slave states to the Union and enforcing the Fugitive Slave Act of 1850. At the peak of his popularity, Hindman's re-election now seemed assured, no matter whom the Family put up as an opponent. With the spring nominating conventions only a few months away, Hindman's new-found national prestige was certainly an advantage.[44]

Like the "Viator" letters, the personal feud with Senator Robert W. Johnson that began in Little Rock the previous fall also dissipated. Personal animosity between the two had intensified, and in December 1859 rumors circulated that a duel was inevitable. The intercession of Washington friends, however, resulted in Johnson's withdrawal of his card branding Hindman a "bully and imposter in the ranks of honor" and in Hindman's disclaimers of any purpose to reflect upon Johnson's "personal character or to give him insult." The issue was thus resolved in a manner which preserved the honor of both antagonists. Despite the settlement of personal difficulties, however, Hindman and Johnson remained political antagonists.[45]

As the 1860 state elections approached, the Family continued to rely on its time-honored technique of holding carefully orchestrated local rallies and nominating conventions to perpetuate its political stranglehold on Arkansas. The plan was to nominate Richard H. Johnson, editor of the *True Democrat*, for governor and slot outgoing chief executive Elias N. Conway to fill the senate seat of Robert W. Johnson who was retiring. In past elections the Family had been able to suppress dissent by claiming that party unity was necessary to defeat the opposition. But in 1860 an opposition party no longer existed; both the Whigs and the Know Nothings had disappeared as political entities. The only dissent was internal. Hindman's open warfare on the Family unleashed and encouraged the aspirations of ambitious men ready to buck the Family favorites in their own try for office. Included in this group was Second District Congressman Albert M. Rust, who desired Robert Johnson's senate seat and allied himself with the Hindman faction.[46]

Although Hindman's coalition had not settled on a gubernatorial candidate to challenge Richard Johnson, it staunchly opposed his nomination. When the nominating convention opened in Little Rock on 2 April, the Hindman forces attempted to block Johnson's nomination but were out maneuvered when the Family-dominated credentials committee seated a competing delegation. Moreover, the convention allowed proxies to cast votes for counties with no delegates present. For example, R. S. Yerkes, co-editor of the *True Democrat* and a resident of Pulaski County, was permitted to cast a vote on behalf of Van Buren County, even though it had not held a convention to elect delegates. As was the case when securing Sebastian's senatorial nomination the previous fall, the usual two-thirds requirement to secure a nomination was changed to make possible the selection by a simple majority vote. As a result of these irregularities, Johnson was nominated on the second ballot.[47]

The selection of Johnson was a bitter pill for Hindman's forces. Thomas Peek of the *Old-Line Democrat* voiced their sentiment when he wrote that the nomination was a "great disappointment to thousands of our party and will cause many to chafe under it even to the verge of

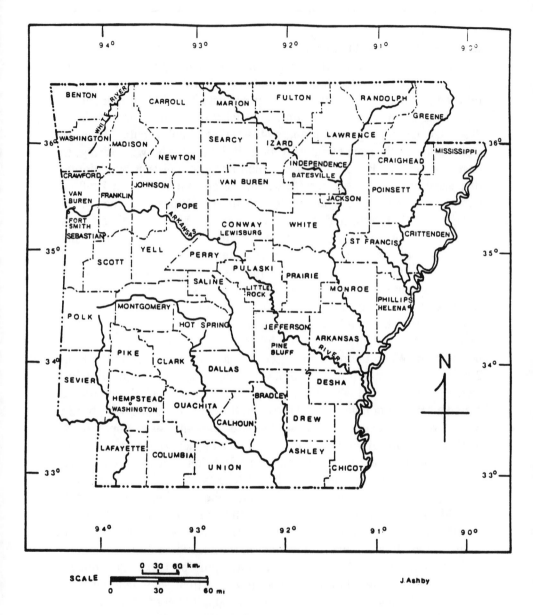

ARKANSAS 1860

Plate 3   *Arkansas (1860)*
J. Ashby, 1990

resistance." Declaring that the nomination was achieved through "improper means and in opposition to the wishes of a large majority of the Democracy of Arkansas," Peek nevertheless urged patience and reluctantly hoisted Johnson's name on the masthead.[48]

Confident that he would easily win the Congressional nomination, Hindman returned home to prepare for the first district nominating convention. The convention opened at Dover in Pope County on 14 May 1860 with Hindman in complete control. Two close associates, W. L. Martin of Phillips County and John A. Price of Independence County, were designated secretaries of the convention. The delegates adopted resolutions endorsing the Dred Scott decision regarding slavery in the territories, condemning efforts to nullify the Fugitive Slave Act, and reaffirming the Batesville platform approved in 1858. With reference to the Batesville meeting, the Dover convention again called upon the legislature to change the date for Congressional elections. As expected, Hindman was nominated on the first ballot, easily defeating A. M. Wilson and William K. Patterson, whose combined total of twelve votes was less than half of his twenty-seven.[49]

Even though his detractors were powerless to prevent his renomination, they vented their anger by accusing him of exercising a "social supervision" over the convention, even to the point of excluding delegates opposed to his candidacy. The *Arkansian* lambasted him for leaving Congress at a time when the "South needed every man at his post" and concluded that Hindman's love for "his own ambitious projects" superseded his devotion to the South.[50]

In contrast to other nominating meetings, neither the "dynasty" nor Hindman's forces were able to prevail at the second district Congressional convention. Family candidate Dr. Charles B. Mitchel and Hindman's ally Edward W. Gantt were locked in such a tight race that no selection was made. In the end, delegates submitted both men to the electorate as bonafide Democratic candidates for Congress.[51]

A Tennessee native, Gantt was the prosecuting attorney for the sixth judicial district. An excellent speaker, he had earned a reputation as a zealous defender of Southern rights whose words "warmed the throbbing hearts of every true Southern man." He vigorously held Congress responsible for protecting slavery in the territories. According to supporters, Gantt was "an eminent statesman, [and] a chivalrous and honest man." In contrast, the Family characterized Gantt as one who possessed a "remarkable" talent for "compressing the fewest ideas into the greatest amount of words" even though he was "somewhat limited in his range of thought." He was a candidate with no ideas of his own and nothing but a "weak, diluted imitation" of Hindman and a "poor self-made miserable man."[52]

Mitchel's stand on slavery and the territories contrasted sharply with that of Gantt. He believed that the Dred Scott decision had made the judiciary, not Congress, responsible for protecting slavery in the territories. Consequently, Congress should adopt a policy of nonintervention. Although Mitchel was perhaps vulnerable on the slavery question, much of the Old-Line rhetoric took the form of vicious epithets relating to his age and connection to the "family." His critics claimed that the "old swamp doctor's" only qualifications for office were that he had lived in Arkansas for twenty-five years and had "danced upon puncheon floors—helped his neighbors roll logs—[and had] worn out a good set of teeth eating jerked beef and hard bread." Lacking in "vigor . . . and profundity," Mitchel was no match for the young and more vigorous Gantt on the stump.[53]

Already hard pressed, the Family received what turned out to be a fatal blow in May 1860 when Henry M. Rector announced his candidacy for governor as an independent Democrat. The announcement of a rival Democratic candidate was hardly unexpected. Dissatisfaction over the tactics employed to engineer the gubernatorial nomination of Richard Johnson still permeated Democratic circles. On 17 May, the *Old-Line Democrat* printed a petition signed by fifty-six men protesting "against political ends attained by sinister means." The petitioners called upon the people to "assert their right and determination to rule," regardless of opposition of cliques "great or small, powerful or weak" and requested that Henry Rector of Little Rock enter the race for governor. Rector, who had been mentioned as a possible candidate as early as March 1859 eagerly entered the race, and on 24 May his name replaced Johnson's on the masthead of the *Old-Line Democrat.*[54]

Rector was no political neophyte. A native of Missouri and a cousin of Governor Conway, he had previously been regarded as a member of the Family organization. A former United States marshall and member of the state legislature, Rector had served on the state supreme court from February 1859 until May 1860. "Pompous, very verbose," and "hot-tempered," he usually acted "from impulse" rather than "from reflection."[55]

Since Rector had not previously been identified with Hindman's political organization and he had been regarded as a loyal member of the

Family, superficially his candidacy appeared to be an anomaly. He was an ambitious man, however, who aspired to higher rank than the Family leadership was ready to accord him in 1860. The Family had placed him on the Supreme Court in the spring of 1860 to restrain his ambition and remove him as a possible challenger to Richard H. Johnson. In June 1859, when the *State-Rights Democrat* suggested Rector as a gubernatorial nominee, the *True Democrat* rushed to acclaim him as a loyal Democrat who would never become a "rough shod" candidate against a regular party nominee. Johnson was wrong. Rector wanted to become the next governor of Arkansas and undoubtedly believed that Hindman would support an independent to oppose Richard H. Johnson.[56]

Rector, with his long residence in the state and important connections (including previous ties to the Family) seemed ideal to Hindman. Old Whigs and dissidents within the Family organization might lend their support. While Rector may not have been Hindman's hand-picked candidate as many Family supporters thought, their relationship was certainly one of mutual convenience. To wrest control of the state Democratic party from the Family, Hindman needed an acceptable candidate, while Rector needed the support of Hindman's organization to win. Pro-Hindman newspapers quickly followed the lead of the *Old-Line Democrat* in linking together the candidacies of Hindman, Gantt, and Rector in common struggle against the powerful clique that had dominated state politics since territorial days.[57]

As engineer of the rebellion against dynastic rule, Hindman closely followed the candidacies of both Gantt and Rector, even though he spent little time on the campaign trail. For most of June he was out of state attending to Congressional duties in Washington and serving as a delegate to the Democratic National Convention in Baltimore. Following the adjournment of Congress on 25 June, he planned to make a quick canvass of the first Congressional district, but Mollie Hindman's illness kept him close to home. Attempting to use the illness to its political advantage, the *True Democrat* stated that Hindman believed that Rector's political ship was sinking and was not campaigning because he could do nothing to save it. One editorial even suggested that Hindman secretly preferred Richard Johnson's election. Even if events in Washington and Baltimore and family matters had not intervened, Hindman had always expected Gantt and Rector to pull their own weight in the campaign. Also, with his own victory over Family-backed Jesse N. Cypert virtually assured, he did not feel compelled to do a thorough canvass. When he finally took the stump, however, his followers declared that his "brilliant" and "forcible" arguments won many followers of the Johnsons to Rector."[58]

The gubernatorial campaign was exceptionally bitter, and although Johnson and Rector discussed the Real Estate Bank and the State Bank debts and internal improvements, the campaign focused mainly on personalities. When issues were debated, the rhetoric was confusing and neither candidate seemed to offer real solutions to pressing problems. Johnson endorsed outgoing Governor Conway's policies regarding the bank debts and opposed internal improvements until the state debt was repaid. Rector dismissed the Family's bank policy as "no policy at all" and proposed funding internal improvements by issuing twenty-five year six percent state bonds to the railroads in an amount equal to the state's outstanding indebtedness. The railroads would transfer their stock to the state, and the state would use the stock to cancel the bonds, "thereby not only paying the State's indebtedness but at the same time building railroads, without its costing the state a cent." The idea seemed so bizarre that a critic writing to the Van Buren *Press* called it a "fantastic intellectual" trick that demonstrated "great want of practicability." The idea of "paying debts and building railroads without money, is in finance, what perpetual motion is in mechanics, something not yet discovered." While many voters questioned the feasibility of Rector's complicated scheme, Johnson's advocacy of deferring internal improvements until the state debt was repaid antagonized many Arkansans who believed internal improvements, especially railroads, were vital if the state was to usher in economic opportunity and prosperity.[59]

Despite the seriousness of the issues, the campaign centered mainly on personalities, the legitimacy of Johnson's nomination, and the alleged ex-Know Nothing support for Rector. Rector and his supporters denounced "the frauds" used at the state convention to select Johnson, especially those relating to proxy votes from Van Buren, Greene, Benton, and Lawrence counties. "Old Line Democrats" had no obligation to obey the dictates of a convention that was Democratic in name only. The people must rise up and slay "a factious combination" that for "the last quarter of a century" had dominated the state by "promot[ing]" and sustain[ing]" their "favorites" in office.[60]

After years of "maneuvering," the blatant "fraud and trickery of the last family convention . . . had brushed the scales from the purblind

Democracy, and manifestations of the public indignation" were reaching a crescendo. Even in areas where "the immaculate and anointed leaders" of the party had been "heretofore worshipped," they were to be overthrown.[61]

Johnson and his backers did not recoil from the Family issue. Instead, they met it head on, reminding voters that dissident candidate Henry M. Rector had been a member of their group. The editor of the Pocahontas (AR) *Advertiser and Herald* caustically noted "this cry of *family*" against Johnson and asked "ought it not rather be made against Rector? He is the last man who should have attempted to disorganize the Democratic party—a party to which he and his family owe so much." According to the Fayetteville *Arkansian*, "all the *buncombe* about *family*" was intended "to put down Democratic nominees in order to exalt a real *oligarchy*." Rector and his supporters were basing their hope of success on tying "their tails [to] credulous Know Nothings." Echoing this argument, a letter to the editor of the Van Buren *Press* stated that "scheming politicians of the Rector school think they can cloud the mind of the people by loudly croaking about the family, the dynasty, etc." The writer assured that the people "know his character," however, and his Know Nothing "seceders" and "disorganizers" will not fool them.[62]

In addition to attacking Rector for using "the old, worn out and low down trick" of crying "Family" and his supposed connection to ex-Know Nothings, Johnson's supporters defended the proceedings of the state convention. Even though the convention "was not in all things as fair as it might have been," it was "humbuggery" to denounce the results. Rector was not the "regular" nominee of the Democratic party but the candidate of "a few discontented politicians and disappointed office-seekers, newly fledged and enthusiastic, but idealess, tricksters." As "the legitimate and regular nominee of the fairest state convention ever held, Richard Johnson was entitled to the faithful vote of the true democracy."[63]

Following the spirited and epithet-laden campaign, voters went to the polls on 6 August and dealt the Family a resounding defeat. Hindman crushed Jesse N. Cypert of White County by a two to one margin, carrying twenty-three of twenty-seven counties. Although the other Congressional race was not as lopsided, Gantt defeated Mitchel by 3,562 votes. The coup was completed when the gubernatorial votes were counted and Rector narrowly defeated Johnson 31,044 to 28,967. The electorate had rejected all three of the Family's candidates, leading

Thomas C. Peek, editor of the *Old-Line Democrat*, to proclaim "the people's majesty" had ended the dynastic rule of the Family, which was now being "taken at reduced prices." Although Charles B. Mitchel was elected to the United States Senate in December 1860 and later served with Family member Robert W. Johnson in the Confederate Senate, the canvass marked the end of Family hegemony in Arkansas. After 1860, civil war and reconstruction brought new issues and new political issues to the forefront, and the Family never again became a dominant factor in state politics.[64]

What motivated the electorate to vote as it did is unclear, although the key factor in Rector's election appears to have been the combined support of former Whigs and dissident Democrats. Although he lost fourteen of the twenty-two traditional Whig counties, the ones he carried were more populous, resulting in an 888 vote margin. Rector's candidacy certainly gave former Whigs an opportunity to vote against one of their old foes. Given the nature of nineteenth century politics, the speaking ability of the various candidates played a major role in the election. Johnson's "slow, dry, and prosy" speeches could not compete with Rector's "graceful," even if verbose, style.[65]

With regard to the Congressional canvass, Hindman had no equal, and Gantt was a better orator than Mitchel. Another factor favoring the dissidents was the past performance of the Family. During its tenure, it had subordinated critical issues to balance intra-sectional rivalries within Arkansas, rather than dealing with them in a meaningful manner. The moment he broke with the Family, Hindman and his followers attacked it for its failure to move the state forward. Many newcomers who had arrived in the state during the 1850s may have been attracted by this argument and voted against those whose inactions they believed had retarded economic development. According to his supporters, the Congressman had "aroused residents from lethargy" and "opened their eyes to the abuses, . . . injuries, . . . and insults" to which they had been subjected by the "immense power" of the monopolistic "junto." Regardless of why it happened, a political revolution had occurred, and the Family had been rebuked at the polls. Instead of crushing the young Helena upstart and the rebellion that he had spawned, the "dynasty" lay near death.[66]

Chapter 4

CHAMPION
OF SOUTHERN RIGHTS

The debate over the Compromise of 1850 left an indelible impression upon Thomas C. Hindman. A sincere exponent of Southern state rights, he believed that slavery was a benevolent institution sanctioned by the Constitution and entitled to legal protection. During his pre-war political career, Hindman never wavered in his belief that slavery must be protected where it already existed and that slaveholders had the legal right to take their slaves with them to any territory of the United States. He also advocated the right of slaveowners to travel through or temporarily reside in free states with their slaves secure in the knowledge that their property rights would be respected. Like many Southerners, he strongly disapproved of the Compromise measures, but agreed to abide by them. The trade-off for allowing California to be admitted as a free state was the passage of a vigorous fugitive slave law. Hindman insisted that the act be strictly enforced and that Northern "personal liberty laws" aimed at nullifying it were placing the Union in jeopardy. There was no doubt in his mind that the Union could be preserved only by guaranteeing the equality of states and protecting slavery. Otherwise, he was quite ready to endorse Southern independence.

During his brief Mississippi political career, he allied himself with the State Rights wing of the Democratic Party. Not content with voting and campaigning for state rights candidates, Hindman was eager to put his beliefs into action by joining Quitman's proposed expedition to liberate Cuba from Spanish rule and to annex it to the United States as additional slave territory. He also endorsed the filibustering efforts of William Walker in Nicaragua. Although he was not among the few thousand Southerners who moved to Kansas in the 1850s to help make that area a slave territory, he supported their efforts and laws designed to ensure that slaveholders could settle in territories with their property protected by law. He believed that slavery should not be an issue when a territory applied for statehood. The only requirements should be the requisite population and a representative government. By the time Hindman took his seat in Congress in December 1859, these beliefs formed the core of his political creed.[1]

Hindman was not only committed to protecting slavery and encouraging its expansion, like many Southerners he believed that actions must be taken to strengthen the "peculiar institution." He heartily championed resolutions approved at the 1856 Batesville congressional nominating convention recommending that free blacks be expelled from Arkansas because they were becoming "too numerous and too trouble- some." This line of thinking reflected the belief of many white Southerners that free blacks constituted an anomaly since they accepted without reservation the concept that servitude was the natural condition for blacks.[2]

The same convention approved a resolution urging Congress to adopt measures aimed at encouraging more citizens to become slaveholders by repealing the prohibition against the international slave trade. Like many Southerners, Hindman saw the repeal of laws against the importation of slaves from both a practical and theoretical viewpoint. The expanding cotton production of the late 1850s had been steadily driving the prices of slaves upwards, with the consequence that only a few whites could afford the large capital outlay to become slaveowners. An influx of slaves would drop the purchase price dramatically and "enable the men, who now are compelled to toil themselves to buy negroes for $250, and thereby prevent the wealthy planters from gathering the negroes to themselves."[3]

Reflecting Hindman's views, Thomas Peek of the *Old-Line Democrat* stated that the question was not whether the international slave trade should be reopened, but rather whether the South would continue to submit by allowing an act of Congress to "slumber upon the statute book that *unnecessarily* and *unconstitutionally* degrades the South by stig- matizing a traffic in her recognized property as *piracy*." This glaring insult to the South should be brushed out, according to Peek.[4]

If Congress exercised its authority to outlaw the importation of slaves into the country, might it also under the guise of regulating interstate

Plate 4   *Thomas C. Hindman (1859)*
Courtesy: Chicago Historical Society

commerce place a ban upon the interstate sale and transfer of slaves? Fearing such a move, Peek declared that the "right to buy and sell slaves rests exactly upon the same high grounds that the right to own and use them rests. The two cannot be separated." Congress had no more right to interfere with the interstate slave trade than with the sale and transfer of "any other kind of property."[5]

Hindman's stand on both the international and interstate slave trade reflected his personal convictions as well as the economic interests of Arkansas. As a developing frontier, Arkansas needed a growing labor supply to cultivate its rich alluvial soil and enable the state to assume its desired place as "the" cotton producing state in the Union. The escalating price of slaves retarded plantation expansion and contributed to a decline in the percentage of the total population that owned slaves. To strengthen slavery within the state, Arkansans needed not only to purchase slaves from other slave states, but to import them from Africa as well.[6]

For the South to avoid shrinking into an ever decreasing minority, it needed to expand into the territories. Popular sovereignty and the Dred Scott decision had theoretically opened territories to slavery, but without slaves to help populate the new lands and work the fields, the territories would not become slave states. The continued right to sell and transfer slaves to residents of the territories was imperative while the opportunity to import them from Africa would provide the labor to make new slave states a reality.[7]

Thomas Hindman was certainly not alone in advocating the renewal of the international slave trade. Many Southerners, including George Fitzhugh of Virginia, supported the proposition in the hope that it would strengthen the position of the South within the Union and, thus, avert the threat of secession. Hindman and others perceived the reopened trade as a means of restoring Southern political power and at the same time permitting the South to protect and preserve Southern rights within the Union. They also believed that even if the attempt failed, it might gain widespread support, help unite the section, and lead to Southern independence.[8]

Given his strong belief in the rightness of slavery and his desire to increase the number of slave states as a way of preserving the South's position within the Union, Hindman naturally manifested a fierce antipathy towards Republicans who were committed to halting the spread of slavery and putting the "peculiar institution" on the road to ultimate extinction. During his Congressional canvasses, he had denounced Know Nothingism and Republicanism as the twin evils of "Sam and Sambo," which threatened the Constitution and the old Union of Washington and Jefferson that he cherished. He was wary of compromise, which he felt had gnawed away at Southern rights. His supporters within Arkansas and across the South applauded his stand as a "powerful bulwark against Northern fanaticism."[9]

Hindman fully met their expectations when the Thirty-sixth Congress convened on 5 December 1859. What in normal times would have been a routine matter of business erupted into a full-scale partisan battle between Democrats, Republicans, and several splinter groups over the choice of the Speaker of the House. Neither the 101 Democrats nor the 109 Republicans could command a majority to select a presiding officer and had to hope for votes from the 26 American Party members or the lone representative who still called himself a Whig. From the first ballot the leading Republican candidate was John Sherman of Ohio, while the Democratic choice was Thomas S. Bocock of Virginia. When Sherman's name was proposed, Democrat John B. Clark of Missouri introduced resolutions condemning the Ohioan for signing a Republican-sponsored compendium of Hinton Rowan Helper's controversial book, *The Impending Crisis of the South*. A letter accompanying the compendium contained explosive headings such as "Revolutionary Appeal to Southern Non-Slave-holders," "The Non-Slave-holders to Strike for Treason," and "Revolution—Peacefully, If We Can, Violently If We Must."[10]

Although Sherman asserted that he had signed the letter without having read Helper's book or the compendium and declared that he was opposed to "any interference whatever by the people of the free States with the relations of master and slave in the slave States," Southern Democrats vigorously denounced him and the other signatories for promoting servile insurrection and bloodshed in the South. Representative Shelton F. Leake of Virginia summarized the Southern viewpoint bluntly:

> We on this side, are entitled to know who it is that we are to elect Speaker, whether we are to elect a man who, while I am here in the discharge of my public duties, is stimulating my negroes at home to apply the torch to my dwelling and the knife to the throats of my wife and helpless children.[11]

The apparent Republican determination to stick with Sherman, even though Southerners regarded his nomination as a threat and a personal insult, touched off a full-scale debate on the merits of slavery and the related sectional issues of the admission of new slave states and enforcement of fugitive slave legislation. Into this fray jumped freshman representative Thomas Hindman. On 19 and 20 January 1860, he delivered a speech subsequently entitled "That Black Republican Bible—The Helper Book." A master of oratory, Hindman's soft voice rose and fell as he flayed Sherman's past "transgressions." According to his supporters, he thoroughly dissected Sherman's record on slavery, causing the Ohioan to pale under the "excoriation inflicted upon him." The same fluent delivery that had made him an unsurpassed stump speaker elicited applause and cheers from the Democratic side of the House and from proslavery admirers in the galleries while the Republicans squirmed in discomfort.[12]

Carefully and methodically, the young Congressman from Arkansas reiterated the rationale behind the Democratic opposition to Sherman and the Republican House leadership. The Republican Party was "synonymous . . . with sectionalism, with hostility to state rights, with disloyalty to the Constitution, and with treason to the Government, and with civil war, bloodshed, murder, and rapine." Employing tactics used successfully in his campaign speeches, he read documents that he claimed substantiated his accusations. They included a petition from New Yorkers urging resistance to the Fugitive Slave Act and a copy of proceedings from textile workers in Massachusetts asserting that they suffered from such exploitation and low wages that "negro slavery is far preferable and death sweet, rather than continued durance vile."[13]

Southerners, still terrified by John Brown's raid at Harper's Ferry, Virginia, the previous October, heartily agreed with his declaration that Republicans by "their maddening and furious abuse of slavery and slaveholders, . . . [had] set on fire the brain of that old fanatic." He concluded that "John Brown was the tool of Republicanism, doing its work; and now, that work is done, Republican politicians cannot skulk the responsibility." To representative John Hickman of Pennsylvania, who had threatened to reenact the conduct of John Brown by marching eighteen thousand Northern men against the South to "whip her into submission to the higher law," Hindman proclaimed that when the invasion came, the price of hemp would rise, "for our whole crop will be needed to hang the Abolition soldiery, but the price of arms will go down, for we will take from our invaders arms enough to equip our whole population." Laughter rang from the galleries and the Democratic side of the House, as Hindman promised that "with bloody hands" Southerners would welcome the invaders to "hospitable graves."[14]

Turning to Sherman, Hindman quoted the Ohioan's remarks supporting Congressional legislation to exclude slavery from certain territories, opposing the admission of new slaveholding states, branding the fugitive slave act as "a savage and unhuman law" and stigmatizing slavery as "an injury to the master and a crime against the slave." Sherman refused to reply directly to Hindman but insisted that he had never sought "to trample upon the rights of citizens of the southern States." When Harrison Blake of Ohio interrupted to assert that there was no one on the witness stand to answer Hindman's questions, the Arkansan pointed to Sherman and shot back, "There may be nobody on the witness stand, but I think there is one here on the mourner's bench."[15]

Hindman urged Democrats to forget their differences and to nominate a candidate for speaker who could appeal to anti-Lecompton Democrats and the Southern opposition (Whig and American Party members). Only in this way, could the Republican candidate be defeated.[16]

At home, Arkansans lauded Hindman's speech as the "ablest thing they [had] ever read" and boasted that he was "the first man from the South, that has ever *floored* the leader of the Black Republican forces." An admirer from Springfield exulted that he had "grappled with the hydra headed monster Black Republicanism with a heroism worthy a political Hercules. We are proud of him." His "burning eloquence" had brought down the "notorious" Sherman "in spite of all the muzzles the Republican phalanx" could put on him. He had become the "LEADER of the State Rights democracy" and had attained the highest rank of any "political debater" or "statesman" from Arkansas.[17]

Accolades also came from Democratic newspapers throughout the United States. The editor of the Somerville (AR) *Democrat* declared that there was not a sentiment in Hindman's speech that he could not endorse. "He is for the Union with the Constitution. Union with honor, disunion, rather than be trampled underfoot, seems to be his motto." Self-made men like Hindman, he concluded, were "the nation's jewels." Praise came from the Ottawa (OH) *Democrat,* which commended his speech for the "truths of wholesomeness" that it contained, while the Portland (ME)

Argus expressed appreciation for the compliments Hindman paid to Northern Democrats for their efforts against Republican domination of the House. Lastly, the Vicksburg (MS) *Sun* proudly noted Hindman's Mississippi heritage and called his address "pre-eminently distinguished" and ranked it among the best in Congress. "That Black Republican Bible—The Helper Book" address was a sensation in Democratic circles. By early March 1860, fifty thousand copies had been sold, and the demand for it remained strong. His premier speech brought Hindman national recognition and acclaim as a spokesman for Southern rights.[18]

Through most of the balloting, Hindman consistently voted for various Democratic candidates in the hope that one of them would be victorious. As a desperate measure, he was willing to vote for one from the so-called Southern Opposition, or as he termed it "the Know Nothing party," as the lesser of two evils, but it would be a "reluctant" ballot. Accordingly, he supported William N. H. Smith, a North Carolina Whig, as a last resort effort to defeat the Republicans. Despite fiery speeches, Democrats were not able to maintain a united front nor attract enough Whig and American party votes to defeat the Republicans. On the forty-fourth ballot, conservative Republican William Pennington of New Jersey, who often described himself as an Old-Line Whig in favor of the Fugitive Slave Act, won over Democrat John McClernand of Illinois. Although gratified that Sherman had gone down to defeat, Hindman could not conceal his anger and disappointment. As the House clerk relayed the news of Pennington's victory, Hindman exclaimed that "a Black Republican Speaker had been elected by the votes of two members of the Know Nothing Party." In contrast to Sherman, who had prompted threats of immediate disunion and withdrawal of several state delegations, Pennington's election sparked no such retaliation.[19]

The tensions that exploded on the floor during the speakership contest persisted into the spring of 1860. On 7 March, Republican Charles H. Van Wyck of New York delivered a lengthy attack on the pro-slavery Democracy, in which he charged that the "peculiar institution" had produced a despotism that oppressed both whites and blacks in the South. He placed the blame for "Bleeding Kansas" squarely upon the shoulders of pro-slavery forces. Southerners such as Hindman seethed with resentment as Van Wyck proclaimed that cowardly Southerners had "quailed and fled before Northern courage and bravery" in Kansas. By implication, he applied the label of coward to his Southern colleagues when he retorted to Reuben Davis of Mississippi that he was not afraid to express his views south of the District of Columbia.[20]

Although stung by Van Wyck's comments, Hindman made no reply on the House floor. A few days later, however, during an encounter outside the National Hotel, Hindman rebuffed the New York Republican's greeting, remarking that Van Wyck's speech had been "insulting to every Southern gentleman." Contrary to subsequent rumors of an "exchange of blows and exhibitions of deadly weapons," no violent altercation occurred.[21]

Finally, after weeks of rancorous debate, the House settled down to the business of appropriations, internal improvements, and individual state concerns. Hindman proposed resolutions along this line to reduce the price of public lands, convert the Little Rock arsenal and the portion of the military reservation at Fort Smith not needed for military purposes to educational use, and finance the construction of a combined courthouse, post office, and federal office building at Little Rock. He also supported his colleague Albert Rust's proposal to fund the construction of a canal to circumvent the Red River Raft that virtually rendered the Red River useless to navigation. In keeping with a campaign pledge, he labored industriously in support of a Pacific railroad that would follow the thirty-fifth parallel from Memphis to Albuquerque via Fort Smith.[22]

As far as his constituents were concerned, Hindman had compiled a glowing record in Congress. Impressed by "his bold and manly efforts to locate the great pacific Railroad on the thirty-fifth parallel," R. F. Colburn of Van Buren exclaimed "well done, Hindman" and suggested calling a public meeting to give him a "declaration of approval." According to J. S. Dunham of the Van Buren *Press*, at no time had Arkansas possessed a "more energetic, working member" of Congress. Crawford County Democrats acclaimed him "the ablest Representative Arkansas has ever had in congress" and called him their "FIRST, LAST, AND ONLY CHOICE for Representative in Congress." From Jackson County Democrats came high praise for Hindman as "a statesman, patriot, and Representative whom we justly may, and do, feel proud to honor." Little wonder then, that in spite of the "Viator" letters and the feud with the Johnson "family," he easily won re-nomination and re-election in 1860.[23]

Although he was not a delegate to the Democratic National Convention that met at Charleston, South Carolina, in April, during the summer of 1860 Hindman's attention, like that of many Americans, focused on the coming presidential election. Fellow Arkansan Thomas Flournoy was chosen president *pro tem* in deference to his strong support for Stephen A. Douglas, the party's presidential front-runner. As Cincinnati reporter Murat Halstead predicted, the convention quickly ruptured as Southerners insisted upon a platform endorsing the protection of slavery in the territories and an unequivocal repudiation of the Douglas doctrine of popular sovereignty. Northerners, on the other hand, pressed for the endorsement of popular sovereignty, which would permit the people of a given territory to abolish or exclude slavery during the territorial stage. Neither side was willing to yield on these critical points.[24]

On the fifth day of the convention (27 April), the platform committee reaffirmed the 1856 platform with the addition of resolutions that advocated popular sovereignty, condemned personal liberty laws, and endorsed a transcontinental railroad and the annexation of Cuba. Debates on the platform threw the convention into an uproar with "a hundred delegates upon the floor, and upon chairs, screaming like panthers, and gesticulating like monkeys." When efforts at compromise failed, Alabama led a Southern stampede from the assembly. At this point, the Arkansas delegation splintered. Six members left, while only two, Thomas Flournoy and John Stirman, remained. The departure of so many Southerners left the convention in a quandary since a two-thirds vote of all delegates was required to nominate a presidential candidate. Unable to choose a standard bearer, the convention was forced to adjourn and to reconvene on 18 June at the Front Street Theater in Baltimore, Maryland.[25]

Back in Arkansas, public opinion was divided as to which set of delegates had acted correctly. Most of the Charleston delegates announced their intention to attend the Baltimore meeting as official delegates. In addition, the congressional nominating conventions at Dover and Arkadelphia named new slates, with Hindman being listed as an alternate by the Dover convention. To further complicate matters, Douglas supporters held a rally in Madison (St. Francis County) and named a three-man delegation headed by Dr. William Hooper. The four overlapping Arkansas delegations all appeared at Baltimore, each claiming to be official representatives from Arkansas. Similar situations existed in several other Southern states which had participated in the

Charleston bolt. The Massachusetts and Missouri delegations also had contested seats.[26]

The rivalry between competing Arkansas delegations erupted into violence while Hindman and Hooper were testifying before the credentials committee. Seeking to convince the committee that the Hooper delegation should not be seated, Hindman claimed that witnesses he was ready to present would testify that less than one hundred and fifty people had attended the Madison mass meeting, some of whom were not citizens of Arkansas. Angrily denying the accusations, Hooper shook his finger "menacingly" at Hindman several times and referred to him as "that man." Hindman pushed Hooper's hand away from his head, but Hooper again pointed or shook his finger at Hindman and declared that the former's statement that the Madison delegation did not represent the Democracy was "false—unqualifiedly false." In response, Hindman stepped forward, struck Hooper in the face, retreated slightly, and then drew a pistol from his pocket. Hooper also "made a movement as if preparing to draw a weapon," but "exhibited none." Committee members and friends immediately surrounded Hindman and pulled him several feet away from Hooper to prevent further confrontation. The congressman then apologized to the credentials committee for the violence. When testimony resumed, Hooper explained that he had not intended to stigmatize Hindman's statement as false, but had rather referred to statements to be made by witnesses Hindman had planned to introduce.[27]

The following day, in an exchange of letters, Hooper demanded redress in the form of a duel, but Hindman refused on the grounds that Hooper was not his "equal." Hooper then retaliated by publishing a card labeling Hindman a bully for striking him and a coward for denying him formal redress. Naturally, Hindman's critics reiterated Hooper's charges and claimed that the affair had detracted from his "hard earned fighting reputation." While his enemies hoped that the episode would tarnish the congressman's image, it did not. Most likely, Hindman's supporters believed that Hooper had provoked the attack and had no right to expect an apology or redress for an affair that he had instigated.[28]

Regarding the Hooper delegation as "bogus" because non-Arkansans had participated in the selection process, the other Arkansas delegates caucused on 18 June to decide on a strategy if the credentials committee admitted the Madison group or denied seating to any of the "regularly" nominated delegates. All delegates, except Thomas Flournoy, signed a letter asserting the right of regular Democrats to seats and protesting the "absurd" claims of the Madison group.[29]

A subsequent caucus adopted a resolution authored by Hindman stating that the Arkansas delegates preferred to "act with Southern men for the South rather than with Northern men against the South" and therefore would join with the majority of regular Democrats from the South in opposing the admission of "Bogus Delegations" and in supporting the protection of slavery in the territories. Senator Robert Johnson and Hindman were selected to confer with other Southern delegations and to inform them of the Arkansas resolution. Happily, Hindman reported on 22 June that a conference of committees from various Southern states had unanimously decided to "make common cause with each other" and to "remain out of the convention if any Regular Democrat is excluded or Bogus Delegate admitted." Proclaiming hearty support for the decision, Johnson announced that he was ready to "battle side by side with his bitterest enemy and against his bosom friend" for the common cause. Hindman concurred, stating that Stephen A. Douglas desired to exclude "Regular Democrats" from the convention in order to repudiate the "just doctrine of protection for slave property in the Territories and to guarantee adoption of a popular sovereignty platform." He could not support such a platform or vote for the nominee of the convention should either of these events occur.[30]

After four days of stormy debate, the credentials committee forced the issue when it submitted a majority report according a number of seats to the competing delegates from Arkansas and other Southern states. The committee also seated the substitutes from Massachusetts and Missouri. These actions completed the rupture of the convention and the national Democratic Party. Having previously agreed to bolt if competing delegates were seated, two hundred thirty-one Southern and pro-Southern members withdrew from the assembly and held their own convention at the Maryland Institute. Unlike the "regular" Arkansas Democrats, Thomas Flournoy and the Madison delegates refused to secede and continued to support Douglas.[31]

After organizing their convention, the seceding delegates adopted a platform affirming the right of citizens to settle "with their property" in the territories and the responsibility of the federal government to protect the "rights of persons and property in the Territories." Amid great fanfare, the newly reconstituted National Democratic Convention nominated John C. Breckinridge of Kentucky and Joseph Lane of Oregon for president and vice-president, respectively. The Breckinridge ticket also received the endorsement of other Southern seceders from the Charleston convention who held a rival convention in Richmond, Virginia.[32]

With their numbers greatly reduced by the bolt, the remaining delegates at the Front Street Theater nominated Stephen A. Douglas for president and Benjamin Fitzpatrick of Alabama for vice president. When Fitzpatrick declined, the second spot on the ticket went to Herschel V. Johnson of Georgia.[33]

In Arkansas, as elsewhere in the South, Abraham Lincoln as the candidate of the hated Republican party could expect no support. Most Arkansans heartily echoed the sentiments of Fayetteville's J. W. Washbourne who exhorted voters to "*Check Lincoln!* Crush abolition sectionalism, combat anti-slavery, if you would preserve inviolate your sovereign liberties." Should the "black Republican party" win, the Van Buren *Press* predicted that it would "commence the mischievous work of trampling upon the South and goading it into a separation from her sisters of the North."[34]

Likewise, the candidacy of Stephen A. Douglas was doomed in Arkansas. Even prior to the rupture of the Baltimore convention, most Arkansas voters had rejected Douglas and his doctrine of popular sovereignty. Phillips County Democrats in March 1860 had approved resolutions abhorring and repudiating "squatter sovereignty, and other heresies which a faction at the North . . . has attempted to engraft on the platform of our party." Not surprisingly, given his prominent role against Douglas at the Baltimore convention, Hindman took the stump against the Illinois Democrat's candidacy. At a rally in Prairie County in late August, Hindman and fellow Congressman Albert Rust, a Douglas supporter, debated the merits of the rival Democratic presidential candidates. Given the political sentiment in Arkansas, Rust's efforts were doomed from the beginning. While the crowd cheered, he "winced and writhed" as Hindman assailed Douglas's policy of popular sovereignty as an "abominable heresy" and a "revolting deformity" that could only lead to "unhappy results."[35]

The audience at a Little Rock Breckinridge and Lane Club meeting applauded as Hindman attacked the nomination of Douglas as one "procured by the most unfair, unjust, undemocratic, and fraudulent means that were ever resorted to, to accomplish an unholy purpose." Declaring that candidates should be measured according to their platform promises, he proclaimed that the Douglas platform had "denied to the people of the South equal rights with the people of the North." Then turning to John Bell of Tennessee, the candidate of the Constitutional Union Party, Hindman passionately asserted that "the simple cry of Union without explanation or interpretation was but as a 'sounding brass and tinkling cymbal,' meaning nothing, or perhaps even worse than nothing." He stated that the Bell-Everett platform was "open to any kind of construction, that southern extremists and northern fanatics could stand side by side upon it." In conclusion, he asserted that "Lincoln was in favor of the Constitution as much as Bell, and that there was no substantial difference between them as to the enforcement of the laws."[36]

At Searcy and Des Arc, "the invincible" Hindman "gloriously held aloft" the Breckinridge banner in a spirited debate with Hugh F. Thomason, who claimed that the only way of saving the Union was by the election of the Constitutional Union ticket. Aiming for Bell's Southern Achilles heel, Hindman castigated the Tennessean for favoring the abolition of slavery in Washington, D. C. and voting against the repeal of the Missouri Compromise. During the course of their remarks, both speakers addressed the issue of state rights and its potential post election ramifications. Citing the Virginia and Kentucky Resolutions, Hindman "asserted the constitutional right of a State to secede from the Union," while Thomason condemned the fallacy of states judging for themselves as to the "mode and means of redress in a contest growing out of a law of Congress."[37]

Hindman's efforts on Breckinridge's behalf brought him into debate with his old antagonist Henry S. Foote, now a resident of Tennessee. On 14 September 1860, Foote spoke to a crowd of several thousand people at a Memphis theater where he condemned Breckinridge's candidacy as the "disunion scheme" of Alabamian William Lowndes Yancey. Aware of Hindman's presence in the audience, Foote alluded to the 1851 gubernatorial race in Mississippi and denounced his opponents as a "band of disunionists and traitors." Looking in Hindman's direction, Foote sneeringly remarked that some of the Mississippi traitors had since emigrated to Arkansas.[38]

Following Foote's remarks, voices in the audience called for Hindman to respond. Arriving on stage, the Arkansas congressman took advantage of the opportunity to attack Foote's "political antecedents," especially his role in the Compromise of 1850. The pro-Breckinridge Memphis *Daily Avalanche* gleefully claimed that Foote emerged from the encounter, his heart "stinging with remorse which [had been] deadened for years," but which Hindman had succeeded in bringing back to him. Foote would no more meet Hindman in debate again than he would "encounter the Anacondin who, embracing him with its folds, would crush him in its convolutions."[39]

As 6 November 1860 dawned, 54,043 Arkansas voters prepared to cast presidential ballots. With a sense of foreboding, Judge John W. Brown of Camden wrote that it was "the most important day to these United States and perhaps to mankind since the 4th of July 1776. . . . The presidential election today will in all probability be made the pretext for destroying the only Republican form of government on earth." Like Judge Brown, many Arkansans felt "great anxiety about the safety of the Union." They also felt that the fate of Southern rights was at stake. Consequently, the results were about as expected.[40]

Breckinridge carried Arkansas, garnering 28,732 votes. Bell finished second with 20,094 votes, and Douglas ran a distant third, polling only 5,227 votes. Generally, with some exceptions, the vote followed previous Whig-Democratic patterns. The wealthy planter counties in the southeast gave their support to Bell, and the mountain counties of the northwest, the traditional bastion of the Democracy, favored Breckinridge. In the southwest where migration from the lower South was increasing, Breckinridge ran very well among small planters, while Bell and Douglas did well in urban areas such as Little Rock, Van Buren, and Fort Smith. Nationwide, however, the results were much different. Lincoln won a clear electoral majority with 180 votes to Breckinridge's seventy-two, Bell's thirty-nine, and twelve for Douglas.[41]

For Thomas Hindman, Lincoln's election signaled that the time for compromise had passed. Southern rights would no longer be safe within the Union when a Republican assumed the presidency on 4 March 1861. "Bold[ly] and unequivocal[ly]," Hindman proclaimed to the Arkansas legislature on 23 November 1860 that the time had come for Arkansas to secede and to join other slave states in forming a separate Southern confederacy. Anticipating that secession could bring on civil war, he recommended that the legislature appropriate $250,000 for arms.[42]

From Little Rock, Hindman traveled to Washington D. C. for the second session of the Thirty-sixth Congress. It was truly a "remarkable" gathering. A "whole array of Southern pluck and talent," including Hindman, favored "precipitate action, with little attempt to compromise." Ohio Congressman Samuel S. Cox characterized the leaders of this group as absolutely irreconcilable. According to him, the most antagonistic was the "offensive" Hindman who "could eat more fire in a given time" than any Southerner in Congress. Others in the group included Virginians Thomas Bocock, who excelled in "parliamentary skirmishing," and Roger A. Pryor, a master of "vituperative phillippic." Mississippi's L. Q. C. Lamar's specialty was "impetuous debate," while the "vain and clever" Laurence M. Keitt of South Carolina treated his audience to "smooth and trenchant dialectics."[43]

Since secession was not yet a reality in any state when Congress convened on 3 December 1860, President James Buchanan sought to avert the threat of disunion by calling for compromise on sectional issues. In response, the next day the House appointed a Committee of Thirty-Three (one member from each state) to consider "the present perilous condition of the country." After a heated debate, the Senate followed suit by appointing a Committee of Thirteen to consider compromise measures.[44]

Efforts at conciliation were destined to fail. Thirty-eight Republicans in the House opposed any compromise and cast the only votes against the establishment of the Committee of Thirty-Three. When Republican Speaker of the House William A. Pennington appointed the committee, he selected sixteen members of his own party, including four who had voted against its establishment. In a move that raised questions about the sincerity of his commitment to resolving the sectional crisis, Pennington excluded Northern Douglas Democrats from the committee even though they had solidly supported its establishment. To make matters worse, Constitutional Unionists were allotted only two members, and Southern Breckinridge supporters were bypassed in favor of Douglas men who "were out of harmony with the vast majority of people in that section." When the committee finally met, it named as its chairman Tom Corwin of Ohio, a man Southerners had distrusted since the Mexican War.[45]

Many Southerners doubted that Lincoln and his party would support compromise proposals and regarded the committees as "a mere [Republican] expedient to gain time and disorganize the South." The tone of the initial meeting of the Committee of Thirty-Three on 11 December left many Southern representatives convinced that it offered little hope that slavery would be protected and that the balance of power between slave and free states would be restored. Two days later, when Republican members of the committee split eight to eight on a resolution as to whether or not slavery was protected by the Constitution, Southerners in Congress became even more convinced that compromise was impossible. They became even more intransigent and insisted that their demands must be met or their states would leave the Union.[46]

Within this framework, Hindman and other state rights Southerners proposed a series of constitutional amendments that they claimed would settle "the agitation of the slavery question on a just and fair basis" and perpetuate "the Federal Union." First and foremost, slavery was to be explicitly protected where it already existed "or may hereafter exist," including Washington D. C. and the territories. When territories met population requirements and drafted constitutions providing for representative government, they were to be admitted as states, regardless of whether they were slave or free. Slaveowners were to be able to travel through or temporarily reside in free states with the assurance that their slave property would be protected. States that had enacted personal liberty laws designed to nullify the Fugitive Slave Act of 1850 were to be deprived of representation in "either House of Congress" until the statutes were repealed. The interstate slave trade was not to be prohibited or restricted, and Southern members of Congress were to be the "absolute" arbiters of "all action of Congress relating to the subject of slavery." Finally, these amendments and the Three-fifths Compromise in the Constitution were to be "forever irrepealable and unalterable."[47]

Cognizant of the Republicans' insistence against adopting any measure that would allow slavery to expand into the territories, Hindman (like most Southern Congressmen) did not expect that his proposals would pass. They represented the only conditions under which Southern states would remain in the Union, however, and their defeat would become the basis for an all out campaign for immediate secession. Hindman introduced his proposals on 11 December, the same day that the Committee of Thirty-Three held its initial meeting. Three days later, on 14 December, Hindman and twenty-two other House members and seven senators representing nine Southern states issued a manifesto to their constituents declaring that "all hope of relief" through Congressional legislation or Constitutional amendments had been exhausted.

> The Republicans are resolute in the purpose to grant nothing that will
> . . . satisfy the South. We are satisfied the honor, safety, and
> independence of the Southern people are to be found only in a Southern
> Confederacy . . . and that the sole and primary aim of each slaveholding
> State ought to be its speedy and absolute separation from an unnatural
> and hostile Union.[48]

Their hope was not long in coming. On 20 December, South
Carolina, acting through a specially called convention, unanimously
approved an ordinance of secession. Four days later, the convention
adopted a Declaration of Causes that stated that the extraordinary action
had been necessitated by the "election of a man to the high office of
President . . . whose opinions and purposes are hostile to Slavery."[49]

To Tom Hindman, South Carolina's action was a clarion for other
states to follow suit. On 21 December, he and Senator Robert W. Johnson
jointly telegraphed the General Assembly of Arkansas that "it is now
manifest that the other cotton states will secede. . . . The spirit of the
present Congress forbids a reasonable hope of any adequate remedy."
They therefore urged the legislature to call a special convention "to
enable the people of Arkansas to join in the COMMON COUNCILS OF
THE SOUTH, FOR HER PROTECTION AND FURTHER SAFETY."[50]

On 8 January 1861, they followed with a jointly published address
"TO THE PEOPLE OF ARKANSAS" that urged the General Assembly
to call a convention "speedily" so that the position of the state could be
made known. They reviewed the sectional crisis and proclaimed that the
"spirit of hostility" to slavery that had surfaced in New England had
spread like "a leaven of poison . . . through Northern sentiments,"
culminating in Lincoln's election to the presidency.[51]

Exercising forbearance, Southerners had delayed any action until
Congress convened in the hope that the North would do "justice" to the
South and "offer . . . ample security for the future." These hopes had
been met with "contemptuous silence, or an insulting refusal" from
Republicans. Hindman and Johnson dismissed Lincoln's "professions of
'conservatism' . . . as empty words, intended to delay action, and reduce
the South into acceptance of her own complete and irreversible ruin and
degredation."[52]

They urged Arkansas to unite with South Carolina and the other
cotton growing states in a Southern confederacy that would protect their

rights. Already, they noted, forces were being readied to coerce South Carolina back into the Union. Arkansans should hasten to "perform their duty towards Carolina, [and] . . . towards every other resisting State" and to place their state in its "proper place in the seceding column, and secure out of the union the rights that have been wrested from her within it."[53]

Once South Carolina set the secession wheel in motion, an almost irresistible force seemed to propel it forward. By the end of January 1861, Mississippi, Florida, Alabama, Georgia, and Louisiana had adopted ordinances of secession. These states then sent delegates to Montgomery, Alabama to draw up a provisional constitution for an independent Confederate States of America.

Arkansas, despite prodding from Hindman, Johnson, and Governor Henry Rector, did not rush headlong into secession. Sentiment over disunion was split; the mountain counties with few slaves resisted secession, while the richer cotton-producing areas of the southeast and southwest pressed for Arkansas to join the seceding states.

Hoping to provide a catalyst for secession, on 6 February 1861, between 800 and 1,000 men from at least nine counties converged on Little Rock determined to seize the United States arsenal. Violence was averted when Captain James Totten agreed to evacuate it and turn it over to Governor Rector on 8 February.[54]

To provide an open forum on the secession question, the legislature passed a bill providing for a popular referendum on 18 February on the holding of a convention and the simultaneous election of delegates should the convention be approved. Voters approved the convention call by a 27,412 to 15,826, but only a minority of delegates favored immediate secession. Most preferred to wait to see what course Lincoln would pursue before initiating any movement toward secession. They also watched anxiously for signs that Congress would agree on an acceptable compromise to protect slavery and Southern rights. Even if Congress failed in this critical mission, many Arkansas Unionists clung to the possibility that a special peace convention that had assembled in Virginia would find a basis for reconciliation.[55]

They were bitterly disappointed. Similar proposals by Senator John J. Crittenden and the Virginia Peace Convention promised protection for slavery where it already existed and in new territories south of the old Missouri Compromise line of thirty-six degrees, thirty minutes. To Southerners such as Hindman, they were "half-way measures" that were "unworthy of the vote of any southern man," and to Republicans such as Lincoln they were unacceptable because they had the potential for allowing the peculiar institution to expand.[56]

With no hope of a settlement on what he considered just terms, Hindman was delighted by the introduction in Congress of various measures that he thought would strengthen disunion sentiment and weaken the United States should civil war come. One such measure, the so-called "force bill" would authorize the president to call out the militia to suppress "insurrections against the authority of the United States." Terming it "one of the best disunion propositions made in this congress," Hindman welcomed a vote on the bill so that the "country may know" the "determination" of the "other side" to subjugate the seceded states.[57]

When the House of Representatives adjourned on 2 March, Hindman rushed to Little Rock where the special convention was in session. Despite his intense lobbying efforts and a speech to the convention, the delegates rejected resolutions calling for immediate secession and, instead, scheduled a special election on 5 August "for the purpose of taking the sense of the people on the question of 'co-operation' or 'secession.'" Following the election, the delegates would return to Little Rock on 19 August and settle the issue. Uncertain of what lay ahead, the convention acted to forestall any unexpected contingencies by authorizing presiding officer David Walker to reconvene the assembly "at any time" before 19 August if an "exigency" requiring immediate action occurred.[58]

After the convention adjourned on 21 March, Hindman returned to his home in Helena to prepare for a thorough canvass of his district to promote "immediate secession." Before his canvass began, events outside Arkansas galvanized secession sentiment in Arkansas. On the morning of 12 April Confederate forces fired on United States troops at Fort Sumter, prompting President Lincoln to issue a call for 75,000 troops to suppress "combinations too powerful to be suppressed by the ordinary course of judicial proceedings." In Arkansas, Lincoln's request for 780 troops from the state fell on deaf ears as Governor Rector notified Washington "that none will be furnished" and that the "demand" added "insult to injury." Interpreting Lincoln's action as coercion of South Carolina, David Walker responded to widespread public pressure and called the convention back into session.[59]

Even though secession was now a foregone conclusion, Thomas C. Hindman, Robert C. Newton (a former Bell-Everett supporter), Robert W.

Johnson, and Edward W. Gantt continued to make speeches in areas where Union sentiment had been strongest during the convention canvass. The attack on Sumter and the cries for war drove many unswerving Unionists underground and converted conditional ones to the Confederate cause. This was clearly obvious when Senator Johnson spoke in the formerly pro-Union stronghold of Van Buren on 20 April. There was no sign of opposition to secession; amid cheering and the booming of cannon, "the masses" raised a Confederate flag with thirteen stars "embracing" the states (including Kentucky and Missouri) that they believed would "soon compose the new Confederacy."[60]

On 6 May, Hindman joined the crowd of excited spectators who packed the gallery of the hall of the state House of Representatives in Little Rock. With secession inevitable, he gleefully watched as the delegates voted sixty-five to five to secede. Four of the dissenting delegates acceded to president David Walker's plea to change their votes so that "the wire [could] carry the news to all the world that Arkansas stands as a unit against coercion." Ignoring Madison County Delegate Isaac Murphy's refusal to switch his vote, Hindman telegraphed his personal friend Confederate president Jefferson Davis that the convention had unanimously passed the ordinance of secession at 4:00 P. M. that day.[61]

For Tom Hindman, 6 May 1861 marked the culmination of almost a decade of labor for secession. In the wake of the furor over the Compromise of 1850, he had entered Mississippi politics convinced that the federal Union had become hostile to Southern interests. Slavery and state rights could only be safeguarded in a separate Southern confederacy. He never wavered in these beliefs. With his dream a reality, Hindman stood ready and eager to prove his dedication to the South on the field of battle.

Chapter 5

FORGING A REPUTATION IN THE WEST

Even before Arkansas joined the Confederacy, the state had become an armed camp. People held resistance rallies across the state, and military companies with colorful names such as the Conway Tigers, Rough and Ready Volunteers, and the Saline Tornadoes sprang up and began drilling for war. In recognition of Tom Hindman's efforts on behalf of an independent Southern Confederacy, one unit in White County honored him by adopting the name "Hindman Guards."[1]

As Henry M. Stanley, a resident of Arkansas in 1861 who later gained fame in Africa, noted, "man after man unresistingly succumbed" to the desire for armed conflict. "Even the women and children cried for war." No matter how "inflamed" men were, their "intense heat" was nothing compared to women who unalterably opposed even the "suggestion of compromise." In many areas of the state, men who did not respond quickly to the call to arms were harassed. When Stanley failed to join a unit being formed in his area, he received a parcel addressed in a feminine hand. Instead of being a "token of some lady's regard" as he had hoped, however, the box contained "a chemise and petticoat," a clear signal of the intolerance he could expect for his lack of "patriotism." Shortly thereafter he joined the "Dixie Grays," which later became part of the Sixth Arkansas Infantry.[2]

Others received firmer warnings. William G. Stevenson, a native New Yorker living in Helena, found himself frequently "sounded on the subject of slavery." Already suspect because of his "Yankee" roots, he came under especially close scrutiny when recruiting began in his area and he failed to enlist. The Phillips County Vigilance Committee accused him of being "a Northern man" and put him on trial as "an Abolitionist whose business was to incite an insurrection among the slaves."[3] Following a prolonged, spirited debate during which opponents taunted him with "a coil of rope" and told him that he deserved to hang, Stevenson was acquitted. Afterwards, he fled to Memphis where a "Committee of

Public Safety" seized him. Realizing that another "trial" might lead to conviction, Stevenson quickly "volunteered" to join the Jeff Davis Invincibles of the Second Tennessee Infantry.[4]

Carried along by the ground swell for war, the secession convention passed a series of ordinances to organize and equip state troops, appropriate money and levy taxes for military purposes, issue war bonds, and punish persons found guilty of giving aid and comfort to the enemy. The most important ordinance created a military board to assist in organizing an army for protection and security of the state.[5]

Although Hindman was not a delegate, his influence was prevalent throughout the convention's deliberations, and "at the request" of several members, he drafted the ordinance to create a military board. Introduced by Jefferson County delegate James Yell on 11 May, the proposed ordinance underwent a few cosmetic changes but emerged with Hindman's main provisions intact. The convention intended for the board (which consisted of the governor and two other members elected by the convention) to be an adjunct to Confederate authority. The ordinance empowered the board to call out the state's militia and volunteer forces, authorize military expeditions, and manage and control forts, arms, and munitions.[6]

The delegates elected James Yell as major general of Arkansas's military forces. They divided the state into a western and an eastern district and named two brigadier generals, N. Bart Pearce and Thomas H. Bradley, to supervise them. Pearce (a graduate of West Point) was to set up headquarters at Fort Smith, organize state troops in the western district, and cooperate with Brigadier General Ben McCulloch of Texas, who had been sent by the Confederate government to defend the Indian Territory.[7]

Empowered to use a draft, if necessary, to raise a militia force, the military board issued a call for 10,000 volunteers for one year's service and began seeking provisions and equipment. McCulloch and Secretary of War Walker also called for volunteers to serve in the Provisional Army of the Confederate States and not in the state militia—actions Governor Rector claimed violated state rights.[8]

Not content to sit on the sidelines while the convention grappled with the cumbersome matters involved in putting Arkansas on a military footing, Hindman immediately obtained permission from Secretary of

War Walker to raise an infantry regiment for service in the Provisional Army of the Confederate States. Because of "heavy demands" for arms from the Confederate government, his authorization required that state officials supply weapons. On 23 May, he notified the convention that he was recruiting a regiment at Helena. He requested muskets, clothing, and ten days rations to allow his men "to fight for our country."[9]

His request was referred to the military board, which failed to send the necessary items. In early June, Hindman telegraphed the military board for shoes and blankets and requested permission to apply to his troops' benefit "the proceeds of sugar stored at Helena," which he had seized from Cincinnati steamboats and turned over to the civil authorities prior to secession. Ignoring Hindman's request, the board invited the troops under his leadership to become a part of the state's militia for twelve months. Hindman angrily spurned the offer and insisted that his troops were in the service of the Confederate States and would remain so until the end of the war, with or without shoes and blankets from the board.[10]

Despite the lack of assistance from the military board, recruitment proceeded rapidly; by 1 June Hindman had raised ten companies, six stationed at Helena and four at Pine Bluff—all subsisting at his personal expense. Since his regiment had just been ordered to Richmond and Federal forces in southern Missouri were threatening northwest Arkansas, however, he was on the verge of losing at least five companies that refused to leave the state to fight in the East.[11]

Still under orders to report to Richmond, Hindman and part of his regiment began the long journey eastward in early June, encamping en route at Knoxville, Tennessee. There he attended a dinner at the home of future Confederate Senator Landon C. Haynes, where the main topic of conversation was the pro-Union canvass of United States Senator Andrew Johnson prior to the 8 June referendum on secession. Hindman excitedly proposed taking a train to Rogersville, about seventy miles east of Knoxville, and arresting Johnson before a scheduled speech. The proposal was thwarted, however, when one of the dinner guests tipped off John H. Branner, president of the railroad. Fearing retaliation by Union men if he cooperated with the Arkansan, Branner sent all available engines out on duty and told Hindman that no trains were available until evening. With such a late start, Hindman had no hope of reaching Rogersville before Johnson left and reluctantly abandoned the plan.[12]

On 11 June, aware of the threat to Arkansas, the War Department rescinded its orders for Hindman to proceed to Virginia. It directed him to move his regiment to northeastern Arkansas near Clark's Bluff in Randolph County and "to adopt defensive measures for the protection of the State," as part of a broader movement to strengthen defenses across Arkansas. On 25 June, the War Department assigned command of "that portion of Arkansas lying west of the White and Black rivers and north of the Arkansas River to the Missouri line" to Brigadier General William J. Hardee and told him to defend all of northeastern Arkansas and the contiguous portion of Missouri. Hardee was promised Hindman's regiment plus an additional 3,000 troops.[13]

A native of Georgia, Hardee's name was a byword in the South. His textbook, *Rifle and Light Infantry Tactics*, written in 1855 under the direction of Secretary of War Jefferson Davis, was the standard of the day. He was an 1838 graduate of West Point, had completed cavalry school in Samur (near Paris, France), and had participated in the siege of Vera Cruz during the Mexican War. When Georgia seceded in January 1861, the tall and wiry Hardee resigned his commission of lieutenant colonel and entered the Confederate army.[14]

The War Department ordered Hindman's unit to be mustered in to service in Memphis, so as to complete its transition to Hardee's command. By the time Hardee arrived, the energetic, dynamic Hindman had recruited seven more companies, raising his total to seventeen. One company, the "Young Guards" of the Fifteenth Tennessee Infantry had received permission "to be detached" to move to Memphis to enlist with Hindman for "three years, or during the war." Commissioned on 12 June as colonel of the Second Arkansas Infantry, the former congressman now commanded what some dubbed "Hindman's Legion." In addition, Charles Swett's Battery moved, at its request, from Vicksburg to Memphis and became part of Hindman's military force. On 10 July Hindman's regiment was ordered to proceed to Pitman's Ferry, Arkansas. En route, he seized two steamboats (the *Ohio Belle* and the *Mars*) on 13 June at Des Arc "in the name of the Southern Confederacy" and sent them to Memphis.[15]

Hardee left for Little Rock on 11 July to meet with Governor Rector and the military board to arrange the transfer of state troops to Confederate service. Under an accord reached on the fifteenth, Arkansas was to transfer its seven infantry regiments, one cavalry regiment, and five artillery batteries (with arms and munitions) to the Confederate States.[16]

The planned transfer was easier to draw up than to implement. Pearce's orders from the military board required him to take a vote of each company "on the question of willingness" before he could turn troops over to Confederate service. Adjutant General Burgevin, along with Generals Yell and Pearce, opposed the agreement because the transfer would deprive Arkansas of its troops and arms and (probably fearing a loss in status) urged Arkansas troops not to join Hardee's forces.[17]

Frustrated, embarrassed, and aware that he must retain the armed and organized troops, Hardee turned to the popular and politically influential Hindman for help, relying on his oratory to turn the tide in favor of the troops' transfer. Unfortunately for Hardee, even the "forcible and attractive" oratory of Tom Hindman could not carry the day. He made several impassioned speeches to the troops in the northwestern part of the state, imploring them to remain and fight, but to no avail. The soldiers had been in service for two to five months "and had never received any pay or clothing." Hundreds were barefoot, and many "were destitute of clothing" to the point that they were scarcely able to "cover their nakedness." Under such conditions, their "natural impulse was to go home." After espousing their loyalty to the Southern cause and promising to "do battle" at a later date when they had clothes and shoes, all but "some 18-20" troops went home. His experience in northwest Arkansas left an indelible impression on Hindman. In the summer of 1862, when he assumed command of the Trans-Mississippi District, he quickly eradicated any semblance of conflicting Confederate and state authority over the military.[18]

After concluding negotiations with the military board and retaining as many troops as possible, Hardee shifted his attention to meeting the Federal military threat in northern Arkansas. Because of Pitman's Ferry's location on the navigable Current River and its proximity to the Missouri border, a location which afforded a reliable line of communications and a springboard to the interior of Missouri, he deployed his forces there.[19]

In late July, Hardee's command, including Hindman's Legion, was supposed to be part of a coordinated effort to expel Union forces from southeastern Missouri. The plan called for Hardee to move north and unite with Brigadier General Gideon Pillow at Ironton. Meanwhile, Major General Sterling Price and McCulloch would march on Union troops under Brigadier General Nathaniel Lyon in southwestern Missouri. After

Price and McCulloch cut off Lyon, Hardee and Pillow would unite with them, occupy St. Louis, and proceed up the Missouri River to raise additional troops.[20]

Never formalized, the plan quickly disintegrated. On 19 July, Price asked Hardee to join him and McCulloch in an attack on Lyon, but Hardee refused, choosing instead to advance toward Ironton to unite with Pillow, then at New Madrid. By 4 August, Hardee reached Greenville, Missouri, in preparation for advancing to Ironton, but Pillow refused to join him, arguing that they should attack Cape Girardeau. Neither relented, and on 26 August Major General Leonidas Polk ordered Hardee to pull back from Greenville and Pillow to abandon his plans to attack Cape Girardeau. The projected invasion into eastern Missouri had ended.[21]

While Southern commanders jockeyed for position in Missouri, Hindman (under orders from Hardee) was busy recruiting additional troops in northern Arkansas. Hardee believed that the war would soon heat up in the state, and on 6 September he urged Hindman to exert his "best energies" and "raise at once" two additional infantry regiments and four companies of cavalry "for twelve months or the [duration of the] war." He promised the colonel that successful completion of the assignment ought to entitle him to "a higher grade," which he would request the President to confer.[22]

Wasting no time, Hindman moved quickly across Arkansas and delivered stirring addresses aimed at encouraging re-enlistments and attracting new recruits. From his headquarters in Fayetteville, he issued an impassioned circular on 17 September urging "the fighting men of the South" to join either the regiments he was raising or those being recruited by McCulloch. "The time for delay" and "dissensions had past." Arkansans must move quickly to defend the state from the "ten thousand Kansas ruffians and cut throats" poised on its doorsteps. If "the patriotic sons of Arkansas" rallied "promptly around the flag of the stars and bars," it would "soon wave triumphantly, not alone over southern soil, but over territory conquered from northern despotism," said Hindman.[23]

While Hindman was busy recruiting, the war in the West greatly intensified. On 10 September, General Albert Sidney Johnston received command of all territory west of the Allegheny Mountains except the Gulf Coast. William Preston Johnston later observed: "Experienced soldier that he was, Johnston must have been appalled by the immense task confronting him."[24] With approximately 20,000 troops, he was to defend an area extending from the mountains of eastern Kentucky and Tennessee across the Mississippi to the Kansas border. The Federals under Major General John C. Fremont controlled Missouri with a force of 60,000 to 80,000 troops, while Major General U. S. Grant had 20,000 troops at Cairo, Illinois, and Paducah, Kentucky. To make the task even more formidable, the Confederates barely held northwestern Tennessee. To oppose Fremont, Johnston had about 6,000 men under Hardee in northeast Arkansas; to confront Grant, he had only 11,000 under Leonidas Polk at Columbus, Kentucky. Also, he had some 4,000 troops under Brigadier General Felix K. Zollicoffer at the Cumberland Gap. Although numerically outnumbered, Johnston was determined to hold the Mississippi. If the Federals succeeded in gaining control of the river, the way would be open for a disastrous Union naval invasion into the heartland of the South.[25]

An adopted Texan born in Kentucky, Johnston seemed the ideal choice for such a challenging assignment. Fifty-eight years old and physically strong, he had graduated from West Point at age twenty-three, had served as commander-in-chief of the army of the Republic of Texas, and had fought in the Mexican War.[26]

Arriving in Nashville on 14 September, Johnston assumed command of his new department and immediately embarked on the task of defending it from Union attack. He dispatched Brigadier General Simon Bolivar Buckner and his 4,500 men to occupy Bowling Green, Kentucky, a strategically important railroad center south of the Ohio River. Buckner arrived on the eighteenth and immediately fortified the city; even though the action was "a mere skirmish line to mask" the weakness of Johnston's forces, the effect was electrifying. According to William Preston Johnston, "Buckner's advance produced the wildest consternation" and "for a time parylze[d] the Federal army and put it on the defensive."[27]

The Confederacy desperately needed additional troops in Kentucky, and Hardee's brigade was ordered to the state in mid-September. Still on recruiting assignment, Hindman did not leave with his regiment when it began its move on 19 September. Choosing to march overland rather than travel by water, the regiment arrived in Columbus on 6 October, and after resting for two days, traveled by rail to join Buckner at Bowling Green. The trip was not without excitement. A combination of mismanagement by railroad officials and a treacherous river crossing turned the trip into a nightmare that included the loss of Hardee's luggage and the drowning of one of his staff members.[28]

In early October, after learning that the Army of the Cumberland under Brigadier General William T. Sherman was advancing toward Bowling Green, Johnston moved his headquarters to the city and divided his army into two divisions. Hardee, who had recently been promoted to major general, commanded the First Division, which was designated as the Army Corps of Central Kentucky. The Second Division was placed under Buckner. Hardee's division consisted of two brigades, the first commanded by Hindman, who had been promoted to brigadier general on 28 September, and the second under Colonel Pat Cleburne.[29]

Hoping to give Sherman an exaggerated impression of his strength and convince him that a Confederate advance was imminent, Johnston ordered Hardee to move about eighteen miles away to Munfordville on the Green River to carry out screening and reconnaissance activities. If the ploy succeeded, Johnston would be able to buy precious time needed to obtain more men and weapons.[30]

In keeping with this strategy, from late October 1861 until early February 1862, Hindman and his men shifted between Bowling Green and the neighboring communities of Cave City, Rocky Hill Station, Oakland, Horse Wells, Chalybeate Springs, and Bell's Tavern. In addition to trying to confuse Union forces about Confederate troop strength and strategy, Hindman simultaneously gathered intelligence about the size and locations of Sherman's divisions and successfully disrupted Federal communications by destroying telegraph lines and railroad track. Although he obtained much of his information through officers and men under his command, Hindman made excellent use of spies and local residents loyal to the Southern cause.[31]

Recognizing that Confederates were not the only ones using spies to supplement knowledge about troop strength and movements, Hindman and his staff interrogated all civilians entering his lines before allowing them to proceed farther. They detained for intense "examination" those without valid credentials attesting to their "*strong Southern* sentiments." Most interviews and "examinations" resulted in permission to proceed on—but not always.[32]

A case-in-point occurred at Oakland on 18 November 1861, when Hindman ordered the arrest of seven men suspected of disloyalty to the Confederacy. Three of the detainees were accused of instigating "depre-

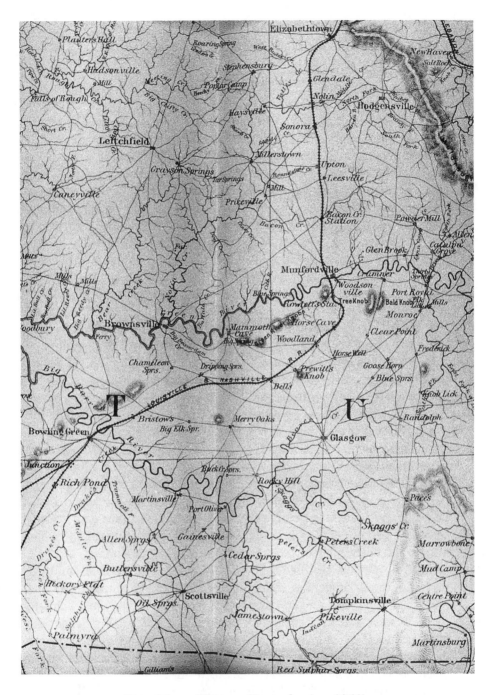

Plate 5.1   *Western Kentucky (ca. 1861)*
Atlas to accompany the *Official Records of the War of the Rebellion*

depredations" against "Southern men near Brownsville," including the attempted assassination of the town sheriff. Labeling them "dangerous and troublesome characters," Hindman held them "as hostages to secure the good conduct of their relatives & friends who have heretofore at their bidding done us so serious damage."[33]

While on assignment to deceive Sherman, disrupt Federal communications, and gather intelligence, Hindman's forces did not participate in any major battles. They did, however, engage in a few skirmishes, the most noteworthy at Brownsville and Woodsonville along the Green River.

On 18 November, Hindman dispatched seven men from Oakland to procure "spirits for hospital use." When they failed to return at the end of the following day, he concluded that they had "been cut off by the enemy" encamped at Brownsville. Personally taking charge, at 8:00 A. M. on 20 November he set out toward Brownsville with one hundred men and one six-pound artillery piece from Swett's Battery. By detaining "all citizens" along the route, the detachment reached the outskirts of town unobserved.[34]

Splitting his force in two, Hindman inspected the area to ascertain the precise strength and locations of Union troops stationed near the town. He detected fifty Federal cavalrymen positioned opposite the river along a narrow road leading across the hills running parallel to the stream. Another fifteen horsemen were 100 yards farther near a small cabin. Fifty more were "partially concealed in timber" along the Litchfield road. Entering the town "as rapidly as possible," the graycoats opened fire from the public square; the first discharge of their six-pounder scattered the fifty cavalrymen across the river. Subsequent blasts of case and "round" shot scattered the squad near the cabin, destroying the structure and killing five nearby horses.[35]

Having driven the Federals directly across the river from their positions, the Confederates shifted their cannon closer to the stream and unleashed a barrage on the cavalrymen stationed along the Litchfield road, dispersing them "instantly." Shaken, but not panic-stricken, the bluecoats took cover behind logs, trees, and fences and opened fire on their attackers. The exchange lasted about fifteen minutes and ended when the Union soldiers retreated downstream.[36]

Casualties were minimal on both sides. Seven Union soldiers were killed, and five (including one "expected to die" by nightfall) were wounded. On the Confederate side, no one was killed, and only one was wounded (a private struck in the shoulder). Hindman's troops detained two civilian pickets, who were later released after he determined that they had furnished their services under force. They also seized a Federal flag, the United States mail from the Brownsville post office, and "sundry articles" belonging to a local merchant who had conducted the Federals into the town. Ever mindful of the chronic shortages that plagued the Confederate army, Hindman ordered his men to take the latter for hospital use.[37]

According to a correspondent of the Nashville *Union and American*, during the skirmish Brigadier General Hindman narrowly escaped serious injury or death while standing near a house in town directing his troops. A bullet "no doubt aimed" at him, whizzed by and "struck a board within a foot of where he was standing." Quickly responding, he grabbed a musket from one of the privates, took "deliberate aim, "killed" the soldier who had shot at him, "and very coolly returned the gun to the private."[38]

One month later on 17 December, Hindman again engaged the enemy. Dissatisfied with Sherman's failure to move aggressively against Southern forces in Kentucky, the United States War Department replaced him on 15 November with Brigadier General Don Carlos Buell. Convinced that Johnston was heavily fortifying the important rail center of Bowling Green and could easily concentrate 20,000–25,000 men there, Buell decided to dislodge the Confederates.[39]

Part of his strategy for capturing Bowling Green involved securing the town of Woodsonville for use as a supply point. Aware of Buell's objective, Hardee confidently informed Johnston that Hindman could keep Federal forces near Munfordville at bay and defend the passage of the Green river. To accomplish this, Hindman received orders in early December to "retard the enemy" by "breaking up the railroad" near Cave City. Noting that "sleepers will be as difficult to replace as iron," Hardee told him to proceed "slowly" and break the road "in spots" rather than continuously. Although Hindman was to avail himself of all opportunities to give the enemy "a wholesome lesson," he was not to endanger his brigade by engaging a superior force.[40]

On 11 December (four days prior to receiving Hardee's instructions), Hindman had learned from Southern loyalists near Woodsonville that Federal troops at Munfordville were repairing a ferry boat previously sunk by Kentucky Confederate Captain John H. Morgan and were measuring the depth of the river. "About the same time, a spy" whom

Hindman had sent to Greensburg returned with the news that six hundred men under Colonel Edward H. Hobson of the Thirteenth Kentucky United States Volunteers, along with two pieces of artillery, were advancing "upon Bowling Green by way of Munfordville."[41]

In response, at 10:00 A. M. Hindman dispatched a scouting party of 30-50 Texas rangers under Colonel Benjamin F. Terry toward Munfordville to observe Union movements. Three hours later, Hindman took ten men with him on a reconnaissance mission to Rowlett's Station, three quarters of a mile from Munfordville. Arriving after sunset, he found that the ferry boat had been repaired and "had the pleasure of hearing" Union band members play "Hail Columbia" and "Yankee Doodle." From there, he traveled over "exceedingly rough" roads to Horse Cave and then via the turnpike to Horse Wells. Anticipating a possible attack, he deployed Terry's rangers at Woodland, his infantry one half mile from camp, Swett's Battery at Middleton's place, and C. W. Phifer's battalion along Mammoth Cave road.[42]

At 8:00 A. M. on 17 December, Hindman, with a force of 1,100 infantry and 250 cavalry supported by four pieces of artillery, started from his camp at Cave City toward Woodsonville to destroy railroad tracks southward from the town. Halting two and one-half miles from town, he stationed Terry's rangers on the heights overlooking the river and dispatched Phifer's cavalry to survey Union troop strength near the railroad tracks. After reaching their positions, neither Terry nor Phifer reported the presence of Federal pickets. Believing his movements concealed from the enemy, Hindman advanced his column to the railroad.[43]

After arriving at the railroad, he ordered Terry and seventy-five rangers up Rowlett's Knob, a small hill, to serve as decoys while the main body of Confederates went around the flanks of the Union troops. Unfortunately for Hindman, when three hundred Federals from the Thirty-second Indiana Infantry appeared on his right and center, Terry suddenly wheeled and charged them rather than continuing up the hill. The impetuous action resulted in Terry's own death and alerted the remaining companies of the Indiana regiment of the Southern presence, thereby destroying the element of surprise.[44]

The rest of the Thirty-second Indiana quickly assembled along the river. The unexpected appearance of Federal reinforcements incorrectly convinced Hindman that "regiments" of bluecoats were now threatening to surround him on both sides, and, after a brief skirmish, he quickly withdrew and returned to Cave City. Casualties on both sides were light. Confederate losses were four killed and ten wounded, while on the Union side eleven men were killed and twenty-two were wounded. Like other officers on both sides early in the war, Hindman's report of the engagement contained a number of exaggerations. Although the skirmish was brief and his troops basically unseasoned, the young brigadier proudly stated that his troops had "displayed courage in excess" and had fought "as steady as veterans." Concurring, Hardee praised the performance of Hindman and his brigade and hailed their "brilliant courage" as a "bright augury" of future valor.[45]

In the few short months since entering Confederate service, Hindman had impressed Hardee and other officers with the tremendous energy and enthusiasm that he brought to every task, from recruiting, to reconnaissance, to destroying the enemy's transportation lines. With resolve and determination, he went to work to master the fine art of drilling his troops. He studied Hardee's drill manual intently but, as late as 13 November, admitted that he was "not yet fully capable" of drilling his brigade alone.[46]

Hindman's concern for the men under his command was not limited to insuring adequate training. As was characteristic of his position throughout the war, in the fall of 1861 he implored authorities in Richmond to correct logistical weaknesses in the system for supplying clothing, equipment, and medicine to troops and to provide adequate pay to make military service "desirable and attractive." On 3 November, he bitterly complained that the combination of inclement weather and the "ill condition of the troops" caused by the lack of clothing, equipment, medicine, and surgeons had "greatly weakened" his force.[47]

Less than two weeks later, he again protested the lack of clothing and supplies and demanded that military pay be increased to provide "superior inducements" for remaining in the army. The lack of sufficient pay involved more than just equity for soldiers. If the Confederacy failed to make military service attractive by increasing compensation, then soldiers would not re-enlist when their enlistments expired and ranks would become "so thinned as to destroy their organization."[48]

Following the skirmish at Rowlett's Station, Hindman continued gathering intelligence, disrupting Union communications, and drilling troops until mid February 1862,. Although preoccupied with military duties and the effects of supply problems, poor pay, and bad weather on his troops, he occasionally found time to relax and enjoy good news from home. His spirits soared when he learned that on 27 November Mollie had given birth to a son, christened Biscoe after her father. Social events such as the "SHYNNEDYGGE MILITAIRE," which his staff organized at Bell's Tavern on 28 January, also helped to brighten the drab routine of camp life. "Let Joy Be Unconfined" was the theme of the evening, which appropriately began with the "Hindman Shynnedygge" to the accompaniment of banjoes. For several delightful hours, Hindman and his staff danced and joked with local residents and laughed at such antics as the "Reel (a-la-Kaintuck)," the "Gallopade (de Woodsonville)," the "Ranger's Quickstep," and the "Break Down (de Rackensack)."[49]

Although no major battles occurred in Johnston's command during the fall and early winter, by the time Hindman and his men settled down for an evening of music and frolic, signs of trouble were already on the horizon. On 17 January, Brigadier General George H. Thomas and his advance Union force had moved to within six miles of Confederate Major General George B. Crittenden's army at Logan's Cross Roads (Mill Springs), Kentucky. Having arrived only a few days earlier to assume command of area troops, Crittenden decided to strike Thomas before the remainder of his army arrived on the scene.[50]

Accordingly on the nineteenth, Felix Zollicoffer with four infantry regiments, Brigadier General William H. Carroll's brigade, and two cavalry companies as a reserve force marched toward Thomas' camp. The weather and the nature of the march set the tone for the battle. After slogging nine miles over muddy roads in a torrential downpour, at 6:30 A. M. the Confederates encountered Union cavalry pickets.[51]

Cold, hungry, and tired after the weary march, the graycoats were completely routed; and "in their desperate panic they left behind their artillery, their wagons, their horses, their supplies, [and] their dead and wounded," including their fallen commander. "Brave to the point of rashness, and conspicuous in a white rubber raincoat, Zollicoffer had ridden far ahead of his troops right up to the enemy." Extremely nearsighted, when he came upon Colonel Speed S. Fry of the Fourth United States Kentucky Infantry, Zollicoffer mistook him for one of his own men. As the Confederate was giving Fry an order, a Union officer shot him to death at point-blank range.[52]

The Confederate setback at Logan's Cross Roads was a crushing one and the first serious defeat for the South since the war began. It sent a shock wave across the entire length of the Confederacy. Disheartened by the trauma, soldiers in Crittenden's army deserted in large numbers.[53]

The disastrous defeat at Logan's Cross Roads was only the beginning of the Confederate nightmare in the West. Less than one month later, Union forces captured two strategically important forts: Henry on the Tennessee River and Donelson on the Cumberland River. Capturing these forts gave an opening to Federal iron clads that were able to convoy and protect troops "an inviting double pathway to the heart of the Confederacy." Curving through western Tennessee across northeastern Mississippi and into northern Alabama, the Tennessee River would enable Union forces to penetrate as far as Muscle Shoals at Florence, Alabama. On the other hand, the Cumberland River led straight to Nashville, a strategically important supply point containing large supplies of food, clothing, and ammunition.[54]

On 8 February, aware that Fort Henry had fallen and that Donelson was likely to fall soon, Johnston ordered Hardee to evacuate Bowling Green and retreat to Nashville, sixty- five miles away. As part of the preparation for abandoning Bowling Green, Hardee ordered Hindman to "draw nearer" so as to be in position to protect the rear flank of the retreating army. To avoid panic, he told the colonel not to discuss the planned evacuation. If he said anything at all, he should "talk loudly of an advance" and of the "determination to hold on to Bowling Green at all hazards and to the last extremity."[55]

After burning the commissary and quartermaster's stores, the Confederates began the evacuation on 11 February, as rain and snow pelted them. While Hardee's main force retreated southward, Hindman and his men remained in the area to obstruct advancing Union forces. On the twelfth, they torched the railroad station and platform on the outskirts of Bowling Green. They destroyed a nearby turnpike bridge two days later.[56]

Before leaving Bowling Green, Hindman's troops struggled to save the city from destruction by arsonists on the night of the thirteenth. Started by "parties never disclosed," a wild fire had turned most of the town into "a raging inferno." In response, Hindman immediately ordered his men "to fall to and fight the rising flames." "Hysterical" residents and the "bitter cold" temperatures, which froze water as it was being transported, turned the night into "an unforgettable experience for the weary soldiers who waged "a desperate fight" against the flames. By daylight the next morning when "the whistle and crash of artillery shells" announced the arrival of Federal forces, the fire was under control. The Confederates were compelled to abandon the few areas still burning when they were driven out by "the boom of exploding shells" echoing among the gutted houses.[57]

Having saved as much of Bowling Green as possible and having completed their demolition work, Hindman and his troops braved biting winds and freezing rain as they plodded steadily through Franklin, Kentucky, and Gallatin, Tennessee, on their way to Murfreesboro, a pleasant town about thirty-five miles southeast of Nashville. Meanwhile, the bulk of Hardee's force pushed on to Nashville, where Albert Sidney Johnston was concentrating his troops. Within a few hours after Johnston's arrival on the morning of 16 February, the city was on the verge of anarchy. News that Fort Donelson had fallen and the fear that the Confederates were planning to abandon the Tennessee capital plunged the local population into a "frenzy of excitement" and "widespread demoralization." Overcome by panic and fear, rioting civilians and soldiers "ruthlessly destroyed" and "appropriated" private and public property before order was restored.[58]

Marching in advance of Johnston's main force, Hindman found Murfreesboro in a similar state of panic when he arrived on 16 February. To restore order and to secure "a proper police and discipline of the troops," he declared martial law on the seventeenth and appointed Colonel John S. Marmaduke military governor and Captain W. L. Martin provost marshal.[59]

Approaching Federals forced Johnston to evacuate Nashville on the twenty-second and Murfreesboro six days later. With Hindman's brigade in the lead, at sunrise on the twenty-eighth the Confederates left Murfreesboro for Shelbyville. From there, they traveled via Decatur, Alabama, to Corinth, Mississippi, arriving in late March to unite with forces under the command of General P. G. T. Beauregard. By moving Major General Braxton Bragg's forces from Alabama, Polk's from Columbus, and scattered units from elsewhere to join with Johnston and Beauregard's armies, the Confederates had assembled 40,355 troops in and around Corinth by April.[60]

With Beauregard as his second-in-command, Johnston divided his forces into three corps commanded by Polk, Bragg, and Hardee, respectively. He combined these corps with a reserve division under Brigadier General John C. Breckinridge and named them the Army of the

Mississippi. Hardee's Third Corps consisted of five artillery batteries and seventeen regiments. He organized them into three brigades commanded by brigadier generals Hindman, Patrick R. Cleburne, and Sterling A. M. Wood.[61]

The newly created army, including Hindman's brigade (consisting of the Second, Fifth, Sixth, and Seventh Arkansas infantry divisions; Third Confederate Regiment; and the batteries of Swett and Miller), was destined to fight soon. Cognizant that Buell was moving southward from Nashville to unite with Grant at Pittsburg Landing twenty-three miles north of Corinth, Johnston determined to strike Grant's army before Buell arrived, even though it meant marching almost forty thousand (mostly untrained) men over narrow dirt roads.

While Johnston was in command, Beauregard was the one who devised the battle plan. His scouts having carefully studied the terrain and having provided fairly accurate maps of the topography of the land and roads, Beauregard prepared instructions for the movement of the troops. Two roads led from Corinth to Pittsburg Landing; one, known as the Ridge or Bark road, ran northward and then swung to the east. The second started eastward, then headed north through Monterey and joined the Ridge Road about five miles from the landing.[62]

According to Beauregard's plan, Hardee's corps was to leave Corinth on the morning of 3 April by the Bark road and camp that night at "Mickey's farm house" at the intersection of the road from Monterey to Savannah. The following day Hardee was to march within sight of Grant's lines and deploy troops on Grant's left at Owl Creek and on his right at Lick Creek. Bragg was to travel the Bark road and occupy a position as the second line of battle one thousand yards behind Hardee. Clark's Division, the only one in Polk's corps at Corinth, was to follow Hardee's line of march to "Mickey's." Polk's second division (Benjamin F. Cheatham's) was to maintain its position at Bethel if attacked, and to join Polk on the battlefield and form a third line on the left if not. Breckinridge, serving as a reserve, was to move from Burnsville to Monterey, once Bragg's corps was well on its way, and then hasten to the battle site by the best available route.[63]

If carried out as envisioned, Beauregard's strategy would deploy Hardee's and Bragg's corps in single parallel lines, one behind the other, with Breckinridge supporting on the right and Polk on the left. As Johnston outlined the plan to Jefferson Davis in a telegram sent on the third:

General Buell is in motion, with 30,000 strong, rapidly from Columbia by Clifton to Savannah; Mitchell behind him with 10,000. Confederate Forces, 40,000, ordered forward to offer battle near Pittsburg. . . . Polk, left; Hardee, center; Bragg, right wing; Breckinridge, reserve. Hope engagement before Buell can form junction.[64]

The strategy required the Confederate army to be in position for battle by the evening of the fourth to strike Grant at daybreak on the fifth. Although it seemed reasonable for Johnston's men to travel the twenty-three miles in two days, confusion and delay plagued the army from the outset. The morning of 3 April was beautiful as Hardee readied his troops for the long march to Pittsburg Landing. By noon they were in motion on the Monterey road. Perfume from wild flowers and peach blossoms filled the air, and Tennesseans cheered as they crossed the border into their home state. Having gotten a late start, they reached their intended destination, Mickey's house, in the early morning hours of 4 April, about twelve hours behind schedule.[65]

Even more problems developed about daylight as Hardee men prepared for the final leg of the march. Polk's corps had blocked the road, and precious time was lost waiting for his men to clear the way. Bragg, with many soldiers who had never made a day's march, was even slower, not reaching the village of Monterey until noon on the fourth. Breckinridge did not leave Burnsville until 3:00 P. M. on the fourth. To make matters worse, "torrents of rain fell on the night of the fourth, making the march over the swollen streams and flooded ravines . . . impracticable." In dismay, Hardee postponed his advance until dawn, instead of 3:00 A. M. as initially intended. Likewise, the "miry roads" that plunged the soldiers knee-deep in mud delayed the arrival of the other commanders until late afternoon on the fifth. Too late to mount an offensive, Johnston ordered an attack "the next morning at the earliest hour practicable."[66]

As the advance troops planned to attack at sunrise, Hardee's men shivered on the wet ground unable to light fires for fear of alerting the enemy across the tangled woodland. As they drifted off to sleep, patriotic tunes from the Federal camp wafted over, breaking the calm of the night. After midnight, a "heavy white mist" settled in and "hung low in the wooded valley between Hardee and the supposed quarter of the enemy."[67]

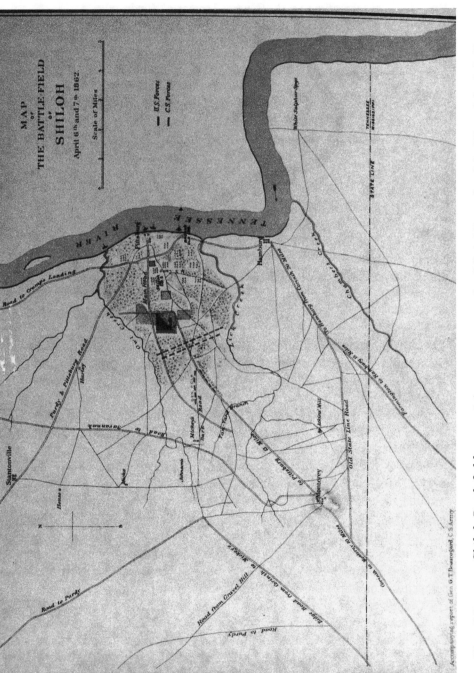

Plate 5.2   Shiloh Battlefield   Atlas to accompany the *Official Records of the War of the Rebellion*

Just before dawn, Johnston gathered his officers for a breakfast of thin crackers and coffee. Usually reserved, the commanding officer "welcomed with exultant joy the long-desired day" and "inspired all who came near him." As final preparations were being made near daylight, Johnston spoke encouragingly to many of the younger officers. To Hindman he said, "You have *earned* your spurs as a major-general. Let this day's work win them." Anticipation of victory rang through the commander's voice as he mounted his horse: "To-night we will water our horses in the Tennessee River."[68]

"Day broke upon a scene so fair that it left its memory on thousands of hearts," Johnston's son later reminisced. "As the sun rose in all its beauty, and as the Southern mocking bird perched on the topmost twig of the magnolia, sending up to heaven its melodious strains, . . . all nature seemed to be rejoicing." Suddenly, the sounds of cannon and musket fire reverberated through the Sunday morning calm and foretold the great battle just ahead.[69]

Although Johnston's army was poised and ready for battle, neither Grant nor William T. Sherman, Grant's second in command, seemed to have anticipated an attack. On the fifth, the very day the Confederates arrived in striking distance with forty thousand men, Grant had told Colonel Jacob Ammen of the Twenty-fourth Ohio Infantry that "there will be no fight at Pittsburg Landing; we will have to go to Corinth, where the rebels are fortified." If the Confederates attacked, Grant stated, "we can whip them, as I have more than twice as many troops as I had at Fort Donelson." Having dismissed the issue for the present, Grant told Ammen to be sure to "call at the brick house on the river to-morrow evening, as I have an engagement for that evening." Unaware that a major battle was imminent, on the morning of the sixth Grant was still at his headquarters in Savannah, nine miles from Pittsburg Landing, and his six divisions were still indiscriminately scattered around their campsites—one of them six miles downstream at Crump's Landing.[70]

Grant's troops were camped in a triangular pattern circumscribed in clockwise fashion by the Tennessee River, Snake Creek, Owl Creek, Oak Creek, Locust Grove Creek, and Lick Creek. Except for a few cleared areas, the ground was covered by forest and undergrowth, much of it impassable for men on horseback. The highest terrain was a ridge running generally east to west about 200 feet above the Tennessee River.[71]

Grant's serenity and that of his ill-prepared troops were shattered at daybreak on the sixth when five companies of Colonel David Moore's Twenty-First Missouri Infantry encountered Hardee's advancing brigade. The dreadful roar of musketry quickly ushered in the battle, and a messenger was immediately dispatched to Brigadier General Benjamin M. Prentiss, Sixth Division Commander, who "promptly sent forward" the rest of the Twenty-first and ordered the remaining regiments of his entire command "into line." The Battle of Shiloh had begun.[72]

Hearing the firing, Sherman moved quickly, posting a battery at Shiloh Church and another on a ridge to the south. Shortly after Sherman established this hastily organized line, Cleburne's second brigade of Hardee's corps (consisting of the Second, Fifth, Twenty-fourth, and Twenty-third Tennessee; Sixth Mississippi; and the Fifteenth Arkansas) unleashed a fierce assault against Prentiss. With "savage yells" transmitting encouragement among his troops, Cleburne's advance scattered the Union forces and seemed to be on the verge of posting a victory when two Union brigades under Brigadier General Stephen A. Hurlbut arrived and turned the tide. Hurlbut quickly deployed his 5,400 men and three well equipped artillery batteries behind a dense thicket on the crest of a hill. Hurlbut, joined by Brigadier General William H. L. Wallace and the residue of Prentiss's troops, held a commanding position on a natural fortress later dubbed the "Hornets' Nest" by Confederates. Under "terrible fire" from a superior force occupying higher ground, without artillery, and bogged down in "an almost impassable morass," confusion entered the ranks and Cleburne's men were quickly repulsed.[73]

While Cleburne was engaging the Federals on the left, Hindman was in the center serving as a pivot, commanding both the second and third brigades. With his horse "at full gallop, his long hair streaming out behind him . . . waving his cap over his head and cheering the men on," he attacked Prentiss "with great vigor." Their bayonets flashing in the sun, Hindman's brigade rushed "pell-mell . . . amidst a shower of bullets" and captured the first line of Union camps by 8:00 A. M., scattering Prentiss' soldiers, who ran like "wild turkies [*sic*]." With little difficulty, the graybacks quickly moved across two ridges and reached the base of a third. Although to some the battle seemed well-nigh over and a complete rout appeared to be the order of the day, the Southerners suddenly encountered the "Hornets' Nest" and joined what Bragg later reported as "the most obstinate resistance of the day."[74]

In order to reach the Union position, Confederates had to cross an open field and subject themselves to "deadly peril" from the "furious storm of bullets" emanating from "ripping, cracking musketry" that resembled "the incessant yapping of terriers" and the murderous fire of cannon whose "deep bass" was like "a great herd of roaring lions." Under orders from Bragg to dislodge the Union soldiers, Hindman commanded his men to charge the Union stronghold. When Major James T. Martin of the Seventh Arkansas Infantry protested that some of his men had "almost expended" their ammunition, Hindman tersely replied they "have their bayonets."[75]

During one of the many charges made by his brigade, a large shell struck Hindman's horse in the breast, tearing "his whole forequarters into shreds." Mortally wounded, the animal crashed to the ground, throwing the general over its head "some ten feet in the air." Convinced that the brigadier had been "blown to pieces," members of his staff cheered when Hindman "disentangled" himself "from the crushed remains," struggled to his feet, "feebly" waved his hat, and yelled "Tennesseans, take that battery." The recovery was only momentary. Weakened by the fall and in excruciating pain from a "shivered" bone in his leg, the gallant Arkansan collapsed and had to be carried from the field.[76]

In considerable pain, Hindman still attempted to carry out some of his duties from the rear while awaiting medical attention. Unaware that a cannon shot had struck fellow brigadier Sterling A. M. Wood, Hindman requested him to remain with the troops if possible and to compel stragglers to return to the field. After apprizing Hindman of his own injuries, Wood promised to return to the command so that the troops might have the benefit of his service.[77]

The intense fighting ended shortly after 6:00 P. M., with Confederates in control of the Union camp and the Federals one mile behind the position they had occupied at the start of the day. To private Sam Watkins of the First Tennessee, the "whole Yankee army" seemed in "full retreat." Jubilant with victory, the Confederates rummaged through the abandoned Federal camp for food and clothing. On the field, "men were lying in every conceivable position; the dead lying with their eyes wide open, the wounded begging piteously for help." Among the dead was the Confederates' beloved commander Albert Sidney Johnston, who bled to death after a minié ball severed the popiteal artery on his right leg just below the knee.[78]

Reporting that thanks to "the Almighty" he had achieved "complete victory," Beauregard, who had assumed command upon Johnston's death, informed Richmond that his troops had moved "like an Alpine avalanche" and were in control of all but one Union encampment lying between Owl and Lick creeks. Moreover, they had captured several pieces of artillery, "about 30 flags, colors, and standards," more than 3,000 prisoners (including General Prentiss), "thousands of small arms," and "a large amount" of transportation. Adding a negative note, he condemned "some officers, non-commissioned officers, and men [who] abandoned their colors . . . to pillage the captured encampments" and those who had "shamefully" hidden when they encountered "thundering cannon" and the "roar and rattle of musketry."[79]

Although Union forces had been driven back, Southern forces had not won a decisive victory. Grant's army was still intact, Johnston's forces had sustained heavy casualties, and Federal reinforcements were en route to Pittsburg Landing. Exhausted and hungry from over twelve hours of fierce combat, both sides settled down to rest for a few hours despite a torrential storm. Seeking refuge under an oak tree, Colonel James S. Wright of Indiana thought of his comrades lying dead and dying on the field. Faint, heartsick, and unable to sleep, he prayed that his men would be spared from "another such day" and that generals Don Carlos Buell and Lew Wallace would arrive with reinforcements by morning.[80]

Buell and Wallace did arrive overnight with 25,000 fresh troops, and at daylight on Monday Grant launched an assault. By 10:00 A. M. Union forces were attacking all along the line. "Hour after hour," Union "shouts of victory filled the air" as the Federals regained positions they had lost the day before. The reinforced Union troops were simply too much for the weary, outnumbered Confederates. His ranks "perceptibly thinned" by "unceasing, withering fire" of musketry and artillery from a superior force, Beauregard ordered a retreat at 2:30 P. M. and by 4:00 P. M. the Army of Mississippi was headed back toward Corinth.[81]

Shiloh was a costly engagement for both sides, and the ghastly results of the slaughter were visible everywhere. According to Henry Stanley, "many bullets found their destined billets" and "the world, . . . bursting into fragments, . . . seemed [to be] involved in one tremendous ruin." Amid the "fearful shambles," lay bodies (many of them "mutilated [and] hacked") strewn willy-nilly "in various postures, each by its own pool of viscous blood."[82]

The battle "mutilated the western army of the Confederacy"; Tennessee was as good as lost, and the capture of Corinth would "only be a matter of time." Although each claimed to have won, the battle was a Union victory. Southern troops had failed to destroy Grant's army and were forced to fall back to Corinth, evacuating much of Tennessee and opening the way for splitting the Confederacy along the Mississippi River. Out of 39,598 troops who were available at Shiloh, Confederates suffered 1,728 killed, 8,012 wounded, and 959 missing. Out of 62,682 effectives, Federal losses were 1,754 killed, 8,408 wounded, and 2,885 missing or captured. What began as an unanticipated Confederate attack on 6 April ended with 3,482 combatants killed, 16,240 wounded, and 3,844 missing or captured.[83]

Juxtaposed against the incredible carnage of the battle, was an exchange between George Wythe Baylor, an aide to General Johnston, and a captured Union lieutenant that offered a succinct summary of the motivation behind many of the belligerents. When Baylor informed the prisoner, "You Yankees are very determined in trying to deny us the right to regulate our own state affairs," the enraged lieutenant immediately "flared up" and emphatically declared that he was "no *Yankee*." He was a "Western man" fighting to preserve the Union.[84]

With the tired and weary remainder of the Army of the Mississippi, Hindman retreated to Corinth. The return was, indeed, a horrible sight. Writing less than six months later, the reluctant Arkansas "volunteer" William G. Stevenson vividly chronicled the scene of "human agony and woe." With roads at time "almost impassable," the wounded, piled into wagons "like bags of grain," groaned and cursed as "the mules plunged on in the mud and water belly-deep, the water sometimes coming into the wagons." Soldiers with broken arms "hanging down" and others with more "fearful wounds" straggled toward Corinth.[85]

The trip became even more ghoulish when "a cold, drizzling rain commenced about nightfall, and soon became harder and faster, [and] then turned to pitiless blinding hail." Many wounded and dying soldiers suffered through the storm "without even a blanket to shield them from the driving sleet and hail, which fell in stones as large as partridge eggs, until it lay on the ground two inches deep." Nearly three hundred soldiers died during the "awful retreat, and their bodies were thrown out" to make room for the wounded who sought "shelter, rest, and medical care."[86]

Although not the only officer singled out for accolades, Hindman's performance at Shiloh drew exceptionally high praise from his superiors. Hardee reported that his leadership "upon the field was marked by a courage which animated his soldiers and a skill which won their confidence." More reserved than Hardee, Beauregard too offered laudatory comments about Hindman's performance at Shiloh. "Conspicuous for a cool courage," he had "efficiently" commanded his troops "ever in the thickest of the fray, until his horse was shot under him and he was unfortunately so severely injured, by the fall that the army was deprived on the following day of his chivalrous example." Even though he and Hindman would later become embroiled in a bitter controversy after the Battle of Chickamauga, Bragg heaped lavish praise on the Arkansas brigadier. "The noble and gallant" Hindman, stated Bragg, "under murderous fire," had led his men "with a heroism rarely equaled."[87]

Chapter 6

TO DRIVE OUT THE INVADER: GENERAL HINDMAN AND THE TRANS-MISSISSIPPI DISTRICT

After the Army of the Mississippi returned to Corinth, Hindman received a leave of absence to return to Helena to recuperate from the serious injuries sustained at Shiloh. Although still wracked by pain and unable to walk without crutches, he was elated at being temporarily reunited with Mollie and the children. This was the first time the proud father had seen his five-month old son Biscoe. Comforted by a loving family and the well-wishes of neighbors, Hindman remained in good spirits, despite overall poor health and surgery to remove several bone fragments from his leg. He may well have reflected that things could have been much worse. According to a story in the Washington *Telegraph* of 16 April, he had "lost his leg—shot away in battle."[1]

While at home, he received the welcome news that his gallant conduct and reputation as a fighter had earned him the major general's spurs promised by Albert Sidney Johnston just before the Battle of Shiloh. Although worried that Tom might ultimately join the ranks of Confederate generals killed in battle, Mollie must have been extremely proud of her husband who had risen to the rank of major general in just under a year.[2]

By the end of the first week in May, Hindman had recovered sufficiently to rejoin the Army of the Mississippi at Corinth. When he reported on 10 May to Major General Bragg, who was then commanding the army, Hindman replaced Brigadier General Daniel Ruggles as commander of the Third Brigade. He had barely settled into his assignment, however, when he was ordered back to Arkansas to command the newly created Trans-Mississippi District.[3]

While he was on duty east of the Mississippi River, Confederate military affairs in Hindman's home state had taken a drastic turn for the worse. Following the defeat of Southern troops commanded by Major General Earl Van Dorn at Pea Ridge on 6–8 March 1862, Federal forces under Major General Samuel R. Curtis controlled southern Missouri and northwest Arkansas. Facing little opposition, he advanced slowly into northeast Arkansas and, moving at will, within three months took Batesville, Searcy, Augusta, and other towns north of the Arkansas River.[4]

After Pea Ridge, Van Dorn withdrew to the Arkansas valley, where he remained until May 1862 when he left with his army and all available military supplies and equipment to reinforce Confederate troops near Corinth. Prior to departing, he appointed Brigadier General John S. Roane military commander of Arkansas on 11 April and authorized him "to organize and put into the field all troops" raised under the conscription law along with cavalry forces from Texas and northern Louisiana that entered the state expecting to report to Van Dorn. In addition, he was to receive all non-Indian troops that could be spared by Brigadier General Albert Pike, Commander of the Department of Indian Territory.[5]

The policy of defending areas east of the Mississippi River by transferring troops from west of the river left southern Missouri and northern Arkansas defenseless. Curtis's seizure of Little Rock was prevented only through a fortuitous combination of circumstances. He found much of northeastern Arkansas barren of forage for his horses, numerous breaks occurred in his lengthy supply lines from St. Louis, and travel over muddy roads and swollen streams was excruciatingly slow. Roane, with a few scattered militia units, one six-gun battery, and fifteen hundred partially armed cavalrymen, certainly would have posed little threat to Curtis had he been able to advance on the capital city.[6]

Although Curtis was unable to launch an immediate attack on Little Rock, he established outposts within thirty-five miles of the city. Thoroughly frightened, Governor Rector fled in panic to Hot Springs in early May and ordered the state treasury and archives moved to Hempstead County. Richard H. Johnson, editor of the *True Democrat*, lambasted Rector for allegedly leaving the state without "any government, whatever, at a time when it was most needed."[7]

Fear gripped Little Rock as bands of thieves and robbers plundered the countryside. Alarmed citizens, including the editors of Little Rock papers, implored General Roane to declare martial law and provide military protection. Uncertain as to what authority he possessed, Roane asked Western Department commander P. G. T. Beauregard for advice. Even though only Jefferson Davis had the power to declare martial law, in view of the emergency Beauregard approved its use. Cloaked with the authority and aware of the need to act swiftly, Roane proclaimed martial law in Little Rock on 17 May, issued orders to raise additional militia units to defend the state, and commandeered four companies of Parsons' Texas cavalry bound for Corinth.[8]

Through a series of special orders, he closed distilleries and prohibited the sale of liquor. He also "earnestly enjoined" Arkansans to assist enrolling officers in implementing the conscription law and to help supply conscriptees with "good effective shot guns or rifles." Persons leaving Little Rock were required to secure passes, and all visitors had to report to military officials upon entering the city. Reacting to rampant profiteering, Roane prohibited "forestalling and huckstering of vegetables" and other items necessary for "daily consumption."[9]

Many elected officials and private citizens solidly endorsed Roane's actions. Reflecting this sentiment, Johnson of the *True Democrat* lauded the extraordinary measures and asserted that they met "with the approval of everyone." If there was a regret, claimed the editor, it was because martial law was not extended over "the entire state." Roane was "taking steps to expel the enemy" and would succeed in less than twenty days if his "patriotic efforts" were sustained.[10]

Apprehensive that Roane's small force could not withstand Curtis's advance, on 15 April the Arkansas congressional delegation wrote to Jefferson Davis protesting the planned removal of troops from the state. Arkansas, they declared, after "having furnished her quota [of Confederate troops] was now to be stripped" of remaining ones "until she was left defenseless and open to the invasion of Yankees." On 15 May, Governor Rector went even further and accused Confederate authorities of trying to subjugate the state by transferring troops to the east. He warned that this situation would not be tolerated and might force Arkansas to secede from the Confederacy. Angered by the apparent abandonment of the state by Richmond authorities, Rector issued a call for militia troops to defend the "sovereign" state of Arkansas. The

Plate 6   *Thomas C. Hindman*
Courtesy: Ivey S. Gladin, Photographer, Helena, Arkansas

governor's militia call had the effect of creating two overlapping military commands, one controlled by state officials and the other by Roane. Like the Arkansas congressional delegation and Rector, Roane was not optimistic about his chances of success. On 4 May, he confided to Van Dorn that "the whole state" was "in danger of being overrun" and that he did not think he was capable of handling his command.[11]

In response to protests from Rector and the Arkansas congressional delegation, on 20 May Davis advised Van Dorn to announce that his transfer was "merely temporary" and that he expected to return "soon" with "at least as many troops as had been temporarily withdrawn." Claiming, however, that Rector's action resulted from "the dung-hill policy of fighting at every State's threshold . . . pressed upon him by shallow politicians" and arguing that the issue was "now at rest," Van Dorn ignored Davis' suggestion and requested Beauregard to name a new commander to replace Roane. Citing "the earnest solicitations of the people of Arkansas" and expressing "sincere regret" at parting with a "gallant officer," Beauregard ordered Thomas C. Hindman to assume command of the military forces in Arkansas and "the Indian Country" on 26 May. The following day, in accordance with General Orders No. 39 of the War Department, he designated Hindman's command as the Trans-Mississippi District encompassing Arkansas, Missouri, Indian Territory, and the portion of Louisiana north of the Red River.[12]

Prior to leaving Corinth, Hindman received permission for his staff to accompany him to Little Rock. For Assistant Adjutant General and Chief of Staff, he selected Major Robert C. Newton, a prewar Little Rock attorney and Bell-Everett supporter who had canvassed the state for secession in early 1861. As Aide-de-Camp, he picked Lieutenant Jerome P. Wilson, a wealthy Mississippi planter, and for Chief Commissary officer, he chose his close friend and former law partner Major John C. Palmer.[13]

Recognizing that he needed an experienced ordnance officer, Hindman obtained the services of Major Francis A. Shoup. A native of Laurel, Indiana, the twenty-nine year old Shoup graduated from West Point in 1855 and had been Hardee's Chief of Artillery at the Battle of Shiloh. Given the task facing Hindman, Shoup's ordnance expertise was not only needed—it was absolutely essential.[14]

Totally committed to the Southern cause, Hindman wasted no time in leaving for his new command. Aware that Confederates were evacuating Memphis in anticipation of a massive Union offensive, en route to Arkansas he detoured by the Tennessee city where he obtained thirty-five Enfield rifles, 400 damaged shotguns and squirrel rifles, and a few hundred rounds of artillery shot and shell. In addition, he acquired percussion caps, blankets, boots, shoes, and medicine and, with Beauregard's permission, impressed one million dollars in Confederate currency from city banks. After leaving Memphis, he seized ammunition, shoes, blankets, and medicine in Helena and Napoleon. While in Helena, he also made arrangements for Mollie and the children to join him in Little Rock.[15]

Besides procuring medicines and other supplies, while in transit Hindman executed contracts for Texas cattlemen to supply beef for future recruits and ordered thousands of bales of cotton along the Mississippi River burned to prevent them from being captured by the Federals. On 17 March 1862, the Confederate Congress had authorized the destruction of cotton, tobacco, military supplies, and other property in danger of falling into the hands of the Union Army. Cotton burning had begun in the state at least as early as March, and Hindman's actions merely accelerated the process. Burning progressed to such a point that on 15 May the *True Democrat* reported that before the paper reached its "more distant subscribers, the last bale of cotton upon the Arkansas River will have been committed to flames." This "glorious offering upon the altar of liberty" and similar actions along the Mississippi River would deprive Federal forces of "fifty million dollars worth of property" torched "by the willing hands of the owners."[16]

Hindman arrived in Little Rock on 30 May and formally assumed his new command the following day, announcing that he had come "to drive out the invader, or perish in the attempt." Considered by many to be the most able general to serve the Trans-Mississippi area, he set out to create and supply an army capable of opening a third front by attacking Union forces in Arkansas and Missouri. Without "even the skeleton of an army" and lacking arms, ammunition, and supplies, he undertook the defense of Arkansas with nothing except his staff and "an order from Beauregard assigning him to the command." Aware that success depended on broad-based support and personal sacrifice, he called on soldiers and citizens to do their "whole duty." Soldiers must serve with "fidelity, and courage" and obey all commands promptly "without murmur," regardless of "the hardships involved." He warned that he would not tolerate lax military discipline. Civilians must "contribute to the army's support" even to their last dollar and stand by the Southern cause "under every difficulty." Arkansans must sustain Confederate currency, "crush out the spirit of extortion and speculation," and be willing to "sacrifice for freedom's sake" any property in danger of falling into Union hands. General Hindman expected much of Confederate Arkansans, but given the desperate situation in the state, to have required anything less would have been too little.[17]

The new commander of the Trans-Mississippi District was appalled by the situation he had inherited from Roane. His command was "bare of soldiers, penniless, defenseless, and dreadfully exposed" as Curtis sat menacingly thirty-five miles outside Little Rock. He immediately dispatched messengers to inform the War Department of the shortage of troops and weapons, the chaotic situation within the state, and his inability to repel Curtis should he move on the capital. Unfortunately for the new commander, his reports fell into Curtis' hands. When news reached him that Curtis had captured the documents, Hindman and his Chief of Staff R. C. Newton resorted to finesse and chicanery to convince the Union general that Confederate troop strength was greater than reported. They recruited approximately one hundred people with sons, brothers, or husbands serving east of the Mississippi River to write letters about "imaginary brigade[s]" that had been raised in, or had been transferred to, Arkansas. Letters written by the fictitious soldiers described their new Enfield rifles "arriving from Mexico," while letters ostensibly from sweethearts talked about dances and other social events involving five thousand Texans who had just arrived to assist in the defense of Little Rock.[18]

Hindman and Newton reviewed all the letters and combined them with pseudo-reports describing new units and their officers and how the scarcity of arms had been quickly overcome by purchasing large numbers from a Mexican firm in Matamoras in exchange for cotton. Augmented by "thousands" of volunteers and suitable weapons, Hindman would soon attack Curtis. Once everything was ready, Lieutenant Colonel Walter Scott, a "daring, handsome" Missourian, volunteered to transport the mail and reports behind enemy lines and insure that they fell into Union hands.[19]

Riding the "fleet limbs" and "strung sinews" of "his beautiful sorrel mare" Princess, Scott traversed swamps, swam bayous, and traveled guarded roads inside Union lines until he reached Curtis' main force. Deliberately encountering thirty Illinois cavalrymen, he opened fire, wheeled around, dashed away, and jettisoned the saddle-bags containing the false letters and reports. Scott returned safely to Little Rock and the ruse "had the desired effect upon Curtis," who became convinced that Hindman's strength was greater than previously reported.[20]

While trying to buy precious time to strengthen his army, Hindman turned his attention to making the Trans-Mississippi a model of efficiency. Arguing that "separate military organizations" could not "exist in the same jurisdiction without causing confusion and provoking dissensions," with the governor's reluctant consent Hindman terminated overlapping jurisdictions in Arkansas and announced that Rector had transferred state troops to Confederate service. Henceforth, there would be no state forces in the Trans-Mississippi District. "All white males between the ages of eighteen and thirty-five" living in Arkansas were to enroll in voluntary infantry companies on or before 20 June or be conscripted.[21]

For several months prior to Hindman's arrival, many Arkansans had complained bitterly that unscrupulous merchants and others were engaging in extortion and speculation. As the war progressed, prices for goods, especially foodstuffs, increased dramatically; money and credit became scarce; and some merchants refused to accept Confederate currency, demanding payment in gold. Although some price increases and tightening of credit were justified because of scarcity and the "deranged condition of currency," many increases resulted from profiteering. Responding to abuses, the editor of the *Daily State Journal* condemned those who "enrich[ed] themselves at the expense of the poor" by taking advantage of deteriorating military conditions. Having "no regard for man or devil," these extortionists and speculators were nothing but "horse-leeches of the body politic" who had entered into a "covenant with hell" to fill their "iron boxes" with gold and silver stolen from a "hissing public."[22]

To stabilize the state's economy and prevent "the devil of extortion" from undermining the Confederate war effort in Arkansas, on 2 June Hindman imposed price controls on various foodstuffs, medicine, and other goods, and required all persons "to take Confederate notes as currency at par, in all business transactions." Those who were "inhuman and disloyal" enough to charge more than the allowable minimum or refused to accept Confederate notes would be arrested and tried by the military.[23]

Although civilians were to make sacrifices, military authorities were not to impress private property without proper written authority from Hindman's staff. Those who seized private property without authorization would be treated as "robbers and marauders" and be "put to death, without hesitation." In addition to issuing orders to regulate impressment, Hindman established a special board to settle claims relating to property illegally seized by the military prior to his arrival.[24]

His initial orders met with wide-spread approval throughout the state. A letter from "VINDEX" in Little Rock to the Washington *Telegraph* predicted that Hindman and his staff would "give the invaders a warm reception" and that Arkansas would soon "become an armed people ready for the conflict on no small scale." Richard H. Johnson of the *True Democrat* lauded the general's policies and exhorted his readers to sustain the new commander who would expel Union forces from the state within "a very short time." C. C. Danley of the *Arkansas State Gazette* praised Hindman and his staff and admonished all to support the new policies "cheerfully." He was especially pleased with the "wise and well time[d]" order governing impressment of private property that would "doubtless[ly] have a restraining influence" on soldiers who had pre-viously "plunder[ed] in the name of patriotism."[25]

To combat marauding bands of outlaws and to end speculation, price gouging, and the refusal to accept Confederate notes in the vicinity of the capital city, on 10 June Hindman declared martial law in Pulaski County and named Benjamin F. Danley, brother of C. C. Danley, post com-mander and provost marshal. Cloaked with sweeping powers, Danley was to maintain order and discipline, enforce all military orders; suppress "vice, disorder, and immorality within the limits of his jurisdiction"; and supervise public property in the county. Like Hindman, Danley believed that strong measures were necessary to reverse Confederate fortunes in Arkansas. Moving quickly to implement martial law in his district, he established maximum prices for goods, ordered merchants to keep their stores open from 6:30 A. M. to 8:00 P. M. every day except Sunday, and warned shoemakers that, if rumors were true that they were overcharging customers, they would "be promptly punished."[26]

Responding to the acute shortage of clothes, shoes, small arms, ammunition, wagons, and other military supplies, Hindman launched a concerted effort to make the Trans-Mississippi District "self-sustaining." Under his direction, lead mines were opened; preparations were made for smelting iron; moulds, furnaces, and lathes were constructed; and machinery was made for manufacturing percussion caps and small arms. In addition, damaged small arms were repaired, condemned artillery pieces were successfully rebuilt, and a chemical laboratory was established to manufacture castor oil, tinctures of iron, and other medicines."[27]

Like most of his initial actions, Hindman's emphasis on home manufacturing drew high praise. C. C. Danley said that the effort was "necessary" for both "present well being" and the "existence" of the state. Home manufacturing would "clothe and shoe" the army during the war, and the development of mining and industry would "yield immense wealth in the future."[28]

While attempting to raise an army and create a supply system capable of meeting its needs, Hindman continued to destroy cotton, tobacco, naval stores, and other materials that were in danger of falling into Federal hands. Acting within the confines of laws passed by the Confederate Congress, on 3 June he ordered "all cotton" within his district—except in the Choctaw Nation—seized and moved to safe locations and, if in danger of capture by the enemy, destroyed. Anyone who concealed cotton earmarked for destruction would be arrested and dealt with as a traitor. While in command of the Trans-Mississippi District, Hindman ordered several tons of cotton burned but mandated that planters and "necessituous persons" be issued parcels of ten pounds per capita to make clothing for their families and slaves.[29]

Confident that his directives would restore order, infuse life into a war-ravaged economy, and promote the production of essential supplies, Hindman turned his attention to building an army capable of repelling Curtis and recovering southern Missouri. The motley forces that he had inherited from Roane were no match for the enemy's fifteen thousand men. Hindman desperately needed soldiers but found himself in a quandary. His orders from Beauregard specified that he was to implement the conscription act but did not authorize the raising of new regiments. Conscripts, by law, were to be used to bring existing regiments up to full strength. Van Dorn, however, had drained Arkansas of troops. Hindman determined that the exigencies confronting him required new units. Waiting for approval from the War Department would have resulted in the fall of Little Rock and the loss of Arkansas and the Indian Territory. In addition to destroying all hope of recovering Missouri, it would have exposed Texas and Louisiana to the "greatest misfortunes." Reasoning that the "main object of law" was the preservation of public safety, the new commander of the Trans-Mississippi resolved to take the responsibility for "raising and organizing a force without authorization of law."[30]

Observers noted that "Hindman worked like a demi-god; small as he was, he seemed like a giant" as he commissioned "daring men to go into north Arkansas and Missouri and bring out recruits." With lightning speed, he divided his command into districts and ordered enrolling officers to enforce the conscription law with vigor. To encourage volunteering, he permitted units formed before 20 June to elect their own company officers. In subsequent units, he appointed the company officers. In all instances, the general personally selected field and staff officers. "Placing devotion to the South on one side and death on the other," Hindman was "relentless against all who hesitated to fight for their State and country." When voluntary compliance failed to achieve the desired results, such as in the Pine Bluff and Little Rock areas, his cavalry transported "skulking conscripts" to induction centers.[31]

Aware that the substitute system was a miserable failure, he violated the conscript law and existing War Department regulations by forbidding the employment of substitutes. Later, when he was criticized for prohibiting their use, the fiery Arkansan made no apologies. He needed troops and the system increased "difficulties, already too great" in enrolling recruits. In spite of his refusal to allow substitution, Hindman also violated existing regulations by expanding the categories of persons who qualified for exemptions in order to enhance efforts to make the Trans-Mississippi self-sufficient.[32]

Even though various editors and other community leaders supported Hindman's policy of strict enforcement of the conscription law, the issue created division in Arkansas, as it did elsewhere in the Confederacy. Men like J. B. Gridley of the Fort Smith (AR) *Tri-Weekly Bulletin* praised the way the law was "being executed." As they "should be," those who tried to "evade" the law were being "unceremoniously marched up to the Captain's office." Such actions were necessary if Arkansans were to "enjoy the blessings of liberty and independence." Johnson of the *True Democrat* agreed, stating that the "right" of "self-preservation" entitled the South to "the services of every arms-bearing man."[33]

The views of Gridley, Johnson, and like-minded Arkansans contrasted sharply with those of John Eakin of the Washington *Telegraph* and others who opposed the law because they believed it an unconstitutional violation of state rights. As early as April, Eakin had endorsed the arguments of congressional critics who claimed that conscription was "contrary to the genius of . . . free government." Conscription was unnecessary since there were enough "volunteers" to fill Confederate ranks. Caught between devotion to the Southern cause and commitment to state rights, opponents of conscription in Arkansas refused to yield, even though the state was on the verge of conquest.[34]

Opposition or not, Hindman enforced the law, enrolled thousands of conscripts, and sent them to camp for instruction. Once in camp, soldiers learned Hardee's military tactics and adhered to strict discipline. Those who failed to observe military regulations received either extra duty or confinement in guard houses.[35]

For various reasons, ranging from a desire to escape the drudgeries of military service or the need to look after their families or to opposition to the Confederate war effort, large numbers of conscripts deserted. At first, those who were arrested for desertion were returned to duty without penalty if they promised to remain in service. When desertions increased, Hindman concluded that his policy of no punishment had been "taken for timidity." Like other commanders, including Braxton Bragg and A. P. Hill, he ultimately ordered deserters shot to death in the presence of other troops. Few such executions actually occurred and then only for those whom the courts martial convicted after permitting them to defend their conduct. The small number of executions, however, had a dramatic impact. During the summer of 1862 "the spirit of desertion was crushed."[36]

To deal with shortages of foodstuffs and war materials and the special needs of certain citizens, Hindman illegally exempted from conscription "persons actually engaged in the manufacture of wool, cotton, arms, powder, salt, leather, breadstuffs, and army clothing or equipment." He also excluded overseers on those plantations that had less than ten black males and that raised mainly grain—if the land was owned by widows, minors, or men serving in the Confederate army when no other white males "capable of managing" were available.[37]

Although a strict disciplinarian who believed that all must sacrifice, Hindman was deeply concerned about the welfare of soldiers and their families. Worried that many families whose husbands and sons had been conscripted or who had voluntarily joined the army were facing starvation, he urged Governor Rector and the Military Board to appropriate at least $250,000 to purchase provisions for them. Extending assistance was not a "gratuity." Instead, it was a "sacred duty" owed to Arkansas' volunteers and conscripts who were fighting for "the cause of their country." Concurring with his recommendations, the *Arkansas State Gazette* suggested that the Military Board consider additional aid "to meet the future wants of the wives and families of the absent soldiers."[38]

Although conscription would eventually provide a substantial military force, Hindman needed trained troops immediately to combat the threat Curtis posed to Little Rock. To acquire them, he asked brigadier generals Paul O. Hebert, Commander of the District of Texas, and Henry McCullough of the Twelfth Texas Cavalry to send as many "unemployed" troops as possible to Arkansas. Both men responded "prompt[ly] and liberal[ly]." Accessions from Texas were supplemented on 13 July when General Braxton Bragg ordered Brigadier General Mosby M. Parsons's Missouri State Guard to report to Arkansas." In addition, on 31 May Hindman ordered Brigadier General Albert Pike to move his entire "infantry force of whites," together with wagons and ammunition and one six-gun battery to Little Rock "without the least delay."[39]

Unlike Hebert, McCullough, and Parsons, Pike did not readily cooperate with Hindman's efforts to find troops to defend Arkansas. Hindman's order arrived on 8 June on the heels of Van Dorn's report of the Battle of Pea Ridge—a report that did not contain even a single line "acknowledging that Pike and the Cherokees were in the action or that the Choctaws and Creeks had helped bring off Van Dorn's train." This, coupled with Pike's earlier disagreements with Van Dorn's policy towards the Indian Territory, made Hindman's order "a blow that Pike could hardly have been expected to accept with equanimity."[40]

Grudgingly, on 8 June Pike ordered Colonel C. L. Dawson's infantry regiment and Captain William E. Woodruff's six-gun battery to Little Rock. He coupled his compliance, however, with a lengthy letter to Hindman protesting the transfer on the grounds that it ruined his command and paralyzed his efforts to defend the Indian Territory. Moreover, the order allegedly negated treaty pledges personally negotiated by Pike and approved by the Confederate government that promised to keep three regiments of white troops available at all times to help defend Indian Territory. Pike argued that he was entitled to "a separate command." Furthermore, the unfair treatment to which he had been subjected had left him "discouraged" and demonstrated Confederate "weakness" to the Indians.[41]

With Curtis poised to strike at "the very heart of Arkansas" and rumors that a Federal advance from Fort Scott in Kansas aimed at northwest Arkansas had begun, Hindman could not afford to wage a war of words with Pike. Waiting impatiently for Dawson and Woodruff to arrive, he sent a follow-up inquiry to Pike on 17 June and ordered him to shift his remaining white troops to Fort Gibson in the Cherokee Nation. Pike replied that he would "obey all lawful orders" and assured Hindman that Dawson and Woodruff would arrive in Little Rock soon. He also promised to move his white regiments to Fort Gibson but warned that the deployment would be delayed due to transportation and supply problems. Bluntly, he labeled the move to Fort Gibson foolhardy and stated that he personally planned to remain at Fort McCulloch drilling troops.[42]

In exasperation, on 8 July Hindman ordered Pike to proceed to Fort Smith to take charge of all Confederate forces in northwest Arkansas and the Indian Territory and "to make the best disposition of them possible to repel invasions, suppress marauding, and maintain our position." The situation was urgent. Bands of Federals were threatening Fort Smith and Van Buren, and unless Pike acted promptly, "the Indian country and all of Northwest Arkansas" could be lost.[43]

Reluctantly, Pike ordered a regiment of Texas cavalry and two companies of artillery to Fort Smith and forwarded his resignation to Hindman. Since Hindman had long thought Pike unfit for a field command, he gladly approved the resignation, sent it to Richmond, and relieved Pike from duty. The matter would have ended had Pike not issued a public address to the Indians that Hindman believed was designed to "disgust and dishearten" the Confederacy's Indian allies. Outraged, Colonel Douglas Cooper, who succeeded Pike as commander of the Indian Territory, ordered his predecessor's arrest. Hindman approved the order and rescinded his endorsement of Pike's resignation so that charges of "falsehood, cowardice, and treason" could be brought before a court martial. Pike, however, escaped to Texas and southwestern Arkansas where he remained until after he learned of Theophilus H. Holmes's assignment on 16 July to command the Trans-Mississippi

Department, superseding Hindman. Returning to Little Rock in late August, he stormed into Holmes's office expecting to be vindicated. When Holmes berated him for criticizing his superior officers in print, Pike issued a series of open letters lambasting both Hindman and Holmes and preferred formal charges of misconduct against them, which the War Department ignored.[44]

Hindman himself moved to fill the void in the Indian Territory and northwest Arkansas. In August, he journeyed to the Cherokee capital at Tahlequah just after the Confederate Cherokees had deposed John Ross and elected Stand Watie chief. There, in response to reports that pro-Union Indians had devastated much of the upper Cherokee country, he ordered nearly two thousand Cherokee refugees who had fled to Arkansas to be subsisted at government expense.[45]

At Tahlequah, Hindman coordinated the troops of colonels Douglas Cooper and Stand Watie with two regiments of Missourians under Brigadier General James S. Raines and three regiments of Arkansans under Colonel C. A. Carroll. Hindman's troops cleared the Cherokee country of pro-Union Indians, moved into southern Missouri, drove back the enemy's advance, and scattered General James Blunt's demoralized force of whites and Indians as they retreated towards Fort Scott. It was a total triumph as Blunt's men ran away "almost without firing a gun whenever attacked." Though outnumbered, Hindman determined to chase Blunt into Kansas and then turn eastward and attack Springfield, Missouri. Preparations were well underway when Theophilus Holmes took command of the Trans-Mississippi and ordered Hindman back to Little Rock.[46]

To augment his regular forces, Hindman organized "independent companies" of guerrillas patterned after the partisan rangers that the Confederate Congress had authorized on 21 April 1862. Like partisan rangers, the independent companies were to operate behind enemy lines "cut[ting] off pickets, scouts, foraging parties and trains, . . . kill[ing] pilots and others on gunboats and transports." As few as ten men could form a company and elect officers without waiting for special instructions. Captains were to make periodic reports to Hindman's headquarters and had authorization to draw "pay and allowance for subsistence and forage for time actually [spent] in the field."[47]

Unlike partisan rangers, Hindman's independent companies consisted of men "not subject to conscription" and were to serve as home guards operating in their own neighborhoods. They were never intended to be full-time soldiers; in fact, they were expected to pursue their usual employment when not in service. As an adjunct to his regular troops, Hindman's independent companies became a controversial and effective fighting force in Arkansas.[48]

Hindman also employed partisan ranger companies. Together with the independent companies, these gray ghosts disrupted Yankee communications, ambushed Federal patrols, blocked roads with trees, cut telegraph lines, tore up railroad tracks, and destroyed bridges. They were so effective in some areas that Union commanders were compelled to deploy larger forces than would normally have been required. Because they gave their enemies no quarter and considered anyone who did not cooperate with them an enemy, they deprived the Union of many "friends."[49]

For the most part, Federal military officials treated these irregulars as outlaws and pirates who, when captured, would not be dealt with as "ordinary prisoners of war." They were to be "hung as robbers and murderers." General James Blunt claimed that he would hang six of these "miscreants" for every one of his men who died at their hands and that "no punishment" would be "too prompt or severe for such unnatural enemies of the human race." Despite their bushwacker status, partisan rangers and independent companies thrived and provided Hindman with much needed logistical support. They proved so effective in harassing the Federals that on 7 July Hindman prohibited the formation of additional companies of partisan rangers and converted several existing units into mounted infantry that could be dismounted as needed.[50]

Although supply problems, heavy rains, and the lack of forage had prevented Curtis's Army of the Southwest from quickly moving on Little Rock, the Union commander was anxious to capture the capital before Hindman completed organizing his forces. Accordingly, on 4 June he requested that additional troops and supplies be sent to him. Four days later, Major General Henry W. Halleck ordered Commodore Charles H. Davis to ascend the White River as far as Jacksonport to resupply Curtis and to capture any Confederate gunboats on the river.[51]

Aware that the Arkansas and White rivers could be used to carry supplies and reinforcements to Curtis, Hindman was determined to prevent Federal gunboats from plying them. Moreover, with the fall of Memphis imminent unless action was taken quickly, the way would be open for Union gunboats to penetrate the large navigable rivers of the Arkansas heartland.[52]

Acting swiftly and decisively, on 3 June he ordered his engineers to study the feasibility of obstructing the Arkansas and White rivers. After a brief reconnaissance, engineers concluded that they could successfully obstruct the White River at St. Charles, about 100 miles from its mouth. The site was ideal because artillery could be placed on a bluff above the river, thereby affording the opportunity to protect the barricades from easy removal.[53]

Under the direction of Captain A. M. Williams, Chief of the Corps of Engineers, and civilians George Brodie and L. Leary, workers transported two pile-drivers to the area and cut large trees from forests along the river. Hindman sent one hundred soldiers from the First Trans-Mississippi Regiment with Williams, but because of a shortage of weapons, only armed thirty-five. As workers felled trees, they took them to the river, formed them into rafts, and floated them to the obstruction site. Bearss described how "Day after day, the dull boom of pile-drivers echoed across the White as Williams's working parties drove hundreds of piles into the river bottom."[54]

While work proceeded on the obstruction, two thirty-two pound Columbiads were removed from the gunboat *Pontchartrain* and a pair of two-inch guns was transferred to the site from Little Rock. Unfortunately for Hindman, on 16 June before obstruction was completed, a Federal flotilla consisting of the ironclad gunboats *St. Louis* and *Mound City*, the timberclads *Lexington* and *Conestoga*, the tug *Spiteful*, and three transports carrying between 1,000 and 1,500 soldiers of the Forty-sixth Indiana Infantry appeared on the White River near St. Charles.[55]

Anticipating an attack, Williams telegraphed Hindman that he had not completed the obstruction and that he was expecting a joint Union naval and land assault. The general ordered two merchant vessels (the *Liza G.* and the *Mary Patterson*) and the Confederate gunboat *Maurepas* (a timberclad that would be no match for the Union ironclads) scuttled. Before sinking the *Maurepas*, the crew removed a twelve-pound howitzer and a rifled gun and placed them on the bluff along with the thirty-two pounders from the *Pontchartrain* and the two guns from Little Rock. Seventy-nine sailors from the *Maurepas* and the *Pontchartrain* manned the battery, and thirty-five of Captain Williams's soldiers were detailed as sharpshooters.[56]

At approximately 6:00 A. M. on the seventeenth, the Union flotilla raised anchors and headed slowly up the river, spraying the woods with grape shot and canisters to kill or drive off any Confederate pickets who might lie in ambush. The engagement at St. Charles began at 9:00 A. M. and lasted almost three hours before the heavily outnumbered and outgunned Confederates withdrew. Even though forced to retreat, the Confederates suffered only six deaths compared to approximately two hundred Union sailors, most of whom died as a result of an explosion onboard the *Mound City* after a projectile fired from one of the thirty-two pound Columbiads "penetrated its steam drum" like "an express train." Following the explosion, survivors tore the clothing from their "scalding bodies" and jumped overboard. Instead of assisting or capturing the "wounded and scaled" seamen struggling in the water, Williams ordered sharpshooters to fire at them and upon the crews of other ships coming to their aid. The "barbarous conduct" outraged Commodore Davis, who predicted that it would lead "to terrible retaliation" from the "excited" men of the squadron who had "vow[ed]" vengeance."[57]

After burying the dead and sending the wounded to Memphis, the remainder of the flotilla began moving up the river towards Devall's Bluff on the eighteenth. Although aided by additional gunboats and transports that arrived on the twenty-sixth, the convoy made little progress in reaching Curtis. Typical for that time of the year, the White River was falling, making navigation difficult at best. As early as 20 June, the *St. Louis* "grounded upon a bar" and had to be freed by a tug, and the *Lexington* had "rubbed bottom." In spite of the treacherous conditions caused by the rapidly falling river, the convoy reached Clarendon on the last day of June.[58]

From Clarendon the transports, accompanied only by the timberclad *Lexington*, proceeded up the river, reaching Aberdeen on 5 July. From there, Colonel Graham N. Fitch of the Forty-sixth Indiana Infantry planned to march overland to join forces with General Curtis. Although he engaged in skirmishes with Confederates at Grand Prairie, after learning that Memphis could not spare the needed reinforcements, Fitch abandoned his plans to reach Curtis by land. Withdrawing, Fitch and his soldiers returned to the river and reboarded their transports.[59]

Curtis, meanwhile, was marching southward still hoping to link up with the Union fleet. To slow his adversary's progress, Hindman ordered Brigadier General Albert Rust to blockade roads, burn bridges, destroy crops, and pollute streams and wells by "killing cattle, ripping the carcasses, and throwing them in." Although Rust failed to carry out his assignment to Hindman's satisfaction, guerrillas more than compensated for his deficiency. Charles D. Field, a soldier who was with Curtis on the long march, wrote that the men suffered horribly from lack of water and food because the "rebels had filled the wells up" and had destroyed foodstuffs for miles along the route.[60]

Despite these obstacles, Curtis crossed the Cache River and inflicted a demoralizing defeat on Rust near Des Arc on 7 July in a thirty minute skirmish that left the Confederates retreating across the White River. Curtis then pressed on through Clarendon to Helena, arriving on 11 July. Aware that the Confederates had strongly fortified Bayou Metre twelve miles from Little Rock, Curtis abandoned any attempts to move against the capital and concentrated his forces in Hindman's hometown. He made his antagonist's new brick house his personal headquarters and freed Hindman's slaves. Piqued by these actions, Hindman still gloated at having thwarted Curtis' threat to the Arkansas capital and breathed a sign of relief that his wife and children were safe in the house he had rented for them across from the Episcopal church in Little Rock.[61]

It was a story of missed connections for Fitch and Curtis. Fitch did not reach Clarendon until 12 July, three days after Curtis had left. Learning of Curtis's plans to drive towards Helena, Fitch reloaded his transports and reached Helena shortly after daylight on the fifteenth to the "cheers and jeers" of Curtis's soldiers. Although Fitch and his troops had finally reached Curtis, the White River Expedition had not accomplished its goal of reinforcing the Army of the Southwest for an attack on Little Rock. At least temporarily, Hindman had made the Arkansas capital city a Confederate stronghold, and Curtis had to be content in Helena.[62]

The White River campaign had demonstrated Hindman's successful use of irregular bands to harass the Union convoy and Fitch's infantrymen. During the entire trip up and down the river, men hiding in the thickets and underbrush along the river constantly fired upon Union sailors and soldiers. This guerrilla warfare was so effective that on 23 June Colonel Fitch halted at Clarendon and warned Monroe County residents that they would be "held responsible in person and property" for future attacks. If such "barbarous" warfare continued, Union forces would send an expedition to the area and "seize and destroy" the personal property of its residents.[63]

Defiantly, Hindman issued an address the next day imploring the citizens of Arkansas to do their part in preventing Curtis's army from reaching the Union fleet. They must lose no time in moving towards the enemy from every direction. Hindman urged them to

> Attack him day and night, kill his scouts and pickets, kill his pilots and his troops on transports, cut off his wagon trains, . . . shoot his mounted officers, destroy every pound of meat and flour, every ear of corn and stock of fodder. . . that can fall into his hands; fell trees as thickly as rafts, in all the roads before him, burn every bridge and block up the fords. . . . This is an appeal of a bleeding country to her sons for deliverance.

Hindman cried, "Our army in the field will do its part. Will you do yours?"[64]

In addition, he informed Fitch on 25 June that he would continue to deploy guerrillas. As Commander of the Trans- Mississippi District, he had the "indisputable" right to "dispose of and use" troops "along the banks of the White River or wherever else" he "deem[ed] proper, even if [they] prove[d] annoying" to Union operations. If Fitch carried out his threat against residents of Monroe County, Hindman promised retaliation "man for man, upon the Federal officers and soldiers who now are, and hereafter may be in my custody as prisoners of war."[65]

As the White River campaign drew to a close, Hindman became convinced that the disruptions of war had resulted in the "virtual abdication" of civil authority throughout Arkansas and that it was necessary to extend military authority over all Arkansans. On 28 June, he ordered an embargo on the shipment of provisions to any point east of the Mississippi River, and on the thirtieth he placed the entire state under martial law and asserted that, if necessary, he would extend it to Indian Territory and Missouri. Under the provisions of General Orders No. 18, Benjamin F. Danley was named Provost Marshal General and Arkansas was divided into four districts, each under a provost marshal. As was the case in Little Rock, citizens were required to procure passes to leave their neighborhoods and "strangers and suspected persons" could be arrested and detained until they provided "a satisfactory account" of their loyalty. Anyone absent from military service without "proper authority" was subject to arrest. Even though provost marshals were not to "subvert the law" and were strictly accountable for their actions, they were cloaked with extraordinary powers.[66]

Reaction to General Orders No. 18 was immediate and dramatic. Claiming that Arkansas was "full of thieves and robbers" and that civil authority was "utterly powerless" to deal with the rampant lawlessness, R. H. Johnson of the *True Democrat* praised Hindman for declaring martial law. Rather than "oppress[ing] or annoy[ing]" loyal citizens, martial law would protect them. With Curtis at the very "doors" and "every nook and corner" of Arkansas filled with "incendiaries and Union spies," martial law was necessary if residents were to "live in peace and safety."[67]

While many Arkansans, including C. C. Danley and W. F. Holtzman of the *Gazette*, agreed with Johnson, strong opposition to martial law came from a number of politically prominent men. Albert Pike, for example, was outraged because he believed such power was the sole prerogative of the president. Clothed with legislative, executive, and judicial power, provost marshals, "like a triple-headed Deity" arbitrarily controlled the state. With regard to Hindman's statement about extending coverage to Indian Territory, Pike told the War Department that no power on earth "short of actual force" could compel him to enforce this "substitution of despotism" for "constitutional government." Judge John W. Brown of Camden condemned what he labeled "tyrannical acts of military power" that had placed the state under a "military despotism."[68]

Even prior to the declaration of martial law, a number of influential Arkansans had accused Hindman of exceeding his lawful authority. Although probably supported by a majority of Confederate Arkansans, Hindman's enforcement of the conscription law, the campaign against profiteering, and cotton destruction drew fire from prewar political opponents such as Judge Brown. A former Whig and Know Nothing who blamed fire- eaters for bringing on the war, he denounced Hindman and his supporters as "upstart political Democratic adventurers" seeking to gratify "their own ambitions" through the prosecution of the war. Opposition also came from men who felt that Hindman's policies were endangering civil liberties. After 30 June, despite strong backing by Richard H. Johnson and other politically powerful Arkansans, criticism of Hindman reached a crescendo, and President Davis decided to replace him. Initially, Davis assigned Major General John Bankhead Magruder to supersede Hindman, designating his command as the Trans-Mississippi

Department. Magruder was recalled to Richmond, however, and Major General Theophilus Holmes was given command of the department.[69]

Arriving in Little Rock on 12 August, Holmes inherited the fruits of Hindman's energetic and dynamic administration. When Hindman began his tenure in Arkansas, he took over an area "stripped" of soldiers and without weapons, ammunition, and other war materials. As he reported to Adjutant General Samuel Cooper, "nearly everything of value" had been taken away by Van Dorn. His artillery amounted "to six bronze pieces, and as many more iron, all condemned." Small arms consisted of "about 2,000 damaged shotguns and rifles, and the same number of pikes and lances." He had 400 rounds of ammunition for the battery, fifteen kegs of powder, 100,000 caps, and 5,000 pounds of lead. His army consisted of 4,000 mounted men and 1,500 infantry.[70]

Starting with virtually nothing, he bequeathed to Holmes an army of about 12,000 effective infantry, 6,000 mounted soldiers, fifty-four pieces of artillery, and 7,000 to 8,000 unarmed draftees in camp receiving military instruction. While simultaneously raising and equipping an army and stimulating home manufacturing, he had, at least for the moment, saved Little Rock and the Arkansas Valley from capture by Union forces. Having stepped into a vacuum created by Van Dorn's departure, in seventy days Hindman had accomplished a miracle.[71]

From the beginning of the war, Hindman recognized that the Confederacy would have to compensate for the Union's superiority in manpower and industrial resources in order to win its independence. Success called for bold, daring military leaders who would not hesitate to depart from accepted procedures and experiment with new tactics and strategies. As commander of the Trans-Mississippi, Hindman proved himself such a leader in his use of guerrillas to operate behind enemy lines and compel the Federals to commit large forces to patrol duty. He was also responsible for "making the cavalry useful instead of ornamental." He detached cavalry from infantry brigadiers and transformed them into separate brigades and divisions capable of covering long distances and striking rapidly. Even Hindman's most severe critics conceded that he was a master at recruiting and organizing soldiers. To overcome the chronic shortages of equipment and vital supplies, he set up factories and repair shops and encouraged home manufacturing.[72]

To Hindman, Confederate success also hinged on political leaders full of revolutionary fervor and a central government ready to break down any barrier in the path of victory. If necessary, state rights and some civil liberties must be sacrificed temporarily for the common goals of victory and freedom. The active cooperation of all citizens was vital. His motto was *"Salus populi est suprema lex*—if the ship were sinking, every body to the pumps."[73]

Unfortunately for Hindman, when he assumed command of the Trans-Mississippi, very few pro-Confederate Arkansans comprehended the magnitude of the fight for Southern independence. Many clung to cherished notions of state rights and personal freedoms, while some succumbed to the age-old lures of speculation and extortion. Others simply did not want to jeopardize their own personal safety and property for the cause. These groups howled in protest over martial law, price controls, cotton destruction, and conscription. Responding to the clamor of "'conscript dodgers,' . . . cotton speculators, . . . and [some] old political opponents seeking revenge for defeats suffered before the war," and the complaints from the champions of state rights, Richmond authorities decided that Hindman's policies had rendered him odious to Arkansans and replaced him with Theophilus H. Holmes.[74]

Chapter 7

STALEMATE
AT PRAIRIE GROVE

Hindman's successor, Theophilus Holmes, often referred to as "Granny" by both officers and enlisted men, was in his late fifties, half-deaf, and was thought by many to lack the boldness necessary to command his new department. Dissatisfied with Holmes' performance in the Seven Days campaign, Robert E. Lee culled him from the Army of the Potomac as soon as the battles ended. After arriving in Little Rock, in spite of attacks on Hindman's policies, Holmes maintained martial law and extended price controls to cover additional items. Although he agreed that Hindman had "transcended" his legal authority, he believed that the extraordinary measures were necessary to guarantee the protection and security of Arkansas. He advised President Davis to ignore criticisms of Hindman lest he should do "great injustice" to "an officer of great merit" totally committed to the Southern cause. Impressed by Hindman's determination to drive Union forces from Arkansas and southern Missouri, Holmes relied heavily on him for advice.[1]

Less than two weeks after arriving, Holmes ordered Hindman to assume command of all Confederate forces in northwest Arkansas, to raise as many additional troops as possible to defend the area, and to extend recruiting into Missouri. Under the Partisan Ranger Act, Hindman had begun recruiting cavalry units in Missouri prior to Holmes's arrival. His endeavors raised several units and brought to the forefront two of the best known Confederate cavalry officers of the war, Joseph O. Shelby and J. Vard Cockrell. He also enlisted the notorious guerrillas William Clarke Quantrill, Bud and Jim Younger, and Jesse and Frank James.[2]

The efforts of Shelby and Cockrell merit special attention since they resulted in the formation of the "Iron Brigade," the most famous cavalry unit in the Trans-Mississippi. Born on 12 December 1830 in Lexington, Kentucky, Shelby had attended Transylvania College before moving to Waverly in Lafayette County, Missouri in the 1850s. By 1861, he was

one of the wealthiest men in the state, owning a rope factory and plantations in Lafayette and Bates counties. With an athletic build, long hair,
and a "square massive lower face" covered by a thick, brown beard, the
gray-eyed Missourian was bold, daring, reckless, and proslavery to the
core. After learning that Southerners had attacked Fort Sumter, he immediately organized a cavalry company, equipped it at his own expense,
and joined the Missouri State Guards. After the Battle of Pea Ridge,
Shelby and his men accompanied Van Dorn across the Mississippi, where
they remained until mid-April when Shelby received permission from the
War Department to raise a regiment of Confederate cavalry. He then took
his unit to Arkansas, where he teamed up with Cockrell near Van Buren.[3]

Departing Frog Bayou, Arkansas, on 15 July, Shelby and Cockrell
moved into Union-controlled Missouri. After a week of hard riding, they
arrived at Grand Rapids, where they split into two groups, with Shelby
heading toward Dover and Cockrell moving in the direction of
Independence. When Shelby and his troops reached Dover, pro-Southern
residents welcomed them as liberators. Young girls "scattered flowers
upon the road and flags among the soldiers," women cried "tears of
intense joy," and fathers offered "half grown sons" for military service.
At his hometown of Waverly, men flocked "from every portion of the
surrounding countryside" to enlist. Within four short days, a thousand
recruits were ready for the treacherous ride back to Arkansas.[4]

While Shelby was busy recruiting at Waverly, on 16 August Cockrell
and his 800 cavalry (reinforced by regiments under Upton Hays and John
T. Coffee) "stirred up a hornet's nest" in the small town of Lone Jack.
With pistols blazing, at daylight they galloped into town "like an
earthquake" and attacked 740 Federals under Major Emory S. Foster. A
wild melee of bloody hand-to-hand combat raged in the streets and from
house to house for five hours before Union forces withdrew, abandoning
two pieces of artillery to the triumphant Confederates.[5]

Each side suffered casualties amounting to about fifty killed and
seventy-five to one hundred wounded. The battle had no impact on the
outcome of the war, but "it was as fiercely contested and as bloody a
fight for the number of men engaged in it as occurred anywhere." During
one phase of the battle, Confederates "cornered a small band of Federal
sharpshooters" in the town hotel and mercilessly "set fire to the building,

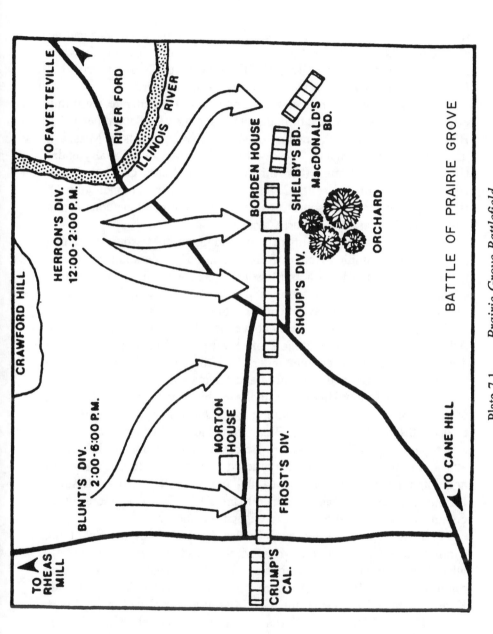

Plate 7.1   *Prairie Grove Battlefield*
Courtesy: Arkansas Department of Parks and Tourism, Prairie Grove Battlefield State Park

roasting the occupants alive." Although victorious, the graybacks had no chance to celebrate. The next day, they abandoned the area quickly when 2,000 Union cavalry under Brigadier General James G. Blunt arrived at Lone Jack and drove them back to the Arkansas border.[6]

Although forced to retreat from Lone Jack, Confederate recruiting efforts in the state continued throughout the summer. By September 1862, Hindman had directed the raising of six cavalry regiments in Missouri, including Shelby's brigade. These were the First Missouri Cavalry under Colonel Joseph C. Porter; the Third Missouri Cavalry, Colonel Colton Greene; the Fourth Missouri Cavalry commanded by Colonel John Q. Burbridge; the Tenth Missouri Cavalry, Colonel Emmett MacDonald; and Colonel H. E. Clark's Missouri Cavalry.[7]

On 24 August, as recruitment was winding up in Missouri, Hindman arrived at Fort Smith to begin full-scale military operations in north-western Arkansas and southern Missouri. His new command, the District of Arkansas, consisted of fourteen pieces of artillery and 9,100 men, including 3,000 Indian cavalry under Colonel Douglas H. Cooper and 2,000 horse soldiers under Shelby concentrated near Newtonia, Missouri. After dispatching one battalion of cavalry to Tahlequah in Indian Territory, he deployed the remainder of his force along the northwestern border of Arkansas, above Elkhorn and Fayetteville.[8]

Poised for action, Hindman established his headquarters at Pineville, Missouri, opened a camp for training recruits near Elkhorn, and prepared to drive the forces of General Blunt from Indian Territory into Kansas and capture Springfield, Missouri. Before he had a chance to launch an attack, on 10 September Holmes ordered him to return to Little Rock to help organize troops near the capital city. Before leaving Missouri, Hindman placed Brigadier General James S. Rains temporarily in command and ordered him not to engage the enemy.[9]

Near the end of August, Brigadier General John M. Schofield, Commander of the District of Missouri, was headquartered at Springfield when he learned of Hindman's planned assault and requested reinforcements. His territory was immediately expanded to include Kansas, renamed the Department of Missouri, and placed under Major General Samuel R. Curtis. Curtis promptly ordered Blunt to reinforce Schofield and designated the combined force as the Army of the Frontier. The addition of Blunt's troops gave Schofield an effective force of 10,800 troops and sixteen pieces of artillery.[10]

Missouri remained quiet until 7:00 A. M. on 30 September, when a Union reconnaissance party under Brigadier General Frederick Salomon encountered 4,500 cavalry under Cooper and Shelby near Newtonia. Salomon immediately ordered his entire force of 6,000 men to engage the Confederates, and what started out as a skirmish turned into a full-scale battle that lasted until near sunset when the Federals fell back to Sarcoxie. In the course of the fighting, Confederates suffered seventy-eight casualties (twelve killed, sixty-three wounded, and three missing), while Union losses were fifty killed, eighty wounded, and 115 missing.[11]

Short of supplies and aware that Schofield was en route with 18,000 men to reinforce Salomon, Cooper and Shelby retreated toward Rains's encampment at Cross Hollow, Arkansas. Unsure of Federal strategy, the retreating Confederates divided their forces. Cooper encamped near Maysville on the Arkansas border and Shelby moved to Cross Hollow. When he arrived there, Shelby discovered that Rains had departed for Huntsville.[12]

After learning that Cooper and Shelby had split their forces, Schofield ordered Blunt's division to attack Cooper and sent brigadier generals Francis Herron and James Totten to Huntsville and Yellville, respectively. On 22 October, Blunt overtook Cooper's force of 1,500 cavalry at Fort Wayne near Maysville and completely routed it in less than thirty minutes. Led by the Second and Sixth Kansas cavalry, Blunt's troops drove the Confederates into Indian Territory and captured all their artillery.[13]

Prior to the setback, Holmes had ordered Hindman back to northwest Arkansas and organized his forces into two corps. He designated Hindman's corps as the First Army Corps, Army of the West; it consisted of all Confederate troops in northwestern Arkansas, southwestern Missouri, and Indian Territory. In addition, he ordered Brigadier General John S. Marmaduke and colonels Francis A. Shoup and James Deshler to report to Hindman.[14]

Marmaduke and Shoup's credentials were impressive. Born in Missouri in 1833 and the son of a former governor of the state, Marmaduke had attended Yale and Harvard and had graduated from West Point in 1857. Prior to the war, he had served on the frontier with Albert Sidney Johnston; after the attack on Fort Sumter, he resigned from the Union Army and volunteered for Confederate service. Like Hindman, he had served with Hardee at Shiloh and was wounded during the battle. A native of Indiana and a West Pointer, the twenty-eight year old Shoup had been Hardee's chief of artillery at Shiloh and later served as Beauregard's inspector of artillery.[15]

Hindman returned to Fort Smith on 15 October and immediately removed General Rains and Colonel John T. Coffee for drunkenness and placed Marmaduke in charge of Shelby's and Bradfute's cavalry brigades. He then departed for Fayetteville and ordered Brigadier General Moseby M. Parsons to shift his force from Yellville and join him there. Before he could complete his move, Hindman received word that Schofield had entered Huntsville with 8,000-10,000 men and was heading toward Fayetteville. Short of ammunition, food, and supplies and in danger of being entrapped, he retreated across the Boston Mountains along the Clarksville and Van Buren Telegraph road to fifty-five miles south of Fayetteville.[16]

Satisfied with the results of his expedition, Schofield returned to Springfield with two divisions and sent Blunt with one division to guard the mountain passes near Fayetteville. On 20 November, in ill health and convinced that hostilities were over until spring, Schofield turned command of the Army of the Frontier over to Blunt and left for St. Louis.[17]

Schofield's assessment that no significant engagements would occur before spring was incorrect. The aggressive Hindman saw no reason to occupy a defensive position and wait for the Federals to attack. If he struck quickly, he might win a decisive battle, drive Blunt's army from northwest Arkansas, and pave the way for an invasion of Missouri. To achieve this objective, he was ready to defy both Jefferson Davis and General Holmes.[18]

After the disastrous Confederate defeat at Corinth in October 1862, Richmond again turned to the Trans-Mississippi for troops, requesting that Holmes send 10,000 men to help reinforce Vicksburg. When Holmes attempted to implement the transfer by ordering Hindman to return to Little Rock, the fiery Arkansan refused, protesting that such a move would sacrifice western Arkansas and Indian Territory to the Yankees. Rather than withdraw, he planned to attack Blunt and drive the Union commander from the state. Hindman's proposal received wide-spread support, especially from newspaper editors who believed that the "insolent invaders" must be expelled. Holmes reluctantly concurred, agreeing to let Hindman undertake an offensive campaign on the expressed condition that, regardless of the outcome, he would then retire south of the Arkansas River.[19]

Having given in to Hindman, on 25 November Holmes notified Lieutenant General John C. Pemberton, Commander of the Mississippi Department, that he could not transfer any troops to Vicksburg. According to Holmes, most of his troops were in northwestern Arkansas and must remain there to protect the valley of the Arkansas and Indian Territory. Sending troops to Vicksburg would result in the loss of his entire department.[20]

To crush Blunt, Hindman planned to deploy Marmaduke's cavalry at Cane Hill as a diversion to attract the Union commander's attention, while he marched his main force to the enemy's rear. Once Blunt responded to the feint and attacked Marmaduke, Hindman would strike before Herron, who was at Wilson's Creek south of Springfield, Missouri, could arrive with reinforcements. Having smashed Blunt, the combined Confederate force would then quickly turn and annihilate Herron, who would doubtlessly be en route to aid Blunt. The bold and daring plan could succeed only if Blunt were fooled by Marmaduke's move to Cane Hill and Herron did not arrive in time.[21]

The scene of the grisly murder of five members of the William Carter Wright family by robbers on 15 June 1839, Cane Hill was situated in southwest Washington County just beyond the north base of the Boston Mountains, about forty-five miles from Van Buren. An attractive area surrounded by farms, it was a ridge about eight miles long and five miles wide. At the top of the hill along the Fayetteville road stood the villages of Russellville, Boonsboro, and Newburg.[22]

Marmaduke's force of 2,500 men (consisting of Shelby's "Iron Brigade," which included Colonel Frank B. Gordon's First Regiment, Colonel Beal G. Jeans's Second Regiment, and Colonel George W. Thompson's Third Regiment; Quantrill's partisan cavalry company under Lieutenant W. H. Gregg; Colonel Charles A. Carroll's Brigade; and Colonel Emmett MacDonald's Missouri cavalry) reached Cane Hill on 25 November. Marmaduke immediately sent out patrols to screen Hindman's main force, which was to begin moving on the twenty-sixth or twenty-seventh. Aas far as the Confederates knew, Hindman's plan was proceeding on schedule at that point.

This was not the case. Warned by spies and Indian scouts, Blunt had not been deceived and was aware of Marmaduke and Hindman's movements. An ardent Kansas abolitionist who had aided John Brown in helping escaped slaves reach Canada before the war, Blunt was determined to take advantage of his information and attack first. By marching two of his three brigades double-quick to Cane Hill, he would annihilate Marmaduke; and, with the help of Herron's troops, he would trap and destroy Hindman's main army.[23]

Moving swiftly and decisively, he arrived within ten miles of Cane Hill at 7:00 P. M. on 27 November with 5,000 men. At 5:00 A. M. the next day, Blunt led as the Eleventh Kansas Infantry, the First and Third (Cherokee) Indian Home Guard Infantry, the Second and Sixth Kansas Cavalry, the Second Indiana Battery, the Second Kansas Light Artillery, and Tenny's Battery headed toward Cane Hill to engage Marmaduke's cavalry.[24]

Approximately one hour later, a small group of mounted men rode up and interrupted Colonel Shelby's breakfast with the news that the Fayetteville road was crawling with bluecoats. The Confederates had been anticipating Blunt's attack, but not so early. Shelby quickly issued orders, and the surprised, grayclad soldiers raced to a hill overlooking the Fayetteville road. There they dismounted and assembled by regiments behind a long wooden fence. Thompson was on the left; Gordon on the right; and Jeans, supported by two six- pounders, anchored the center. Carroll's brigade, still to the rear, was ordered to form a second line north of Boonsboro. Marmaduke had just sent MacDonald's brigade to Kidd's Mill, a few miles northeast of Carroll when the sound of muskets and cannon came from his north. Gathering his staff and heading toward the scene, he arrived in time to witness the Federal advance recoiling from Shelby's canister fire and musketry.[25]

Undaunted by the initial Confederate success, Blunt rallied his troops, within an hour formed a battle line, and launched a counter-attack. Heavily outnumbered in both men and artillery and in danger of being encircled, Marmaduke dispatched MacDonald's regiment and Shelby's brigade to join Carroll and began retreating through a valley southeast of Boonsboro. The withdrawal was orderly and well executed and demonstrated the tactical brilliance of Jo Shelby, who arranged his thirty companies in two columns on each side of the road. When the enemy approached within point-blank range, the two end companies opened fire and then quickly rode to the head of the column to reload and prepare for their next appearance. As a result of the superb rear-guard action, Blunt's forces faced a constant barrage from Shelby's cavalry during the retreat. As they withdrew to the base of the Boston Mountains, the Confederates periodically deployed to make stands but could not check the Union advance. When the fighting ended and the combination of rain and a cold November wind set in, the exhausted Southern troops sought refuge anywhere they could—under trees, behind rocks, in ditches, and on the road. At 5:00 A. M. the next day, Marmaduke and his weary men withdrew to Dripping Springs to await further orders.[26]

"Hotly contested" and fought over "every foot" of a fifteen mile area, the Battle of Cane Hill produced very few casualties when measured against the number of men engaged. Out of a force of 5,000, Blunt suffered only eight dead and thirty-two wounded, while Confederate losses, although not clearly reported, probably did not exceed those of the Federals. Had the battle been waged in open country rather than in heavy brush and timber, ridges, and valleys, casualties would have been much greater. Trees and brush deflected much of the shot and shell and made it difficult to use artillery effectively, a definite advantage for Marmaduke's greatly outnumbered and outgunned cavalry.[27]

Although Blunt reported that Marmaduke had been "badly whipped" and that Hindman's infantrymen had "gone back to their hole" and "probably would not venture north of the Boston Mountains" until spring, the reversal at Cane Hill made Hindman even more determined to expel the invader. On the thirtieth, when Marmaduke arrived at Van Buren to inform Hindman of the reversal at Cane Hill, he was stunned when Hindman ordered him to return to Dripping Springs and prepare for an immediate all out attack on Blunt, who had retired to Newburg. Hindman's reaction to defeat was another attack, this time by the entire First Corps.[28]

Aware of the power of rhetorical frenzy and convinced that a heightened spirit among his men could bring forth a superior effort, Hindman borrowed a tactic used by Albert Sidney Johnston at Shiloh. Prior to beginning his movement, he penned a stirring address and had printed copies distributed to his troops. A clarion to battle, the circular exalted the Southern cause and condemned Union soldiers as dreadful fiends with no redeeming qualities. Hindman told them that when the fighting began, the Confederates must remember that the enemy you engage has no feeling of mercy or kindness toward you. His ranks are made up of Pin Indians, free negroes, Southern tories, Kansas jayhawkers, and hired Dutch cut-throats. These bloody ruffians have invaded your country; stolen and destroyed your property; murdered your neighbors; outraged your women; driven your children from their homes, and defiled the grave of your kindred. If each man of you will do what I have urged upon you, we will utterly destroy them. We can do this; we must do this; our country will be ruined if we fail. A just God will strengthen our arms and give us a glorious victory.[29]

Conscious that his supply of ammunition was limited to a one day battle, Hindman warned his troops not to fire merely because their comrades did or because they saw the foe. They were to wait until the enemy was in range of their guns and take careful aim before firing. They were to single out for targets the mounted officers and artillery horses in order to demoralize the Federals and weaken the effectiveness and mobility of their artillery. Hindman pledged to enforce discipline strictly and to shoot "on the spot" those who straggled or broke ranks to plunder.[30]

At dawn on 3 December, Hindman started toward Cane Hill with 9,000 infantry, 2,000 cavalry, and twenty-two pieces of artillery to attack Blunt. Due to a scarcity of shoes and arms, he was forced to leave almost 1,000 infantrymen at Van Buren. Moreover, because neither the War Department nor the state military board had provided adequate uniforms, most of his troops wore summer clothing and suffered terribly from the bitterly cold December weather. To make matters worse, the men had been on half rations for more than a month.[31]

The line of advance followed the three parallel roads that ran north toward Fayetteville over the Boston Mountains. The main force consisted of brigadier generals Francis A. Shoup and Daniel M. Frost's divisions, which marched along the Telegraph road with Colonel Emmett MacDonald's cavalry brigade in their front. About a mile to their west, Shelby's cavalry brigade moved along the Cove Creek road to protect the left flank, while Carroll's cavalry brigade under Colonel J. C. Monroe advanced a mile east of the Telegraph road down the Frog Bayou road to cover the right flank. Hindman's plan of attack was perfectly adapted to the terrain. It called for Shelby and Monroe to secure the mountains south of Newburg and then to harass the bluecoats from the front, while the infantry divisions and Monroe's cavalry fell on their exposed rear and flanks. Confident of victory, Hindman had ordered Stand Watie and his Cherokees to Evansville, just west of Cane Hill, to strike Blunt should he try to escape in that direction.[32]

Unfortunately for Hindman, his advance did not surprise Blunt. Soon after the march began, spies and deserters informed the Union commander of his movements and strategy. On 2 December, he telegraphed Major General Samuel R. Curtis, Commander of the Department of Missouri, that Hindman was poised to attack with a force of 25,000 strong and requested that reinforcements under Herron be sent immediately. Having decided to remain and fight, on the following day Blunt moved his first brigade to Rhea's Mill, eight miles north of Cane Hill, to protect supply wagons from Fort Smith and ordered his second and third brigades across the Fayetteville road two miles south of Newburg. Once these movements were completed, he dispatched pickets from the Second Kansas Cavalry to Morrow's farm and Reed's Mountain to cover the Van Buren road.[33]

Blunt's knowledge of his plan was not the only problem facing Hindman. The combination of having to travel up a winding creek bed road that crossed the creek twenty-five times in a mile, intermittent rain and snow flurries, and draft animals so starved by a lack of forage that guns often had to be pushed by hand delayed the progress of his main force, which advanced less than twenty miles in three days. When Hindman camped near Oliver's Store on Friday 5 December, he was already one day behind schedule, a critical factor since timing was vital to the success of his plan. The following evening, as he was reviewing last minute battle strategy with division commanders at his headquarters in John Morrow's house, a dispatch rider burst in with a message that Herron was already at Fayetteville.[34]

The news certainly came as an unwelcome surprise. Holmes had promised to send Parsons's cavalry brigade and J. H. Pratt's artillery battery to detain Herron in Missouri while Hindman's troops demolished Blunt. "Old Granny" failed to follow through, either because he thought Herron had retreated from the Springfield area or because he feared an attack on Little Rock from the direction of Helena. Regardless of reason, Holmes "simply drew his troops about him like an old man drawing on an overcoat against the cold, and did nothing."[35]

While Hindman had marched fifty difficult miles in five days, with "untiring strength" Herron moved his army 135 miles in three and one-half days. He had received Blunt's telegram on 4 December at Wilson's Creek and by forced marches moved six brigades, including 2,000 cavalry and thirty guns, in record time to reinforce Blunt. One regiment had marched fifty-seven miles in the last thirty-seven hours, while another had marched sixty-six miles in thirty-six hours. Writing to his wife on 10 December, Colonel William Ward Orme of the Ninety-fourth Illinois Infantry stated that during the "fatiguing march" he did not take off his spurs and overcoat and had slept with his "harness on." He added that had anyone told him prior to the march that he could have endured "so much," he would not have believed him.[36]

Hindman predicated his strategy on Herron's inability to reach Blunt before Southern forces had crushed him at Cane Hill. The last report to Hindman had placed Herron near Springfield, too far away to help. With Herron now present, he had either to withdraw without fighting or attack a much larger force than anticipated. Convinced that abandoning the area without engaging the enemy would demoralize his troops and "so embolden" the enemy that it would follow and attack him from the rear, Hindman did not waver. Rather than confronting Blunt at Cane Hill, a new plan called for only a feint by a small cavalry force under Colonel Monroe, while the main Confederate force attacked Herron. Once Herron's force was smashed, the graycoats would turn and unleash their full fury on Blunt. To succeed, the plan depended on speed and surprise.[37]

While their leaders hammered out a revised plan, the hungry, weary Confederates clustered near their glowing campfires, as the wind fluttered the trees and the "snowy phantasm of the frost crinkled and rustled its gauze robes under foot." Thanks to an eclipse of the moon, "pale, ghost-like phantoms" seemed to appear, as clouds drifted past the "crimson disc" producing an eerie effect. Was this an augury of good or bad things to come, the soldiers wondered before snatching a few precious hours of sleep.[38]

Jolted awake Sunday morning with orders to be ready to march at three o'clock, the Confederates began the last leg of their journey toward Fayetteville to meet Herron. Problems developed from the outset, and it was four o'clock when they finally got underway. By then, the moon had set and a dim, ominous red light shone from the twinkling stars in the frosty sky. Only the crunch of leaves and twigs broke the silence as Hindman's army, with Marmaduke's cavalry in the lead, surged forward.[39]

In the darkness, the men of Shelby's brigade strained to catch a glimpse of the "first defined object with semblance of a man" as they made their way toward Herron's sentinels. Artillerymen struggled to repair snapped harnesses while foot-sore infantrymen "toiled up" incredibly rough roads at a pace of two miles per hour. All were hungry, having eaten nothing since Saturday. Many, debilitated from the lack of food, fell by the wayside.[40]

As "a great, red sun" rose over the tree tops, Shelby and his brigade, far in advance of the other cavalrymen, made contact with the enemy. The initial encounter was a complete rout, as Federal horsemen of the Seventh Missouri and part of the First Arkansas (USA), "bearheaded [*sic*], . . . without saddles and arms having lost their entire equipments," fled in terror toward Fayetteville, where they encountered Herron's divisions moving southward. Captain Chester Barney of the Twentieth Iowa Volunteer Infantry described the conduct of the men of the First Arkansas as "ludicrous" and disgusting. "They were utterly panic-stricken—honor, glory, shame, [and] duty were alike forgotten, and their only thought" was "an ignoble desire to save their worthless carcasses." When shouted at as "coward[s]," they "admitted all and dashed on."[41]

By "hard talking" and "shooting one cowardly whelp off his horse," Herron halted the retreating cavalrymen. Even so, damage had occurred and confusion had overtaken his men, some of whom thought that a force of perhaps 40,000 men was attacking them. Almost immediately, the sound of Confederate howitzers announced the arrival of the gray clad cavalrymen who emerged from the woods, dismounted, and prepared to attack. Amid the confusion, Federal officers shouted orders and the First Missouri Light Artillery, supported by the First Missouri Cavalry, raced from the rear and began firing.[42]

On the Confederate left, Marmaduke and his staff appeared. As he yelled out orders, bugles sounded, muskets opened fire, and the tempo of the battle quickly picked up, and all along the Union line troops fell into position and began to advance. As the bluecoats began to move in earnest, Marmaduke wondered what had happened to Shoup's infantry that was supposed to have moved up as soon as the cavalry made contact with Herron. Facing at least 5,000 advancing Federals, Marmaduke and his cavalry quickly mounted and galloped southward.[43]

Instead of rushing to support Marmaduke and take advantage of the initial Union confusion, Shoup made a "fatal blunder" and took up a defensive position on a wooded hill behind the Illinois River near Prairie Grove to wait for an attack by Herron. The location provided an elevated, commanding battle position and controlled the Cane Hill and Fayetteville road. After surveying the area, Hindman agreed that it was "an exceedingly strong one" and approved Shoup's choice. Even though he hated to fight a defensive battle, Hindman elected to do so at Prairie Grove.[44]

The line of battle resembled the shape of a horseshoe, conforming to the configuration of the hill. Shelby's brigade and Shoup's division took position opposite Herron's troops, while Frost's division (reinforced by Walker's Texas Cavalry Regiment and Clark's Missouri Infantry Regiment) were held in reserve pending Blunt's expected advance. Lane's Texas Cavalry and MacDonald's Missouri Cavalry also waited in readiness to cover the Confederate flanks.[45]

At the summit along the Cane Hill and Fayetteville road stood the Prairie Grove Church that gave the battle got its name. Within the shadows of the spire of this peaceful country church, the armies of Herron and Hindman collided like two locomotives. Believing that Hindman's forces greatly outnumbered his, Herron maneuvered a superior position by cutting a road through a thicket a half mile below the ford of the Illinois River and establishing his artillery facing Hindman's center. Protected by the surrounding thicket, the Union battery rained shell and canister at the graycoats and almost demolished the Confederate artillery. In mute testimony to the effectiveness of Herron's cannon, by nightfall Confederate horses "lay dead in heaps of four to six in every position taken."[46]

All morning the battle raged. Warmed by the whiskey that their commander had provided as they forded the icy Illinois River, Herron's men fought "like tigers," while the graycoats battled their foes with "desperation" and seemed resolved on "victory or death." Entrenched on a hill with sharpshooters posted in houses and outbuildings and infantrymen behind fences, Hindman's forces repeatedly drove back Union advances. George Griffith of the Thirty-seventh Illinois later recalled that the Confederates poured "volley after volley" into the

Federal ranks as "though they thought we liked it." The deadly fire of the Union artillery seemed to be the only factor preventing a Confederate sweep. As Griffith explained, "The timely arrival of General Blunt from Cane Hill is all that saved our bacon . . . The Johnnies had done us up to a frazzle until Blunt showed up." Charles Dewolf of the Seventh Missouri Cavalry concurred, stating that Blunt's arrival had come "just in time to save us from utter defeat."[47]

Salvation for the Union came about 1:45 P. M. when Blunt's men burst from the woods like a "long-confined flood" with the "rush and roar . . . of storm-driven seas." Announcing his arrival with two cannon shots, Blunt immediately moved into position beside Herron. Although now greatly outnumbered, the Confederates continued to fight "desperately and seemed no more to regard a shower of grape than if [it] had been a summer wind." "With deafening yells," they poured to fill vacancies left by "solid shot [that] ploughed its through their columns." Although the Union troops fought with "great vigor and determination" until sunset, they were unable to overrun the Confederates, who stubbornly held their positions. When dusk settled over the battlefield twelve hours after the initial fighting began, the sound of musketry and the fierce booming of cannon finally ceased. The Battle of Prairie Grove was over, and Hindman's heavily outgunned, undernourished, and ill-clad soldiers had battled the combined forces of Blunt and Herron to a draw.[48]

Hindman had battled a superior force to a stalemate, but he might have achieved victory had he not allowed Shoup to maintain a defensive position and wait for Herron to attack. Shoup should have struck immediately after Marmaduke dispersed and confused the Union troops. Instead, he took a defensive position, which Shelby's adjutant John N. Edwards likened to the "dilly-dallying" of "some asthmatic lover wheez[ing] about his darling." Shoup blundered, but the fault lay with Hindman. Although he was the greatest organizer to serve in the Trans-Mississippi, he made a ghastly mistake by uncharacteristically approving a passive strategy at Prairie Grove. As Edwards later observed, "Waiting for Herron's attack meant waiting for Blunt."[49]

At the time, Hindman believed that he had no choice but to approve Shoup's decision. Most of his infantry was still to the rear and in no condition to move rapidly to join Marmaduke. Because of supply problems, their rations had been insufficient for a month, and they had not eaten since the previous day. Some troops "had not tasted food for three days." His troops were exhausted from marching nearly fifteen miles that day over bad terrain, and worn out shoes and socks had left many soldiers with feet so blistered and sore that walking was no longer possible. He could not have changed the course of events—by then the element of surprise was gone; at 9:30 A. M. Herron's troops had brought eighteen guns to bear on the position, and Blunt was moving north to unite with them.[50]

Casualties were high on both sides, and evidence of the day's carnage was everywhere, especially in the peach orchard. Close to two hundred wounded Union soldiers who had crawled into haystacks for warmth were burned to death when Federal artillery fire turned stacks of straw into blazing infernos. Edward's memoirs describe how afterwards, the men lay "half consumed in one vast sepulcher," being eaten by hogs that were attracted by the smell of burning flesh. When the fighting ceased that evening, all around

> the gory field . . . in every direction lay the dead and the dying, the full glare of a cold battle moonshining white on their upturned faces, and the chilling wind singing freezing dirges among the naked and melancholy trees. . . . Great heart sobs wrung from strong men, in their agony, while the white hoar-frost hardened the fever drops into ice that oozed from clammy brows. Death stalked in silently amid the sufferers and plied his busy sickle with cold, unerring hands.

When daylight came, "many wounded were dying slowly and lingering in dark and lonesome places." The net results of the horrors of the battle were 167 Union soldiers killed, 772 wounded, and 252 missing, and 164 Confederates killed, 817 wounded, and 336 missing.[51]

The next morning "a loud shrieking wail" from the direction of the peach orchard pierced the cold air. It was a cry that would "never be forgotten by those hearing it." Motivated by a spirit of "love and mercy," a group of women who lived in the area came to "nurse the wounded and to soothe the sick." The wail came from one of the women when she

> found her only son upon the gory field, lying stark and ghastly, clutching his musket in rigid grasp—a swift, hot bullet through his heart having left upon his features the same expression they bore in life, except the fixed stare of the eyeballs, which had been dimmed by frost.[52]

After the battle ended and Union soldiers began removing the dead and wounded of both sides, the extremely under-nourished state of Hindman's troops was patently obvious. Lieutenant Charles Dewolf of the Seventh Missouri Volunteer Cavalry "was struck" by the "sallow cadiverous [sic] look" of the Southern dead. Even if they were covered by blankets, he could pick out the Confederate dead by looking only at faces. The "thin and yellow" graybacks stood in stark contrast to the "fresh and healthy" Federal troops.[53]

After surveying the battlefield and weighing his options, Hindman decided to withdraw toward Van Buren. With supply wagons thirty miles to the rear, his men destitute of food and down to less than twenty rounds of ammunition per man, his battery animals dying of starvation, and rumors abounding that General Schofield and 7,000 men had arrived at Fayetteville, he felt that he had no choice. Another day of fighting would have been suicidal.[54]

After nightfall, Hindman took advantage of a cease-fire with Blunt to treat the wounded and bury the dead by silently and secretly withdrawing his remaining force. Keeping Marmaduke's cavalry on the field as a ruse and staying to meet with Blunt the following day, he ordered fires kindled and blankets tied to the wheels of artillery and wagons to muffle their sound. Thus, while Union forces rested anticipating more fighting, Hindman successfully withdrew the remainder of his army toward Van Buren. After completing his negotiations with Blunt, Hindman rode at the head of Marmaduke's cavalry and rejoined his command.[55]

While Hindman and his beleaguered troops marched toward Van Buren, Union soldiers continued the "melancholy task" of burying the dead. Bodies of comrades were "deposited . . . amid the muffled roll of drums and solemn funeral services," while fallen Confederates, some of whom had been "partly eaten by hogs," were "thrown but with little ceremony" into "long trenches" and covered with dirt.[56]

Although Herron declared that Union forces had "given Hindman & Co. a damned sound thrashing," the battle had been a stalemate. Even so, Prairie Grove was in reality a defeat for the Confederates because they failed to destroy Blunt's army and drive Federal forces from Arkansas and southern Missouri. The Union Army was now in complete control of all of Missouri and northwest Arkansas to the Arkansas River.[57]

In spite of deficiencies in supplies and equipment, Hindman had to gamble and hope for victory at Prairie Grove. His situation was typical of that faced by other Southern field commanders. "Only by bold, if often desperate strokes could their handicaps be offset." The Confederate plan was well-conceived and, even with the lack of resources, might have succeeded had it not been for the unexpected arrival of Herron and Hindman's decision to support Shoup's defensive strategy. Obviously, his critics used the opportunity to renew their attacks on him and to demand that he be transferred east of the Mississippi.[58]

On 8 December, the weary troops crossed the Arkansas River. Marmaduke and Shelby went into winter headquarters at Lewisburg, while Hindman and the infantry set up camp just east of Van Buren. Although they did not initially pursue the retreating Confederates, on the twenty-seventh Blunt and Herron began a forced march toward Van Buren with at least thirty pieces of artillery. The following morning at 10:00 A. M., they overran two cavalry regiments stationed at Dripping Springs and "dashed" into Van Buren, forcing the First Corps into retreat. Withdrawing in haste, Hindman's army left over 25,000 bushels of grain, forty-two wagons filled with supplies, camp and garrison equipment, ammunition, five steamers, and a ferry boat. What Union forces could not carry, including the boats, they burned before leaving for Springfield, Missouri.[59]

Led by Hindman, the hungry and exhausted soldiers began the long trek to Little Rock. The nightmare grew even worse as "a dreadful snow-storm came on suddenly, and the weather grew bitter cold in a night." Supply wagons mired in mud, and the troops, many of them barefoot, "were not clad to withstand the snows and rains of winter." "Sickness [quickly] entered the ranks and depleted them fearfully, while plain visible starvation glared from behind every cottonwood, and mingled with the soldiers' dreams and their desolate camp fires." Desertion became a serious problem, as hundreds of men (mainly conscripts) sought refuge behind enemy lines, became bushwackers, or returned to their homes.[60]

As the tattered army trudged wearily toward Little Rock, a Union force of thirty thousand men under Major General John A. McClernand was moving up the Mississippi River to capture Fort Hindman at Arkansas Post, fifty miles above the mouth of the Arkansas River. Situated 117 miles south of Little Rock, Arkansas Post was one of the key defenses for the capital city and also served as a base from which the Confederates could launch gunboats into the Mississippi. Garrisoned by only five thousand men under the command of Brigadier General Thomas J. Churchill, Fort Hindman surrendered on 11 January after a combined assault by McClernand and thirty gunboats under the command of Rear Admiral David Porter. Hearing of the planned attack on the fort which bore his name, Hindman while en route to Little Rock turned the First Corps toward Arkansas Post to reinforce Churchill. At Pine Bluff, however, he learned that the fort had surrendered and led his five thousand "emaciated, frozen, and exhausted" men back to Little Rock, where they went into winter quarters.[61]

Despite widespread desertion by conscripts, many of Hindman's soldiers remained deeply committed to the Southern cause. For example, after reaching Little Rock, a South Carolina officer wrote his wife that he would "never be part of a conquered people" or "accept the infamy of subjugation." Convinced that Hindman's address correctly portrayed the enemy, he implored her to hate "those who recreant to our cause, and teach our children to do the same."[62]

Following Prairie Grove, Hindman convinced Holmes to approve another cavalry raid into Missouri. Operating as a strategic force, Marmaduke's division would strike Blunt's rear and force the Union to concentrate on defending Missouri rather than pushing further into Arkansas. On a cold 31 December, Jo Shelby, accompanied by J. C. Monroe and Joseph Bledsoe, led 2,370 men into Missouri. Although they suffered terribly from the bitter January weather, the cavalrymen accomplished their purpose. After splitting forces at the base of the Boston Mountains, they burned several Union forts, destroyed bridges, attacked Springfield, and returned to Arkansas having suffered only 136 casualties.[63]

The raid was one more indication of the revolution in cavalry tactics that Hindman forged. Thanks to him, "a new day had dawned for the cavalry." Earlier raids, Cane Hill, Prairie Grove, and this latest move had proved that mounted units could operate effectively independent of infantry, instead of being a courier and escort service for generals. The cavalry in the Trans-Mississippi had become "a most effective arm of the service."[64]

Even while Hindman was preparing to move against Blunt, criticism of his earlier policies was reaching new heights. In November, the state House of Representatives unanimously passed a resolution condemning martial law as "illegal, oppressive, and unconstitutional." Although

Governor Rector admitted that it had "accomplished much good," in his annual message to the legislature on 3 December, he lambasted martial law as an "unnecessary" and improper evil. When Hindman's efforts at Prairie Grove failed to drive Union forces out of Arkansas, verbal attacks against him reached a crescendo. On 29 January 1863, the entire Arkansas congressional delegation demanded that President Davis transfer him east of the Mississippi River, on the grounds that "his presence" was "very objectionable to the public feeling of the State." Davis granted the request the following day, ordering Hindman to Vicksburg to await further instructions.[65]

Hindman balked at his new assignment, requesting instead that he be transferred "without delay" to duty with General Braxton Bragg's command. According to Hindman, the services he had rendered to the Confederacy "entitle[d]" him to be assigned to a command where he could be the most "useful." As matters turned out, he went neither to Vicksburg nor to Bragg's command when he left Arkansas. By mid February he had been named senior officer of a court of inquiry to investigate the loss of New Orleans.[66]

Prior to his departure on 13 March, many officers and enlisted men who had served under General Hindman organized meetings and a serenade to pay "merited tribute" to his "genius and self-sacrificing patriotism." On 13 March, the officers of Parsons's Brigade adopted a series of resolutions expressing "profound regret" about his departure and lauding him for his commitment to the "welfare" of the South. They lamented the loss of a "patriotic leader" they held in "high esteem."[67]

In addition to formal outpourings of sentiment, individual soldiers also expressed appreciation for Hindman's efforts to expel Union forces from Arkansas and southern Missouri and regret about his transfer. Writing to his daughter on 15 March 1863, Captain Elijah Petty of Walker's Texas Brigade called General Hindman "one of the best officers" ever to serve in Arkansas. Although "able and efficient," Hindman had become "the most slandered man in the Confederate Government." He was "worst sinned against than sinning." In spite of the attacks against him, Petty hoped that someday General Hindman would be "properly appreciated."[68]

Petty's admiration for Hindman was indicative of the feeling among many people (both soldiers and civilians) who believed that the general's policies were the only ones that could have succeeded. In spite of Pike's

Plate 7.2 *Thomas C. Hindman and Children (1865)*
Courtesy: Ivey S. Gladin, Photographer, Helena, Arkansas

bitter verbal attacks on him for his actions toward Indian Territory, Hindman had strong support among the Cherokees. Following the battle of Prairie Grove, Elizabeth Pack, daughter of a former Cherokee chief, presented him with a saddle ornament that was made in France about 1815 and a set of holster cases. The gifts were "in token of the high esteem" in which he was held by both "the humble giver" and "by the Southern Cherokees generally." Her father had acquired the items in Washington in 1816 and had never used them. She had kept them until she found someone "worthy of them." Mrs. Pack was "well acquainted" with the general's parents from her younger days and had known them to be "friends of the Cherokees." Hindman, too, had "proved himself" to be a friend and it afforded her "the greatest pleasure" to present him with a "humble tribute of respect" on behalf of "the sons and daughters of Southern liberty."[69]

Prior to leaving, the general issued a written farewell address to his troops. He stated that his departure in no way reflected "dissatisfaction" with the men under his command and assured them of his continuing affection. Ignoring "all allusion to the true causes" of his departure, he concluded his brief remarks by asking God to bless his former troops and enable them to serve "worthily."[70]

When Hindman and his family left Little Rock together on 13 March amid rumors that he might resign from the army, the controversy surrounding him continued. Detractors and defenders debated the merits of his policies into the summer and fall. On 14 April 1863, an exceptionally vitriolic attack occurred in the Confederate House when Hindman's old foe, Henry S. Foote of Tennessee, denounced the general "in unmeasured terms." Quoting from a pamphlet written by Albert Pike, Foote claimed that while serving "in his official capacity, in the Trans-Mississippi District," Hindman had been guilty of "high crime[s] and misdemeanor[s]." The House, argued Foote, must guard the rights of the people against "their violation by military usurpers." Based on Foote's comments and other alleged infractions of the law by military commanders, the House ultimately approved a series of resolutions denouncing martial law. Only one member of the Arkansas delegation, Grandison D. Royston of Washington in Hempstead County, voted to sustain Hindman. Not wanting to miss an opportunity to condemn Hindman and his supporters, James D. Butler, editor of the *Arkansas Patriot* and a vocal critic of Hindman's policies from their inception, applauded the resolution and suggested that voters "remember" Royston at the next election.[71]

Butler's verbal assaults became even more caustic just before Hindman left and continued long after he departed the state. On 19 February, he facetiously praised the general as "a man of very considerable ability, a fine stump speaker and a most decided politician" with "untiring perseverance and unflagging industry." Thereupon he added the venomous phrases "but Alas! All his labor proves abortive. He never effects anything." Less than three weeks later, he accused Hindman of subjecting "the people of Arkansas to all manner of degradation" and of riding "rough-shod" over "civil and individual rights." Commenting on Hindman's farewell remarks to his troops that his "heart was too full to say more," Butler rhetorically asked "full of what?"[72]

Responding to the attacks of Foote and other politicians opposed to martial law, C. C. Danley of the *Gazette* defended Hindman and offered readers his "history of Martial Law in Arkansas." Emphasizing the lack of sufficient troops to defend the state from Federal forces, the failure to enforce the conscript law, the evacuation of the capital by Governor Rector and other officials, and the "anarchy" that prevailed prior to Hindman's arrival, Danley staunchly defended the general's policies. Foote's "hue and cry against" martial law in Arkansas was the "veriest humbuggery that was ever attempted." Martial law was not unique to Arkansas and its only critics were "fools, grumblers, and enemies to the country."[73]

Danley's assessment was shared not only by many Arkansans, but by large numbers of people outside the state. In June 1863, commenting on "the excellency of discipline and drill" of troops in Holmes's command, a correspondent of the Jackson *Mississippian* credited the success solely to Hindman. The "vigorous efforts" of Hindman, "one of the most abused men" in the South, had completely reversed the "state of disorganization and confusion" that had existed in troops of the Trans-Mississippi. "He [had] brought order out of chaos—he had made an army. He was a rigid disciplinarian—but circumstances [and not military usurpation] made him one." He had "many enemies," but most who served under him were not numbered among them.[74]

Danley and others who endorsed Hindman's policies were correct. Regardless of its legal merits, martial law in Arkansas had (at least for the time being) prevented the capture of Little Rock by the Union;

forestalled military, political, and economic collapse; and was a viable alternative to the lackluster state rights approach of Governor Rector and others whose policies produced chaos and anarchy. In an open letter to the *True Democrat*, "A Missouri Soldier" in Parsons's Brigade castigated the editor for the "disgusted" tone of the *Patriot* and recommended that men like him, undoubtedly "anti-conscription," should leave the state. As Charles W. Adams, an aide to Hindman noted, it sometimes appears true that "those who try the most earnestly to do their duty; meet with the least favor."[75]

Chapter 8

RIVER OF DEATH: THE CHICKAMAUGA CAMPAIGN

Public outcry over the fall of New Orleans to Federal forces in April 1862 led Secretary of War James Seddon, on 18 February 1863, to order a court of inquiry to review Major General Mansfield Lovell's defense and evacuation of the city. As the senior officer assigned to the court, Hindman presided over its proceedings; other members were brigadier generals Thomas F. Drayton and William M. Gardner and Major L. R. Page, who served as judge-advocate and recorder. The court convened on 4 April in Jackson, Mississippi, and began the lengthy process of hearing testimony and examining affidavits. Drawing on his experience as an attorney, Hindman carefully adhered to established legal procedures; noting that Lovell was under "no accusation or imputation," the court prohibited the word "accused" during the inquiry. Due to the dispersal of witnesses after the Federal occupation of New Orleans, the Court met in four locations to collect evidence. It sat in Jackson from 4–18 April and in Vicksburg from 22–25 April before returning to Jackson for a session on the twenty-seventh. Additional hearings followed in Charleston, South Carolina, from 18–21 May and in Richmond from 2 June–9 July.[1]

After more than three months of listening to testimony and questioning witnesses, the court rendered its opinion on 9 July. Although the members agreed that Lovell had made "a serious error" in giving instructions for the evacuation of Chalmette, they exonerated him, stating that he had "displayed great energy and an untiring industry in performing his duties." Moreover, he had demonstrated "a high capacity for command and the clearest foresight in many of his measures for the defense of New Orleans."[2]

As the court of inquiry moved into the final stages of its work, Hindman changed his mind about being assigned to duty with General

Bragg east of the Mississippi. Believing that he would be more useful in Arkansas, he proposed that the War Department create a new Western Department, consisting of the Indian Territory and eight counties in northwest Arkansas, and assign it to him along with one division of troops currently serving in the Trans-Mississippi.[3]

Based on previous antipathy to his declaration of martial law and other policies, the War Department rejected his request and assigned him to replace Major General Jones M. Withers as one of Lieutenant General Leonidas Polk's division commanders in the Army of Tennessee.[4]

Under the command of General Braxton Bragg, the Army of Tennessee controlled Chattanooga, the gateway to the heart of the South. Corinth had fallen to Union forces in May 1862, and Vicksburg capitulated on 4 July 1863, leaving only Chattanooga and Richmond as the two remaining bastions of the Confederate frontier. If Chattanooga were lost, the Confederacy would be deprived of the copper, saltpeter, and grain of east Tennessee; the nitre mines of northern Alabama; and possibly the munitions complexes in Georgia and Alabama.[5]

In early July, as Hindman was completing his work on the court of inquiry, Bragg's two corps under Hardee and Polk contained less than 29,000 effectives. Without reinforcements, he would be hard-pressed to resist Major General William Rosecrans's Army of the Cumberland, which was sitting menacingly at Murfreesboro and moving toward his outposts at Tullahoma, Tennessee. Rosecrans reputedly had almost twice as many men and was on the verge of being strengthened by idle troops from U. S. Grant's army. To make matters worse, intelligence reports indicated that Major General Ambrose Burnside was in Kentucky preparing to move against east Tennessee with at least 25,000 men. In late August, Bragg and Major General Simon B. Buckner, commander of the Department of East Tennessee at Knoxville, alerted Richmond of their fears that Rosecrans and Burnside were planning a joint assault designed to capture Chattanooga and Knoxville.[6]

Although the War Department had known of Bragg's precarious situation for over six months, it did not move to strengthen his command until after the fall of Vicksburg and Lee's repulse at Gettysburg. In a belated response to Bragg's petitions, the War Department began the work of reinforcing the Army of Tennessee in August. It eventually sent

9,000 troops under major generals John C. Breckinridge and W. H. T. Walker from Joseph E. Johnston's Department of Mississippi and East Louisiana; Buckner and 8,000 men from Knoxville; and Lieutenant General James Longstreet's Virginia Corps. The various transfers carried with them as many problems as they did blessings. While he down played his desire, Longstreet wanted to command Bragg's army. Although Buckner was theoretically under Bragg's command, the War Department stipulated that he would continue to "correspond directly" with Richmond. When Buckner's troops arrived and became the Third Corps of the Army of Tennessee, they were officially referred to as "Buckner's Corps." In addition, the War Department transferred William J. Hardee to Johnston's command and replaced him with Daniel Harvey Hill, recently promoted to the rank of lieutenant general.[7]

The massing of forces to decide the fate of Chattanooga brought together friends from the "old army" of pre-war days and pitted former comrades against each other. Longstreet and Rosecrans had been roommates and members of the 1842 class at West Point, where the former was voted most handsome and the latter most studious. Other future members of the Army of Tennessee in the class of 1842 were D. H. Hill and A. P. Stewart. Hill, along with Bragg and George H. Thomas (now serving with the Army of the Cumberland), had been messmates at Fort Moultrie in 1845.[8]

Hill's fond memories of his pre-war association with Bragg were quickly supplanted on 19 July when he met with his new commander. Bragg, according to Hill, had grown old prematurely, was "silent and reserved," and seemed "gloomy and despondent." Hill's opinion of Bragg after their initial interview did not change. If anything, he became even more critical, believing that the recent retreats from Murfreesboro and Tullahoma had dampened the enthusiasm of most soldiers in the Army of Tennessee and had "alienated" many of them. Moreover, he concluded that because Bragg often issued "impossible orders," the "mutual confidence" between the commanding general and his subordinate officers necessary to "insure victory" was lacking. Bragg's disposition to find a "scapegoat" for his own failures, claimed Hill, had made his subordinates "cautious about striking a blow . . . unless they were protected by a positive order." He was especially dismayed by what he perceived to be the "hap-hazard" state of affairs, which included the absence of a "well-organized" system of spies and other informants.

Unlike General Robert E. Lee, Bragg suffered from the "want of information" needed to formulate sound military strategy. The lack of precise intelligence resulted in Bragg's becoming "bewildered" when Rosecrans' widely dispersed troops popped out of the mountain passes like rats out of holes.[9]

As acquaintances in the "old army" well knew, Bragg had an "irascible temper" and was, as U. S. Grant put it, "naturally disputatious." An oft-repeated story, perhaps apocryphal, illustrates Bragg's reputation as a cantankerous man. While serving as a temporary post commander, he submitted a requisition for supplies to the quartermaster. Then, as quartermaster, denied the request, leading his superior to exclaim, "Bragg, you have quarreled with every officer in the army, and now you are quarreling with yourself."[10]

Poor health exacerbated Bragg's faults, which in turn intensified the internal strife within the Army of Tennessee. By late summer, a cadre of anti-Bragg men had developed, including lieutenant generals Polk and Hill, and major generals Patrick Cleburne, Benjamin F. Cheatham, and John C. Breckinridge.[11]

Tom Hindman entered this quagmire on 13 August 1863 when he arrived in Chattanooga ready to assume leadership of Withers's division. Although disappointed that the War Department had not given him an independent command in Arkansas, he was optimistic about his new assignment. During the Shiloh campaign, he had won lavish praise from Bragg, leading him to expect that their future relationship would be harmonious. Even the train trip from Richmond to Chattanooga seemed to be a portent of good things to come. At several stations along the way, he encountered soldiers from his old command who seemed "much pleased at seeing him again." On the train, he visited with Kate Cumming, a nurse with the Army of Tennessee, and swapped stories of their Scottish heritage. Hindman was in such good humor that he teasingly claimed that his middle name was Culloden in honor of the services of his ancestors in the cause of Bonnie Prince Charlie. Impressed with his remarks about "the state of the country," Miss Cumming noted in her journal that it was "a pity that a man who could arrange every thing so nicely" was "not at the *head of affairs*." In spite of these omens, by the end of September Hindman and Bragg had become bitter antagonists, and Hindman cast his lot with the growing faction of anti-Bragg men.[12]

Three days after Hindman arrived, three of Rosecrans' army corps (under major generals George H. Thomas, Alexander McCook, and Thomas L. Crittenden) began moving toward Chattanooga. Counting the cavalry and the reserve corps under Major General Gordon Granger, the Army of the Cumberland totaled about 67,000 men. Even though Richmond had begun reinforcing Bragg, when the advance began neither Johnston's brigades nor Longstreet's corps had been ordered to join him. Lacking sufficient strength to engage the Army of the Cumberland, Bragg evacuated Chattanooga on 8 September and retreated to La Fayette in northern Georgia to await the arrival of additional troops. While he had abandoned Chattanooga, Bragg was determined to attack Rosecrans at the first favorable opportunity.[13]

He did not have to wait long, for after occupying Chattanooga, Rosecrans had carelessly over extended his army by stringing it out from Chattanooga to Alpine, Georgia, along a circuitous route through several mountain passes. Thomas's Fourteenth Corps had crossed the Raccoon-Sand Mountain range and had entered Lookout Valley. Major General James S. Negley, commanding the Second Division, had passed through Stevens Gap to Davis Crossroads in McLemore's Cove, the valley between Lookout and Pigeon mountains near the headwaters of Chickamauga Creek. Unaware of where Bragg was concentrating his forces, Negley planned to move across Pigeon Mountain into Dug Gap and attack La Fayette.[14]

Cognizant of Negley's position and convinced that other Union troops were too far away to provide support, on 9 September Bragg decided to attack. That evening he summoned Hindman to his headquarters at Lee and Gordon's Mills and outlined his plan to trap Negley in McLemore's Cove. Hindman was to march his division through Worthen's Gap on Pigeon Mountain at the north end of McLemore's Cove and move south to Davis Crossroads. At his discretion, Hill was simultaneously to send or accompany Cleburne's division across Pigeon Mountain at Dug Gap and unite with Hindman at Davis Crossroads. The combined forces were to move "upon the enemy" (reported to be 4,000 or 5,000 strong) encamped at the foot of Lookout Mountain at Stevens Gap. At 11:45 P. M., Bragg followed up his verbal instructions to Hindman in writing and sent a copy to Hill.[15]

Bragg's cleverly conceived plan soon turned into a fiasco for which he, Hill, and Hindman share the blame. Acting on schedule, Hindman had his men in motion by 1:00 A. M. on the tenth, and before daylight they had covered nine of the thirteen miles to the proposed rendezvous site at Davis Crossroads. While Hindman had immediately carried out his instructions, Bragg's courier did not locate Hill until 4:30 on the morning of the tenth. After receiving his orders, Hill promptly notified Bragg that the movement of Cleburne's division to Davis Crossroads was "impracticable" since Cleburne "had been sick in bed all day" and two of the division's regiments were still out on picket duty. He also stated that both Dug and Catlett's gaps were "blocked" by fallen timber that would "require twenty-four hours" to remove. Hill advised Bragg that, due to the delay, the element of surprise would be gone before he could reach the rendezvous site.[16]

Hill's message did not reach Bragg's headquarters until about 8:00 A. M. 10 September; by then Hindman had been idling for two hours waiting for Hill to open communications with him. Eager for information, he had sent out a cavalry detachment to investigate reports from local residents that Federal divisions were already at Davis' Crossroads and Stevens' Gap and that Dug and Catlett's gaps were impassable due to fallen trees. In addition, at 6:00 A. M. he dispatched a message informing Hill of the reports and stated that he would not advance until he had heard that Cleburne's division was in motion. A half hour later, Hindman sent a copy of the message to Bragg and asked for alternative instructions. Awaiting word from Hill or Bragg, Hindman continued to send out scouting parties and pickets while he formulated strategy in case he had to retreat.[17]

Meanwhile, upon receipt of Hill's message at 8:00 A. M., Bragg acted to salvage his plan of attack by ordering Buckner's corps to march to Davis Crossroads to replace Cleburne division. Leaving immediately, Buckner pressed his men along the same route that Hindman had taken earlier in the day and junctioned with him about 4:45 P. M., too late to launch an attack. Shortly after Buckner's arrival, Hindman received copies of dispatches that Hill had written at noon and 1:30 stating that Cleburne was moving toward Dug's Gap. Should the Federals attack Cleburne in force, Hill recommended that Hindman attack in the rear. Both messages were routed to Hindman through Bragg's headquarters and were marked for "his information and guidance."[18]

At this point, because of conflicting cavalry reports, Bragg was uncertain as to the "relative strength and position of the Federals in McLemore's Cove and southward toward Alpine." Therefore, he did not directly order Hindman to attack. He feared that Rosecrans's Fourteenth and Twentieth Corps might be massing south of La Fayette. If so, the Confederates, instead of Negley, would be trapped in McLemore's Cove. Moreover, by late afternoon new reports placed a large segment of Crittenden's corps marching directly south from Chattanooga, causing Bragg to worry that Polk might be caught in the middle as part of Crittenden's corps moved up from Ringold toward La Fayette. Hence, at 6:00 P. M. Bragg told Hindman to "finish the movement now going on as rapidly as possible." Then, at 7:30 P. M. he notified Hindman that the enemy was divided and could be crushed if he moved vigorously. The message implied that Hindman should attack, but did not specify when the attack should begin; neither did it order him to proceed to Davis Crossroads or another point.[19]

Unfamiliar with the terrain and new to his command, Hindman was reluctant to attack without explicit instructions from Bragg, especially since a Federal force of unknown number was "within striking distance" at Stevens Gap on his right and another, equal in number to his own troops, imperiled his front. As far as he knew, Dug and Catlett's gaps were still obstructed; if Crittenden blocked the approach to Worthen's Gap, Hindman worried that his own force might be trapped in McLemore's Cove. In view of the risks involved, he met with Buckner and his own brigade commanders to plan the next move. After careful consideration, they decided unanimously not to advance until they received "more definite information" about enemy troop strength and assurance that Hill would be able to cut through Dug Gap and join them at Davis Crossroads.[20]

Following the meeting, Hindman dispatched Major James Nocquet of Buckner's staff to inform Bragg and Hill of the decision not to attack without additional information. Hindman sent a series of questions for Hill to answer, indicating that negative responses to the questions or proof that "the enemy [is] on our flank . . . in such force as to render it hazardous," would result in Hindman moving against Crittenden rather than proceeding to Davis Crossroads.[21]

Hindman could not have made a worse choice than Nocquet. French by birth, he spoke little English and had openly criticized the Southern war effort. He and Bragg had been on bad terms ever since the general removed him as his chief engineer in November 1862. At midnight, Nocquet attempted incoherently to explain Hindman's concerns about launching an attack at Davis Crossroads. Bragg refused to relent and told Nocquet to inform Hindman "there would be no change of orders." He also sent a courier to Hindman with orders to attack Negley at daylight on the eleventh. Polk was to cover Hindman's rear, and Cleburne was to attack in front when "Hindman's guns were heard."[22]

Hindman received Bragg's written orders at 4:30 A. M. and Nocquet's verbal version at 6:30 A. M. According to Hindman, Nocquet told him that Bragg had given him "the discretion" to execute his "own plans" and had promised to "sustain" him if he did, a claim Bragg later denied. Discretionary powers or not, at 7:00 A. M. on the eleventh, still uncertain as to whether Cleburne's path was blocked and fearing entrapment by a numerically superior force, Hindman began moving toward Davis Crossroads. Given the absence of exact information about Cleburne's movement and seemingly contradictory instructions from Bragg, Hindman moved deliberately through the densely wooded country, covering only one and a half to two miles in four hours. As his troops advanced, he sent out scouting parties to ascertain the position and strength of the enemy, and Buckner dispatched a team of engineers to clear Catlett's Gap, unaware that Cleburne's men were already at work clearing Dug and Catlett's gaps. Two miles into the march, cavalry skirmishes broke out along Hindman's front, further slowing his progress.[23]

At 11:10 A. M. about two and a half miles from Davis Crossroads, infantry skirmishes forced Buckner to deploy his corps on the "spurs of Pigeon Mountain." Patton Anderson, one of Hindman's brigade commanders, then moved in to support Buckner's right where the enemy was concentrating. According to Hindman, "the enemy's skirmishers were now driven in" and his "whole line about to advance" when he received a message from Bragg written at 11:00 A. M. ordering him to "fall back at once" on La Fayette by Catlett's Gap if he found the enemy in "such force as to make an attack imprudent." A 12:30 P. M. note from Bragg's chief of staff, W. W. Mackall, stated that a Federal force of between 12,000 and 15,000 was forming in front of Dug's Gap, where Bragg had established his headquarters and was waiting anxiously to hear from Hindman, who was to report to headquarters hourly by courier. Other reports said that the enemy was moving from Graysville to La Fayette.[24]

Upon receipt of the communiques about mid-afternoon, Hindman halted his advance and again conferred with Buckner and Anderson, who agreed that further advance would be "imprudent" as their rear flank was "insecure." Hindman then ordered his men to retire through Catlett's Gap to La Fayette. Before his order could be implemented, a scouting party brought news that the enemy was retreating through Stevens Gap. Hindman immediately ordered a pursuit to "intercept the retreating column." Darkness halted the Confederates' "ineffectual pursuit," and the Union force escaped Bragg's intended trap. Bromfield Ridley, an aide to General A. P. Stewart, aptly assessed the situation: when the Confederates finally offered battle, the Federals had fled and "the Southern wolves had lost their supper."[25]

Exasperated at Hindman's delay in launching an attack and letting the Union forces escape, Bragg angrily ordered him to report to Davis Crossroads. After a stormy meeting, Bragg himself decided the Confederate position was untenable and ordered Hindman to retire through Catlett's Gap and Buckner through Dug Gap.[26]

Although Bragg faulted Hill and Hindman, he deserves much of the blame for the failure at McLemore's Cove. His imprecise orders virtually compelled Hindman to exercise his own discretion. Furthermore, conflicting reports about the location of Rosecrans's corps made Bragg unsure of his strategy. If Hindman's worries about the strength and location of various Federal forces had proved correct, then the Confederates would have been trapped in the cove. This uncertainty pervaded Bragg's communications and encouraged Hindman to await further instructions. Bragg also erred by relying on a courier to deliver his initial orders to Hill instead of coordinating the plan with Hill and Hindman simultaneously at headquarters. Finally, Bragg's previous practice of holding subordinates responsible for his own mistakes made Hindman wary of launching an attack without specific orders.[27]

Certainly, Hill and Hindman were not blameless in the affair. Hill bungled the early stages of the plan by not opening communications with Hindman as ordered. Hindman's excessive caution was a mistake. Had he struck at daylight on the eleventh with Polk and Cleburne in support, he may well have hemmed in the Federals in the cove and destroyed them.[28] When Bragg returned to La Fayette the evening of the eleventh, he was still uncertain of the precise location of Rosecrans's Fourteenth and Twentieth Corps. He was positive, however, that Crittenden's Corps, isolated from the remainder of Rosecrans's army, was advancing toward La Fayette along the main road from Chattanooga via Lee and Gordon's Mills and the Pea Vine Road. Determined to take advantage of the situation, at 3:00 A. M. on the twelfth he ordered Polk to attack at daylight.[29]

The planned attack never materialized. After evaluating the situation, Polk concluded that he lacked sufficient troop strength to engage the enemy and asked Bragg to send reinforcements. The two generals then engaged in an exchange of messages that culminated at midnight with a planned assault on the thirteenth. By this time, they had lost the opportunity because Crittenden had slipped away. As had been the case in McLemore's Cove, Bragg gave vague instructions that left room for discretion. His last instructions told the bishop "to fight at the earliest moment," but "to avoid all danger."[30]

In spite of the failure in McLemore's Cove and the inability to trap Crittenden, Bragg was still determined to launch an assault against Rosecrans, who was concentrating his forces north of Lee and Gordon's Mills along Chickamauga Creek. The creek flowed in a northeasterly direction, parallel to Missionary Ridge, to the Tennessee River four miles above Chattanooga. By cutting around the Union left and moving up the right bank of the creek, Bragg hoped to place himself between Rosecrans's army and Chattanooga, thereby disrupting the Federal commander's communications. To extricate himself, Rosecrans would have to expose himself to an attack by traveling through mountain passes to reach the Tennessee River at Bridgeport.[31]

Initially Bragg hoped to attack on 18 September, but he was unable to get all of his units into position in time to launch an assault. Reinforced by Longstreet's first three brigades under John Bell Hood on the eighteenth, Bragg devised a plan that called for advancing on Crittenden's left, severing the routes to McFarland's Gap and Rossville, and cutting off the three Union corps to the south from their bases of supply at Chattanooga. Brigadier General Bushrod Johnson's division (Hood's Corps), accompanied by Brigadier General Nathan Bedford Forrest's cavalry and supported by W. H. T. Walker's division, would move down Chickamauga Creek, cross at Reed and Alexander's bridges, and assault Rosecrans's left flank. Simultaneously, Buckner's Corps would cross farther upstream at Thedford's Ford, Polk would cross and attack at Lee and Gordon's Mills, and Hill's Corps would guard the northern exit of McLemore's Cove to prevent George H. Thomas and Alexander McCook from using that route to come to Crittenden's aid.[32]

Excitement quickened the Confederates' steps on the morning of 18 September as they set out upon the last leg of their journey in the quest

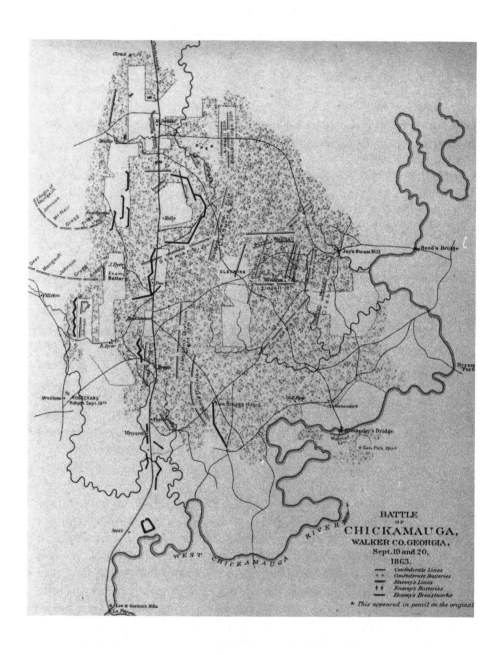

Plate 8   *Chickamauga Battlefield*
Atlas to accompany the *Official Records of the War of the Rebellion*

to destroy Rosecrans. With "determination . . . written on every brow," Bragg's men remarked to each other, "Boys, we have retreated far enough; we will whip 'em this time or die." While the troops were eager for the coming fray, progress along the rugged mountain roads was slow; stiff resistance from Union cavalry also retarded the Confederates. By late afternoon, Hood had crossed Reed's Bridge, and Walker had crossed at Byram's Ford. Now west of Chickamauga Creek, Hood and Walker bivouacked and waited for the remaining Confederates who reached the creek by nightfall. During the night, the graycoats captured two of the important creek fords. In the meantime, alerted by Confederate movements during the day, Rosecrans moved Thomas and McCook into position to support Crittenden.[33]

Troops in both armies spent the night of the eighteenth poised for the next day's battle and pondering the possibility that this could be their last evening on earth. "The morning of the nineteenth (Saturday) opened cloudy but the sun soon lifted the veil to look down upon the awful scenes in progress" as the armies of Bragg and Rosecrans collided. The fighting began between eight and nine o'clock when Thomas dispatched Brigadier General John M. Brannan toward Alexander's Bridge to attack what he thought was only a single brigade across the creek. As Brannan encountered Forrest's cavalry and Walker's infantry division, "a salvo of musketry" poured forth. All day long, the lines of both armies "moved to and fro like the advancing and receding waves of the sea."[34]

From that moment until after sunset, "thunderbolts shot forth in flashes . . . like forked lightning from the clouds," sweeping "death and destruction before them." At times, "like meeting clouds in the darkness of the storm, the smoke from the firearms in the dense woodland almost concealed the combatants." With accuracy and rapidity, the "unabated fury [of] 'the death shot'" and "sulphurous flames" blanketed the area like a hail storm, producing heavy casualties. The wounded crying out in agony, the dead, mangled horses, field surgeons, and litter forces were everywhere. In some areas, nests of yellow jackets added "to the horror of the galling fire" by attacking willy nilly. In spite of heavy losses on both sides, the engagement on the nineteenth never developed into more than a series of inconclusive and sporadic clashes fought mainly in the woods. It was as D. H. Hill said, a day of "desultory fighting from left to right, without concert, and at inopportune times. It was the sparring of the amateur boxer, and not the crushing blows of the trained pugilist."

Some units (including Hindman's division), although in position to participate in the battle, spent most of the nineteenth in reserve.[35]

Exhausted from battle, Saturday night the Southerners threw up log breastworks, knowing that "the sound of the ax" in the distance indicated that the Yankees were doing the same. Although the night was "cold and chilly" and many men's clothes were still wet from having waded the Chickamauga, no fires were allowed until nearly 3:00 A. M. Heavy frost covered the ground, where "hundreds of ghastly corpses [lay] mangled and torn." While "ghouls and stragglers" hovered over the dead and dying hoping to find watches and other valuables, other weary soldiers rested on their arms and whispered about "the fearful mortality" in their ranks. Having been on half rations, the men were hungry, and some even plundered fallen comrades' haversacks for crackers, stopping only to chip away sprinkles of blood before devouring them.[36]

Longstreet reached Bragg's headquarters about 11:00 P. M. that night. Delighted to see him, Bragg reorganized his army by dividing it into two wings; Longstreet commended the first and Polk the second. Bragg gave Longstreet a map of the area and briefly described the Confederate plan of attack, which was to begin at daylight. Significantly, he did not give Hill (also a lieutenant general) similar status but placed him under Polk in charge of Cleburne and Breckinridge's divisions.[37]

Sunday morning dawned crisp and cold with a heavy fog still hanging over the battlefield. In the Confederate camps, "every arm [stood] in readiness for a 'hand all around'. . . 'hilt to hilt' and 'breast to breast'" fight. As usual with Bragg, however, plans went awry. Unaware that they were to lead the attack at daylight, Hill's divisions lingered over breakfast, while Longstreet—having been with his command only a few hours—began to align his left flank.[38]

Also, planning to renew the battle at daylight, Rosecrans was frantically trying to fill a number of gaps in his line. Had Bragg's army moved as scheduled, the Confederates could have quickly penetrated these gaps and "dismembered" the Federals. Hour after hour passed, however, with troops waiting restlessly for an explanation. Had the enemy retreated or had the order of battle been changed? To Arthur Manigault, one of Hindman's brigade commanders, "everything was quiet as though no human being was within miles."[39]

Finally, at 9:30 Polk gave the order to attack. During the first hour, fighting was heavy but inconclusive; then about 10:30 a dramatic error in Union intelligence turned the tide in favor of the Confederates. Incorrectly told that a gap had developed between the divisions of Brigadier General Thomas J. Wood and Major General Joseph Jones Reynolds, Rosecrans ordered Wood to move to the left to close the supposed hole in the Federal line. Wood did as ordered, and the results were devastating—instead of closing the alleged opening between Wood and Reynolds, the move opened one between Brannan and Brigadier General Jefferson C. Davis.[40]

As the gap opened, Longstreet was beginning an assault against the Union line just to the right of its center. "Like the breaking of a levee and the rushing in of the tide," the divisions of Bushrod Johnson and brigadier generals Evander McIver Law and Joseph B. Kershaw, supported by Major General Alexander P. Stewart on the right and Hindman on the left, poured into the gap left by Wood. "Rushing on at a double quick, through a storm of bullets, shot and shell," one of Hindman's brigades under the command of Zachariah Deas, "swept like a whirlwind" over the Federal breastworks and, joined by Manigault's men, drove the bluecoats from the field.[41]

Hindman and Johnson's combined assault completely destroyed the Union right wing. Isolated from the rest of Rosecrans' army, J. C. Davis and Phil Sheridan's divisions had to withdraw through McFarland's Gap; with their commands disintegrating, Crittenden and McCook followed. In utter panic, Rosecrans' legions fled "in one confused mass through the large cornfields and roads" raising a "cloud of dust unequalled any-where." It was, as one Confederate soldier rejoiced, a "total rout."[42]

The retreating Federals left behind dead and dying soldiers scattered over miles of the battlefield. During the "splendid advance," Hindman's forces took over 1,100 prisoners and captured 1,400 small arms, 165,000 rounds of ammunition, forty horses and mules, a battery wagon, five caissons, one ambulance, and seventeen artillery pieces. Caught up in the intensity of the battle, Hindman paid little attention to the prisoners except to order them stripped of their shoes for the benefit of his men, about two thousand of whom were barefoot.[43]

Riding in front of his staff, Rosecrans drew his sword and tried to rally his troops, but to no avail. As men raced by him, "Old Rosy" listened with his ear to the ground for any sounds that would indicate continued resistance. Hearing scattered musketry without artillery, he believed that his army was "entirely broken" and decided to ride on to Chattanooga to reorganize the troops as they straggled in.[44]

As a result of the panic within the Union lines, by 1:00 P.M. Thomas was left in command. Joined by Brigadier General James B. Steedman and the reserve corps under Granger, he collected the remaining troops of Rosecrans's right wing at Snodgrass Hill, "a frowning fortress almost impregnable to attack," on Missionary Ridge. Greatly outnumbered, the determined and resolute Thomas (later dubbed "The Rock of Chicka-mauga") held out against repeated Confederate assaults in the most stubborn fighting of the day, thereby preventing a devastating Union defeat.[45]

Although wounded in the neck by a piece of shrapnel at midday and "suffering much pain," Hindman remained on the field to direct what Hill later described as "some of the severest fighting" of the day. In command of his own brigades and two of Johnson's, from about 3:30 until just before 7:00 P. M. Hindman attacked Thomas's position "again and again" in fierce "close quarters" fighting, in which many soldiers were killed by bayonets and muskets used as clubs. Several times the men of Mani-gault's brigade exhausted their ammunition but, being unwilling to fall back, "supplied themselves from their dead or wounded comrades" or from the Yankees. When the ammunition did not fit their guns, they threw them aside and seized their opponents' weapons.[46]

Both sides fought valiantly throughout the afternoon. As they assaulted Thomas' entrenchments, the Confederates faced "the whirlwind of lead and iron with the steadiness and composure of a summer rain." Likewise, the Union forces "struggled like men who had cast their last die in the balance, and were resolved 'to meet the shuddering battle shocks until their lives ran ruddy rain.'" Impressed by the bluecoats' determined obstinacy, Hindman declared that he had never known "Federal troops to fight so well."[47]

Thomas stubbornly held his position until late afternoon. He could not withstand the combined onslaught, however, as Polk and Longstreet brought their wings together. When Preston and Stewart dashed at Snodgrass Hill and Confederate artillery poured shot and shell into his ranks, Thomas knew he was beaten. As darkness came, he withdrew toward Chattanooga via the Rossville road.[48]

With Thomas in retreat, both wings of the Army of Tennessee burst into loud, continuous "huzzas" as they celebrated their "first grand victory." "The dews of twilight hung heavy about the trees as if to hold down the voice of victory," but as the two lines converged, their voices united in a "tremendous swell . . . that seemed almost to lift from their roots the great trees of the forest.[49]

As darkness fell, cries of agony from the wounded competed with shouts of victory along Chickamauga Creek. Years earlier, the Cherokees had given the stream its name, which meant "River of Death," after scores of tribal members had died along its banks from small pox. On the night of 20 September the name seemed appropriate, as glittering moonbeams illuminated "the ghastly faces of the dead, distorted in expression from the wounds of their torn and mangled bodies." Piled in heaps, the dead and wounded were strewn everywhere, as were "broken artillery carriages and caissons, [and] dead horses." Wild hogs rooted among the dead and carried off amputated arms and legs. Hundreds of wounded were burned beyond recognition when sparks from artillery charges ignited trees and grass parched from months of summer drought. The creek even took on a pink tinge from the blood of the wounded who crawled down its banks for water.[50]

The casualty reports attest to the "desperate and bloody character" of the fighting and the "heroism" of troops from both armies. Total Confederate casualties were estimated at 17,800 out of approximately 50,000 effectives, and Union losses were roughly 16,500 out of 67,792 available soldiers. Among individual Confederate regiments, at least twelve suffered casualty rates of fifty percent or higher. This group included the Tenth Tennessee (68%), the Fifth Georgia (61%), the Second Tennessee (60%), the Fifteen Tennessee (60%), and the Thirty-Seventh Tennessee (60%). Hindman's three infantry brigades commanded by brigadier generals Patton Anderson, Zachariah Deas, and Arthur Manigault incurred heavy losses. In Deas's six Alabama regiments 123 men were killed and 271 were wounded, while in Anderson's six Mississippi regiments eighty were killed and 219 wounded. The total losses for Hindman's entire division (including artillery batteries) were 277 killed, 841 wounded (562 severely), and 112 missing or captured. In less than two hours on the second day of battle, Longstreet estimated that his command lost nearly forty-four percent of its strength, while on the Union side Steedman and Brannan lost forty-nine and thirty-eight percent in less than four hours.[51]

In spite of the horror that surrounded them, the Confederates celebrated wildly and looked forward to an early morning pursuit of the retreating Yankees. Much to their amazement and counter to the advice of Longstreet, however, Bragg decided against pursuit, arguing that it would be "fruitless" since Rosecrans's main body was already safely back in Chattanooga. "Exhausted by two days' battle, with very limited supply of provisions, and almost destitute of water," the Confederates were in no condition to march. No reserves were available to replace tired troops, and a third of Bragg's artillery horses had been lost during the fighting. They would have to rebuild bridges destroyed by the Federals, and they needed railroads to transport wounded soldiers to hospitals and prisoners to other locations. Under the circumstances, Bragg argued, pursuing the enemy was simply impractical.[52]

Although unwilling to confront Rosecrans's retreating army immediately, Bragg aggressively entered into one of his customary post-battle condemnations of subordinates. On 22 September, he demanded that Polk justify his failure to attack Crittenden on time. Exactly one week later, he suspended Polk for "neglect of duty" and "noncompliance" and Hindman for "disobedience of the lawful command of his superior officer" in the McLemore's Cove affair. He ordered both men to proceed to Atlanta to await further instructions. Bragg's actions were unwarranted, ill-timed, and failed to take into account his unpopularity with other generals and the support in Richmond for Polk and Hindman.[53]

Hindman received notification of his suspension while in Newnan, Georgia, recuperating from the wound he suffered on the twentieth. He had never known such humiliation and was outraged by what he felt was a ploy by Bragg to distract attention from his own leadership failure in not pursuing Rosecrans on the twenty-first. Because of Bragg, for an indefinite period of time he would be without command of his division and have to witness the campaign in Georgia as a spectator. Hindman reported to Atlanta as ordered, and after arriving, received permission to return to Newnan to continue his convalescence and rejoin Mollie and the children, who had gone there when he was transferred to the Army of Tennessee.[54]

By 7 October, Hindman felt well enough to "write without much difficulty" and launched a spirited counter-attack. He wrote to his close friend and Assistant Adjutant General J. P. Wilson, telling him that his services and those of Colonel Charles W. Adams, another aide, were "indispensable." They must immediately bring all available correspondence and papers relating to Chickamauga to Newnan and obtain a copy of the "report of the McLemore Cove business" written by Brigadier General Patton Anderson of his division. Although Wilson had sent a copy of Anderson's report earlier, it had been "lost," leading Hindman to conclude that it looked "as if the very devil" was trying to prevent him from mounting a defense of his actions in the cove. In addition, Wilson and Adams were to secure copies of reports written by Major General Benjamin F. Cheatham and brigadier generals Bushrod Johnson, Joseph Kershaw, and William Preston. Confident that Wilson and Adams would obtain the information necessary to blunt Bragg's charge, Hindman turned his attention to family matters. Mollie was expecting their fourth child in late November, and he wanted to move her to a more suitable location as soon as possible. With the army's consent, he moved his family to Madison, Georgia, about fifty miles from Atlanta and remained there awaiting action on the charges pending against him.[55]

Convinced that an impartial review of the facts would vindicate his conduct, Hindman acquired all needed records, proofread his report one last time, and on 8 November demanded that a court of inquiry be convened, sending the War Department his report and supporting documents. Resembling a legal brief to an appellate court, his report and exhibits presented his argument that any problems in the cove resulted from Bragg's vague and confusing orders rather than his own misconduct.[56]

Although Hindman and Polk made errors in judgment, their suspensions in part appear to have been motivated by Bragg's desire to rid his command of some of his critics. Moreover, as Polk claimed, Bragg was trying to find a "scapegoat" for his own failure to pursue Rosecrans. Polk's disdain for his commanding officer was well-known since he had been openly critical of Bragg's leadership for a long time. For his part, Bragg had formed a negative impression of the bishop-general in 1861; subsequent events had simply reinforced his opinion. By ousting Polk, Bragg would eliminate one of his most prominent detractors.[57]

Although Hindman had not been a vocal critic, Bragg believed that he shared the views of dissidents within the Army of Tennessee. If nothing else, the Arkansan's close friendship with Patrick Cleburne, who had told Bragg that he lacked "the confidence of the army" necessary to "secure success," made him suspect. Even if Bragg was incensed about the incident in McLemore's Cove, as Longstreet correctly pointed out, Hindman's "brave" conduct on the twentieth "would have relieved him of any previous misconduct according to the customs of war."[58]

With respect to Hindman's action, in 1873 Bragg himself indicated that he believed Polk's "querulous, insubordinate spirit" resulted in the failure to send Cleburne's division to join Hindman in McLemore's Cove. He might also have mentioned his own contradictory and confusing orders and messages that were permissive rather than preemptive, as well as his lack of precise information about the location of Union forces. As Longstreet noted years later, if any one had blundered at Chickamauga, it was Bragg who failed to follow up success "and capture or disperse" Rosecrans's army. Hill concurred, stating that "whatever blunders each in authority committed before the battles of the 19th and 20th, the greatest blunder of all was that of not pursuing the enemy on the 21st."[59]

The suspensions intensified opposition to Bragg and, on 4 October, resulted in the submission of a petition to President Davis by Longstreet, Buckner, Hill, Preston, and several other generals in the Army of Tennessee condemning the failure to pursue "the panic-stricken" and confused enemy to win "the most fruitful" victory of the war. As a result of Bragg's inaction, "the beaten enemy" had regrouped and was rapidly being reinforced. The "complete paralysis" caused by Bragg's decision might well mean "disaster" for the Army of Tennessee. Not "entering into a criticism" of Bragg's "merits," the petitioners asked that he be relieved because his "health" made him "totally" unfit for command. Polk and Hindman, in Atlanta awaiting action on their requests for courts of inquiry, did not sign the petition. Longstreet and others also wrote individual letters to Davis and the Secretary of War criticizing Bragg's overall performance and recommending his replacement.[60]

In addition to dissident generals, Davis received letters criticizing Bragg's action from private citizens, including close personal friends such as Howill Hinds of Jefferson County, Mississippi. Commenting on the suspensions, Hinds noted that "it looks strange to see officers who have worn their laurels on so many bloody fields under arrest," parenthetically asking "what can it mean?" He closed his letter by expressing the desire to see Hindman and Polk soon back at work helping to "whip all the armies the Yankees . . . bring against us."[61]

Hindman's suspension had an interesting and, in some respects, a surprising effect in Arkansas. Some who had criticized him for his use of martial law and other policies while in command of the Trans-Mississippi District were quick to defend him against Bragg's charges. John Eakin of the Washington Telegr*aph* cited a letter from the Atlanta *Appeal* that claimed Hindman had proof that he had "complied" with Bragg's orders both "in letter and spirit to the utmost practical extent." Rallying to the defense of a fellow Arkansan, Eakin stated that he hoped to soon hear that the "brave" Hindman had been "sustained."[62]

Aware of Bragg's standing with many of his subordinates and not wanting to see morale jeopardized by unnecessary controversy, Davis declared that Bragg's suspensions were "punishment without trial" and should be countermanded. When his aide Colonel James Chesnut went to Georgia to investigate the situation, it became evident that Bragg was going to ignore the president's advice and allow the situation to fester. Davis immediately boarded a train for Atlanta to resolve the crisis of command personally by bringing about a reconciliation between Bragg and his generals. Arriving on 8 October, he spent five days with the army and visited Bragg's headquarters at Marietta. As a result of the president's intervention, a compromise was reached whereby charges were dismissed against Polk in exchange for his transfer to Johnston's command and Hardee's return to the Army of Tennessee.[63]

On 15 November, agreeing with Davis that "the facts" indicated Hindman should not have been suspended and that neither the general's "honor" nor the "interests of the public" would be served by a court of inquiry, Bragg dropped all charges and asked that Hindman be restored to duty. In recommending the reinstatement, Bragg praised Hindman for "conspicuously distinguished" conduct and "gallantry" at Chickamauga and expressed full confidence in Hindman's abilities to make a continued contribution to the Southern war effort. Although exonerated of misconduct charges and returned to active duty status, Hindman received authorization to remain at Madison until Mollie bore their child.[64]

On 23 November, eight days after Bragg dropped the charges against her husband, Mollie gave birth to the Hindman family's second son. He was named Tom in honor of his father, but was usually referred to as "Tinker" or "Tink." The general's elation at "Tinker's" birth immediately turned to fear and apprehension when Mollie became "precarious[ly]" ill on the twenty-sixth and almost died. With the prospect of her recovery "very doubtful," he received permission to remain in Madison and spent several days at her bedside anxiously hoping for improvement in her condition. Fortunately for the family, by mid December the crisis had passed, and Mollie began to recover.[65]

With his wife out of danger, on 15 December Hindman returned to the Army of Tennessee then under William J. Hardee, who had replaced Bragg on 30 November. Although he had been offered command, Hardee had agreed to serve as commanding general only until President Davis had selected a permanent replacement for Bragg. In recognition of his gallantry at Chickamauga, Hardee assigned Hindman to head one of his two corps. The assignment was only temporary, however, until John Bell Hood arrived. With his arm maimed at Gettysburg and the loss of a leg at Chickamauga, Hood had become a popular hero in the Confederate Capital. Moreover, Hood was a West Pointer, and at least until very late in the war, Davis generally appointed only graduates of the academy as permanent corps commanders.[66]

Chapter 9

FROM DALTON TO
KENNESAW MOUNTAIN

On 27 December, less than two weeks after Hindman's temporary assignment began, General Joseph E. Johnston arrived at Dalton to take command of the Army of Tennessee. A veteran of the Seminole, Black Hawk, and Mexican wars, Johnston had served in the cavalry and artillery and had been Quartermaster General of the United States Army. He had been a full general since August 1861, ranking in seniority behind Samuel Cooper, Albert Sidney Johnston, and Robert E. Lee. Believing that his senior position in the "old army" entitled him to the same status in the Confederacy, Johnston's protest to Jefferson Davis touched off a feud that lasted the rest of their lives. Based upon Hardee's reports, Davis had told Johnston that the Army of Tennessee was "tolerably" well clothed and contained "an effective total that exceeded in number 'that actually engaged on the Confederate side in any battle of the war.'" Johnston's assessment contrasted sharply with Hardee's. He found that the Army of Tennessee had less than 36,000 effectives, 6,000 of whom "were without arms" and as many more without shoes. In addition, there was a deficiency of blankets. "The morale of the army was gone, the spirit of the soldiers was crushed," and "men were deserting by tens and hundreds." Discipline had disappeared, and a "feeling of mistrust pervaded the whole army." To make matters worse, artillery horses were "too feeble to draw the guns in fields, or on a march," and forage was so inadequate that the animals had to be sent to the Etowah Valley where "long forage" was available. Although under orders from Davis "to commence active operations against the enemy" as quickly as possible, Johnston decided against an offensive until discipline and order were restored, additional troops had arrived, and ample supplies of "field transportation, subsistence stores, . . . and fresh artillery horses" were available.[1]

As the war neared the end of its third year, the Union's thundering guns and vast armies were pressing along Southern seacoasts and land frontiers from the Rappahannock to the Rio Grande. Federal forces controlled nearly half of the Confederacy. Believing that the South was on the verge of losing the war because of a severe shortage of troops, Hindman wrote an open letter to the Memphis *Appeal* (then being published in Atlanta) in which he outlined a series of steps to reverse the tide of retreat and defeat. Since he had just returned to command in the wake of the McLemore's Cove incident, he decided to write under a pseudonym. Significantly, he chose the name "Culloden" to indicate the parallel to another lost cause—that of his Scottish ancestors under the banner of Bonnie Prince Charlie in 1746. Hoping for a favorable reception to his suggestions, which appeared in the *Appeal* on 3 December, he planned to submit a formal proposal to the Confederate Congress.[2]

Any hope of Confederate success in the field, he asserted, rested on the principles that "the entire white male population" be placed in military service for the duration of the war and that exemptions be limited to essential employees of the Confederate and state governments. Whenever possible, only those "not able for duty in the field" should fill government positions. To encourage soldiers to remain in service, he recommended generous bounties for re-enlistment, higher pay, and increased chances for promotion. When the 1864 spring campaign began, Hindman estimated that the Confederacy would need nearly 400,000 additional troops to repel the enemy's advances. They could raise half of this number by enrolling men between the ages of eighteen and forty-five who were currently exempt from conscription or had employed substitutes.[3]

Faced with a struggle for life itself, the Confederacy could not afford to overlook a single resource. "The ghosts of legions of Southern heroes, . . . [would] haunt our pillows" if the Confederacy did not employ its "uttermost strength." As a last resort, it might even have to draw upon the services of those between sixteen and eighteen and between forty-five and sixty. To avoid turning to the "seed corn" and "grain well nigh over ripe," Hindman made a bold and daring proposal: the Confederacy should arm slaves and free those who served in its ranks.[4]

Cognizant of the furor that the proposition would provoke, he carefully rebutted anticipated objections. To those who would argue that property rights in slaves must remain inviolate, he stated that horses were also property and could be impressed by the government. Likewise, white

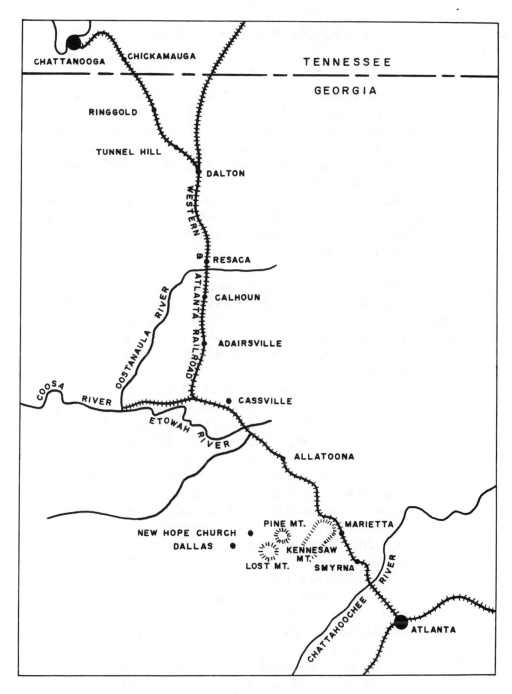

Plate 9   *Atlanta Campaign*
Pam Belote, 1991

men in the army were the property of God, themselves, and their families. Was property in slaves "any more sacred," he rhetorically asked.[5]

To those who would claim that blacks would not fight, he pointed out that similar remarks about Northerners had been proved false. Blacks, he contended, were courageous and endured "pain and hardship" as well as whites. If they were put "by the side of white Southern soldiers," allowed "a little monthly pay," and assured of "freedom for good conduct," he was confident that they would "display a determined bravery" in fighting for the Confederacy and their homes. Contrary to the unfounded fears of Southern whites, arming the slaves would not result in "servile war" nor "ruin farming."[6]

To Hindman, no sacrifice was too great in the struggle for Southern independence. Urging fellow Confederates to support his proposal, he bluntly asked, "Are we fit to be free?" Although a slaveowner himself and a pre-war, fire-eating defender of the peculiar institution, he now was ready to support emancipation for blacks who would agree to fight in the Confederate army.[7]

The idea of arming and enlisting slaves did not originate with him. As early as 17 July 1861, William S. Turner, a prosperous farmer from Hindman's hometown of Helena, had written to Secretary of War L. P. Walker and inquired if "Negro regiments . . . officered, of course by white men," could be "received" for Confederate service. According to Turner, at least one man near Helena was willing to provide his son as a captain and "arm 100 of his own" slaves. In a curt letter, Walker rejected the idea on the grounds that there was a "superabundance" of whites "tendering their services to the government." Although isolated suggestions to arm slaves continued to come from private citizens, the Confederate government and the military spurned the idea. Until Hindman's letter appeared in the *Appeal* on 3 December, no Confederate officer supported it as a means of offsetting Union numerical superiority.[8]

The week following the publication of his letter, Hindman left Madison for Atlanta to make preparation for reporting to Dalton as temporary corps commander. Arriving at camp, he found many of his fellow officers equally disturbed about the steady depletion of the Confederate ranks, and on 17 December he joined eleven other generals, including Hardee and Cleburne, in petitioning the Confederate Congress to curtail draft law exemptions. Noting that the Army of Tennessee lacked the men to repel Sherman's anticipated spring advance, they suggested ending the use of substitutes and limiting exemptions to civil officers and state and national employees. "All other white males between eighteen and fifty" who were capable of "perform[ing] any military duty" should be placed in service.[9]

Other recommendations included eliminating discharges, except for "permanent disability," and detailing blacks (both bond and free) to replace white soldiers as "cooks, laborers, teamsters, and hospital attendants." If these measures were "promptly enacted," the army could replenish its ranks, improve its organization, and restore discipline. As a result, it would become "invincible" and "conquer a peace."[10]

The generals also suggested taking measures to ease the dissatisfaction caused by short rations and depreciated currency. They proposed offering "bounties" that provided bonuses for re-enlistment, increasing military pay, and compensating soldiers for any rations not issued to them. Such reforms would enhance morale and greatly reduce desertion.[11]

Deeply concerned about the welfare of his troops, Hindman recognized that wide-spread desertion in the Army of Tennessee reflected more than a mere desire to return home or lost confidence after the Battle of Missionary Ridge. In the midst of the "bitter[ly] cold" winter, over 1,500 officers and men in his corps were without blankets or "other bedding," and hundreds of others had only a single blanket. Moreover, large numbers of his men lacked shoes, boots, and socks, and many who had them were not much better off since theirs were "so worn as to be worthless."[12]

Knowing that the army was unable to provide assistance any time soon, on 2 January he ordered his medical director to issue an open appeal for help to the "kind ladies" of north Georgia to provide cotton comforters, socks, and gloves to his soldiers. Although unable to pay for any items, Hindman promised reimbursement for shipping costs.[13]

As the Army of Tennessee camped in the cold north Georgia winds, its dwindling strength was painfully obvious to officers and enlisted men. Without substantial reinforcements, Joe Johnston could not repel Sherman's advance when the spring campaign began. More ground would be lost, and total defeat seemed likely. As they drilled their troops, Hindman and his close friend and former law partner Pat Cleburne exchanged ideas for strengthening the Confederate forces. Cleburne decided to follow up on Hindman's proposal to arm and enlist slaves. Like his friend, Cleburne was totally committed to the Confederate cause, which he viewed as a struggle for Southern rights and independence.[14]

For several days in late December, Cleburne seemed very "preoccupied" as he put his thoughts into draft form after consulting with Hindman, Hardee, and several members of his own staff. He then requested permission to read the final version at a special meeting of corps and division commanders on 2 January 1864. Entering Johnston's headquarters with Hindman at his side, Cleburne presented his ideas to his fellow officers.[15]

After three years of war in which much of the South's "best blood" had been spilled, soldiers could see no end in sight except their own exhaustion. Sinking into "a fatal apathy," they were "weary of hardships and slaughters which promise[d] no results." Desertion was a logical consequence of the wide-spread despair. If the current state of affairs continued, "total subjugation" would soon follow. Cleburne listed three factors that would lead to the Confederacy's ultimate demise: dependence on a single source of supplies, the numerical superiority of the enemy, and the preservation of slavery.[16]

Moving beyond Hindman's suggestion of offering freedom to slaves who would fight for Southern independence, he proposed guaranteeing "freedom within a reasonable time to every slave in the South" who "remain[ed] true to the Confederacy." In addition, "a large reserve of the most courageous of our slaves" must be trained for military service. With freedom for themselves and their families, black men, he predicted, would fight valiantly for the South. Great Britain and France would respond with moral "support and material aid," while Northerners, stripped of the "most powerful and honestly entertained plank in their war platform," would soon tire of a fight.[17]

The proposal generated instant controversy. Forewarned by the opposition of Major Calhoun Benham of his staff, Cleburne told his adjutant Captain Irving Buck that he was determined to make his presentation regardless of personal consequences. He was quite willing to accept that his action might result in his being passed over for promotion to lieutenant general. Should the proposal result in a court martial and cashiering, he would simply re-enlist in the ranks of the Fifteen Arkansas, his original unit. Like Captain Thomas J. Key of his staff, he was ready to "sacrifice everything for the Confederacy."[18]

At the close of the presentation, Hardee and Johnston seemed "favorably disposed," but did not publicly announce their support. As planned, Hindman declared that he favored putting blacks in the ranks and "freeing the most courageous." In contrast, Patton Anderson, William Bate, C. H. Stevens, and W. H. T. Walker exploded in anger and disbelief. Stevens bluntly stated later that he did not "want independence, if it is to be won by the help of Negroes. . . . If slavery is to be abolished, then I take no more interest in our fight." Outraged, Anderson wrote to Leonidas Polk that he considered the project "revolting to Southern sentiment, Southern pride, and Southern honor." "If this thing is once openly proposed to the Army, the total disintegration of that Army will follow in a fortnight," he predicted.[19]

Convinced that Cleburne had joined the "abolition party of the South," Walker led the opposition at the meeting and asserted that they send a copy of the paper, along with the names of anyone who supported it, to the War Department. Labeling the paper "more political than military in tenor," however, Johnston denied Walker's request and ordered the proposal kept "confidential."[20]

Walker was not mollified by Johnston's decision and sent a copy of the "incendiary" document to Jefferson Davis. He also addressed letters to each of the generals present at the meeting asking if they favored Cleburne's ideas. Hardee and several other generals ignored Walker's inquiry, but Hindman answered tersely that he did not intend to be interrogated by a junior officer, even though he had "no opinions to conceal and . . . [would] evade no responsibility." Prepared to reply to queries from his superiors on the matter, he told Johnston that he was ready to meet "the looked-for- thunderbolts . . . by a distinct avowal at the proper time and in the proper way."[21]

Believing that even mere discussion of the paper would generate "discouragement, distraction, and dissension," Davis rejected Cleburne's proposal outright. In accordance with the president's instructions, Seddon informed Johnston that the matter must remain "private" and ordered him to suppress the "memorial itself," and all "discussion and controversy respecting or growing out of it."[22]

In spite of opposition from other generals and the Confederate government, Hindman was convinced that blacks must be enrolled as soldiers, and he risked his career to advance the concept. On 16 January, he wrote a personal letter to Davis discussing the issue and other matters relating to the state of affairs in the army. According to his calculations, if "Negroes were allowed as teamsters, cooks, hospital attendants, laborers, and for the pioneer companies of divisions and engineer companies of the army, it would swell our ranks, *at once*, [by] about *20,000* men." Such a revitalization of the armies "ought to ring in the ears of [every] Congressmen" like the oratory of Cato.[23]

Reiterating arguments made in the December memorial to the Confederate Congress, Hindman discussed the need to amend the exemption law and to eliminate the use of substitutes in order to improve the fighting capability and morale of the army. Moving to the specific needs of his division, he noted that his men were "suffering" from the lack of shoes and "subsistence." Although his troops had "borne" the deficiencies "well," the shortages had resulted in "some desertions."[24]

In addition to supporting the use of blacks as soldiers and commenting on logistical problems, Hindman directly confronted the temporary nature of his assignment and the eventual arrival of Hood to replace him. Asking that his remarks not be taken as "a complaint or a demand" or be interpreted as transcending "the kind personal relationship" between them, he requested to be reassigned before Hood arrived. He suggested a transfer to non-field duty in south Georgia or Florida or appointment as "Inspector General." A change of command would avoid the awkward situation of serving under his successor. Although he "really prefer[red] duty in the field," he felt that he had "no other alternative" than reassignment to a non-field command. He would "acquiesce cheerfully," however, if Davis denied his request.[25]

While awaiting word about his transfer request, Hindman continued to work aggressively at enhancing the discipline of his soldiers and obtaining re-enlistments. Although "deeply mortified" by the conduct of his division at Missionary Ridge, he had not lost faith in its ability to "win back its lost laurels." To this end, he used the time in winter quarters to drill his men and instill in them a renewed sense of pride and purpose. His efforts paid off handsomely as discipline improved and large numbers re-enlisted. For example, Brigadier General Otho Strahl's entire brigade and the Thirteenth, Forty-seventh, and Fifty-fourth Tennessee Infantry Divisions all re-enlisted "for the [duration of] the war." In spite of the suffering caused by shortages and the ravages of winter, these soldiers had delivered "an eloquent rebuke to the despondent," according to Hindman. Their brave actions echoed throughout the "homes and firesides" of the South, bringing strength and encouragement to its leaders.[26]

Despite increased re-enlistments and efforts to improve morale, desertion was still a problem, and Hindman approved execution orders when necessary. A case in point occurred on 8 January when he signed an order for the execution of three men convicted by court martial. Although death by firing squad was "a terrible fate," Hindman considered it sometimes necessary to punish those who had "abandoned their flag" and fellow soldiers.[27]

In his capacity as temporary corps commander, he continued to drill and instruct his troops until 25 February, when Lieutenant General Hood arrived at Dalton and assumed permanent command. Although he had told Davis that he would "acquiesce cheerfully" if his transfer request were denied, Hindman decided to force the issue. Three days after Hood arrived, the Arkansan tendered his resignation, which Johnston with "much regret" forwarded to the War Department. Hindman had no intention of leaving the army, and submission of his resignation was a long-shot gamble. Because he was a twice-wounded, experienced field commander who was respected for his bravery and unflinching loyalty to the Confederate cause, it was most unlikely that his resignation would be accepted. He hoped that Davis would reject it and assign him to a new command, preferably with a promotion to lieutenant general.[28]

While waiting to hear from Richmond, he spent much of his time in Madison with Mollie and the children. The experience provided him with an opportunity to soothe his troubled mind away from the front and to look after his wife who was still recovering from her December illness. Although rumors abounded that he would be promoted and reassigned to a command in the Trans-Mississippi, such was not the case. His strong support for the unpopular idea of arming and enlisting slaves precluded both a transfer and promotion. He had spoken in favor of Cleburne's proposal and had written Davis about the matter. Moreover, Davis close personal friend, Braxton Bragg, was serving as his military adviser, and the former commanding general of the Army of Tennessee had not forgotten the incident in McLemore's Cove. Finally, continuing hostility expressed by prominent politicians dissatisfied with his administration in Arkansas, especially the use of martial law, made re-assignment in the Trans- Mississippi and promotion unlikely. On 13 March, Hindman himself gloomily predicted that although "'played out' on this side of the [Mississippi] river," he would be "ordered back" to his division rather than be promoted or reassigned.[29]

He was correct. Concurring with Secretary Seddon's recommendation, on 18 March Davis declined to accept the resignation and ordered

Hindman to return to Hood's Corps. Five days later, Seddon notified Hindman that President Davis "high[ly]" appreciated his outstanding service to the Confederacy and declined to accept his resignation. His bluff having been called and as committed as ever to Southern independence, on 3 April Hindman resumed command of his division consisting of four brigades commanded by Zachariah C. Deas, Arthur M. Manigault, William F. Tucker, and Edward C. Walthall.[30]

One month later on 4 May, the anticipated advance against Johnston began. On 12 March 1864, U. S. Grant was promoted to lieutenant general and named General in Chief of the Armies of the United States, and William T. Sherman replaced him as commander of the Military Division of the Mississippi. Consisting of the armies of the Cumberland commanded by George H. Thomas (numbering 60,773), the Tennessee under James B. McPherson (24,465), and the Ohio under John M. Schofield (13,559), Sherman's force totaled 98,757. Under orders "to move against Johnston's army, break it up, and to get into the interior as far as you can inflicting all the damage you can against" Southern "war resources," Sherman started toward Dalton. Johnston immediately telegraphed Richmond for reinforcements and withdrew to Resaca, a village of a few dozen houses clustered around a freight station along the Western and Atlantic Railroad.[31]

About midday on 13 May, Hood and Hardee arrived in Resaca to reinforce Polk, who had preceded them on the seventh. They quickly assumed defensive positions and awaited the arrival of McPherson's advancing troops. Only a few hours of daylight remained, however, when Federal soldiers, slowed by rain, finally pressed their way to within sight of the town and began skirmishing with the outposts of Polk's corps. Nightfall brought a few hours of nervous sleep as men on both sides anticipated battle the next day.[32]

Fighting began at daylight on the fourteenth, and by six o'clock intense firing reverberated all along the lines. Federal divisions under brigadier generals Jacob Cox and Henry Judah charged Hardee's position and met a "deadly fire right in their faces." Judah found himself suddenly "pinned down and helpless," but Cox, despite heavy casualties, pushed forward and after nearly two hours forced Hardee to withdraw to a new position.[33]

Other Union troops under Schofield launched a "very vigorous attack on Hindman's division . . . which was handsomely repulsed." While

Hindman was holding off Schofield, Confederate cavalry discovered that the Union's left flank was exposed. Seizing the initiative, Johnston immediately sent two of Hood's divisions under A. P. Stewart and C. L. Stevenson to press the advantage. Under the furor of their combined assault, the Federals abandoned their entrenchments, leaving behind guns, knapsacks, and haversacks.[34]

With Hindman having repulsed Schofield and Stevenson and Stewart wreaking havoc on the Union left, a Confederate victory seemed in the offing when Federal reinforcements arrived and checked the Southern advance about sunset. As darkness fell, heavy fighting ceased, although desultory firing continued through the night and made rest impossible for exhausted men on both sides.[35]

Fighting resumed at sunrise as bluecoats under Joseph Hooker launched a series of vigorous attacks on Hindman's line. The Arkansan's pride in his division was well-placed as his "first line alone" repelled Hooker's onslaught. Hood, meanwhile, ordered Stevenson and Stewart to resume their positions of the previous evening in preparation for another assault on the Union line. Just before the attack began, Johnston learned that Sherman had sent a large portion of his army across the Oostanaula River, west of Calhoun. With his mainline of communications threatened, Johnston decided that further "occupation of Resaca [was] exceedingly hazardous," immediately countermanded his attack orders to Hood, and ordered evacuation towards Calhoun. Unaware of the change, Stevenson and Stewart surged forward only to be repulsed by a storm of bullets and the deafening thunder of artillery.[36]

While the Union troops celebrated their victory, Johnston's army began its retreat after midnight on the fifteenth. Hood's corps crossed the Oostanaula above Resaca, while Hardee and Polk moved across the railroad bridge on the edge of town. They were to meet south of Calhoun, where Johnston hoped to regroup and establish a "favorable position." Dissatisfied with Calhoun, he retreated southward through Adairsville, Cassville, and finally to Allatoona.[37]

The morning following the battle, Benjamin Harrison's Eighty-sixth Indiana regiment began burying the dead and collecting abandoned weapons. The battlefield was scarred by evidence of the "great struggle" that had taken place. "Thickets of brush, even great saplings, were literally mown down by the storm of musket balls, shot, shell, grape, and canister." While total casualties were not accurately reported, Resaca had been a bloody battle. Alabama private W. A. Stephens aptly wrote, "We have had a heap of hard fiten [*sic*] . . . and have lost a heap of men and kild [*sic*] a heap of Yanks."[38]

Retreating from Resaca, Johnston deliberately placed his army squarely between Sherman and Atlanta, with the intention of giving battle when the odds seemed favorable. In anticipation of an engagement, on the twenty-fourth he deployed Hardee and Polk's corps southeast of Dallas and Hood's four miles from New Hope Church. Before Johnston had a chance to devise a plan of attack, Sherman struck. Just before 6:00 P. M. on the twenty-fifth, Major General Joseph Hooker's Twentieth Army Corps "fiercely" assaulted Stewart's Division of Hood's Corps. "Without lull or pause," fighting raged for two hours until Hooker withdrew after suffering heavy casualties. Johnston assessed

> This engagement was one of the most spectacular of the whole war. In the midst of it a severe thunderstorm came on with [a] blinding downpour of rain. Through the waning hours of the day the booming thunder kept pace with the roar of artillery and the lightning vied with flashes of the guns as the rain pelted down on men struggling in the thick underbrush.[39]

In preparation for additional fighting, during the night both sides hastily threw up breastworks, but except for intermittent skirmishing, no action took place on the following day. On the twenty-seventh, however, at approximately 5:30 P. M. Sherman's Fourth Corps under Major General Oliver Otis Howard and a division of the Fourteenth Corps under Major General John M. Palmer launched an unsuccessful assault against Cleburne's division in an engagement that cost the Union 1,500 casualties. Skirmishing in and around New Hope Church continued until 4 June, when Johnston, much to Sherman's chagrin, fell back to a new line along the Brush, Pine, and Lost mountains around Marietta near Kennesaw Mountain.[40]

Following the Confederate shift, until 22 June Johnston and Sherman devoted most of their attention to getting troops into position and strengthening their lines. Although no general engagements occurred during this period, at 11:30 A. M. on the fourteenth Polk was killed on Pine Mountain while on a reconnaissance tour with Johnston and Hardee. After the generals concluded their "examination" and reached a decision to abandon the mountain that night, "a few shots" came screaming through the air from a battery of Parrot rifles a quarter of a mile away. The third shot "passed through General Polk's chest, from left to right, killing him instantly."[41]

In keeping with the decision to abandon Pine Mountain, Johnston established a new line at Kennesaw Mountain on the nineteenth. He positioned Hardee on the left just west of the mountain, Polk's Corps (temporarily under Major General William J. Loring) in the center on the mountain, and Hood on the right posted toward Marietta. This deployment provided both a strong defensive position and an excellent location for observing Union movements.[42]

The lull in the fighting ended on the twenty-second when Hooker's Twentieth Corps and Schofield's Twenty-third pushed forward and encountered Hood's pickets at Kolb's Farm. Acting on his own initiative and without analyzing the situation carefully, Hood "suddenly sallied" and launched a fierce assault, sending wave after wave of Hindman and Stevenson's division against the Federals. Each time they attacked, the gray coats were repulsed by heavy artillery fire. After suffering almost 1,000 casualties, "either by" Hood's orders "or by the discretion of the troops," the Confederates gave up the poorly planned and mistaken assault.[43]

During the debacle, Hindman and Hood became embroiled in an argument over tactics. At one point in the fighting, Hood pointed to a hill and announced to Hindman that "when you see the enemy crown that eminence, take your division and charge them off." Believing that it made more sense to occupy the hill before the Federals, Hindman suggested that his division proceed there first. "Hood replied: 'Why is it that I can never give an order but that you have some suggestion to make?' Hindman replied: 'Because you never give me an order with any sense to it.'"[44]

Kolb's Farm marked the beginning of intense fighting that culminated in Sherman's assault on the Confederates entrenched on Kennesaw Mountain on 27 June. "It was one of the hottest . . . days of the year," private Sam Watkins of the First Tennessee recalled. As the sun rose in a cloudless sky, the "heavens seemed made of brass, and the earth of iron." The attack began about eight o'clock when blue coats poured from a wooded, swampy area directly in front of the Confederate line. Guns on both sides spewed forth volleys of shots with deadly fury. "The blinding smoke" filled eyes and mouths, and the "awful concussion" caused blood to gush from ears and noses."[45]

Soldiers blue and gray fought furiously with bayonets and fists and clubbed each other with muskets. From on top of Little Kennesaw, the Confederates hurled huge rocks on the attacking Union troops and beat them in the faces with sticks. As the Federals responded in kind, "the rocks came . . . like a perfect hail storm." By about noon, when the Yankees fell back, the scene of "carnage and death" was indescribable.[46]

With the failure of his assault, Sherman resumed his steady flanking movements and on 3 July forced Johnston to abandon Kennesaw Mountain and to retreat towards Smyrna Station. On the fourth and fifth, as the Army of Tennessee began moving toward Smyrna, Sherman "pushed a strong skirmish line down the main road" and "made strong demonstrations along Nickajack Creek and about Turner's Ferry." During the retreat, as he was riding through a wooded area on 4 July, the branch of a tree struck Hindman across his eyes and threw him from his horse. Beginning with the Atlanta *Southern Confederacy*, newspapers across the South flashed the news that " Gen. Hindman was thrown from his horse and was severely injured." As a result of being thrown from his mount, he suffered severe bruises and the blow from the branch caused a serious inflammation of the eyes that rendered him unfit for service in the field for an indefinite period of time. Unable to command his division, Hindman went to Atlanta and thence to Macon to recuperate.[47]

Chapter 10

EXILE IN
A LAND UNTRIED

The eye injury received when he was thrown from his horse on 4 July left Hindman's vision severely impaired for several months and compelled his withdrawal from the field. He hoped to be reassigned west of the Mississippi River upon full recovery, and he applied for a transfer to the Trans-Mississippi Department with this in mind on 10 July. In response, Secretary of War Seddon stated that he could not approve a transfer because no suitable opening existed in that command. Even if a vacancy had existed, intense opposition to the request from members of the Arkansas Congressional delegation and other influential opponents of his earlier policies in the Trans-Mississippi precluded approval by the War Department. When Congressman Augustus H. Garland heard rumors that "a move was being made to bring General Hindman" to Arkansas, he advised Seddon that such a plan would be "productive of evil." Even though the general was "a valuable officer," his "earlier course" was "still fresh in the minds of the people" and a transfer to Arkansas would "revive bad and evil feelings."[1]

The War Department rejected the transfer request but, at the suggestion of Jefferson Davis, offered Hindman a leave of absence until he recovered from his "physical disability." Seddon's offer was not what Hindman wanted, but he believed that it afforded a means to the desired end. Since he would be unable to resume active duty for several months, he planned to spend his leave in San Antonio, Texas, where he would be in position to receive an assignment in the Trans-Mississippi when his injury healed. Convinced that things would work out as he hoped, when his leave of absence was approved in August he began preparing for the long, arduous trip from Georgia to Texas.[2]

In need of money and unable to take all of the family slaves, Hindman offered to hire out two families to Dr. Samuel H. Stout, Medical Director of the Army of Tennessee, on the condition that they be "kindly treated." Using funds borrowed from several members of his staff, he purchased tobacco in Selma, Alabama, and had it shipped to Texas, where he hoped to sell it for specie. He anticipated receiving enough money from the sale to repay the debt and to leave a balance sufficient to cover family expenses for the duration of the war. Due to Hindman's injury, a junior officer volunteered to take charge of the transaction and to ship the tobacco in his own name from Selma to Vaiden, Mississippi, where Hindman would assume ownership.[3]

After completing last minute arrangements, in late August Hindman, accompanied by Mollie and the children, departed the Atlanta area bound for San Antonio. As they trekked across the South, sickness plagued the entire family. Near Meridian, Mississippi, illness turned to sorrow and anguish when five-year old Sallie, their second daughter, died.[4]

After burying Sallie along the road, the grief stricken family continued the journey toward Texas. At Vaiden, Hindman's staff arranged with generals Mosby M. Parsons, J. Bankhead Magruder, and other Confederates operating in southern Arkansas and northern Mississippi to furnish escorts and wagons to haul the tobacco, which had arrived by rail, across the Mississippi River and Bayou Bartholomew. The Mississippi crossing in early November at Catfish Point just below Bolivar, Mississippi, was especially treacherous since federal gunboats were patrolling the river and a Union cavalry detachment was operating in the area. The party effected the crossing with "great difficulty" and arrived in Shreveport on 14 November. While in Shreveport, Hindman learned that complaints had been made about the propriety of using military wagons to transport his luggage and tobacco. He assured Confederate authorities that he would reimburse the government for the expenses that it had incurred, even though he considered the use of the wagons a proper courtesy since the army frequently furnished transportation to civilians when the public interest was not jeopardized. Should not an officer who "had fought for the Confederacy and had been impoverished in the service" be entitled to the same kindness?[5]

After a brief stay in Shreveport, the weary Hindmans angled across Texas, reaching San Antonio in January 1865. By then the Confederacy was on the verge of collapse. Atlanta had fallen to Union forces in

Plate 10.1   *Thomas C. Hindman (1865)*
Courtesy: Walter J. Lemke Papers, Special Collections Department,
University of Arkansas Libraries

September 1864, and the following December a proud William T. Sherman presented Savannah to Abraham Lincoln as a Christmas present. Replacing the intrepid Hood, Joe Johnston could only annoy Sherman as he marched through the Carolinas. Robert E. Lee's Army of Northern Virginia was withering under U. S. Grant's war of attrition. Only the Trans-Mississippi under the command of Edmund Kirby Smith offered any hope of continued resistance to federal troops. Even in "Kirby Smithdom," the Confederacy faced overwhelming financial problems. Soldiers went for as long as fourteen months without pay, while unpaid civilian claims against the Richmond government amounted to $40,000,000. Early March 1865 brought news that General E. R. S. Canby was preparing to invade Texas with 40,000 men.[6]

In the twilight of the Confederacy, "San Antonio, in the full drift of the tide [of supplies] which flowed in from Mexico, was first an island and afterwards an oasis." Here everything that European markets could provide was found in abundance. "Cotton, magnificent even in its overthrow, had chosen this last spot as the city of its refuge and its caresses." Situated on the western edge of the Confederacy, San Antonio became a haven for Confederate refugees as the cordon of Union troops brought General Winfield Scott's "Anaconda Plan" to fruition.[7]

San Antonio was an ideal spot for Hindman to relax with his family while he waited for his eye to heal before assuming a new field command. Although he had enemies in Arkansas and elsewhere in the Confederacy, San Antonio welcomed Hindman as a hero. On 26 January, military officials and local residents honored him with a ball commemorating his "distinguished services" and to raise funds for the families of indigent soldiers. Being singled out for accolades and the opportunity to raise money for needy soldiers greatly pleased Tom and Mollie.[8]

Letters and newspapers arriving in the city carried wild rumors about Hindman's westward journey. According to C. V. Meador, editor of the Little Rock *National Democrat*, Hindman was coming to Little Rock to give himself up and to apply for a presidential pardon. Given Hindman's oratorical talent, Meador predicted that, once pardoned, he would emerge as the leader of the Unconditional Union faction in the attempt to restore loyal government to Arkansas.[9]

Another story reported that Kirby Smith had ordered Hindman's arrest at Shreveport, presumably over the tobacco, which was incorrectly thought to have been the property of the Confederate government. This rumor was quickly discredited and supplanted by the claim that Hindman was on his way to Mexico to join the Duke of Sonora (former California Senator William Gwin) in a colonization scheme. The Richmond (VA) *Dispatch* noted that Yankees had alleged that Hindman had gone to join Mexican Emperor Maximillian's army. A variation of this rumor asserted that, while en route to Mexico, Hindman had been shot and killed by Confederate stragglers near the Rio Grande who believed "he had a number of wagons and ambulances freighted with tobacco and . . . a considerable quantity of plate and coin." Regardless of destination, a common theme running through the various accounts was the allegation that Hindman had a "heavy box of specie" with him. Writing to the Memphis *Bulletin*, P. J. Kelly of Mississippi surmised that the box contained funds that the general had confiscated from Memphis banks in 1862 when he assumed command of the Trans-Mississippi District. This claim was absurd since the money Hindman had impressed was Confederate currency long since spent while he was on duty in Arkansas. Moreover, by July 1864 a lack of funds forced him to borrow money to finance the trip to San Antonio.[10]

Hindman laughed off most of the rumors but felt called upon to respond to the charge that he had abandoned the Confederacy to enter Maximillian's service. On 9 April, he indignantly denied the allegation in an open letter in various newspapers. "Southern-born, always a secessionist, a soldier since the war began . . . and never yet reduced to the thoughts of subjugation, it humiliates me that such a rumor must even be denied." He would be gratified to "lead our veteran troops against the common enemy on Mexican soil," if Yankee forces invaded Mexico after Confederate independence was secured or if an alliance existed between the Confederacy and Mexico. In the absence of these contingencies, "my services will be given and my life offered, as heartily as in 1861, in the defence of our flag and territory."[11]

Within a few weeks, service with Maximillian in Mexico did not seem as far-fetched as it had on 9 April. The same day that Hindman penned his reaffirmation of loyalty to the Confederacy, Robert E. Lee surrendered his tattered army to U. S. Grant at Appomattox Courthouse, Virginia. Faced with massive desertions and convinced that Southerners were tired of war, seventeen days later Joe Johnston surrendered the Army of Tennessee to William T. Sherman at Durham Station, North Carolina. When the news of Lee and Johnston's surrenders reached

Edmund Kirby Smith at Shreveport, he decided that further resistance was futile. Trying to avoid unconditional surrender, he urged his troops to stand by their colors and maintain discipline in the hope that the resources and numbers of the Trans-Mississippi would secure capitulation terms that a "proud people" with honor could accept.[12]

As the shock of the surrenders in the East spread, civilians and soldiers in the West knew the Confederate cause was lost. Yet in the face of the obvious and despite the impossible odds, there was a spontaneous call for continued resistance. Governors Henry Watkins Allen of Louisiana and Pendleton Murrah of Texas addressed mass meetings and urged Southerners to "rally around the battle scarred and well known flag of the Confederacy." Within his own command, Kirby Smith faced bitter opposition to surrender from generals Sterling Price and Jo Shelby.[13]

Likewise, Hindman declared that the disasters east of the Mississippi should not produce a "factious or a despondent spirit." If Kirby Smith launched a "vigorous and steady offensive campaign . . . in Arkansas and Missouri" it could offset the defeats in the East. The recent approval by the Confederate Congress of the "negro bill" providing for the arming of slaves meant that white Southerners were finally ready to maximize their available human resources. Although encouraged by the action, Hindman could not resist pointing out that he had proposed "making soldiers of negroes" eighteen months ago, but the military affairs committee in Congress had quietly suffocated the plan. With time of the essence, state legislatures must implement the bill immediately, Hindman argued. With the promise of freedom for themselves and their families, he thought that blacks would volunteer to fight for Southern independence.[14]

As the Confederacy collapsed around him, Hindman continued to rally support for the Southern cause. On 15 May, he published an impassioned address in which he proclaimed that the spirit of liberty was "not dead nor dying. . . . The resolute intention to be free is freedom itself." If the people of the South dedicated themselves "anew and utterly to the cause," their independence would be assured and "the gates of hell" could not prevail against them. Hindman appealed that the people of the Trans-Mississippi must

> appal [*sic*] our foes, startle christendom, revitalize our crushed
> co-sovereigns, and make our name immortal by kindling such volcanic
> fires as shall set the land ablaze, and showing such desperate energy

and courage as will extort victory from reluctant fate and establish our independence on imperishable foundations.[15]

The Confederate constitution and government were too conservative and complex for a state of war, he argued. "Petty measures and petty men" that had "throttled the revolution" must be replaced by a provisional government full of revolutionary fervor. The Trans-Mississippi was an "imperial dominion, worthy of a distinct nationality." With the men it already had in the field and others "white and black" who might be put into the field, Hindman contended, Southerners could prolong the struggle against the enemy until

the present generation of boys shall be of age to go to war. . . . A people so numerous and with such resources, holding a territory so extensive and difficult of access, cannot be subdued unless deficient in intelligence and manly fortitude.[16]

Eloquent rhetoric failed to stay the tide of Union victory, but Kirby Smith stalled for time and clung to frail hopes that Jefferson Davis would reach the Trans-Mississippi and rally the troops or that Emperor Maximillian of Mexico would send aid. Convinced that the war was lost, however, soldiers began deserting en masse. Others mutinied and seized public and private property in a spirit of desperate abandon. Quickly, Kirby Smith became a general without an army. With hope gone, on 26 May generals Simon B. Buckner, Sterling Price, and Joseph Brent met with E. R. S. Canby in New Orleans where they signed a surrender document similar to that between Lee and Grant. On board the federal steamer *Fort Jackson* in the Galveston harbor on 2 June, Kirby Smith finalized the agreement.[17]

Committed to Southern independence since 1851, Hindman refused to surrender. In a letter to his mother, he explained that "he had fought too long and too hard for the South to remain under the flag of her conquerors." With Kirby Smith's surrender of the Trans-Mississippi Department imminent, Hindman pondered the suggestion of his friend J. E. Barkley in Cotton Gin, Texas, that he join a "company for the purpose of colonizing in Mexico."[18]

While Hindman contemplated his post-war future, news reached San Antonio that Jefferson Davis had been captured near Irwinville, Georgia, on 10 May and imprisoned at Fort Monroe. Vice-president Alexander H. Stephens had been incarcerated at Fort Warren in the Boston harbor. A number of Confederate cabinet officers including John H. Reagan, Stephen R. Mallory, and James A. Seddon had been arrested and imprisoned. Orders had even gone out for Robert E. Lee's arrest, despite the lenient parole terms of the surrender accord with Grant. Hindman, himself, was under indictment for treason. The April term of the United States District Court for the Eastern District of Arkansas indicted him along with a host of prominent Arkansas Confederates, including governor Harris Flanagin, generals James F. Fagan and Thomas J. Churchill, and Hindman's former adjutant Robert C. Newton. From Washington President Andrew Johnson had emphatically declared that treason must be made odious and traitors must be punished. Like Edmund Kirby Smith, Hindman decided to place the Rio Grande between himself and "harm" and to join the Confederate exodus to Mexico.[19]

As the Hindmans scurried to make preparations for a move that they thought would be permanent, Confederate refugees heading toward Mexico flooded San Antonio. From the collapsed Trans-Mississippi streamed in General Jo Shelby (with part of his Iron Brigade), generals J. Bankhead Magruder, Edmund Kirby Smith, and Cadmus Wilcox. Three displaced governors—Thomas C. Reynolds of Missouri, Henry Watkins Allen of Louisiana, and Pendleton Murrah of Texas—briefly sought respite in the city of the Alamo before embarking on the long dangerous trek into Mexico.[20]

The vacuum of authority left with the demise of the Confederacy proved irresistible to bands of desperadoes, "sententious of speech and quick of pistol" who took possession of the city upon their arrival. They plundered a dozen stores and sacked and burned a commissary train before they decided to "smoke out Tom Hindman." Hammering at his door, they yelled, "It is said you have dealt in cotton, that you have gold, that you are leaving the country. We have come for the gold—that is all." With cool courage, Hindman's usually soft, musical voice turned "harsh and guttural" as he replied, "Then, since you have come for the gold, suppose you take the gold. In the absence of all law, might makes right." Although he spoke "not another word [to them] that night, . . . no man advanced to the attack upon the building."[21]

In early June the Hindmans, with their worldly possessions loaded in an ambulance and a wagon pulled by six mules, left San Antonio.

Accompanied by other exiles, including Colonel James B. Sweet, Major Charles Russell, Colonel and Mrs. James Duff, and Major John McMurtry, they crossed the Rio Grande at Laredo and pushed on through Sabinas, Vialdama, Palo Blanco, and Salinas. Writing to his friend Dr. J. C. Lee of San Antonio, Hindman described their journey as uneventful. The "rumors of Indians, robbers, etc. amount[ed] to just [that]," and the "extravagant reports" that they had been robbed and murdered were without foundation.[22]

The Hindman experience was in sharp contrast to that of many other exiles. Pursued by Union cavalry under Colonel E. J. Davis and a band of Mexican robbers, his friends Alexander W. Terrell and William P. Hardeman determined to cross the Rio Grande a few miles from Roma. According to their guide, there was a small boat on the Mexican side of the river that could ferry as many as four horses across at one time. Terrell and three companions stripped and swam the cold stream to bring the boat over for their horses and their comrades. All reached the other bank safely, and Terrell remained on the Mexican side to indicate the landing site. Hardly had the boat returned to the Texas side when two Mexicans menacingly appeared on the bluff above where he stood. "Naked and alone," Terrell realized his peril and resorted to diplomacy, exclaiming *"Muchos Americanos poco tiempo."* Fortunately, the sounds of his friends returning in the boat deterred the would-be attackers, and Terrell escaped unmolested.[23]

Jo Shelby and his cavalrymen had to fend off an attempt to steal their horses at Piedras Negras across the river from Eagle Pass. Before marching southward toward Monterey, Shelby and his men gathered with bowed heads around the "old tattered battle flag" of their division. They held the blood-stained banner, "rent and bruised," aloft for a few brief moments before lowering it "slowly and sadly" beneath the "swift waves of the Rio Grande." Hindman was not present for the ceremony, having crossed the river several days earlier, but he certainly could have echoed the sentiments of Colonel A. W. Slayback who wrote:

> A July sun, in torrid clime, gleamed on an exile band,
>> Who, in suits of gray,
>> Stood in mute array
> On the banks of the Rio Grande.
> They were dusty and faint with their long, dear ride,

And they paused when they came to the river side,
For its wavelets divide,
With their flowing tide
Their own dear land, of youth, hope, pride,
And comrades' graves who in VAIN had died,
From the stranger's home in a land untried.[24]

At Salinas, the Hindmans separated from the rest of their party and went to Cadarita where they hoped to rent a house and obtain medical aide for little Tinker, who was "suffering violently from diarrhoea." Unable to find housing in Cadarita, they pushed on to Monterey, arriving on 24 June. After a three week search, Hindman rented a three room house with a kitchen and a stable for thirty dollars a month, about one third the cost he had paid in San Antonio. Their new home was "well ventilated, new, clean, and entirely comfortable." All of their former slaves who had accompanied them from San Antonio, except Charlie, had left immediately after arrival in Mexico. Charlie was expected to leave the following day. Claiming that blacks were "worse than worthless in this country," Hindman advised his friend Dr. Lee to bring Mexican servants from San Antonio if he decided to emigrate.[25]

As his own experience indicated, bringing furniture was a mistake since it broke up along the road. Furniture, tableware, and kitchen utensils were easily obtainable in Monterey. If he had to make the trip again, Hindman informed Lee that he would bring only clothing, bedding, cooking utensils for the road, and as much "good flour and bacon" as he could haul."[26]

Hindman quickly discovered that Mexico was "a harder country to make a start in than the United States." He expected to cover immediate living expenses by selling the tobacco that he had brought from San Antonio. He hoped that by the time he ran out of tobacco he would have mastered Spanish well enough to establish a thriving law practice that would provide a suitable income for the family. Although he applied himself diligently and within three months was able to write and speak Castilian Spanish fluently," the hoped for flourishing legal practice did not materialize.[27]

Although things were not working out as planned, Hindman remained convinced that eventually he and Mollie would prosper in Mexico. Full of optimism, he and the other Confederate exiles looked past portents of

MEXICO, 1865-1867

Plate 10.2 *Mexico (1865–1867)*
Pam Belote, 1991

the dim fate that awaited them. Under the leadership of Napoleon III, the French had placed Emperor Maximillian and his wife Carlota on the Mexican throne in June 1864. In December 1861, when the Mexican government of Benito Juarez failed to meet its financial obligations, Great Britain, Spain, and France had dispatched troops to Vera Cruz to exact payment of the debts. Britain and Spain withdrew, however, upon discovering that Napoleon was using the debts as a pretext for establishing a revived French empire in North America. French troops toppled Juarez's government and forced his "Liberal" followers to move to the country's northern provinces where they continued to wage a fierce guerrilla war against the invaders.[28]

Napoleon then persuaded Austrian Archduke Maximillian to accept the Mexican throne, assuring him that the Mexican people truly desired his leadership in forging a modern state. Amid staged popular demonstrations and lavish floral canopies, Maximillian and Carlota entered Mexico City on 12 June 1864 and soon implemented plans to encourage immigration and to revitalize the country's agriculture. With time the new Emperor and Empress expected resistance from Juarez to collapse. The reality, of course, was that Juarez was the choice of the masses who saw the rulers as outsiders propped up by the hated French invaders.[29]

Naively, Maximillian feared no action on the part of the United States, despite its dire warnings that the Monroe Doctrine forbade European colonization or intrigue in the Americas. Writing to President Andrew Johnson, Maximillian explained, "The state which I am erecting is not intended to be an Empire on the European model, but a state of freedom and progress and the home of the most liberal institutions." He was eager to restore friendly relations between the United States and his adopted country.[30]

The complexity of Mexico's internal affairs was not readily apparent to the Confederate exiles pouring into Mexico in the summer of 1865. The Empire appeared to be taking hold, "the Liberal cause seemed hopeless. Nowhere did Juarez hold a sea port, an outlying mine, a foot of grain-growing territory, a ship, an arsenal, a field large enough to encamp an army." But he held on.[31]

Maximillian's approach to the Confederates was contradictory. On the one hand, he welcomed them with open arms. Worried that too warm a reception would jeopardize any hope for a friendly accord between his government and the United States, however, he held them at arm's length. He was also concerned that the exiles might prove to be a Trojan horse. To allow the Southerners to settle along Mexico's northern border, as William Gwin had proposed, might in the long run prove ruinous because, like earlier Texans, they would desire independence once they became wealthy. To forestall such a calamity, the exiles would be permitted to settle in central Mexico but not in large numbers in any single locality. To avoid arousing the ire of the United States, he decided not to accept ex-Confederates into the Imperial Army; they could keep their arms, however, and form a militia for protection against thieves.[32]

Through July and early August, Hindman remained in Monterey studying Spanish and awaiting news as to how Maximillian and his French advisers would receive the exiles. Almost daily, additional parties of Confederate refugees arrived in the city. Soon his companions included generals J. Bankhead Magruder, Jo Shelby, and Sterling Price, as well as former governors Henry Watkins Allen of Louisiana and Thomas C. Reynolds of Missouri. Though no official word had come from the Emperor, the exiles were cheered when General Pierre Jenningros, who commanded French troops in the northern provinces, invited prominent Confederate officers to a lavish banquet on 29 June.[33]

Just promoted to brigadier general following his victory over Juaristas near Buena Vista, Jenningros was a superb host. The banquet was long remembered for "its contrast, both in its plate, liquids, and cuisine to the camp-fare" to which the refugees had become accustomed. Though Jenningros spoke no English and the guests, except Magruder, knew no French, the conversation through interpreters was lively. Jenningros delighted his guests with talk of the Crimean War and all the great generals he had known. "He was profuse in his expressions of praise for the long and heroic struggle made by the South," and the Confederates were "charmed with his open bearing and hospitality."[34]

Wine flowed freely until dawn as the tales of adventure gave way to frank discussions. Shelby, having sold his artillery to Juarez's troops at Piedra Negras, was queried as to his motive in coming to Monterey. The Missourian informed Jenningros that the transaction was purely monetary since his men were penniless. Furthermore, they had declared their desire "for service under Maximillian." Shelby then bluntly asked their host about the Emperor's statesmanship. Candidly, according to John Edwards, Shelby's adjutant, the French general described his majesty as "more of a scholar than a king . . . honest, earnest, tender-hearted and sincere. . .

His soul is too pure for the deeds that must be done." Continuing, Jenningros exclaimed, "He knows nothing of diplomacy . . . Bah! his days are numbered; nor can all the power of France keep his crown upon his head, if, indeed, it can keep that head upon his shoulders." The Americans should have heeded the warning, but faced with the likelihood of arrest and imprisonment if they returned to the United States, they felt that they had no other choice than to tie their fate to Maximillian.[35]

Like Hindman, most of the Confederate refugees in Monterey found themselves strapped for cash, and several, out of necessity, sold their horses and wagons. Poverty did not dim the spirit of comraderie that existed among the Confederate generals and their staffs. Shelby divided the proceeds from the cannon sale among his staff, while Magruder divided "the money in his possession" among his men, saving three hundred dollars to fund a magnificent fourth of July banquet for about fifty Confederate officers. Toasts were "drunk to the host, to [Robert E.] Lee, to [Stonewall] Jackson, and to the Sovereignty of the States."[36]

Although they were "destitute almost of money . . . [and had] no rational hope of speedy relief," the Confederate exiles displayed little gloom or bitterness as they discussed the recent war. Some such as Colonel George Flournoy, former attorney general of Texas, felt the war had been retribution for the South's failure to protect the sanctity of the slave family. He concluded that slavery was "cursed in the sight of a just God, and our success was never possible." Dissenting, Hindman and others declared that slavery was only an incident of "the over-shadowing question of the right of states to regulate their own domestic affairs." Vigorously, Hindman voiced his long-held belief that the "triumph of federal coercion against an oppressed state had made a consolidated power, under which civil freedom would soon disappear." As such, he had no desire to return to the United States.[37]

In accordance with an imperial decree which ordered the refugees to leave Monterey and to "domicile themselves in San Luis Potosi or points further in the interior," in late July, the Hindmans departed for Saltillo, where Tom intended to practice law. Evidently they found Saltillo unsuitable as a new home, and by late August they had relocated in Montelise. Thus far they had fared poorly in Mexico. As Hindman explained to an old friend, his letters seemed to be "records of sorrow." Mail service was virtually nonexistent, and he was "almost crazed with grief and anxiety," not having heard "one word from home."[38]

The whole family had been sick with fever all summer, and his own health seemed to worsen everyday. Several close friends, including Mrs. Sophie Watkins, the wife of Judge George Watkins of Little Rock, had died. Hindman's heart ached as he described her "nervous prostration brought on by over exertion and anxiety of mind." She was, indeed, "another sacrifice offered upon War's hideous altar, as though her precious life had been breathed out upon the battlefield."[39]

Many of his closest refugee friends, such as Judge Watkins and General Thomas Churchill and his family, had already returned to the United States. Virtually alone in a strange land, Hindman longed for "words of Christian consolation" and hoped that his friend Bishop Henry C. Lay of Little Rock would "come down" to Mexico. Immense loneliness and homesickness spilled from his pen, as the general concluded that God in "His wisdom, love & mercy" had seen fit for him to bear "great sorrow and affliction *Alone* with Him."[40]

Shortly after Tom wrote Lay, the Hindmans left for Mexico City, where Tom hoped to confer with the Emperor regarding land for the refugees. After a long, rough trip that was especially trying for Mollie, who was pregnant, they arrived in the capital city on 10 September. By then, several of the exiles had departed for various colonies that were to be organized in the Cordova Valley between Vera Cruz and Mexico City.[41]

During their sojourn in the City of Mexico, the Hindmans again enjoyed the company of their old friend Henry Watkins Allen, who was now editing the *Mexican Times*, an English language newspaper aimed at the Confederate exiles. The Hotel Iturbide was a mecca for Confederates waiting to see the Emperor or to transact business in the capital. Ornate, velvet chairs held Southerners who played cards or chatted for hours about the battles in which they had been involved, their harrowing experiences south of the Rio Grande, and Mexico's miserable roads. Colonel A. W. Slayback often regaled his listeners with poems commemorating their hegira.[42]

The Empress Carlota took a keen interest in the Confederate refugees, since she too knew what it was like to be "far from home." "Lonely and secluded" in her new home, she invited the exiles to court receptions and teas. They even sensed a special warmth in her nods to them from behind the curtains of her coach as she traveled about the streets of Mexico City. Reciprocating her feelings, they proclaimed the Empress "the most perfect woman of the nineteenth century."[43]

The Hindmans found favor with both the Emperor and Empress. At the request of Maximillian, Hindman authored two treatises: "The Government of Troops in Time of War" and "The Government of Troops in Time of Peace." The money from this work helped the general support his family until his law practice yielded an income. Carlota became a close personal friend of both Tom and Mollie Hindman, and when their fifth child was born on 2 December, virtually in the shadows of Chapultepec Palace, they named her Blanche Carlotta. The Empress graciously consented to serve as godmother to her namesake.[44]

Although the Hindmans enjoyed cordial relations with Maximillian and Carlota, they did not like living in Mexico City. Disturbing to Mollie, a devout Presbyterian, was the practice of Mexican Catholics kneeling and crossing themselves as the coach of the bishop passed. She refused to cross herself.[45]

Leaving Mexico City, the Hindmans sought the camaraderie of their friends who had established several small colonies in the Cordova Valley, the "queen" of which was called Carlota. In the vicinity of Cordova lay an abundance of uncultivated land that had belonged to the Catholic Church prior to its confiscation by Juarez. Maximillian decided against returning the land to the church and, instead, opened it to colonization by the American immigrants. Men with families, such as Hindman, could purchase 640 acres at one dollar per acre from the Imperial government, payable in five annual installments. Single men were allowed 320 acres. Settlers were permitted to bring in duty-free their tools, agricultural implements, farm animals, and seeds. They were to be exempt from taxes for one year, promised religious freedom, and could form militias for their protection from robbers.[46]

Acclaimed by Jo Shelby as "the finest agricultural country in the world," Carlota was located on the railroad route between Vera Cruz and Mexico City. The climate was enthusiastically described as healthful and the well-watered soil so fertile that the slightest labor would meet with "abundant returns." Confident that the colonies would succeed, Commissioner of Immigration Matthew F. Maury exulted, "We are going to have happy times, a fine country, and a bright future."[47]

Good times did seem to lie ahead. Carlota buzzed with activity. Every vacant house in the village was taken by refugee families, and the town was "noisy with the preparation of the house builders." Men were "happy and sang at their toil," the eloquent John N. Edwards wrote.

Birds of beautiful plumage flew near and nearer to them while they plowed, and in the heat of the afternoons they reposed for comfort under orange trees that were white with bloom and golden with fruit at the same time. . . . The village had begun to take on the garments of a town.[48]

Sent by the Emperor to "examine lands and assist emigrants in getting horses, etc," Hindman had bright hopes for the future as he settled his family in Cordova, where he ultimately planned to combine the practice of law with farming. Nearby Carlota neighbors included Sterling Price, who built a bamboo house and settled into the life of a coffee planter. Jo Shelby and John McMurtry became freight contractors and established a route between Paso del Macho and Mexico City. The future looked so promising that all three men even sent for their families to join them. In neighboring Orizaba, General Hamilton Bee raised cotton and General James E. Slaughter and Captain Herbert Price established a saw mill. Close contact remained with Henry Watkins Allen, who stayed in the capital to edit the *Mexican Times*, and Thomas C. Reynolds, who was appointed superintendent of two short railroad lines. Best of all to Mollie Hindman, her younger brother, Cameron Biscoe, settled in Mexico City and took a job as a railroad engineer.[49]

Despite glowing descriptions of their ideal locations, the colonies offered a dismal existence. The beautiful city that settlers planned to build at Carlota never materialized. "Shabby clapboard rooming houses, crumbling adobe offices, and ramshackle shops arose everywhere out of the slimy, vine- infested surroundings. Criss-crossed by red dirt roads that exuded mud in April and dust in July, 'downtown' Carlota never lost its air of impermanence," was Rolle's description of the conditions there. Neighboring settlements at Omealco and Orizaba also remained "make-shift communities."[50]

Farming in a land overgrown with bamboo and banana trees proved difficult, as Hindman and many other Confederate refugees who had counted on growing coffee for export discovered. While prices for coffee were good (Sterling Price's neighbor's crop sold for $16,000), few Confederates ever realized a return on their labor because it took three years to bring a coffee crop to maturity. Although fresh fruits and vegetables grew abundantly, and cattle, hogs, and poultry did well, they failed to yield an income for the poverty-stricken Southerners.[51]

Even nature itself seemed to frown on their efforts. Heavy rain clouds hung over the Cordova Valley, turned well-plowed furrows into rivulets of mud, and made plowing impossible for days at a time. The heavy rains also contributed to infestations of mosquitoes that spread yellow fever. Diarrhea and dysentery were chronic problems. Plagued with illnesses, the Confederates often could not obtain proper medical care. As Hindman noted, good doctors were hard to find and hospitals were virtually non-existent.[52]

Like farming, Hindman's attempts to establish a successful law practice proved disappointing, even though there was a need for attorneys who could write and speak Spanish and English as fluently as he did. While W. G. Johnson, who operated the Confederate Hotel in Carlota, estimated that a lawyer with these abilities could "make a pile soon," he failed to consider that many Confederates—however much they might need legal advice—simply could not afford to pay for it. Despite energy, initiative, and hard work, Hindman never realized more than a meager income from either his law practice or farming efforts.[53]

Hoping to encourage further emigration from the United States, the exiles down played reports of robberies and armed attacks by bandits and Juaristas. As early as August 1865, however, the Confederate refugee communities were shocked by the brutal robbery and murder of General Mosby M. Parsons and four companions by the notorious Cortina band. The New York *Herald*, openly hostile to the Southern *emigres*, warned other Americans not to follow the misguided Confederates south of the Rio Grande. In reply to the *Mexican Times*, which promoted the Confederate colonies, the *Herald* commented on the absence of stories concerning the "midnight assassinations, the daily robberies, and the operations of the guerrilla bands."[54]

On the morning of 15 May 1866, the tiny colony of Omealco, about thirty miles from Cordova, was attacked by Juaristas under Luis Figueroa. His followers ransacked houses and stole personal belongings, livestock, and agricultural implements. They then marched the captured Americans to Vera Cruz, where they permitted them to leave the country or to seek shelter in Carlota.[55]

Little wonder then, in the spring of 1866 Hindman was ready to try new horizons. He formed a partnership with several other refugees to establish a colony in the Yucatan. If the Emperor approved the plan and the Empire survived, Hindman told Mollie, the profit of the American

Colony of the Yucatan would be at least half a million dollars, his share of which would enable them to "live again in comfort" and to educate their children properly. He anticipated approval, since there was "no opposition to it of any weight," and assured Mollie that he was working with "all the energy and prudence" of which he was capable to secure Maximillian's backing. As the attorney for the company, Hindman drew up the documents for its legal organization; the withdrawal of French troops from Mexico that began in the summer of 1866 and pressure from the United States on Maximillian, however, forced the abandonment of the project.[56]

Thoroughly disenchanted with Cordova and Carlota, following the collapse of the Yucatan project, Hindman moved his family to nearby Orizaba, "a pretty and pleasant" compact city of about ten thousand people. Attracted by the impressive scenery of nearby mountains and cool temperatures, Hindman found Orizaba a "healthy and sociable place, full of amusements and business." Neighbors included Judge Augustus Jones of Texas, who operated an auction and commission office; Daniel J. Warwick of Virginia, who established a tobacco factory; and George B. Clarke of Texas, who published a local newspaper.[57]

While residents described Orizaba as a "thriving place," such was not the case. The soil was not as productive as that in the Cordova area, and, since there was no dry season, days were often rainy and gloomy. In consequence of the heavy rainfall, the dirt roads were "awful to behold" with huge mudholes that "literally swallow[ed] up stage, passengers, mules, and all!" An ancient town that predated Cortez's explorations, Orizaba's old walls and deserted houses were constant reminders of the years of "revolution" and "decline." Its one-story stone houses and stores, topped with red tile roofs and iron grates on the windows, resembled "an immense collection of private jails."[58]

Luckily for the Hindmans, they left the Cordova area just in time. On 1 June, Carlota, the "queen" of the Confederate colonies was attacked by over one thousand supporters of Juarez. As houses and shops were set ablaze, residents fled to Vera Cruz in whatever conveyances they could find. Some were shot as they tried to flee, while about one hundred were captured and marched into the nearby hills. A few died from food deprivation and beatings, but most managed to escape to the shelter of French troops. Carlota, as they had known it, however, vanished. Primitive homes and shops were gone, crops destroyed, and livestock slaughtered.

"In a night the labor and toil of a long year were utterly broken up and destroyed." Hearing the news in Orizaba, Hindman initially thought of taking an armed force and going in search of the captives, in the hope of securing their release, but decided pursuit would be fruitless.[59]

By June 1866, every endeavor that Hindman had undertaken in Mexico had resulted in frustration and disappointment. Still, his spirit was not broken. By chance, he received a copy of *The War of the Rebellion*, written by his old nemesis Henry S. Foote. Outraged by what he labeled Foote's "willful misstatements, false innuendoes and malicious perversions," he decided to reply in an open letter to the New York *News*. In contrast to Foote's assertion that his initial commission as colonel and subsequent promotions were due to the "undue partiality" of Jefferson Davis, Hindman reviewed his military career and argued that his advancement was "worthily won." He defended the imposition of martial law in Arkansas as necessary to the war effort and declared that "a similar system, made universal, might have saved the Confederacy." Admittedly, as Foote had charged, he was "an exile and a wanderer in Mexico—poor, [i]solated, well nigh friendless." He was, however, "as free in spirit as when the starry cross floated above me, and Confederate shouts of victory rang in my ears. Of the Conquering North I ask no pardon, and to Southern renegades I offer no apology."[60]

In spite of his comments, within a few months Hindman was forced to abandon Mexico. The withdrawal of French troops and Maximillian's military reverses convinced Hindman and most of the Confederate exiles that the Empire was on the verge of collapse. What had been unthinkable a short time earlier—return to the United States—now seemed the only alternative. On 31 October, the Brownsville (TX) *Daily Ranchero* reported that crowds of women and children were crossing "from modern Egypt to the security of the greenback side" of the Rio Grande. "The exodus amounted to almost a perfect rush, and the boats could but ill accommodate the panic-stricken flee-ers from the wrath to come."[61]

For Hindman, the safety of Mollie and the children was paramount. He made arrangements for them to leave Orizaba for Arkansas on 6 November. He planned to follow as soon as he could get the money to pay his passage home and received assurance that authorities would not molest him. Promising to abide by the "existing order of things," he requested his friend S. H. Tucker of Little Rock to intercede directly with Governor Isaac Murphy on his behalf.[62]

Tucker apparently replied in the affirmative, and Hindman began planning for his departure. According to John Edwards, Hindman was expected to leave Mexico in late March or early April "to practice law in Memphis or merchandise in New York." Edwards explained that

> with evacuation of Mexico by the French, the rest of the foreigners think it best to leave the country . . . . The great idea in the Mexican mind is to get rid of foreigners . . . and whether it is the French this year, or the people of the United States next, it makes but little difference to them.[63]

On 11 April, the *Arkansas State Gazette* reported that Hindman had arrived in Arkansas within the past few days and was again at his home in Helena. He left Mexico in the nick of time. Following the departure of French troops, Maximillian's few Mexican supporters made little effort to sustain him. The Liberals routed the Imperial forces and captured the Emperor and his two closest lieutenants. All three were executed by a firing squad on 19 June.[64]

Chapter 11

BACK HOME IN HELENA

In the spring of 1867 when Hindman returned to Arkansas, the political situation was in a state of flux. Following the surrender of Lee and Johnston in the East, President Andrew Johnson on 29 May 1865 extended amnesty to Southerners who had not held political or civil office under the Confederacy, military personnel below the rank of colonel in the army or lieutenant in the navy, and persons whose taxable wealth in 1860 had not exceeded $20,000. Even those exempt from the general amnesty could apply to the president for a special pardon. By 2 March 1867, nearly two hundred Arkansas Confederates including generals Albert Pike, Thomas Churchill, James F. Fagan, N. B. Pearce, and Daniel H. Reynolds had received pardons, as had Confederate congressmen Augustus H. Garland, Robert W. Johnson, Grandison D. Royston, and Thomas B. Hanly (as well as secession convention president David Walker). Persons who were pardoned or covered by the general amnesty could not be prosecuted in federal courts for their wartime activities and were exempt from the provisions of the confiscation acts.[1]

At the state level, political disabilities imposed by the Arkansas legislature in May 1864 were stricken down in May 1865 when the state Supreme Court declared unconstitutional a statute requiring voters to swear that they had not voluntarily borne arms against the state of Arkansas or the United States government since 18 April 1864. With the test oath dead and federal restrictions lifted by President Johnson, no obstacle stood to prevent large numbers of former Confederates from flocking to the polls for the August 1866 biennial state election. Hoping to defeat the Unconditional Union faction that had dominated state government since the spring of 1864, Confederate loyalists billed themselves as Conservatives in an effort to build a coalition of pre-war Democrats, Whigs, and Constitutional Unionists. The Conservatives characterized themselves as champions of President Johnson's amnesty program and as opponents of black suffrage, which Republicans in Congress were promoting. Recognizing the unpopularity of the Republican Party and black suffrage in Arkansas, Unconditional Unionists avoided the Republican label and campaigned solely on the issue of "undisguised loyalty" that embraced "full, free, and perfect obedience to the Constitution and laws of the United States."[2]

Since a majority of Arkansas voters had supported Southern independence, the election results came as no surprise. Conservatives won landslide victories in most legislative races and captured the offices of auditor, treasurer, and chief justice of the state supreme court. Among ex-Confederates elected to the legislature were Hindman's close friend and former adjutant Colonel Robert C. Newton, who was elected to the lower house, and General Daniel H. Reynolds (who had served with Hindman in the Atlanta campaign), who won a seat in the state senate.[3]

Securely in control of the General Assembly, the Conservatives quickly passed bills providing for the purchase of artificial limbs for disabled Confederate soldiers and pensions for destitute and disabled Confederate soldiers and their families. Other measures prohibited assessment and collection of state taxes prior to 1865 and extended "full and free pardon and amnesty to all persons who [had] committed any crime or misdemeanor, with the exception of rape," between 6 May 1861 and 4 July 1865.[4]

Given the poor mail service in Mexico, Hindman may not have known about these developments in November 1866 as he was making plans to send Mollie and the children back to Arkansas and to return himself. As encouraging as events in Arkansas seemed to ex-Confederates, they did not mirror reality. Since early 1866, President Johnson and Congress had been at odds over reconstruction of the Southern states. Moderate and Radical Republicans favored extension of basic civil and economic rights to blacks and the imposition of political disabilities upon leading Confederates. Johnson, on the other hand, seemed determined to restore the Southern states to the Union once they had ratified the Thirteenth Amendment abolishing slavery and had repudiated secession and Confederate war debts. The president's vetoes

Plate 11   *Hindman Family Home in Helena, Arkansas*

Courtesy: Walter J. Lemke Papers, Special Collections Department, University of Arkansas Libraries

of the Civil Rights Bill of 1866 and the second Freedmen's Bureau Bill, along with his initial generous granting of special pardons intensified the conflict and ultimately led Congress to pass its own plan for reconstructing the former Confederate states.

On 2 March 1867, Congress overrode Johnson's veto of the First Reconstruction Act, which divided the former Confederate states (except Tennessee) into military districts and clothed the generals commanding them with authority to register voters to elect delegates to conventions for framing new state constitutions. Voters and delegates were to be male citizens, at least twenty-one years old, and not disfranchised for participation in the rebellion as specified by the proposed Fourteenth Amendment. Arkansas and Mississippi constituted the Fourth Military District under the command of Major General E. O. C. Ord. Assuming command on 15 April, Ord notified Governor Isaac Murphy that the legislature, which had recessed on 23 March, was not to reconvene in July as previously scheduled.[5]

Uncertainty and confusion reigned in Arkansas as Hindman returned in the spring of 1867. Prior to leaving Mexico, he had requested friends such as John C. Palmer (his former law partner), S. A. Tucker, and George C. Watkins to intercede with Governor Murphy on his behalf in the hope that the governor would endorse his application for a presidential pardon. Remembering Hindman's fiery speeches in Congress, leadership in the secession movement, and enforcement of the Confederate draft—which compelled many residents of northwest Arkansas to flee their homes to avoid Confederate service—Murphy merely forwarded Hindman's application with no endorsement, unlike the glowing letters he wrote for old friends such as David Walker.[6]

Palmer also wrote directly to President Johnson in support of Hindman's petition, stressing the general's sufferings in Mexico and his wish to return to the United States as a paroled officer. According to Palmer, Hindman desired to "pursue the quiet and peaceful avocations" of a private citizen. Echoing this theme, Mollie Hindman wrote to Johnson, noting that she and "four little helpless children" had just returned to Arkansas "without home or money." Appealing for the president's sympathy, she stated that while in Mexico they had failed "to make a support" and now desired to live in the United States with his permission. She assured him that her husband had "faithfully" promised to be a "quiet citizen and devote his life to domestic duties." Lieutenant

Colonel James H. O'Connor of the Third Illinois Cavalry, who had married Mollie's stepmother Laura Biscoe, also appealed to Johnson and emphasized Hindman's intention to become a "peaceful and loyal citizen."[7]

These endorsements and petitions fell on deaf ears as the president refused to pardon Hindman. Although Johnson did not indicate why he rejected the request, a number of factors probably accounted for his decision. Johnson and Hindman had served in Congress together, and the president was familiar with the Arkansan's impassioned speeches on the House floor in support of slavery and state rights. In addition to his prewar activities, Hindman's plan to capture Johnson while he was attempting to rally Tennessee Unionists in June 1861, his use of partisan rangers in Arkansas and Missouri, and his refusal to surrender and subsequent exile in Mexico undoubtedly worked against him. Since wide-spread arrests of ex-Confederates had ceased in the fall of 1865, although unpardoned, Hindman decided to return to Arkansas. Prior to Tom's arrival in Helena, Mollie and the children stayed with her stepmother and Colonel O'Connor until she was able to regain possession of the family's home, which had been used as a headquarters for various Union commanders since the summer of 1862. Upon his return, Hindman resumed his law practice in partnership with John C. Palmer and M. T. Sanders (later) and turned his attention to trying to put his family on a sound financial footing.

The law practice claimed much of his attention, but even so Hindman found time to serve as the featured orator at a local charitable tournament and to involve himself in Helena's perennial problem—the almost annual flooding of the Mississippi River. In a letter to the Helena *Clarion*, he proposed to solve the problem by construction of a drainage system that would channel overflow from the Mississippi through several outlets to the seacoast.[8]

As always, he found politics irresistible. He had scarcely unpacked his bags when an editorial in the *Arkansas State Gazette* about a recent Union meeting in Little Rock regarding the Reconstruction Acts drew his attention. According to the *Gazette*, the platform adopted at the rally indicated that the Republican Party planned to deprive "the people of Arkansas" of all rights except those that Thaddeus Stevens, Benjamin Butler, "and that ilk" considered they were entitled to receive. If Republicans had their way, former Confederates would have only one right—to be hanged as "traitors." As the work of registering voters for the election of delegates to the coming constitutional convention proceeded, the passions of ex-Confederates were inflamed when they read that persons who had served in the Confederate states in any capacity—from governor down to county coroner and mayor—would be disfranchised. Voting and office-holding would also be denied to men who as members of Congress, state legislators, judges, or executive officials of any state had taken an oath to support the Constitution of the United States and had subsequently violated it by engaging in the rebellion.[9]

Should former Confederates who were eligible register and vote, or should they abstain from any political activity that could be interpreted as countenancing the Reconstruction Acts? Never one to remain on the sidelines, Hindman eagerly plunged into the fray. On 22 May, he joined a large crowd of citizens, "without distinction of party or color," who assembled at the Phillips County Courthouse. So rarely did meetings bring together such "extremes of color and opinion" that every face manifested "intense . . . curiosity." Hindman was appointed to the resolutions committee along with Major Henry Sweeney, a Freedmen's Bureau agent, and three other Phillips County residents.[10]

The members of the committee recommended that the people of Phillips County accept the Reconstruction Acts without hesitation and that they carry out the requirements in good faith as "a full and final settlement of the issues growing out of the late war." Efforts to impose additional penalties or conditions or "to keep up sectional bitterness, or to create a war of races" should be opposed. The resolutions further pledged to secure blacks "every right that belongs to them" under the acts. According to the committee, these resolutions constituted a platform upon which all Arkansans, without distinction of party or race, could unite. Following the presentation of the resolutions, Hindman made a few "forcible and effective" remarks, as did Dr. T. M. Jacks (a pre-war Unionist) and William H. Grey, a black Helena minister well-known for his speaking ability and advocacy of political rights for ex-slaves. Consideration of the resolutions was postponed until the following week after several prominent Republicans pressed for an endorsement of confiscation.[11]

Between three and four thousand black residents attended the follow-up rally on 28 May, which according to the Little Rock *Daily Republican* attracted "a sprinkling of ex rebels" and "a few true and tried Union men." Hindman addressed the gathering, advising ex-Confederates, not disfranchised as he was, to register and "enter sincerely and honestly into the work of reconstructing the state" under the Reconstruction laws. He stressed that the acts were the best that could be obtained and declared himself willing to support the Congressional plan "fairly, squarely, and honestly." He announced opposition to confiscation and urged his listeners to devote their energies to building up and repairing the losses of the country "rather than engaging in a political crusade."[12]

At the close of the meeting, substitute resolutions were adopted pledging support for reconstruction under the "military bill" and public education for the "rising generation, of all colors." Missing, however, were affirmations to oppose the imposition of disabilities for former Confederates. Hindman considered the omission a bad omen that would inflame sectional tensions and promote racial discord in the state.[13]

Hindman's speeches at the Helena mass meetings certainly placed him back in the thick of Arkansas politics and elicited immediate responses from both supporters and detractors. Under the pseudonym of "Loyalist," an anonymous letter writer to the *Daily Republican* praised the general's stance on the Reconstruction Acts as manifesting "good sense and cultivated taste." Others interpreted his remarks as a condemnation of the Republican Party, while still others saw them as an indication that Hindman had affiliated with the Radical Republicans.[14]

Seeking to clarify his position, Hindman wrote several open letters in which he emphatically denied the rumor that he had become a "radical." Regarding the policies of the Republican Party as an anathema, he had merely spoken at non-partisan meetings where he had urged whites to register and vote and blacks "to shun all radical men and doctrines." "Perhaps, as 'thrift follows fawning,'" he continued, if he were willing to barter "honor and consistency for a place in the radical ranks," the disabilities that were "illegally enforced" against him might be removed and the "avenue to political distinction reopened." But he could not "pay such a price for such rewards." Men who thought otherwise did not know his "true character."[15]

He exhorted "every friend of the south" who was eligible to register and vote for "good and true men" [those who opposed "radical" Republicanism] as delegates to the constitutional convention and to acquiesce in the military bills of Congress since the power behind them was greater than they could resist. The registration certificates might possibly be the basis for voting for years to come. "Holding them, we may refuse to vote when we like; but if we do not hold them, we will be powerless to help our best friends, although our worst enemies may thereby be elected."[16]

Hindman recommended that Conservatives throughout the state organize for the "purpose of resisting radicalism." "If boldly met," he declared, "paltry tricksters" would be defeated and "the negro, notwithstanding his ignorance and credulity, may yet be saved from following radical leaders into a hopeless crusade." Had the non-partisan approach that he and the resolutions committee advocated been followed, he contended that controversy could have been avoided. Radicals in Phillips County, however, had thrown off their mask and had set themselves up as "the sole representatives of the government, holding out confiscation as a bribe to the negro and as scourge to the southern white man." If Conservatives organized, they could elect a decisive majority of the convention delegates and shape the future policy of Arkansas. "The exotic weed of radicalism will die out in our midst, its white teachers and preachers will disappear, and its deluded colored converts will be glad to labor quietly with and for their old masters, who are their best friends."[17]

Even though he was playing a major role in the canvass, Hindman stated that he had no plans to seek political office. He had "no animosities to gratify" and cherished no ambition except to preserve his own self-respect and the good will of his neighbors as he labored to support his family and "settle honest debts contracted before the war." He had no plans to reenter politics, he assured Arkansans. "If the law did not in effect debar me, I would voluntarily exclude myself from politics for the attainment of these objects, and therefore hope that this may be the end of my association with political matters."[18]

While Hindman advocated registering and voting, most Conservatives favored a decidedly different approach to the convention issue. They agreed with Albert Pike that Southern whites would only worsen their situation by "returning into the Union on grossly unequal terms, and with such shameful compromises of principle. . . . If our States can only return upon such terms as these . . . it will be infinitely better for them to remain out of the Union altogether."[19]

Thomas Churchill, Robert C. Newton, James F. Fagan, and John M. Harrell, friends and former military colleagues, headed a list of prominent Arkansans who issued an address "To the People of Arkansas" condemning restoration under the Reconstruction Acts as an "impossibility." Reconstruction under any terms which did not give "our people equal rights with others" would be a "cruel mockery, and would result . . . in the certain degradation, prostration, and complete ruin of our State." They preferred military rule to what would follow from restoration under the Congressional plan.[20]

In the midst of the heated debate over which approach Conservatives should follow, registration proceeded apace. Either because they were disfranchised or because they opposed restoration under the Congressional plan, many Conservatives did not register. Of those who did, many voted against the constitutional convention in hopes that it would be defeated. The latter strategy failed, and General Ord announced on 5 December that a majority of registered voters had voted for the convention and designated 7 January 1868 as the date for convention delegates to assemble in Little Rock.[21]

The convention met as scheduled and drafted a new constitution that would confer the elective franchise on all male citizens or those who had declared their intention to become citizens who had reached the age of twenty-one and had resided in Arkansas for six months preceding the next election. It would disfranchise those who during the war had taken a oath of allegiance to the United States and had violated it and those disqualified by the proposed Fourteenth Amendment or the Reconstruction Acts. Persons in these categories who openly advocated or voted for Congressional reconstruction, however, could register. In order to register or to vote, persons were required to swear on penalty of perjury that they were not disfranchised by the new constitution, would accept the civil and political equality of all men, and would not attempt to deprive anyone on account of "race, color or previous condition, of any political or civil right . . . enjoyed by any other class of men."[22]

Outraged by the disfranchising clauses and the requirement that white voters must accept political and civil equality of blacks, Conservatives immediately began formulating strategy to defeat the proposed constitution. The newly formed Democratic State Central Committee called upon all citizens, irrespective of previous party affiliation, who were opposed to black suffrage to unite behind the Democratic party. Committee members openly proclaimed that the majority of registered voters were determined to maintain a "white man's government" in Arkansas and recommended that each county hold a convention to decide the best mode of opposing the constitution, whether by voting full strength against it or by staying away from the polls to prevent the required percentage of votes from being cast. Although Hindman was not on the committee, his close friends Robert C. Newton and John M. Harrell were. They urged him to canvass his old Congressional district for the cause. Fearing the power of his oratory, John G. Price, editor of the Little Rock *Daily Republican*, castigated Hindman's wartime recruiting activities in Arkansas and claimed that his canvass would not "set well with the people to-day."[23]

Republicans launched a strong campaign to secure ratification of the proposed constitution, which they defended as the best possible for the freedmen and poor whites. They pointed with pride to the system of common schools that the constitution established. Once reconstruction was an accomplished fact, they predicted that outside capital would pour into Arkansas and peace and prosperity would follow. They nominated a full slate of candidates for state and local offices, slotting for governor General Powell Clayton, who had commanded Kansas troops stationed near Pine Bluff during the war.[24]

The vote on ratification of the constitution and simultaneous balloting to select state and local officials began on 13 March and continued through the end of the month. To no one's surprise during and after the canvass, both Conservatives and Republicans accused each other of voting irregularities. According to Republicans, opponents of the constitution had attempted to intimidate blacks by threatening to harm them physically or deny them employment if they went to the polls. Conservatives charged that "friends of the constitution resorted to dressing negro women in men's clothes and voting them at the election, besides moving them around from precinct to precinct in battalions, and voting them over and over again."[25]

As a result of the Conservative boycott and possible irregularities by Republican election officials when counting ballots, the Constitution was narrowly ratified by a vote of 27,913 to 26,597. The *Daily Republican* rejoiced, proclaiming that the "rule of the Johnsons, the Watkins, the Hindmans . . . and the men of that class . . . has at last terminated."[26]

Hindman's efforts to defeat the constitution were not only in vain, but they brought him into direct conflict with powerful Republicans. On the night of 23 March, in Helena, he "berated, confounded, and utterly annihilated" Republican gubernatorial candidate Powell Clayton in debate over ratification. Even before the confrontation with Clayton, Hindman's re-emergence in politics after his return to Arkansas had given Republicans just cause for fear. His powerful oratorical skills and prewar career made him a force to be reckoned with in the state. Apparently in a move to silence him, Republicans dredged up the treason indictment filed against Hindman on 23 May 1865 and had him arrested on 20 March. The arrest did not remove Hindman from the canvass since Deputy United States Marshall Q. K. Underwood permitted him to remain "at liberty on his personal recognizance" until his trial in the United States Circuit Court at Little Rock on the second Monday in April.[27]

Speculating on the reason for the arrest, William Woodruff of the *Gazette* commented that since he had heard no explanation of the cause, he could only presume it was made for the "benefit of whom it may concern." The Memphis *Avalanche* was more explicit: "General Hindman was guilty of the great crime of raising his eloquent voice against the ratification of the recent constitution . . . and hustled off to prison on the most frivolous pretexts hatched up by the tyrants [i. e. leading Arkansas Republicans], who are determined to stifle liberty, and, if possible consign to a dungeon every noble spirit who dares to war upon corruption and despotism."[28]

Hindman appeared in court as scheduled, but his case was postponed until the next term. Bond was set at five thousand dollars, which Augustus H. Garland, U. M. Rose, E. H. English, and a host of other prominent Arkansans immediately posted. Not surprisingly, his attorneys constituted an elite of former Confederates including Garland, George C. Watkins, and the firm of Robert C. Newton and George A. Gallagher.[29]

With treason proceedings pending against him, Hindman found himself excluded from Andrew Johnson's third amnesty proclamation (4 July 1868) that granted "full pardon and amnesty" to all former Confederates except "such person or persons as may be under presentment or indictment in any court of the United States . . . upon a charge of treason or other felony." Thus, Hindman was placed in the category with Jefferson Davis and a handful of other ex-Confederates who remained unpardoned and excluded from presidential amnesty.[30]

Undaunted by his impending trial, Hindman emerged as the leader of the Young Democracy, which advocated taking the oath required under the new constitution and voting in the upcoming presidential and congressional elections. As such, he devised a plan for organizing the various townships and counties under the direction of the Democratic State Central Committee. By this means, he explained, the Democratic strength could be utilized, its volume enlarged, and "its impetus quickened so as to be irresistible." United on a common basis, the people would surge forward "like a grand army, with fixed bayonets, to rescue Liberty from her ravishers."[31]

To those who said that the Democrats should let the Republicans win by default, Hindman rhetorically asked if it were not

> a more monstrous crime to continue Radicals in power by refusing the oath, than to eject them and instal [*sic*] democrats by taking it. . . . Shipwrecked—an angry sea threatening to devour us—pirates bearing down upon us to torture and kill—may we not righteously take any oath that saves from such perils? May we not gratefully grasp any hand—even that of the democratic negro—that snatches us from the fury of the elements and the more fearful fury of cruel men! . . . Ceasing to differ, let us win the fight, though the heavens fall! . . . Forward! Charge! With a yell at the double quick! Organize—register—work—vote! He that dallies is a dastard, and he who doubts is damned.[32]

In resolutions he presented at a rally of the Democracy of the First Congressional District, Hindman told blacks that the Democrats he represented wanted their relationship to be based upon "kindly feelings, . . . and mutual confidence, assistance, and fair dealing." He urged blacks to cooperate with the Democrats to "secure peace and prosperity to both races, rather than follow the lead of strangers who array whites and blacks against each other . . . solely to get offices out of our division, and to prosper out of our losses and suffering."[33]

Republicans, aware of the persuasiveness of Hindman's oratory and his skill as a political organizer, tried to offset his efforts by ridiculing his arguments and recalling his tenure as commander of the Trans-Mississippi District during the war. Who was Hindman to propose a plan for rescuing liberty from the hands of ravishers, queried John G. Price of the *Daily Republican*.

> He who not only violated, but murdered and slaughtered that weeping, helpless, and defenceless [*sic*] virgin, and cut her bleeding, quivering form into ten thousand pieces that he might hang up a bloody fragment at the door post of every cottage and cabin in the land, as a reminder of his fearful and omnipotent power!

Price declared that the recollection of Hindman's "reign of terror" was "too fresh in the minds of the people of Arkansas, for them to listen with any degree of patience to his canting appeals in behalf of Liberty."[34]

The *Republican's* attempts to belittle and discredit Hindman failed to diminish the crowds who flocked to his speeches in Phillips and adjacent counties. In every quarter, throngs of black and white listeners fell under the spell of Hindman's soft, musical voice as he appealed for cooperation in restoring peace and prosperity to Arkansas. For example, at Trenton, southwest of Helena, his powerful stump speaking one night convinced forty-eight black Republicans to join the Democratic Party and to pledge support for Horatio Seymour's presidential candidacy. Events such as these prompted the Helena *Clarion* to proclaim precipitously that the Democracy would "grease the head of radicalism with its own oil and swallow it."[35]

If Hindman had lived, he might have been successful in forging a biracial Democratic coalition strong enough to combat the initial strength of the Republican party among the freedmen. One thing is certain. In the short period since his return from Mexico, Tom Hindman had again emerged as the pre-eminent figure in Arkansas Democratic politics. As was expected, he championed political rights for ex-Confederates and opposed property confiscation. With respect to the freedmen, he was much more moderate than many of his contemporaries. Paternalistic in his personal and political associations with blacks, Hindman was ready to cooperate with them in battling what he considered the malevolence of the Republicans. If the two races worked together for their mutual interests, Hindman truly believed that the South could be rebuilt and that peace and prosperity would result.

Chapter 12

THE WARRIOR'S
FIRE IS EXTINGUISHED:
THE MURDER
OF GENERAL HINDMAN

Tom Hindman did not live to see the results of Reconstruction in Arkansas. At approximately nine thirty on the night of 27 September 1868, as he sat quietly relaxing with his family in the sitting room of his Helena home, he was shot by an unknown assassin. The warm moonlit night had prompted him to open a window to let in fresh air as he read the newspaper and smoked his pipe. The children were playing happily near the fireplace where their father sat in a rocking chair, his feet propped in another chair. Mollie, who was resting across the room, glanced over at her husband as one of the boys, probably Tinker, crawled up in the general's lap for a few minutes before scampering off to play.[1]

Without warning, less than eight feet away, musket shots rang out from a window. Shot and ball struck Hindman, passing through his neck and jaw, severing his windpipe and causing massive hemorrhaging and internal bleeding. He would have been killed instantly had not his left hand, which was holding the pipe, deflected part of the load. Aroused by the sound of gunfire piercing the night air, neighbors quickly gathered in the front yard to find out what had happened. The answer was not long in coming. Within minutes, Mollie helped her wounded husband to the porch for fresh air.[2]

Realizing that he had been fatally wounded, in the brief time left to him Hindman spoke with friends and family and attempted to make arrangements to help Mollie and the children adjust to their new and shocking circumstances. Although becoming weaker and weaker, "with perfect composure," he urged his listeners to "unite their courage and determination to bring peace to the people." Indicating that he believed his shooting may have been politically motivated, Hindman alluded to the recent debates with Powell Clayton and said, "I do not know who killed me; but I can say, whoever it was, I forgive him."[3]

Spotting Colonel James H. O'Connor, the husband of Mollie's stepmother, Hindman apologized for harsh words that had previously passed between them about Reconstruction and the war and requested forgiveness. O'Connor replied, "I freely forgive you, general." Hindman then said, "I ask you then to take care of my family and be a protector to my wife and dear little ones." When O'Connor agreed, Hindman uttered the statement "I forgive everybody, and hope they will forgive me." Too weak to continue, he was carried to a lounge just inside the hallway. After kissing Mollie and the children, he sank into the lounge, where he remained until he died just before sunrise the next morning.[4]

The assassination shocked and outraged friends and political admirers across Arkansas. With "unmingled sorrow and regret," William Woodruff of the *Gazette* announced the death of the "able and distinguished man" whose "short but splendid career" as an orator, politician, and soldier had unalterably affected the state.

> No man ever listened to Tom Hindman even of those who differed with him in politics to the utmost extreme, who did not acknowledge to himself that in natural gifts he was the ablest and best beloved of the children of the state. . . . As a military man he has always been underrated. He was an able general, one of the best the Confederacy ever had. . . . Arkansas loved him living and mourns him dead.

Although most outpourings of grief and adulation came from Conservatives, a few Republicans openly praised his career and condemned his murder. An obituary in the *White River Journal* eulogized him as "a man of great energy and marked ability."[5]

From the pen of an unknown poet came this tribute:

> Thy heart was fearless as thy mind was clear,
> Nor did'st thou make a willing compromise
> With that which seemed a wrong, however near
> The peril lay; and in thy earnest eyes

To alter was to fail; no doubt might sear
Thy vision, and thy mournful fate implies
That in the assassin's craven arm
Alone thine enemies found power to do thee harm.

And who that listened ever can forget
Thy noble and impassioned eloquence,
The costly gems of wisdom fitly set
In gorgeous languages, or the opulence
Of thy proud scorn, which yielded not, nor yet
Allowed a truce to any vain pretense—
An ever ready weapon, keen and bright,
A terror for the wrong, a defense for the right.

Besides the gifts that caught the eyes of men
With wide glare, there was something better still;
A gentleness beyond the rabble's den;
A deep, unwanting sympathy did fill
Thy spirit, and with speech or ready pen
Thou did'st its quiet lessons oft instill;
Not for the din of war was thy desire,
Though never all unconscious of the warrior's fire.[6]

Initial reports from Helena indicated that no apparent motive existed for the shooting and that the only clue at the murder scene was two sets of footprints near the window where the fatal shots were fired. Even though evidence was scant, there was no absence of speculation about why the general had been killed. Most Conservatives believed that he had been assassinated by a "political enemy." Woodruff of the *Gazette* bluntly asserted that "strong suspicion exists" that the "jaws" of the Republican party were "red with the blood of the murdered Hindman," while the Memphis *Appeal* angrily denounced the deed as the "work of the hellish loyal leagues." Hindman's close friend and law partner M. T. Sanders, who edited the Helena *Clarion*, stated that the general's heavy blows against radicalism had made him the Republican Party's "most formidable opponent."[7]

James S. Dunham of the Van Buren *Press* likewise placed the blame squarely upon the shoulders of the Republicans. According to him, "Radicals have, in many instances, resorted to the knife [and] the musket

. . . to rid themselves of a formidable opponent." Hindman "had become
a 'strong man' against the Radical party" in Arkansas. He "had gained
the confidence of the negroes and they would go to hear him speak."
Because "none desired his death but Radicals," Republicans must have
been behind the murder. Although he stopped short of actually accusing
Republican Reverend Joseph Brooks of Marianna of planning the crime,
he came very close to pointing the finger of guilt at him. Hindman had
recently "annihilated" Brooks in a debate, and curiously, on the day that
General Hindman was killed, Brooks was conveniently in Fort Smith for
a political rally. As a resident of Phillips County, Brooks could not hope
to "advance his own [political] interests" by attending a rally and
barbeque in western Arkansas. Why then, asked Dunham, had the "bitter
and vindictive" and "cowardly" Brooks made "the long and tedious trip"
to Fort Smith? Having all but named Brooks as the person behind the
crime, Dunham stated "we do not say the creature (Brooks) had any
knowledge of this murder, but only forward the facts in the case."[8]

Republicans vehemently denied that the assassination had been
politically motivated. Party members in Phillips County held a mass
meeting at Helena and declared that Hindman's death was not attributable
to his "course in the present canvass" and disputed claims that
Republicans had "ever counselled or countenanced personal violence or
assassination." In addition, a correspondent to the *Southern Shield* who
claimed to be a "Democrat" asserted that Helena members of his party
did not believe that Republicans were behind the murder.[9]

Conservatives were not mollified by these protestations and continued
to hold Republicans responsible for Hindman's death, especially since
Governor Powell Clayton had not immediately offered a reward for
information leading to the arrest of the general's murderer. A
gubernatorial reward offer in cases involving prominent citizens was
customary, and Clayton's inaction fueled arguments that Republicans had
planned and carried out the assassination. Claiming that he "did not wish
to offer inducements for the conviction of innocent people" and was
waiting for "the results of the judicial investigation," Clayton delayed
offering a reward until 15 October, more than two weeks after the
shooting. The belated action and Clayton's explanation did not satisfy
Conservatives. The editor of the Memphis *Avalanche* believed that the
governor's timing was part of an overall Republican plot. According to
him, detectives had uncovered information that proved beyond a doubt

that "leading radicals" in Little Rock had planned the murder. The assassin was a white man who received eight hundred dollars for killing Hindman. He was "stealthily" taken to Helena and "furnished all needed information" about Hindman, including "the most practical method of committing the murder." After killing the general, he was ushered to Mexico via Texas. It was only after he was safely out of the country that Clayton offered a reward for the apprehension of the general's assassin.[10]

Hoping to blunt accusations that leading members of their party were behind the killing, Republicans put forth their own explanations. Some suggested that the perpetrator was a soldier who had served under Hindman during the war who retaliated against his former commander's mistreatment or that it might have been someone avenging wrongs committed during the general's tenure in the Trans-Mississippi District.[11]

In seeking to shift attention elsewhere, some Republicans assigned a purely family motive to the killing. Repeating a totally unbelievable rumor, a few Arkansas Republicans alleged that during a visit to St. Louis one of Hindman's sons had accused Mollie's brother Cameron N. Biscoe. According to this account, Tom was going to file for a divorce on 28 September and Cameron Biscoe killed him to get even. This argument probably injured rather than helped Republican efforts to disavow complicity in the murder. Hindman's elder son Biscoe was only eight years old and was in Helena with his mother at the time he supposedly accused Cameron of murdering his father. Already discredited, the story seemed even more preposterous two years later when Cameron and his wife named a son James Hindman Biscoe in honor of Mollie's dead husband.[12]

Investigation into the murder continued well into the 1870s, and although numerous accounts tried to tie specific individuals to the crime, no conclusive evidence ever linked anyone to the murder. On 15 March 1869, Charles Williams, a white prisoner in the Phillips County jail, told authorities that he had overheard two black inmates, Sip Cameron and Heyward Grant, discussing the crime. On the following day, Grant told a justice of the peace that the murder was part of a larger plot to avenge the lynching of Lee Morrison, a black resident of Helena who had been hanged on the morning of 27 September 1868. According to Grant, blacks planned to retaliate by burning several Helena homes and by killing a number of prominent whites, including Hindman. Although the mass violence did not occur, Grant claimed that Sip Cameron and

Charles Porter carried out part of the plot by murdering Hindman. Although nine blacks, including Porter, were indicted, they were freed when subsequent evidence indicated that Williams and Grant had fabricated the story in hopes of being released from jail.[13]

Cognizant that Conservatives were still accusing them of masterminding the murder, Republicans continued to offer nonpolitical explanations for the crime. In the summer of 1870, John G. Price of the *Daily Republican* informed readers that he had received a letter from a man who contended that Hindman was killed by "the husband of the lady whose reputation and happiness he had destroyed." Although Price claimed to have affidavits to support his allegation, he did not make them public. Reflecting the belief of most Conservatives, the Helena *Monitor* labeled Price's assertion a "base and slanderous" falsehood designed to shift suspicion from the Republican loyal league and to "tarnish the fair reputation of the honored dead."[14]

The idea of romantic roots resurfaced in March of 1873 when Mollie Hindman received a mysterious letter with a return address of the "Dominion of Satan" from a man who later identified himself as Frank Burdett. He told her that if she wished to learn who killed her husband and why, she should place a coded message in the Memphis *Appeal*. She did so, and he responded with another letter naming John P. Moore of Helena as the instigator of the crime. In the same letter, he asked Mollie to meet him in Memphis if she wished further details which would enable her to have the perpetrators prosecuted and convicted.[15]

In an ensuing meeting at the Peabody Hotel in Memphis, Burdett asserted that Moore and Dr. Daniel A. Linthicum, also of Helena, had hired the assassin and described in detail the scene in the Hindman home just before the shooting. Burdett claimed to have witnessed the assassin loading a double- barrel shotgun in a blacksmith shop near the Hindman home and stated that the killer escaped on a horse that Linthicum had held for him in a nearby vacant lot. Burdett refused to give the name of the man who actually fired the shots but promised to do so later.[16]

Burdett was subsequently arrested for complicity in the murder, whereupon he claimed that his real name was Louis (Lewis) D. Vaughn and that he had no involvement in the crime. He claimed that he had been hired to write the letters to the general's widow by two men, Frank Burdett and Clem Denning. Following his arrest, Vaughn was taken to Mollie's room, where she identified him as the man she had met earlier

Plate 12   *Mary Biscoe Hindman*
Courtesy: Walter J. Lemke Papers, Special Collections Department,
University of Arkansas Libraries

and declared that his description of the murder scene and the events surrounding the crime was so accurate that he must have been present. In fact, at one time she was convinced that he was the killer. Wringing her hands, she exclaimed,

> Would to God that you, villain, had murdered me and my children, and spared him! I have never since known a moment's peace. I am friendless, weak, broken in health and spirit. Often have I gone half-starved to bed, that my children might have a crust of bread. You wretch, brought all these woes upon me.[17]

Based on his detailed knowledge of the crime, Vaughn was arraigned in Memphis and a hearing was held in circuit court. Dressed in "deep mourning" clothes, Mollie, though visibly affected by the recent events, testified in a clear, distinct voice concerning the letters and her meetings with the accused. Protesting his innocence, Vaughn brought in witnesses who supported his claim that he had been working near Clarksville, Tennessee about two hundred miles from Helena at the time of the murder. The vividness of his description of the crime scene, however, convinced the judge that there was sufficient evidence to have him bound over for trial and extradited to Arkansas.[18]

In spite of his elaborate knowledge about the murder scene, Vaughn's complicity in the crime was doubtful. Although the risk of being prosecuted and convicted was great, he apparently made up the entire story to get even with Linthicum for exposing him as a bigamist when he began courting a woman in Helena. The incident had occurred two years earlier, and Vaughn decided to retaliate by attempting to tie Linthicum to the Hindman murder. After reviewing a letter from Linthicum and comparing known facts to Vaughn's testimony, the editors of the Memphis *Appeal* were convinced discrepancies in Vaughn's confession clearly demonstrated that he was not involved in the killing. Rather than being a murderer, he was "a consummate scoundrel [and] unmitigated liar" who should be sent to the penitentiary for all the "unnecessary pain and trouble" he had caused Mrs. Hindman and Dr. Linthicum.[19]

The assessment of the *Appeal* was apparently shared by most Arkansans. When Vaughn was tried in Helena during September 1873, the case ended in a mistrial when jurors determined that he had made a mistake in "the person he said he killed or was concerned in the killing of Gen. Hindman." After the trial, he remained in custody until 5 February 1874, when he was released and the case closed. Reflecting on the case, the editor of the Helena *World* concurred with the jury's decision and concluded that the "whole yarn was spun from his notorious propensity for lying and was . . . nothing but a myth from the beginning."[20]

Speculation about the cause of Hindman's murder did not end with Vaughn's acquittal. In July 1876, Heyward Grant, who had claimed that the murder was part of a broader plot to avenge the lynching of a Helena black, was hanged in Rome, Georgia for arson. Shortly before his execution, he claimed to have murdered six men, including Hindman, since 1865. There were several discrepancies in his story. Although he stated that the lynching victim was his cousin, he referred to him as Morris instead of Morrison and incorrectly claimed that Hindman was present during the hanging. In addition, he claimed that the murder weapon that supposedly belonged to his uncle was an Enfield rifle. The fatal shots fired at Hindman came from a musket. Grant's remarks constituted the last public comments relating to the assassination. No further leads in the case developed, and it was never re- opened.[21]

Regardless of who killed the general and why, members of the Hindman family were convinced that Republicans were responsible for his murder. Their love and grief continued unabated and are reflected in the words on the marble shaft that marks Hindman's grave. The inscription on one side reads " We miss thee sadly husband and father at home," while the other side contains the words "My Papa."

Helena residents continued to hold Hindman in high esteem as a man and as a martyr to the Southern cause. Fellow attorneys praised him as "a true and loyal gentleman, of chivalrous disposition, faithful to the trusts reposed in him, zealous in defense of right, fearless in denouncing wrong, eminently a man for the times."[22]

In 1870 when Hindman's remains were moved to the Confederate burial grounds within the Evergreen Cemetery (later renamed Maple Hill), a large crowd accompanied the body to the new site. At the dedication of the Confederate Monument in the cemetery in 1892, keynote speaker John R. Fellows singled out Hindman and his close friend and comrade in arms General Patrick Cleburne for special commendation. Quoting Samuel S. Cox, Fellows eulogized Hindman as "perhaps the most efficient Confederate Major General of the war" and praised him for devoting "his energies and talents to the deliverance of his people from 'carpet-bag rule.'"[23]

EPILOGUE

Hindman's death left his family in dire straits. At the time of his assassination, he was striving to repay debts contracted before the war and to support his wife and children. While they retained a number of town lots in Helena that produced income to supplement Tom's law practice, like many Arkansas families during the post war years, the Hindmans faced economic hardships exacerbated by declining land values. Mollie Hindman was thirty years old when her husband died, leaving her with four children, the oldest of whom was eleven year old Susie. Susie helped with household chores, and Biscoe, a sprightly boy of eight, delivered newspapers and gathered and sold mint to local saloons to augment the family's meager income. Times were hard, and Mollie often went to bed hungry so that she could feed the children and provide for their education. She was proud to see Biscoe excel in school and was delighted when he won a scholarship to the preparatory department of St. John's College in Little Rock. When he was twelve years old, Biscoe's oratorical abilities earned him a twenty dollar prize for the best recital of the Declaration of Independence. At graduation, he was awarded the "only certificate of high distinction for splendid conduct and example."[1]

Mollie died on 19 August 1876, after a long bout with tuberculosis. A faithful mother to the end, she entrusted the children to the care of James and Laura O'Connor and appointed Captain B. Y. Turner trustee of her estate.[2]

Although the children lived with the O'Connors, the means for their support and education was derived from the income generated from land holdings of their deceased parents. In 1859, Tom had deeded over to Mollie five blocks of land in Helena and what later became New Helena, and in spite of hard times she was able to retain them until her death. Even though greatly depreciated in value, they became her chief legacy to the children.[3]

To supplement earnings from rental properties, in early 1877 Susie became a traveling sales representative marketing *Tom Sawyer*, *Women of the Country*, and other popular literary works of the day in Little

Rock, Marianna, and Helena. The *Arkansas State Gazette* happily noted that Susie's energetic efforts had met with success and commended her for the "noble effort to place herself and family beyond the needs of friendly charity."[4]

This effort and rental income were not enough to offset educational expenses for the younger children, and in January 1881 Captain B. Y. Turner, trustee of Mollie's estate, decided to sell the Hindman home and adjacent land. The property was purchased at an auction by Laura O'Connor for $5,000.00, less a tax lien of $896.87. Unable to pay the full amount in cash, she executed promissory notes for the balance. In keeping with terms of the agreement, she paid the final installment on 11 April 1887.[5]

Susie's income and revenue derived from real estate enabled Biscoe to complete his preparatory work at St. John's and to enter West Point at the age of seventeen. Although he was the youngest member of his class, he diligently applied himself and, by his third year, ranked among the top ten in his class. He almost certainly would have graduated with high honors had he not dropped out when officials at the academy refused to allow him leave to visit Susie, who was terminally ill. Orphaned at a young age, the Hindman children were devoted to each other. Mindful of his older sister's sacrifice, when his request was denied, Biscoe left West Point and came home to Helena to comfort Susie, who died 8 November 1882.[6]

After leaving West Point, Biscoe worked briefly as an engineer in Pennsylvania before entering the Kentucky Military Institute, where he earned bachelor's and master's degrees in mathematics. He returned to Helena to serve as superintendent of schools for a year before affiliating with the Mutual life Insurance Company of New York. He quickly rose to the rank of general agent and enjoyed phenomenal success before retiring to pursue a real estate career in Chicago. Like his father, Biscoe was active in public life, serving as colonel in the Kentucky militia, national commander of the United Sons of Confederate Veterans, and as park commissioner.[7]

Likewise Tinker benefitted from Susie's hard work. Following his graduation from high school in Helena, he worked as a reporter in his hometown and was elected president of the local Press Association in 1883 at the age of nineteen. In this capacity, he delivered the opening address at the association's grand ball, leading his contemporaries to remark that young Hindman was "like his father, a natural orator." Following his graduation from the University of Mississippi, he joined Biscoe in Chicago, where he also became a successful real estate entrepreneur.[8]

As adults, Biscoe, Tinker, and Blanche sought to regain the family home that Laura O'Connor had purchased in 1881. They filed suit in the Phillips County Circuit Court in 1890 alleging fraud in the original transaction. Mrs. O'Connor responded that all of her actions towards them had been characterized by "fair dealing, honesty, and desire" to promote their interests. Special Judge James P. Brown found no evidence to sustain the allegations of fraud and dismissed the suit. The Hindmans appealed to the state Supreme Court, which reaffirmed the judgement of the lower court as it related to Biscoe and Blanche. Due to an error in proceedings involving Thomas, Jr. (Tinker), however, it reversed the judgement against him and remanded the case to the circuit court, which subsequently ordered Mrs. O'Connor to pay him sixty dollars.[9]

While the Hindman children failed to regain their homestead, they did much to perpetuate their father's memory. During his lifetime, Biscoe erected a magnificent marble obelisk at the grave site of his parents and funded the construction of a concrete drive in the Maple Hill Cemetery leading to the Hindman family plot. He gave generously to the Helena Public Library and in his will bequeathed $250,000 to the city as a memorial to his father. Part of this legacy went to establish a Hindman exhibit in the Phillips County Museum featuring family portraits; General Hindman's epaulets, uniform buttons, and boot hooks; and a pocket-size family Bible. Biscoe also left $100,000 for the construction of a memorial at the Prairie Grove battlefield and $50,000 to the City of Little Rock, a portion of which went to fund the establishment of a public park named for the general. Biscoe died in Chicago on 17 June 1932, and Tinker followed on 1 November 1934.[10]

Blanche died in 1952 at the age of eighty-six. Although she had barely known her father, the godchild of Empress Carlota remained true to his memory. She was active in the United Daughters of the Confederacy, serving as president of her local chapter in Monteagle, Tennessee. Even when she was old and infirm, Blanche's dedication to her "dear Papa" led her to make personal appearances at ceremonies commemorating the Battle of Prairie Grove.[11]

With Blanche's death, the direct line of Thomas C. Hindman's descendants came to an end. Like their father, the Hindman children looked boldly to the future, but always cherished the legacies of the past. His military service to the Confederacy was a point of pride, and Biscoe, Tinker, and Blanche were filled with joy when in 1887 Jefferson Davis penned a final tribute to him:

> General Hindman was certainly endowed with high military attributes. Both in his civil and military career he displayed zeal and energy, marked by unswerving fidelity. Daring, without being rash, and looking beyond the event of the moment to the future result to be achieved, he possessed the instincts of a soldier, without which no amount of education can make a general.[12]

BIBLIOGRAPHY

Manuscripts

Binford, George. Letters. Virginia Historical Society. Richmond, Virginia.

Bragg, Braxton. Papers. Western Reserve Historical Society. Cleveland, Ohio.

Brown, John W. Diary, 1820–1865. Arkansas History Commission. Little Rock, Arkansas.

Buckner, Simon Bolivar. Papers (SB 214). The Huntington Library. San Marino, California.

Closing Exercises of the Lawrenceville Classical Commercial High School, September 25, 1843. John Dixon Library. The Lawrenceville School. Lawrenceville, New Jersey.

Coolidge, H. P. Mrs. Scrapbook. Maple Hill Cemetery. Helena, Arkansas.

Hill, Daniel Harvey. Papers. Virginia State Library and Archives. Richmond, Virginia.

Hindman, Thomas C. Collection. Phillips County Museum. Helena, Arkansas.

_____. Papers. Record Group 109. National Archives and Records Administration.

_____. Papers. Frederick M. Dearborn Collection. The Houghton Library. Harvard University. Cambridge, Massachusetts.

Holmes, Theophilus Hunter. Papers. Duke University Library. Military Documents, 1862–1863 (Microfilm) in University of Arkansas Library. Fayetteville, Arkansas.

Jackson, Andrew. Papers. Library of Congress (microfilm). Washington, D. C.

Johnson, Andrew. Papers. Library of Congress (microfilm). Washington, D. C.

Lemke, Walter J. Papers. Special Collections Department. University of Arkansas Library. Fayetteville, Arkansas.

Nineteenth Century Letters (MC726). Special Collections Department. University of Arkansas Library. Fayetteville, Arkansas.

Oldham, Kie. Collection. Arkansas History Commission. Little Rock, Arkansas.

Orme, William Ward. Papers. Photocopies of letters in the Illinois State Historical Society on deposit in the Special Collections Department. University of Arkansas Library. Fayetteville, Arkansas.

Sons of Temperance, Minutes, 1852–1854. Ripley Public Library. Ripley, Mississippi.

Quitman, John A. Papers. Houghton Library. Harvard University. Cambridge, Massachusetts.

———. Papers. Mississippi Department of Archives and History. Jackson, Mississippi.

Wassell, Mrs. Samuel. Collection. Arkansas History Commission. Little Rock, Arkansas.

Wilson, J. P. Papers. Special Collections. Robert W. Woodruff Library. Emory University. Atlanta, Georgia.

Wright, J. C. "Major General T. C. Hindman." Collected by Omer R. Weaver in Individual File of Thomas C. Hindman Materials. Arkansas History Commission. Little Rock, Arkanss.

Newspapers

Arkansas:

Batesville *Independent Balance*, 1856, 1868.

Batesville *North Arkansas Times*, 1866–1868.

Des Arc *Citizen*, 1858–1860.

Des Arc *Constitutional Union*, 1861.

Des Arc *Semi-Weekly Citizen*, 1861.

Fayetteville *Arkansian*, 1859–1860.

Fort Smith *Tri-Weekly Bulletin*, 1862.

Helena *Democratic Star*, 1854–1855.

Helena *Southern Shield*, 1855–1857.

Helena *State-Rights Democrat*, 1856.

Little Rock *Arkansas Patriot*, 1862–1863.

Little Rock *Arkansas State Gazette*, 1855–1862, 1866–1868, 1870, 1873–1874, 1877, 1879, 1883, 1885–1886, 1890, 1892, 1966.

Little Rock *Daily Republican*, 1867–1868, 1873.

Little Rock *Daily State Journal*, 1861–1862.

Little Rock *National Democrat*, 1864–1865.

Little Rock *Old-Line Democrat*, 1859–1860.

Little Rock *True Democrat*, 1855–1863.

Little Rock *Unconditional Union*, 1865.

Ouachita Herald (Camden), 1859.

Pine Bluff *Daily Graphic*, 1934.

Van Buren *Intelligencer*, 1858.

Van Buren *Press,* 1859–1861, 1867–1868.
Washington *Telegraph,* 1862.

Mississippi:

Holly Springs *Gazette,* 1847.
Holly Springs *Guard,* 1846.
Holly Springs *Mississippi Palladium,* 1851–1852.
Natchez *Mississippi Free Trader,* 1846–1848.
Jackson *Flag of the Union,* 1850–1851, 1853.
Jackson *Mississippian,* 1846–1847, 1851–1853.
Ripley *Advertiser,* 1844–1846, 1856.
Vicksburg *Sentinel,* 1850.
Yazoo (Yazoo City) *Democrat,* 1850–1851.

Tennessee:

Chattanooga *Rebel* (Griffin, Georgia), 1864.
Memphis *Appeal,* 1849, 1860, 1863, 1867, 1881.
Memphis *Avalanche,* 1860, 1868
Memphis *Bulletin,* 1863.

Other:

Alexandria *Louisiana Democrat,* 1867.
Atlanta (Georgia) Southern Confederacy, 1865.
Baltimore (Maryland) *American and Commercial Advertiser,* 1860.
Brownsville (Texas) *Daily Ranchero,* 1866.
Galveston (Texas) *Daily News,* 1865–1866.
Macon (Georgia) *Telegraph,* 1864.
Marshall (Texas) *Republican,* 1862.
Matamoras (Mexico) *Daily Ranchero,* 1865.
Mexican Times (Mexico City), 1865.
New Orleans (Louisiana) *Picayune,* 1862, 1865.
New York *Herald,* 1865.
New York *Times,* 1865, 1867–1868.
New York *Tribune,* 1862.
Richmond (Virginia), *Daily Dispatch,* 1863–1864.
Shreveport (Louisiana) *Southwestern,* 1863.
Washington, D. C. *Evening Star,* 1860.

Printed Diaries, Letters, and Memoirs

Anderson, John Q., ed. *Campaigning with Parsons' Texas Brigade, CSA: The War Journals and Letters of the Four Orr Brothers, 12th Texas Cavalry Regiment.* Hillsboro, Texas: Hill Jr. College Press, 1967.

Barnes, James. *The Eighty-Sixth Regiment of Indiana Volunteer Infantry: A Narrative of its Services in the Civil War of 1861–1865.* Crawfordville, Indiana: Journal Co., Printers, 1895.

Barney, C. *Recollections of Field Service with the Twelfth Iowa Infantry Volunteers: or What I Saw in the Army . . . .* Davenport Iowa: Gazette Job Rooms, 1865.

Box, Sam. "End of the War—Exiles in Mexico." *Confederate Veteran* 11:3 (March 1903): 121–23.

Baylor, George Withe. "With Gen. A. S. Johnston at Shiloh." *Confederate Veteran* 5:12 (December 1897): 609–13.

Britton, Wiley. *The Civil War on the Border.* 2 vols. New York: G. P. Putnam's Sons, 1899.

____. *Memoirs of the Rebellion on the Border, 1863.* Chicago: Cushing, Thomas & Co., Publishers, 1882.

Brown, Norman D., ed. *Journey to Pleasant Hill: The Civil War Letters of Captain Elijah P. Petty, Walker's Texas Division, C. S. A.* San Antonio: University of Texas for Institute of Texan Cultures, 1982.

Buck, Irving. *Cleburne and his Command.* Edited by Thomas Robson Hay. Jackson, Tennessee: McCowat-Mercer Press, 1959.

"Captain Cameron N. Biscoe." *Confederate Veteran* 33:10 (October, 1925): 385.

Cate, Wirt Armistead, ed. *Two Soldiers: The Companion Diaries of Thomas J. Key, C. S. A. December 7, 1863–May 17, 1865 and Robert J. Campbell, U. S. A. January 1, 1864–July 21, 1864.* Chapel Hill: University of North Carolina Press, 1938.

Clayton, Powell. *The Aftermath of the Civil War in Arkansas.* New York: The Neale Publishing Company, 1915.

Coons, John W., comp., *Indiana at Shiloh.* n.p.: Indiana Shiloh National Park Commission, 1904.

Cox, Jacob. D. *Atlanta.* New York: Charles Scribner's Sons, 1898.

Cox, Samuel S. *Three Decades of Federal Legislation.* Providence, Rhode Island: J. A. & R. A. Reid, Publishers, 1895.

Cumming, Kate. *Kate: The Journal of a Confederate Nurse.* Edited by Richard Barksdale Harwell. Baton Rouge: Louisiana State University Press, 1959.

Cypert, Jesse N. "Secession Convention." In *Publications of the Arkansas Historical Association* 1 (1906): 314–23.

"Daughters of Confederacy at Monteagle." *Confederate Veteran* 16:9 (September 1908): 474.

Davis, Jefferson. *Jefferson Davis, Constitutionalist: His Letters, Papers, & Speeches*. Edited by Dunbar Rowland. 10 vols. Jackson: Mississippi Department of Archives and History, 1923.

_____. *The Papers of Jefferson Davis*. Edited by Haskell M. Monroe, Jr. and James T. McIntosh. 4 Vols. Baton Rouge: Louisiana State University Press, 1971–.

Davis, Reuben. *Recollections of Mississippi and Mississippians*. rev. ed. Oxford: University and College Press of Mississippi, 1972.

Dorsey, Sarah, ed. *Recollections of Henry Watkins Allen, Brigadier-General Confederate States Army, Ex-Governor of Louisiana*. New York: M. Doolady, 1866.

Duke, Basil. *Reminiscences of General Basil W. Duke, C. S. A.* Garden City, New York: Doubleday, Page & Company, 1911.

Edwards, John N. *Shelby and his Men: or, The War in the West*. Cincinnati: Miami Printing and Publishing Company, 1867.

_____. *Shelby's Expedition to Mexico, An Unwritten Leaf of the War*. Kansas City: Kansas City Times Steam Book and Job Printing House, 1872; Reprint, Austin: The Steck Company, 1964.

Estill, Mary, ed. "Diary of a Confederate Congressman, 1862–1863." *Southwestern Historical Quarterly* 39: (July 1935): 33–65.

Featherstonhaugh, G. W. *Excursion Through the Slave States, From Washington on the Potomac to the Frontier of Mexico; with Sketches of Popular Manners and Geological Notes*. New York: Harper and Brothers, 1844.

Field, Charles D. *Three Years in the Saddle From 1861–1865: Memoirs of Charles D. Field*. n.p., n.d.

Foote, H. S. *War of the Rebellion: or Scylla or Charybdis*. New York: Harper and Brothers, 1866.

Force, M. F. *From Fort Henry to Corinth*. New York: Charles Scribner's Sons, 1898.

Gaughan, T. J. Mrs., ed. *Letters of a Confederate Surgeon*. Camden, Arkansas: Hurley Co., Inc., 1960.

Guild, George B. *A Brief Narrative of the Fourth Tennessee Regiment: Wheeler's Corp, Army of Tennessee*. Nashville, Tennessee: n. p., 1913.

Harrell, John M. "Arkansas." In *Confederate Military History*. Edited by Clement A. Evans. 12 vols. Atlanta: Confederate Publishing Co., 1899.

Heartsill, William M. *Fourteen Hundred and 91 Days in the Confederate Army*. Edited by Bell I. Wiley. 2nd ed. Jackson, Tennessee: McCowat-Mercer Press, 1954.

Hesseltine, William B., ed. *Three Against Lincoln: Murat Halstead Reports the Caucuses of 1860*. Baton Rouge: Louisiana State University Press, 1960.

Hill, Daniel H. "Chickamauga—The Great Battle of the West." In *Battles and Leaders of the Civil War*. Edited by R. U. Johnson and C. C. Buell. 4 vols. New York: Thomas Yoseloff, 1888.

"Hindman's Reply to Hood." *Confederate Veteran* 8:2 (February 1900): 69.

Johnston, William Preston. "Albert Sidney Johnston at Shiloh." In *Battles and Leaders of the Civil War*. Edited by R. U. Johnson and C. C. Buell. 4 vols. New York: Thomas Yoseloff, 1888.

Jones, Samuel. "The Battle of Prairie Grove." *Southern Bivouac* 1:4 (September 1885): 203–11.

Jordan, Thomas. "The Battle of Shiloh." in *Southern Historical Society Papers*. 35 (January–December 1907): 204–23.

Longstreet, James. *From Manassas to Appomattox: Memoirs of the Civil War in America*. Edited by James I. Robertson, Jr. Bloomington: Indiana University Press, 1960.

Love, Thomas N. "Remarks on Some of the Diseases Which Prevailed in the Second Mississippi Rifles." In *Chronicles of the Gringos: The U. S. Army in the Mexican War, 1846–1848*. Edited by George W. Smith and Charles Judah. Albuquerque: University of New Mexico Press, 1968.

McPherson, Edward. *The Political History of the United States of America, During the Great Rebellion*. Washington, D. C.: Philip & Solomons, 1865.

"Memoirs of Mildred Stanfield Hindman Doxey." *News and Journal* 8 (December 1982): 76–82.

Monnett, Howard, ed. "A Yankee Cavalryman Views the Battle of Prairie Grove." *Arkansas Historical Quarterly* 21:4 (Winter 1962): 289-304.

Moore, Frank, ed. *Rebellion Record: A Diary of American Events*. Garden City, New York: G. P. Putnam, 1864–1868.

Moore, John C. "Missouri." In *Confederate Military History*. Edited by Clement A. Evans. 12 Vols. Atlanta: Confederate Publishing Company, 1899.

Nash, Charles Edward. *Biographical Sketches of Gen. Pat Cleburne and Gen. T. C. Hindman Together with Humorous Anecdotes and Reminiscences of the Late Civil War*. Little Rock: Tunnah & Pittard, Printers, 1895: Reprint, Dayton, Ohio: Morningside Bookshop, 1977.

Nisbet, James Cooper. *4 Years on the Firing Line.* Edited by Bell Wiley. Jackson, Tennessee: McCowat-Mercer Press, 1963.

"Nominated for Commander in Chief." *Confederate Veteran* 8:5 (May 1900): 205.

Oliphant, William J. "Arkansas Post." *Southern Bivouac* 1:11 (April 1886): 736-39.

"A Patriotic Bequest." *Confederate Veteran* 40:9–10 (September–October, 1932): 365.

Pike, Albert. *Albert Pike's Letter Addressed to Major-General Holmes, Dec. 30, 1862.* Little Rock: J. D. Butler, 1862.

Pike, Albert. *Charges and Specifications Preferred August 23, 1862, by Brigadier General Albert Pike, Against Major Gen. Thos. C. Hindman.* Richmond: Smith, Bailey & Co., Printers, 1863.

Pilcher, M. B. Mrs. "U. D. C. Day at Monteagle." *Confederate Veteran* 15:8 (August 1907): 377.

Pollard, Charleen Plumly, ed. "Civil War Letters of George W. Allen." *Southwestern Historical Quarterly* 83: (July 1979): 48-52.

Ray, Johnette Highsmith, ed. "Civil War Letters from Parsons' Texas Cavalry Brigade." *Southwestern Historical Quarterly* 2: (October 1965): 210–23.

Ridley, Bromfield L. *Battles and Sketches of the Army of Tennessee.* Mexico, Missouri: Missouri Printing and Publishing Company, 1906; Reprint, Dayton, Ohio: Morningside Bookshop, 1978.

Ross, John. *The Papers of Chief John Ross.* Edited by Gary E. Moulton. 2 vols. Norman: University of Oklahoma Press, 1985.

Ruiz, Ramon Eduardo, ed. *An American in Maximillian's Mexico, 1865–1866: The Diaries of William Marshall Anderson.* San Marino, California: The Huntington Library, 1959.

Russell, Tom. "Adventures of a Cordova Colonist." *The Southern Magazine* 11 (August–September 1872): 90–102, 155–66.

"Sketch of General Felix K. Zollicoffer." *Southern Bivouac* 2:11 (July 1884): 492–94.

Snead, Thomas L. "The Conquest of Arkansas." In *Battles and Leaders of the Civil War.* Edited by R. U. Johnson and C. C. Buel. 4 vols. New York: Thomas Yoseloff, 1888.

Sorrell, G. Moxley. *Recollections of a Confederate Staff Officer.* Edited by Bell I. Wiley. Jackson, Tennessee: McCowat-Mercer Press, 1958,

Staley, James. "[Letter] to Editor, May 21, 1893." *Confederate Veteran* 1:6 (June 1893): 172.

Stanley, Dorothy, ed. *The Autobiography of Sir Henry Morton Stanley.* Boston: Houghton Mifflin Company, 1937.

Stevenson, William G. *Thirteen Months in the Rebel Army.* New York: A. S. Barnes, 1862.

Temple, Oliver P. *Notable Men of Tennessee* (New York: Cosmopolitan Press, 1912.

Terrell, Alexander Watkins. *From Texas to Mexico and the Court of Maximillian in 1865.* Dallas: The Book Club of Texas, 1933.

Thompson, Ed Porter. *History of the Orphan Brigade.* Louisville, Kentucky: Lewis N. Thompson, 1898.

Thorndike, Rachel Sherman, ed., *The Sherman Letters: Correspondence between General Sherman and Senator Sherman from 1837 to 1891.* New York: Da Capo Press, 1969.

Turner, R. Lockwood, ed., *A Carolinian Goes to War: The Civil War Narrative of Arthur Middleton Manigault.* Columbia: University of South Carolina Press, 1983.

Wallace, Lew. "The Capture of Fort Donelson." In *Battles and Leaders of the Civil War.* Edited by R. U. Johnson and C. C. Buell. 4 vols. New York: Thomas Yoseloff, 1888.

Waterman, Robert E. and Thomas Rothrock, eds. "The Earle- Buchanan Letters of 1861–1876." *Arkansas Historical Quarterly* 33: (Summer 1974): 99–174.

Woodruff. W. E. *With Light Guns in 61–65: Reminiscences of Eleven Arkansas, Missouri, and Texas Light Batteries in the Civil War.* Little Rock: Central Printing Company, 1903.

Worley, Ted R., ed. "A Letter Written by General Thomas C. Hindman in Mexico." *Arkansas Historical Quarterly* 15:4 (Winter 1956): 365–68.

Wright, John C. *Memoirs of Colonel John C. Wright.* n.p.: A. L. Scallion, 1982.

Wright, Thomas E., ed. "The Capture of Van Buren, Arkansas, During the Civil War from the Diary of a Union Horse Soldier." *Arkansas Historical Quarterly* 38:1 (Spring 1979): 72-89.

Published Addresses and Reports

Hindman, T. C. *Address of Hon. Thos. C. Hindman of Arkansas to his Constituents.* Washington, D. C.: Lemuel Towers, 1860.

_____. *Report of Major General Hindman, Of His Operations in the Trans-Mississippi District.* Richmond: R. M. Smith, Public Printer, 1864.

_____. *Speech of Col. T. C. Hindman, on Federal and Arkansas Politics: Made in Representatives Hall, on February 15, 1859.* Little Rock: James D. Butler, 1859.

_____. *Speech of Hon. Thos. C. Hindman, at Helena, Arkansas, November 28, 1858.* Washington, D. C.: Lemuel Towers, 1860.

Johnson, R. W. and T. C. Hindman. *To the People of Arkansas.* Washington, D. C.: W. H. Moore, Printer, 1861.

Government Documents

Arkansas. *Acts* (1866–1867).

_____. *Biennial Report of the Secretary of State* (1907).

_____. *Constitution* (1868).

_____. *Journal of Both Sessions of the Convention of the State of Arkansas* (1861).

_____. *Message of Gov. Henry M. Rector to the General Assembly of the State of Arkansas: Delivered Nov'r, 1862.*

_____. *Message of Gov. Henry M. Rector to the General Assembly of Arkansas in Extra Session, November 6, 1861.*

_____. *Ordinances of the State Convention Which Convened in Little Rock, May 6, 1861.*

_____. *Reports of Cases at Law and in Equity Argued and Determined in the Supreme Court of Arkansas.*

Indictment of Thomas C. Hindman, May 24, 1865. United States District Court for the Eastern District of Ark. Vol. D. Case O. United States District Court. Little Rock, Arkansas.

Journal of the Congress of the Confederate States of America, 1861–1865. 7 vols. Senate Doc. No. 234, 58 Cong., 2 sess., 1904–1905.

Military Service Record of Robert H. Hindman (Mexican War). National Archives and Records Administration. Washington, D. C.

Military Service Record of Thomas C. Hindman (Civil War). National Archives and Records Administration. Washington, D. C.

Military Service Record of Thomas C. Hindman, Jr. (Mexican War). National Archives and Records Administration. Washington, D. C.

Mississippi. *House Journal* (1854).

Phillips County. Abstract and Index of Deeds, 1857–1869. Book 2. Arkansas History Commission. Little Rock, Arkansas.

_____. Circuit Court Record in Chancery. Book L. Phillips County Courthouse. Helena, Arkansas.

_____. Marriage Transcript Record. T. C. Hindman and Mollie Biscoe. Book. 1, File No. 1018975. Phillips County Courthouse. Helena, Arkansas.

_____. Probate Record. Book 5, 1874–1880. Arkansas History Commission. Little Rock, Arkansas.

____. Probate Records. Volume 45. Phillips County Courthouse. Helena, Arkansas.

____. Tax Records, 1850–1860, 1866–1867. Arkansas History Commission. Little Rock, Arkansas.

Proceedings of the First Confederate Congress. In *Southern Historical Society Papers* (New Series). 44 vols. Richmond: Southern Historical Society, 1923–1959.

Richardson, James D., ed. *Compilation of the Messages and Papers of the Presidents, 1789–1897.* 53d Cong., 2 sess., 1907, House Miscellaneous Document No. 210. Pts 1–10, 10 vols. Washington, D. C.: Government Printing Office, 1907.

Tippah County. The State of Mississippi v. William C. Falkner. Circuit Court. Tippah County Courthouse. Ripley, Mississippi.

United States. Bureau of the Census. Manuscript Census for Phillips County, Arkansas, 1860.

____. Manuscript Census for Phillips County, Arkansas, 1870.

____. Manuscript Census for Tippah County, Mississippi, 1850.

____. Manuscript Slave Schedules for Tippah County, Mississippi, 1850.

____. *The Statistics of the Population of the United States.* Washington, D. C.: Government Printing Office, 1872.

United States. Congress. *Acts and Resolutions.* 39 Cong., 2 sess. ____.

Congressional Globe. 46 vols. Washington, D. C., 1834–1873.

____. House of Representatives. *Executive Documents.* 39 Cong., 2 sess. (Serial 1289, No. 31).

____. *Executive Documents.* 39 Cong., 1 sess. (Serial 1263, No. 99).

____. *Executive Documents.* 39 Cong., 1 sess. (Serial 1293, No. 116).

____. *Executive Documents.* 39 Cong., 2 sess. (Serial 1294, No. 76).

____. *Executive Documents.* 40 Cong., 2 sess. (Serial 1343, No. 274).

____. *Executive Documents.* 40 Cong., 2 sess. (Serial 1343, No. 278).

____. Department of the Navy. *Official Records of the Union and Confederate Navies in the War of the Rebellion.* 31 vols. Washington, D. C.: Government Printing Office, 1884–1927.

____. War Department. The Adjutant General's Office. Amnesty Papers. Record Group No. 94. National Archives and Records Administration. Washington, D. C.

____. *The War of the Rebellion: Official Records of the Union and Confederate Armies.* 128 vols. Washington, D. C.: Government Printing Office, 1880–1902.

Secondary Articles

Anders, Leslie. "Fighting the Ghosts at Lone Jack." *Missouri Historical Review* 29:3 (April 1985): 332–56.

Bailey, Anne J. "Henry McCullough's Texans and the Defense of Arkansas in 1862." *Arkansas Historical Quarterly* 46:1 (Spring 1987): 46–59.

Barr, Alwyn. "Confederate Artillery in Arkansas." *Arkansas Historical Quarterly* 22:3 (Fall 1963): 238–72.

Bearss, Edwin C. "The White River Expedition June 10-July 15, 1862." *Arkansas Historical Quarterly* 21:4 (Winter 1962): 305–62.

Bourne, Edward. "The 'Young Guard.'" In *The Military Annals of Tennessee.* Edited by John Berrien Lindsley. Nashville, Tennessee: J. M. Lindsley & Co., 1886.

Brent, Robert A. "Mississippi and the Mexican War." *Journal of Mississippi History* 31:3 (August 1969): 202–14.

Brown, Maud Morrow. "William C. Faulkner, Man of Legends." *Georgia Review* 10:4 (Winter 1956): 421–38.

"County Officials." *Alabama Historical Quarterly* 6:2 (Summer 1944): 138–239.

Crenshaw, Ollinger. "The Speakership Contest of 1859–1860: John Sherman's Election A Cause of Disruption?" *Mississippi Valley Historical Review* 29:4 (December 1942): 323–38.

Dougan, Michael B. "A Look at the 'Family' in Arkansas Politics." *Arkansas Historical Quarterly* 29:2 (Summer 1970): 99–111.

____. "Thomas C. Hindman: Arkansas Politician and General." In *Rank and File: Civil War Essays in Honor of Bell Irvin Wiley.* Edited by James I. Robertson, Jr. and Richard M. McMurry. San Rafael, California: Presidio Press, 1976.

Finger, John R. "The Abortive Second Cherokee Removal, 1841–1844." *Journal of Southern History* 47:2 (May 1981): 207–26.

Gregory, Ival L. "The Battle of Prairie Grove, Arkansas, December 7, 1862." In *Civil War Battles in the West.* Edited by LeRoy H. Fisher. Manhattan, Kansas: Sunflower University Press, 1981.

Harmon, George D. "Confederate Migrations to Mexico." *Lehigh University Publications* 12:2 (February 1938): 458–87.

Hartsell, Henry F. "The Battle of Cane Hill, Arkansas, November 28, 1862." In *Civil War Battles in the West.* Edited by LeRoy H. Fisher. Manhattan, Kansas: Sunflower University Press, 1981.

Hay, Thomas Robson. "The South and the Arming of the Slaves." *Mississippi Valley Historical Review* 6:1 (June 1919): 34–73.

Hindman, Biscoe. "Thomas Carmichael Hindman." *Confederate Veteran* 38:3 (March 1930): 97–104.

Hoar, Victor. "Colonel William C. Falkner in the Civil War." *Journal of Mississippi History* 27:1 (February 1955): 42–62.

Huff, Leo E. "The Martial Law Controversy in Arkansas, 1861–1865: A Case History of Internal Confederate Conflict." *Arkansas Historical Quarterly* 37:2 (Summer 1978): 147–67.

Hulston, John K. and James W. Goodrich. "John Trousdale Coffee: Lawyer, Politician, Confederate." *Missouri Historical Review* 77:3 (April 1983): 272–95.

Lemke, W. J. "The Hindman Family Portraits." *Arkansas Historical Quarterly* 14:2 (Summer 1955): 103–108.

Logan, Robert R. "Address at Dedication of Prairie Grove Battlefield Monument December 7, 1956." *Arkansas Historical Quarterly* 16:3 (Autumn 1957): 257–80.

Monnett, Howard N. "A Yankee Cavalryman Views the Battle of Prairie Grove." *Arkansas Historical Quarterly* 21:4 (Winter 1962): 289–304.

Moneyhon, Carl H. "Economic Democracy in Antebellum Arkansas, Phillips County, 1850–1860." *Arkansas Historical Quarterly* 40:2 (Summer 1981): 154–72.

McMurry, Richard M. "The Affair at Kolb's Farm." *Civil War Times Illustrated.* 7: (December 1968): 20–29.

_____. "Kennesaw Mountain." *Civil War Times Illustrated* 8:9 (January 1970): 20–25, 28–35.

_____. "Resaca: 'A Heap of Hard Fiten.'" *Civil War Times Illustrated* 9:7 (November 1970): 4–12, 44–48.
National Cyclopedia of American Biography, 1967 ed. S. v. "Biscoe Hindman."

Oates, Stephen B. "The Cavalry Fight at Cane Hill." *Arkansas Historical Quarterly* 20:1 (Spring 1961): 65–73.

_____. "The Prairie Grove Campaign, 1862." *Arkansas Historical Quarterly* 19:2 (Summer 1960): 119–41.

Reid, Bill G. "Confederate Opponents of Arming the Slaves." *Journal of Mississippi History* 12: (October 1960): 249–70.

Rister, Carl Coke. "Carlota, A Confederate Colony in Mexico." *Journal of Southern History* 11:1 (February 1945): 32–50.

Roberts, Bobby L. "Thomas C. Hindman and the Trans-Mississippi District." *Arkansas Historical Quarterly* 32:4 (Winter 1973): 297–311.

Robinett, Paul M. "Marmaduke's Expedition Into Missouri: The Battles of Springfield and Hartville, January, 1863." *Missouri Historical Review* 58:

(January, 1964): 193–212.

Ruby, Barbara C. "General Patrick Cleburne's Proposal to Arm the Southern Slaves." *Arkansas Historical Quarterly* 30:3 (Autumn 1971): 193–212.

Scroggs, Jack B. "Arkansas in the Secession Crisis." *Arkansas Historical Quarterly* 12: (Autumn 1953): 179–224.

Secrist, Philip L. "Prelude to the Atlanta Campaign: The Davis-Bragg-Johnston Controversy." *Atlanta Historical Bulletin* 17 (Spring–Summer 1972): 9–20.

_____. "Resaca: For Sherman a Moment of Truth." *Atlanta Historical Journal* 22 (Spring 1978): 9–41.

Smith, Harold T. "The Know Nothings in Arkansas." *Arkansas Historical Quarterly* 34:4 (Winter 1975): 291–303.

"Tippah County Deed Book 'D' and Index." *News and Index* 11:2 (1985): 44.

Wilder, Jeremy H. "The Thirty-Seventh Illinois at Prairie Grove." *Arkansas Historical Quarterly* 49:1 (Spring 1989): 3–19.

Windham, William T. "The Problem of Supply in the Trans- Mississippi Confederacy." *Journal of Southern History* 27: (May 1961): 149–68.

Worley, Ted R. The Arkansas State Bank: Ante-bellum Period." *Arkansas Historical Quarterly* 23:1 (Spring 1964): 65–73.

_____. "The Control of the Real Estate Bank of the State of Arkansas, 1836–1857." *Mississippi Valley Historical Review* 37:3 (December 1950): 403–26.

_____. "Helena on the Mississippi." *Arkansas Historical Quarterly* 13:1 (Spring 1954): 1–15.

Secondary Books

Andrews, J. Cutler. *The South Reports the Civil War.* Princeton, New Jersey: Princeton University Press, 1970.

Bailey, Anne J. *Between the Enemy and Texas: Parsons's Texas Cavalry in the Civil War* (Fort Worth, Texas: Texas Christian University Press, 1989.

Bettersworth, John K. *Mississippi: A History.* Austin: The Steck Company, 1959.

Biographical and Historical Memoirs of Eastern Arkansas. Chicago: The Goodspeed Publishing Company, 1890.

Blotner, Joseph. *Faulkner: A Biography.* 2 vols. New York: Random House, 1974.

Brown, Andrew. *History of Tippah County, Mississippi: The First Century.* Ripley, Mississippi: Tippah County Historical and Genealogical Society, Inc., 1976.

Brown, P. Hume. *A Short History of Scotland.* Revised by Henry W. Meikle. Edinburgh: Oliver and Boyd, Ltd., 1951.

Brownlee, Richard S. *Gray Ghosts of the Confederacy: Guerrilla Warfare in the West, 1861–1865.* Baton Rouge: Louisiana State University Press, 1958.

Cassidy, Vincent H. and Amos E. Simpson. *Henry Watkins Allen of Louisiana.* Baton Rouge: Louisiana State University Press, 1964.

Cavaliers and Pioneers: Abstracts of Virginia land Patents and Grants, 1623–1666. Abstracted and Indexed by Nell Marion Nugent. Vol. 1 Baltimore: Genealogical Publishing Co., Inc., 1974.

Collier, Calvin C. *First In—Last Out: The Capitol Guards, Ark. Brigade.* Little Rock: Pioneer Press, 1961.

Commager, Henry Steele. *The Blue and the Gray.* 2 vols. Indianapolis: Bobbs-Merrill Company, Inc., 1950.

Connelley, William Elsey. *The Life of Preston B. Plumb, 1837–1891.* Chicago: Browne & Howell Company, 1913.

Connelly, Thomas Lawrence. *Autumn of Glory: The Army of Tennessee, 1862–1865.* Baton Rouge: Louisiana State University Press, 1971.

Crowley, William J. *Tennessee Cavalry in the Missouri Cavalry Major Henry Ewing, C. S. A., of the St. Louis Times.* Columbia, Missouri: Kelly Press, Inc., 1978.

Dorris, Jonathan Truman. *Pardon and Amnesty under Lincoln and Johnson: The Restoration of the Confederates to their Rights and Privileges, 1861–1865.* Chapel Hill: University of North Carolina Press, 1953.

Dougan, Michael B. *Confederate Arkansas: The People and Policies of a Frontier State in Wartime.* Tuscaloosa: University of Alabama Press, 1972.

Dumond, Dwight L. *The Secession Movement, 1860–1861.* New York: Macmillan Company, 1931.

Eaton, Clement. *Jefferson Davis.* New York: The Free Press, 1977.

Esposito, Vincent J., Chief ed. *The West Point Atlas of American Wars.* 2 vols. New York: Frederick Praeger Publishers, 1959.

Fellman, Michael. *Inside War: The Guerrilla Conflict in Missouri During the American Civil War.* New York: Oxford University Press, 1989.

Franks, Kenny A. *Stand Watie and the Agony of the Cherokee Nation.* Memphis: Memphis State University Press, 1979.

Galloway, B. P. *The Ragged Rebel: A Common Soldier in W. H. Parsons' Texas Cavalry, 1861–1865.* Austin: University of Texas Press, 1988.

Hall, Hugh Levis Jr. *Those Who Came Before Us.* Sherman, Texas: A–1 Printing Company, 1982.

Hamilton, Holman. *Prologue to Conflict: The Crisis and Compromise of 1850.* New York: W. W. Norton. 1966.

Hanna, Alfred Jackson and Kathryn Abbey Hanna. *Napoleon III and Mexico: American Triumph over Monarchy.* Chapel Hill: University of North Carolina Press, 1971.

Haynes, Jane Isbell. *William Faulkner; His Tippah County Heritage.* Columbia, South Carolina: The Seajay Press, 1985.

Hickerson, Thomas Felix. *The Falkner Feuds.* Chapel Hill: North Carolina: Colonial Press, Inc., 1964.

Horn, Stanley F. *The Army of Tennessee.* Norman: University of Oklahoma Press, 1952.

Hughes, Nathaniel Cheairs, Jr. *General William J. Hardee: Old Reliable.* Baton Rouge: Louisiana State University Press, 1965.

Ingenthron, Elmo. *Borderland Rebellion: A History of the Civil War on the Missouri-Arkansas Border.* Bransom, Missouri: Ozarks Mountaineer, 1980.

Kerby, Robert L. *Kirby Smith's Confederacy: The Trans-Mississippi South, 1863–1865.* New York: Columbia University Press, 1972.

Knight, Wilfred. *Red Fox: Stand Watie and the Confederate Indian Nations during the Civil War Years in Indian Territory.* Glendale, California: Arthur H. Clark Company, 1988.

Lamers, William M. *The Edge of Glory: A Biography of General William Rosecrans.* New York: Harcourt, Brace & World, Inc., 1961.

McMurry, Richard M. *John Bell Hood and the War for Southern Independence.* Lexington: University of Kentucky Press, 1982.

May, Robert E. *John A. Quitman: Old South Crusader.* Baton Rouge: Louisiana State University Press, 1985.

Moore, Albert Burton. *Conscription and Conflict in the Confederacy.* New York: The Macmillan Company, 1924.

Mulford, Roland. *History of the Lawrenceville School, 1810–1935.* Princeton: Princeton University Press, 1935.

Oates, Stephen B. *Confederate Cavalry West of the River.* Austin: University of Texas Press, 1961.

O'Flaherty, Daniel. *General Jo Shelby: Undefeated Rebel.* Chapel Hill: University of North Carolina Press, 1954.

Overdyke, W. Darrell. *The Know-Nothing Party in the South.* Baton Rouge: Louisiana State University Press, 1950.

Parks, Joseph Howard. *General Edmund Kirby Smith, C. S. A.* Baton Rouge: Louisiana State University Press, 1954.

Purdue, Howell and Elizabeth Purdue. *Pat Cleburne: Confederate General.* Hillsboro, Texas: Hill Jr. College Press, 1973.

Polk, William M. *Leonidas Polk: Bishop and General.* 2nd ed. 2 vols. New York: Longmans, Green, and Co., 1915.

Powell, William, H. *List of Officers of the Army of the United States from 1779 to 1900.* New York: L. R. Hamersly & Co., 1900.

Rippy, J. Fred. *The United States and Mexico.* New York: Alfred A. Knopf, 1926.

Robertson, James I., Jr. *General A. P. Hill: The Story of a Confederate Warrior.* New York: Random House, 1987.

Roland, Charles P. *Albert Sidney Johnston: Soldier of Three Republics.* Austin: University of Texas Press, 1964.

Rolle, Andrew. *The Lost Cause: The Confederate Exodus to Mexico.* Norman: University of Oklahoma Press, 1965.

Rowland, Dunbar. *History of Mississippi: The Heart of the South.* 2 vols. Chicago-Jackson: The S. J. Clarke Publishing Company, 1925.

_____. *Military History of Mississippi, 1803–1898.* With a New Index by H. Grady Howell, Jr. Spartanburg, South Carolina: The Reprint Company, 1988.

Seitz, Don C. *Braxton Bragg: General of the Confederacy.* Columbia, South Carolina: State Company, 1924.

Shinn, Josiah H. *Pioneers and Makers of Arkansas.* Washington, D. C.: Genealogical and Historical Publishing Company, 1908.

Slaymaker, S. R., II. *Five Miles Away: The Story of the Lawrenceville School.* Lawrenceville, New Jersey: The Lawrenceville School, 1985.

Smith, Gene. *Maximillian and Carlota: A Tale of Romance and Tragedy.* New York: William Morrow and Company, Inc., 1973.

Staples, Thomas S. *Reconstruction in Arkansas, 1862–1874.* New York: Columbia University, 1923.

Sword, Wiley. *Shiloh: Bloody April.* New York: William Morrow & Company, 1974.

Takaki, Ronald T. *A Pro-Slavery Crusade: The Agitation to Reopen the African Slave Trade.* New York: The Free Press, 1971.

Thomas, David Y. *Arkansas in War and Reconstruction, 1861–1874.* Little Rock: Arkansas Division of the United Daughters of the Confederacy, 1926.

Tucker, Glenn. *Chickamauga: Bloody Battle in the West.* Indianapolis: Bobbs-Merrill, 1961; Reprint, Dayton, Ohio: Morningside House, 1984.

Wakelyn, Jon L., ed. *Biographical Dictionary of the Confederacy.* Westport, Connecticut: Greenwood Press, 1977.

Woods, James M. *Rebellion and Realignment: Arkansas's Road to Secession.* Fayetteville: University of Arkansas Press, 1987.

Unpublished Theses and Dissertations

Brown, Walter Lee. "Albert Pike, 1809–1891." Ph. D. diss., University of Texas, 1953.

Duclos, Donald Philip. "Son of Sorrow: The Life, Works, and Influence of Colonel William C. Falkner, 1825–1889." Ph.D. diss., University of Michigan, 1961.

Harvin, Edwin Lawrence. "Arkansas and the Crisis of 1860–1861." M. A. thesis, University of Texas, 1926.

Huff, Leo Elmer. "Confederate Arkansas: A History of Arkansas During the Civil War." M. A. thesis, University of Arkansas, 1964.

Jennings, Thomas A. "San Antonio in the Confederacy." M. A. thesis, Trinity University, 1957.

Lewis, Elsie M. "From Nationalism to Disunion: A Study of the Secession Movement in Arkansas, 1850–1861." Ph. D. diss., University of Chicago, 1947.

Roberts, Bobby L. "Thomas Carmichael Hindman: Secessionist and Confederate General." M. A. thesis, University of Arkansas, 1972.

NOTES

Notes to Chapter 1

[1]Little Rock *Arkansas State Gazette*, 29 September 1868. (Although the name of the newspaper varied, we have used *Arkansas State Gazette* throughout this book.)

[2]Biscoe Hindman, "Thomas Carmichael Hindman," *Confederate Veteran* 38:3 (March 1930): 97; *Cavaliers and Pioneers: Abstracts of Virginia Land Patents and Grants, 1623–1666,* abstracted and indexed by Nell Marion Nugent (Baltimore: Genealogical Publishing Co., Inc., 1974) 1: 231; Kate Cumming, *Kate: The Journal of a Confederate Nurse,*
ed. Richard Barksdale Harwell (Baton Rouge: Louisiana State University Press, 1959) 125; P. Hume Brown, *A Short History of Scotland*, rev. Henry W. Meikle (Edinburgh: Oliver and Boyd, Ltd., 1951) 306–308; Hugh Levis Hall, Jr., *Those Who Came Before Us* (Sherman, Texas: A-1 Printing Company, 1982) 101.

[3]Biscoe Hindman, "Thomas Carmichael Hindman," 97; William H. Powell, *List of Officers of the Army of the United States from 1779 to 1900* (New York: L. R. Hamersly & Co., 1900) 373; Thomas C. Hindman to Andrew Jackson, 26 March 1816, Andrew Jackson Papers, Library of Congress (LC), Washington, D. C.

[4]Receipt, 21 June 1818 in Andrew Jackson Papers, LC; "County Officials," *Alabama Historical Quarterly* 6:2 (Summer 1944): 169; Biscoe Hindman, "Thomas Carmichael Hindman," 97.

[5]Mildred Stanfield Hindman Doxey, "Memoirs," reprinted in Jane Isbell Haynes, ed., *William Faulkner: His Tippah County Heritage* (Columbia, South Carolina: Seajay Press, 1985) 61–62.

[6]Ibid., 62–63.

[7]Certificate of Thomas C. Hindman, 16 February 1820, Andrew Jackson Papers, LC; Elizabeth Pack to Maj. Gen. Thomas C. Hindman, 15 December 1862, Thomas C. Hindman Collection, Phillips County Museum, Helena, Arkansas; John Ross to R. K. Call, 30 July 1821; John Ross et al to Andrew Jackson, 6 March 1829; John Ross to Andrew Jackson, 24 June 1829, all reprinted in *The Papers of Chief John Ross*, ed. Gary E. Moulton, 2 vols. (Norman: University of Oklahoma Press, 1985) 1:41–42, 157–58, 165–66.

[8]Gary E. Moulton, *John Ross: Cherokee Chief* (Athens: University of Georgia Press, 1978) 105; Doxey, "Memoirs," 65–66.

⁹Doxey, "Memoirs," 67; John R. Finger, "The Abortive Second Cherokee Removal, 1841–1844," *Journal of Southern History* 47:2 (May 1981): 211–15.

¹⁰Doxey, "Memoirs," 67–68; Thomas C. Hindman to John Ross, 14 April 1841, Oklahoma Historical Society (OHS), Oklahoma City, Oklahoma.

¹¹Doxey, "Memoirs," 68–70; "Tippah County Deed Book 'D' and Index," *News and Journal* 11:2 (1985): 44.

¹²Roland Mulford, *History of the Lawrenceville School, 1810–1935* (Princeton: Princeton University Press, 1935) 6, 9, 49; S. R. Slaymaker II, *Five Miles Away: The Story of the Lawrenceville School* (Lawrenceville, New Jersey: The Lawrenceville School, 1985) 27. Biscoe Hindman claims that his father entered Lawrenceville at the age of fourteen and graduated four years later. Lawrenceville records, however, list him as part of the class of 1843, which would have him entering the institute at age eleven. Biscoe Hindman, "Thomas Carmichael Hindman," 97.

¹³Slaymaker, *Five Miles Away,* 64–67.

¹⁴Ibid., 64–65.

¹⁵Mulford, *History of the Lawrenceville School,* 62–63.

¹⁶Slaymaker, *Five Miles Away,* 29, 71, 88; Mulford, *History of the Lawrenceville School,* 16.

¹⁷Slaymaker, *Five Miles Away,* 68.

¹⁸Ibid., 87–88, 98.

¹⁹Closing Exercises of the Lawrenceville Classical Commercial High School, 25 September 1843, John Dixon Library, The Lawrenceville School, Lawrenceville, New Jersey; Biscoe Hindman, "Thomas Carmichael Hindman," 97.

²⁰Doxey, "Memoirs," 72–73.

²¹Ripley (MS) *Advertiser,* 2, 30 March 1844; 1 November 1845.

²²Jackson *Mississippian,* 15 April 1846.

²³Holly Springs (MS) *Guard,* 8, 29 May 1846; Robert A. Brent, "Mississippi and the Mexican War," *Journal of Mississippi History* 31:3 (August 1969): 204–205.

²⁴Dunbar Rowland, *Military History of Mississippi, 1803- 1898* with a New Index by H. Grady Howell, Jr. (Spartanburg, South Carolina: The Reprint Company, 1988) 19; Ripley (MS) *Advertiser,* 6 June 1846.

²⁵Ripley *Advertiser,* 30 May; 6, 27 June 1846.

²⁶Robert E. May, *John A. Quitman: Old South Crusader* (Baton Rouge: Louisiana State University Press, 1985) 149- 62; John K. Bettersworth, *Mississippi: A History* (Austin: The Steck Company, 1959) 219–20; Rowland, *Military History of Mississippi,* 18–28; Clement Eaton, *Jefferson Davis* (New York: Free Press, 1977) 63–64.

²⁷Brent, "Mississippi and the Mexican War," 207.

[28]Natchez *Mississippi Free Trader,* 2, 23, 30 December 1846; 13 January 1847; Jackson *Mississippian,* 8 December 1846; Military Service Record of Thomas C. Hindman, Jr., National Archives and Records Administration (NARA), Washington, D. C.; Military Service Record of Robert H. Hindman, NARA; Rowland, *Military History of Mississippi,* 29.

[29]Reuben Davis, *Recollections of Mississippi and Mississippians,* rev. ed. (Oxford: University and College Press of Mississippi, 1972) 253; Thomas N. Love," Remarks on Some of the Diseases Which Prevailed in the Second Mississippi Rifles," in George W. Smith and Charles Judah, eds., *Chronicles of the Gringos: The U. S. Army in the Mexican War, 1846–1848* (Albuquerque: University of New Mexico Press, 1968) 49; Natchez *Mississippi Free Trader,* 27 January; 3 February 1847; Holly Springs (MS) *Gazette,* 8 January 1847.

[30]Love, "Remarks on Some of the Diseases Which Prevailed in the Second Mississippi Rifles," 51; Natchez *Mississippi Free Trader,* 3 February 1847; Vicksburg (MS) *Sentinel,* 17 February 1847; Rowland, *Military History of Mississippi,* 30.

[31]Love, "Remarks on Some Diseases Which Prevailed in the Second Mississippi Rifles," 52; Natchez *Mississippi Free Trader,* 3 March 1847; Jackson *Mississippian,* 26 March 1847.

[32]Davis, *Recollections,* 243–45, 253; Dunbar Rowland, *History of Mississippi: The Heart of the South,* 2 vols. (Chicago: The S. J. Clarke Publishing Company, 1925) 1:683; Jackson *Mississippian,* 22 October 1847; Rowland, *Military History of Mississippi,* 30–31.

[33]Military Service Record of Robert H. Hindman; Military Service Record of Thomas C. Hindman, Jr.; T. C. Hindman, Jr. to Jacob Thompson, 10 May 1850, reprinted in Donald Philip Duclos, "Son of Sorrow: The Life, Works, and Influence of Colonel William C. Falkner, 1825–1889" (Ph.D. diss., University of Michigan, 1961) 422; Rowland, *History of Mississippi,* 1:684; Natchez *Mississippi Free Trader,* 19 July; 2 August 1848.

[34]Ripley *Advertiser,* 10 May 1849, reprinted in the Memphis (TN) *Tri-Weekly Appeal,* 17 May 1849; The State of Mississippi vs. William C. Falkner, Circuit Court, Tippah County Courthouse, Ripley, Mississippi. Galloway's version of the feud appeared in the 10 April 1881 issue of the Memphis (TN) *Daily Appeal,* and C. J. Frederick, Falkner's law partner retold the tale of the killing of Robert Hindman and Erasmus Morris in a letter to the Memphis *Daily Appeal,* 20 April 1881. Numerous accounts of the Hindman-Falkner feud exist. See Thomas Felix Hickerson, *The Falkner Feuds* (Chapel Hill, North Carolina: The Colonial Press, Inc., 1964) 12–15; Joseph Blotner, *Faulkner: A Biography* (New York: Random House, 1974) 1:16–19; Duclos, "Son of Sorrow," 71–85; Maud Morrow Brown, "William C. Falkner,

Man of Legends," *Georgia Review* 10:4 (Winter 1956): 424–25; Victor Hoar, "Colonel William C. Falkner in the Civil War," *Journal of Mississippi History* 27:1 (February 1955): 44.

[35]Sons of Temperance, Minutes, Term Ending 30 September 1852, Items 4, 13, 27, 39; Term Ending 31 December 1852, Items 45, 52, 57; Term Ending 30 June 1853, Items 39, 45, 64. Ripley Public Library, Ripley, Mississippi.

[36]Ibid., Term Ending 31 December 1852, Items 6, 12, 32, 34, 54.

[37]Ibid., Term Ending 31 December 1853, Items 32, 41; Term Ending 31 March 1854, Item 64.

[38]May, *John A. Quitman*, 214; Jackson *Flag of the Union*, 22 November 1850.

[39]Vicksburg (MS) *Sentinel*, 24 September 1850; Yazoo (Yazoo City, MS) *Democrat*, 26 September 1850; Eaton, *Jefferson Davis*, 74; Holman Hamilton, *Prologue to Conflict: The Crisis and Compromise of 1850* (New York: W. W. Norton, 1966) 139.

[40]Eaton, *Jefferson Davis*, 73, 77; Mississippi, *House Journal* (1854), 18; Hamilton, *Prologue to Conflict*, 148. The Holly Springs *Mississippi Palladium*, 16 May 1851, reprinted the legislative resolutions of 30 November 1850, condemning Foote's course.

[41]Yazoo *Democrat*, 19 March; 16 July; 17 September 1851; Jackson *Flag of the Union*, 7 February; 9 May; 20 June; 19, 26 September 1851; Holly Springs *Mississippi Palladium*, 9, 16 May; 12 September 1851; Eaton, *Jefferson Davis*, 79.

[42]Jackson *Mississippian*, 3 October 1851; Yazoo *Democrat*, 16, 22 October 1851; *Flag of the Union*, 7 November 1851.

[43]Holly Springs *Mississippi Palladium*, 27 June 1851.

[44]Ibid., 6 June 1851; H. S. Foote, *War of the Rebellion; or Scylla and Charybdis* (New York: Harper & Brothers, Publishers, 1866) 362; Memphis (TN) *Avalanche*, 15 September 1860, reprinted in Des Arc (AR) *Citizen*, 19 September 1860; Thomas C. Hindman to the Editor of the New York *News*, 25 June 1866, reprinted in the *Arkansas State Gazette*, 3 August 1866; Eaton, *Jefferson Davis*, 79; Yazoo *Democrat*, 14 January 1852.

[45]Joel H. Berry and T. C. Hindman, Jr. to Jefferson Davis, 10 September 1853, in *Jefferson Davis, Constitutionalist: His Letters, Papers and Speeches*, ed. Dunbar Rowland, 10 vols. (Jackson: Mississippi Department of Archives and History, 1923) 2:263–64; Jackson *Mississippian*, 28 October 1853; Jackson *Flag of the Union*, 25 November 1853.

[46]Mississippi, *House Journal* (1854), 111, 158, 207, 252, 499–500, 517, 532, 695.

[47]Ibid., 239.

[48]Ibid., 287, 304.

[49]Ibid., 133–37, 612.

[50]Ibid., 151–55, 161–63.

[51]Ibid., 130–31; Yazoo *Democrat,* 18 January 1854.

[52]Message of Governor Henry S. Foote, 2 January 1854, in Mississippi *House Journal* (1854), 14–27.

[53]Ibid., 28–29.

[54]Mississippi *House Journal* (1854), 32, 183, 185, 187.

[55]Yazoo *Democrat,* 17 October 1850; Jackson *Mississippian,* 28 October 1853.

Notes to Chapter 2

[1]Josiah H. Shinn, *Pioneers and Makers of Arkansas* (Washington, D. C.: Genealogical and Historical Publishing Company, 1908) 265.

[2]G. W. Featherstonhaugh, *Excursion Through the Slave States, From Washington on the Potomac to the Frontier of Mexico; with Sketches of Popular Manners and Geological Notes* (New York: Harper and Brothers, 1844) 94–95; Ted R. Worley, "Helena on the Mississippi," *Arkansas Historical Quarterly* 13:1 (Spring 1954): 4–5 (Hereafter cited as *AHQ*).

[3]*Biographical and Historical Memoirs of Eastern Arkansas* (Chicago: The Goodspeed Publishing Company, 1890) 747; *The Statistics of the Population of the United States* (Washington, D. C.: Government Printing Office, 1872) 1:87; Carl H. Moneyhon, "Economic Democracy in Antebellum Arkansas, Phillips County, 1850-1860," *AHQ* 40:2 (Summer 1981): 159.

[4]Worley, "Helena on the Mississippi," 6–9.

[5]Ibid., 3, 13–14; Helena (AR) *Democratic Star,* 29 March, 7 June 1854.

[6]Memphis (TN) *Appeal,* n. d., reprinted in the Helena *Democratic Star,* 14 June 1854; Helena *Democratic Star,* 14 June 1854.

[7]Helena *Democratic Star,* 5 July 1854.

[8]Charles Edward Nash, *Biographical Sketches of Gen. Pat Cleburne and Gen T. C. Hindman Together with Humorous Anecdotes and Reminiscences of the Late Civil War* (Little Rock: Tunnah & Pittard, Printers, 1895; Reprint, Dayton, Ohio: Morningside Bookshop, 1977) 57; Helena *Democratic Star,* 5 July 1854.

[9]Nash, *Biographical Sketches,* 57–58.

[10]Ibid.,59.

[11]Ibid.,60.

[12]Helena *Democratic Star,* 26 July 1854; Helena (AR), *Southern Shield,* n.

d., reprinted in the Helena *Democratic Star,* 26 July 1854.

[13]T. C. Hindman, Jr. to John A. Quitman, 31 January 1855, John A. Quitman Papers, Mississippi Department of Archives and History (MDAH), Jackson, Mississippi; Sam W. Williams, "Recollections," in Nash, *Biographical Sketches,* 149.

[14]J. W. McDonald to John A. Quitman, 26 March 1854, John A. Quitman Papers, Houghton Library (HL), Harvard University, Cambridge, Massachusetts; T. C. Hindman, Jr. to J. S. Thrasher, 12 June 1854; T. C. Hindman, Jr. to John A. Quitman, 31 January 1855, both in John A. Quitman Papers, MDAH.

[15]T. C. Hindman, Jr. to John A. Quitman, 31 January 1855, John A. Quitman Papers, MDAH.

[16]T. C. Hindman, Jr. to John A. Quitman, 31 January 1855, John A. Quitman Papers, MDAH; Helena *Democratic Star,* 1 February 1855.

[17]Holly Springs (MS) *Democrat,* n. d., reprinted in the Helena *Democratic Star,* 1 March 1855.

[18]Helena *Democratic Star,* 26 April; 3 May 1855.

[19]Ibid., 17 May 1855.

[20]Ibid., 24 May; 7 June 1855.

[21]Harold T. Smith, "The Know Nothings in Arkansas," *AHQ* 34:4 (Winter 1975): 292–93.

[22]Ibid., 293–94.

[23]W. Darrell Overdyke, *The Know-Nothing Party in the South* (Baton Rouge: Louisiana State University Press, 1950) 113; Little Rock (AR) *True Democrat,* 12 June; 11 December 1855.

[24]Helena *Democratic Star,* 24, 31 May 1855.

[25]Ibid., 9 August 1855.

[26]*True Democrat,* 16, 30 October; 13 November 1855; Helena *Democratic Star,* 18 October 1855; Memphis (TN) *Appeal,* n. d., reprinted in the Helena *Democratic Star,* 22 November 1855.

[27]Helena *Democratic Star,* 15 November 1855; *True Democrat,* 13 November 1855.

[28]Helena *Democratic Star,* 29 November 1855; Howell Purdue and Elizabeth Purdue, *Pat Cleburne: Confederate General* (Hillsboro, Texas: Hill Jr. College Press, 1973) 48.

[29]Helena *Democratic Star,* 29 November 1855.

[30]Ibid.   [31]Ibid.

[32]Ibid.

[33]Memphis *Appeal,* n. d., reprinted in the *True Democrat,* 11 December 1855.

[34]*True Democrat,* 18 December 1855.

[35]Nash, *Biographical Sketches,* 52–54.

[36]Helena *Democratic Star*, 4, 11 October 1855.

[37]Nash, *Biographical Sketches*, 10, 56–57; Helena *Southern Shield*, 29 December 1855.

[38]*True Democrat*, 8 January; 26 February; 4 March 1856; Helena *Southern Shield*, 23 February 1856; Van Buren (AR) *Intelligencer*, 16 February 1856, reprinted in the *True Democrat*, 26 February 1856.

[39]*True Democrat*, 18 March 1856.

[40]Ibid., 11 March; 13 May 1856; Memphis (TN) *Eagle and Enquirer*, n. d., reprinted in the *True Democrat*, 15 April 1856.

[41]*True Democrat*, 20 May 1856; Batesville (AR) *Independent Balance*, 9, 16 May 1856.

[42]*True Democrat*, 20 May 1856.

[43]Ibid.

[44]Helena (AR) *State-Rights Democrat*, 29 May 1856; *True Democrat*, 13 May 1856.

[45]Helena *Democratic Star*, n. d., reprinted in the *True Democrat*, 12 June 1855; The text of Hindman's 18 October 1855, speech is in the *True Democrat*, 11 December 1855.

[46]*True Democrat*, 11 December 1855.

[47]Ibid.   [48]Ibid.

[49]Ibid.

[50]Nash, *Biographical Sketches*, 63-64; Helena *State-Rights Democrat*, 15 May 1856.

[51]Helena *State-Rights Democrat*, 29 May 1856; Little Rock *Arkansas State Gazette*, 14 June 1856; Nash, *Biographical Sketches*, 65.

[52]Helena *State-Rights Democrat*, 29 May 1856; *True Democrat*, 10 June 1856; Nash, *Biographical Sketches*, 66.

[53]Nash, *Biographical Sketches*, 66–69.

[54]Helena *State-Rights Democrat*, 10, 17 July 1856; *True Democrat*, 12 August; 18 November 1856.

[55]Nash, *Biographical Sketches*, 76–79.

[56]Ibid., 77; Marriage Transcript Record, T. C. Hindman and Mollie Biscoe, Phillips County, bk. 1, file no. 1018975.

[57]Nash, *Biographical Sketches*, 78; Hall, *Those Who Came Before Us*, 116–17.

[58]Manuscript Census for Phillips County Arkansas (1860), 396, Abstract and Index of Deeds, 1857–1869, Phillips County, Arkansas, bk. 2, 320.

Notes to Chapter 3

[1]Nash, *Biographical Sketches,* 75; Helena *Southern Shield,* 30 July 1857; *True Democrat,* 8 September; 24 November 1857.

[2]*True Democrat,* 29 December 1857.

[3]Ibid., 19 January; 16 February; 23 March; 13, 20, 27 April 1858.

[4]Ibid., 19 January; 23 March; 6 April 1858.

[5]Ibid., 18 May 1858; Van Buren (AR) *Intelligencer,* 21 May 1858; Fort Smith (AR) *Times,* 9 June 1858, reprinted in the Batesville (AR) *Independent Balance,* 24 June 1858.

[6]*True Democrat,* 28 July 1858.

[7]Helena *State-Rights Democrat,* 31 July 1858, reprinted in the Van Buren *Intelligencer,* 13 August 1858; *True Democrat,* 18 August 1858; Nash, *Biographical Sketches,* 75.

[8]*True Democrat,* 21 July; 18 August 1858.

[9]John Hallum, *Biographical and Pictorial History of Arkansas* (Albany: Weed, Parsons and Company, 1887) 45–47. Michael B. Dougan, *Confederate Arkansas: The People and Policies of a Frontier State in Wartime* (Tuscaloosa: University of Alabama Press, 1972) 8, 12; Michael B. Dougan, "A Look at the 'Family' in Arkansas Politics, 1858–1865," *Arkansas Historical Quarterly* 29:2 (Summer 1970): 99; Margaret Ross, *Arkansas Gazette: The Early Years, 1819–1866* (Little Rock: Arkansas Gazette Foundation, 1969) 129–32.

[10]Dougan, *Confederate Arkansas,* 15–16; James M. Woods, *Rebellion and Realignment: Arkansas's Road To Secession* (Fayetteville: University of Arkansas Press, 1987) 39–40; Napoleon *Planter,* n.d., reprinted in the *Arkansas State Gazette,* 26 June 1858.

[11]Dougan, *Confederate Congress,* 12.

[12]*True Democrat,* 21 July 1858.

[13]Batesville *Independent Balance,* 1 July 1858.

[14]Napoleon *Planter,* n.d., reprinted in the Little Rock *Arkansas State Gazette,* 26 June 1858.

[15]*Ouchita Herald* (Camden, AR), 29 July; 5 August 1858.

[16]Batesville *Independent Balance,* 24 June 1858; T. C. Hindman to Editor, 8 June 1858, Smithville (AR) *Plaindealer,* 16 June 1858, reprinted in the *True Democrat,* 29 June 1858.

[17]T. C. Hindman, *Speech of Col. T. C. Hindman, on Federal and Arkansas Politics: Made in Representatives Hall, on February 15, 1859* (Little Rock: James D. Butler, 1859) 14–15, 17; T. C. Hindman, *Speech of Hon. Thos. C.*

Hindman, at Helena, Arkansas, November 28, 1859 (Washington, D. C.: Lemuel Towers, 1860) 2–3.

[18]Hindman, *Federal and Arkansas Politics,* 18–21.

[19]*True Democrat,* 16, 30 March; 6 April 1859; Batesville (AR) *Sentinel,* n.d., reprinted in the *True Democrat,* 6 April 1859.

[20]*True Democrat,* 9, 16, 30 March; 22 June 1859.

[21]Fayetteville *Arkansian,* 30 July; 22 October 1859.

[22]Hindman, *Speech . . . at Helena,* 16–17.

[23]Ibid., 17–18.

[24]Ibid., 18–20.

[25]Ibid., 20–21.

[26]Ibid., 17, 21–25.

[27]*True Democrat,* 16 February; 9, 16, 30 March; 13, 20, 27 April; 18 May; 1 June; 10 August 1859.

[28]Ted R. Worley, "The Control of the Real Estate Bank of the State of Arkansas, 1836–1855," *Mississippi Valley Historical Review* 37:3 (December 1950): 403–405.

[29]Worley, "The Control of the Real Estate Bank," 403–26; Ted R. Worley, "The Arkansas State Bank: Ante-Bellum Period," *AHQ* 23:1 (Spring 1964): 65–73.

[30]Hindman, *Speech . . . at Helena,* 26–27; *True Democrat,* 14 September 1859.

[31]Hindman, *Speech . . . at Helena,* 26–31.

[32]*True Democrat,* 14, 21 September; 5, 19, 26 October 1859; Little Rock *Old-Line Democrat,* 13 October 1859.

[33]Hindman, *Speech . . . at Helena,* 26, 31.

[34]Ibid., 32; *True Democrat,* 19, 26 October 1859.

[35]Hindman, *Federal and Arkansas Politics,* 19; Hindman, *Speech . . . at Helena,* 12; *True Democrat,* 15, 29 June 1859.

[36]Hindman, *Federal and Arkansas Politics,* 18–19; Hindman, *Speech . . . at Helena,* 33.

[37]*True Democrat,* 25 May 1859.

[38]Ibid., 12 October 1859; *Old-Line Democrat,* 27 October 1859.

[39]*Old-Line Democrat,* 22 September 1859.

[40]R. W. Johnson to William F. Douglass, Editor, The *Independent,* 28 November 1859, reprinted in the *Old-Line Democrat,* 8 December 1859.

[41]*Old-Line Democrat,* 17 November 1859; R. W. Johnson to William F. Douglass, Editor, The *Independent,* 28 November 1859, reprinted in the *Old-Line Democrat,* 8 December 1859; Fayetteville *Arkansian,* 27 January 1860.

[42]*Old-Line Democrat,* 8 December 1859; Hindman, *Speech . . . at Helena,*

9, 11; Des Arc (AR) *Citizen*, 18 February 1859; *True Democrat*, 22 June 1859.

[43]*Arkansian*, 28 October; 18, 25 November; 16, 23 December 1859; 24 February 1860; W. L. Martin, alias Viator, 22 November 1859, reprinted in the *Old-Line Democrat*, 1 December 1859; *True Democrat*, 21 December 1859; T. C. Hindman to Jno. A. Price, 21 January 1860, reprinted in the *Old-Line Democrat*, 9 February 1860.

[44]Van Buren *Press*, 25 November 1859; 27 February 1860; *Old-Line Democrat*, 9 February 1860; Des Arc *Citizen*, 7 December 1859.

[45]*Arkansian*, 30 December 1859; *True Democrat* 18 January 1860; Van Buren *Press*, 20 January 1860; Des Arc *Citizen*, 21 December 1859. Hindman's Congressional career will be covered in the succeeding chapter.

[46]Woods, *Rebellion and Realignment*, 77–78; Dougan, *Confederate Arkansas*, 12.

[47]*Old-Line Democrat*, 3 May 1860.

[48]Ibid., 5 April 1860.

[49]Ibid., 31 May 1860; Van Buren *Press*, 1 June 1860.

[50]*Arkansian*, 25 May 1860.

[51]*True Democrat*, 19, 26 May 1860; *Old-Line Democrat*, 24 May 1860; Hempstead *Democrat*, n.d., quoted in the *True Democrat*, 26 May 1860.

[52]*Old-Line Democrat*, 1, 8 December 1859; 8 March; 10 May; 10 July 1860; *True Democrat*, 7, 14 1860.

[53]Ibid., 10 May; 5, 10, 27 July 1860.

[54]Ibid., 17, 24 May 1860; Des Arc *Citizen*, 11 March 1859.

[55]Pocahontas *Advertiser and Herald*, n.d., reprinted in the *Arkansian*, 4 August 1860; Dougan, "A Look at the 'Family' in Arkansas Politics, 1858–1865," 101–103.

[56]Des Arc *Citizen*, 11 March 1859; *True Democrat*, 29 June 1859.

[57]*Arkansian*, 14 July 1860; *True Democrat*, 30 June 1860. *Old-Line Democrat*, 24 July 1860.

[58]Helena *Southern Shield*, n.d., reprinted in the *True Democrat*, 14 July 1860; Washington D. C. *Evening Star*, 19–25 June 1860; Williams, "Recollections," 153–54; *True Democrat*, 21 July 1860; *Old-Line Democrat*, 24 July 1860; Nash, *Biographical Sketches*, 62–63.

[59]*Old-Line Democrat*, 31 May, 7 June; 5, 27 July 1860; Van Buren *Press*, 29 June 1860.

[60]*Arkansas State Gazette*, 23 June; 28 July 1860; Van Buren *Press*, 13 July 1860; *Old-Line Democrat*, 21, 28 June; 10 July 1860.

[61]*Arkansas State Gazette*, 23 June 1860.

[62]Pocahontas *Advertiser and Herald*, n.d., reprinted in the *Arkansian*, 4 August 1860; Van Buren *Press*, 13 July 1860; *Arkansian*, 23 June; 28 July 1860.

[63]Van Buren *Press*, 27 July 1860; *Arkansian*, 23 June; 21 July 1860.

[64]Van Buren *Press*, 7 September 1860; *Old-Line Democrat*, 16 August 1860; *Arkansian*, 14 September 1860; *True Democrat*, 1 September 1860; 14 November 1861; John W. Brown, Diary, 14 August 1860, Arkansas History Commission (AHC), Little Rock, Arkansas; Woods, *Rebellion and Realignment*, 120; Dougan, "A Look at the 'Family,'" 111. Hindman polled 20,051 votes to Cypert's 9,699, while Gantt garnered 16,599 votes to 13,007 for Mitchel. An independent candidate, James A. Jones polled 891 votes. Van Buren *Press*, 7 September 1860.

[65]*Arkansas State Gazette*, 28 July 1860; John M. Harrell, "Arkansas," in *Confederate Military History*, ed., Clement A. Evans, 12 vols. (Atlanta: Confederate Publishing Co., 1899) 10:3; Dougan, *Confederate Arkansas*, 21–22; *Old-Line Democrat*, 28 June 1860; *True Democrat*, 25 August 1860; Helena *Southern Shield*, n.d., reprinted in the *True Democrat*, 25 August 1860.

[66]*Old-Line Democrat*, 10 November; 8 December 1859; 5, 27 July 1860.

Notes to Chapter 4

[1]T. C. Hindman to John A. Quitman, 31 January 1855, John A. Quitman Papers, MDAH; Mississippi, *House Journal* (1854), 130–31, 183–87; Helena (AR) *State-Rights Democrat*, 13 November 1856.

[2]Des Arc (AR) *Citizen*, 18 December 1858; Little Rock (AR) *True Democrat*, 18 May 1858; Van Buren (AR) *Intelligencer*, 21 May 1858; Fort Smith *Times*, 9 June 1858, reprinted in Batesville (AR) *Independent Balance*, 24 June 1858.

[3]*True Democrat*, 28 September 1859; 4 January 1860; Des Arc *Citizen*, 22 February 1860; Van Buren *Press*, 13 July 1860.

[4]Little Rock (AR) *Old-Line Democrat*, 29 September 1859.

[5]Ibid., 15 September 1859.

[6]Ronald T. Takaki, *A Pro-Slavery Crusade: The Agitation To Reopen the African Slave Trade* (New York: Free Press, 1971) 35–36, 65–67.

[7]Ibid., 26–27.

[8]Ibid., 27–28.

[9]*True Democrat*, 28 July 1858.

[10]*Congressional Globe*, 36 Cong., 1 sess., 1–3, 21, 427, 547–48.

[11]John Sherman to W. T. Sherman, 24 December 1859, in *The Sherman Letters: Correspondence Between General Sherman and Senator Sherman from 1837 to 1891*, ed. Rachel Sherman Thorndike (New York: Da Capo Press, 1969)

78–79; *Congressional Globe,* 36 Cong., 1 sess., 21.

[12]*Appendix to the Congressional Globe,* 36 Cong., 1 sess., 81–87; St. Louis (MO) *Republican,* n.d., quoted in the Des Arc *Citizen,* 7 March 1860; *Old-Line Democrat,* 9 February 1860.

[13]*Appendix to the Congressional Globe,* 36 Cong., 1 sess., 82.

[14]Ibid., 83; *Old-Line Democrat,* 10 November 1859.

[15]*Appendix to the Congressional Globe,* 36 Cong., 1 sess., 85–86.

[16]Ibid., 84.

[17]*Old-Line Democrat,* 23 February; 8, 29 March 1860; Van Buren *Press,* 10 February; 16 March 1860.

[18]*Old-Line Democrat,* 8 March 1860; Somerville *Democrat,* n. d.; Ottawa (Ohio) *Democrat,* n. d.; Portland (Maine) *Argus,* n. d., all reprinted in the *Old-Line Democrat,* 1 March 1860; Vicksburg (MS) *Sun,* n.d., reprinted in the Des Arc *Citizen,* 22 February 1860; St. Louis *Republican,* n.d., reprinted in Des Arc *Citizen,* 7 March 1860.

[19]*Congressional Globe,* 36 Cong., 1 sess., 614, 650–55; Des Arc *Citizen,* 25 January 1860; Van Buren *Press,* 17 February 1860; Ollinger Crenshaw, "The Speakership Contest of 1859–1860: John Sherman's Election A Cause of Disruption?" *Mississippi Valley Historical Review* 29:4 (December 1942): 333–35.

[20]*Congressional Globe,* 36 Cong., 1 sess., 1027–34.

[21]Des Arc *Citizen,* 11 April 1860.

[22]*Congressional Globe,* 36 Cong., 1 sess., 818, 1116, 2677; *Old-Line Democrat,* 27 October 1859.

[23]*Old-Line Democrat,* 23 February; 1, 8, 29 March; 31 May; 16 August 1860; Van Buren *Press,* 10 February; 16, 30 March; 5 April; 1 June; 7 September 1860.

[24]William B. Hesseltine, ed., *Three Against Lincoln: Murat Halstead Reports the Caucuses of 1860* (Baton Rouge: Louisiana State University Press, 1960) 19, 32, 34–35. Proceedings of the Charleston convention were reprinted in the *True Democrat,* 28 April; 5, 12 May 1860.

[25]Hesseltine, ed., *Three Against Lincoln,* 45–46, 55, 82–88.

[26]*Old-Line Democrat,* 24 May 1860; *True Democrat,* 19, 26 May 1860; Washington (D. C.) *Evening Star,* 19 June 1860; Dwight L. Dumond, *The Secession Movement, 1860–1861* (New York: MacMillan Company, 1931) 76–78.

[27]Washington *Evening Star,* 20 June 1860; Baltimore (MD) *American and Commercial Advertiser,* 20 June 1860; *True Democrat,* 11 August 1860; *Old-Line Democrat,* 17 July 1860; Des Arc *Citizen,* 25 July 1860.

[28]*Baltimore American and Commercial Advertiser,* 21 June 1860; The correspondence was reprinted in the *True Democrat,* 30 June 1860. See also *True Democrat,* 11 August 1860; Louisville (KY) *Journal,* n.d., reprinted in the *True Democrat,* 21 July 1860; Fayetteville *Arkansian,* 7 July 1860.

[29]*Old-Line Democrat,* 13 July 1860; Des Arc *Citizen,* 25 July 1860.

[30]*Old-Line Democrat,* 13 July 1860.

[31]Washington D. C. *Evening Star,* 23 June 1860; Dumond, *The Secession Movement,* 86–89.

[32]Hesseltine, ed., *Three Against Lincoln,* 274, 278; Washington D. C. *Evening Star,* 25 June 1860.

[33]Washington D. C. *Evening Star,* 25 June 1860; Dumond, *The Secession Movement,* 90.

[34]Fayetteville *Arkansian,* 21 July 1860; Van Buren *Press,* 18 November 1859.

[35]*Old-line Democrat,* 29 March; 30 August 1860; Des Arc *Citizen,* 22 August 1860.

[36]*True Democrat,* 1 September 1860.

[37]Des Arc *Citizen,* 5 September 1860; *Arkansas State Gazette,* 8 September 1860.

[38]Memphis (TN) *Daily Appeal,* 15, 18 September 1860; Memphis (TN) *Avalanche,* 15 September 1860, reprinted in the Des Arc *Citizen,* 19 September 1860.

[39]Memphis *Avalanche,* 19 September 1860.

[40]John W. Brown, Diary, 1821–1865, 22 October; 6 November 1860, AHC.

[41]*Arkansas State Gazette,* 8 December 1860; Dougan, *Confederate Arkansas,* 33–34.

[42]*Arkansas State Gazette,* 1 December 1860; 12 January 1861. Heeding his advice, the legislature appropriated $100,000 to purchase arms for the state. See Des Arc *Constitutional Union,* 25 January 1861; *Arkansas State Gazette,* 26 January 1861.

[43]Samuel S. Cox, *Three Decades of Federal Legislation* (Providence, Rhode Island: J. A. & R. A. Reid, Publishers, 1885) 74, 96.

[44]David M. Potter, *The Impending Crisis 1848–1861* (New York: Harper and Row, 1976) 492.

[45]Dumond, *The Secession Movement,* 155–56; Potter, *The Impending Crisis,* 492.

[46]Dumond, *The Secession Movement,* 157; Potter, *The Impending Crisis,* 492.

[47]*Congressional Globe,* 36 Cong., 2 sess., 63, 78–79.

[48]Washington D. C. *Evening Star,* 15 December 1860; Edward McPherson, *The Political History of the United States of America, During the Great*

Rebellion (Washington, D. C.: Philip & Solomons, 1865) 37.

[49]South Carolina, Ordinance of Secession, 20 December 1860, and South Carolina, Declaration of Causes, 24 December 1860, reprinted in Henry Steele Commager, *The Blue and the Gray*, 2 vols. (Indianapolis: Bobbs-Merrill Company, Inc., 1950) 1:7–9.

[50]*Arkansas State Gazette*, 29 December 1860.

[51]R. W. Johnson and T. C. Hindman, *To the People of Arkansas* (Washington, D. C.: W. H. Moore, Printer, 1861) 1.

[52]Ibid., 2–3.

[53]Ibid., 5–6.

[54]*The War of the Rebellion: Official Records of the Union and Confederate Armies*, 128 vols. (Washington, D. C.: Government Printing Office, 1880–1902) 1st. ser., 1: 638–47. Hereafter cited as *OR*. Unless otherwise noted, all volumes cited are Series 1.

[55]Fayetteville *Arkansian*, 24 November 1860; 1 February 1861; Woods, *Rebellion and Realignment*, 122, 130–32.

[56]*Congressional Globe*, 36 Cong., 2 sess., 114, 509, 1264, 1333.

[57]Ibid., 1001, 1032–33.

[58]Des Arc *Constitutional Union*, 15 March 1861; Arkansas, *Journal of Both Sessions of the Convention of the State of Arkansas* (1861), 27–30, 90–91, 102.

[59]*True Democrat*, 18 April 1861; Arkansas, *Journal of Both Sessions*, 114; "Proclamation Calling Militia and Convening Congress," in *The Collected Works of Abraham Lincoln*, ed. Roy P. Basler, 9 vols. (New Brunswick, New Jersey: Rutgers University Press, 1953–1971) 4:331–32; Copy of Governor Rector's Letter to Simon Cameron, Secretary of War, n. d., L. C. Gulley Collection (AHC).

[60]Van Buren *Press*, 24 April 1861.

[61]Arkansas, *Journal of Both Sessions*, 120–24; Jesse N. Cypert, "Secession Convention," in *Publications of the Arkansas Historical Association* 1 (1906): 318–19; *OR*, 1: 690.

Notes to Chapter 5

[1]Little Rock (AR) *True Democrat*, 11, 25 April; 9 May 1861; Van Buren (AR) *Press*, 1 May 1861; *Arkansas State Gazette*, 20, 27 April 1861; Van Buren *Press*, 24 April 1861; Des Arc (AR) *Constitutional Union*, 5 April 1861; Des Arc *Semi-Weekly Citizen*, 14 May 1861; Leo Elmer Huff, "Confederate Arkansas: A History of Arkansas During the Civil War" (M. A. thesis,

University of Arkansas, 1964) 45.

[2]Dorothy Stanley, ed., *The Autobiography of Sir Henry Morton Stanley* (Boston: Houghton Mifflin Company, 1937) 165–66.

[3]William G. Stevenson, *Thirteen Months in the Rebel Army* (New York: A. S. Barnes and Company, 1862) 20–23.

[4]Ibid., 24–34.

[5]Arkansas, *Ordinances of the State Convention Which Convened in Little Rock, May 6, 1861* (Little Rock, AR, 1861) 7–12, 16–18, 20–22, 24–26, 40–42, 62–66.

[6]*True Democrat*, 19 December 1861; Arkansas, *Journal of the Convention*, 190–91; Arkansas, *Ordinances*, 20–22; Huff, "Confederate Arkansas," 34–35.

[7]Harrell, "Arkansas," in 10:17; David Y. Thomas, *Arkansas in War and Reconstruction, 1861–1874* (Little Rock, AR: Arkansas Division, United Daughters of the Confederacy, 1926, 85–86; *The War of the Rebellion: Official Records of the Union and Confederate Armies* (Washington D. C.: Government Printing Office, 1880-1902) 1st ser., 3: 576 (hereafter *OR*).

[8]*OR*, 3: 710–11; Thomas, *Arkansas in War and Reconstruction*, 89.

[9]*OR*, 3: 578; *Journal of the Convention*, 325; *Arkansas State Gazette*, 1 June 1861.

[10]Helena *Shield*, n.d., reprinted in the *Arkansas State Gazette*, 15 June 1861.

[11]*OR*, 53: 694; 3: 588, 590.

[12]Oliver P. Temple, *Notable Men of Tennessee* (New York: Cosmopolitan Press, 1912) 402–405.

[13]*OR*, 3: 590, 592, 598; Helena *Shield*, 29 June 1861, reprinted in the Des Arc *Semi-Weekly Citizen*, 10 July 1861.

[14]Jon L. Wakelyn, ed., *Biographical Dictionary Of The Confederacy* (Westport, CT: Greenwood Press, 1977) 216.

[15]Nathaniel Cheairs Hughes, Jr., *General William J. Hardee Old Reliable* (Baton Rouge: Louisiana State University Press, 1965) 878; Edward Bourne, "The 'Young Guard,'" in *The Military Annals of Tennessee*, ed. John Berrien Lindsley (Nashville, TN: J. M. Lindsley & Co, 1886) 600; Military Service Record of Thomas C. Hindman (NARA); Des Arc *Semi-Weekly Citizen*, 17 July 1861.

[16]*OR*, 3: 609–10, 638.

[17]Thomas, *Arkansas in War and Reconstruction*, 94; *Message of Gov. Henry M. Rector To The General Assembly Of Arkansas In Extra Session, Nov. 6, 1861* (Little Rock, AR, 1861) 12; Huff, "Confederate Arkansas," 40; *True Democrat*, 12 December 1861.

[18]*OR*, 3: 691–92, 715–16; Van Buren *Press*, 4 September 1861; Basil Duke, *Reminiscences of General Basil W. Duke, C. S. A.* (Garden City, New York:

Doubleday, Page, & Company, 1911) 59.

[19]*OR*, 3: 615.

[20]*OR*, 3: 616; Hughes, *Old Reliable*, 78.

[21]*OR*, 3: 617–20, 626–27, 629, 634–35, 682–83.
Hughes, *Old Reliable*, 78.

[22]*OR*, 3: 736–37.

[23]Van Buren *Press,* 11 September: 2 October 1861; *True Democrat*, 3 October 1861.

[24]William Preston Johnston, "Albert Sidney Johnston At Shiloh," in *Battles and Leaders of the Civil War*, eds. R. U. Johnson and C. C. Buell, 4 vols. (New York: Thomas Yoseloff, 1884–1888) 1: 543.

[25]Johnston, 1:540–43; Stanley F. Horn, *The Army of Tennessee* (Norman: University of Oklahoma Press, 1952) 55.

[26]Charles P. Roland, *Albert Sidney Johnston Soldier of Three Republics* (Austin: University of Texas Press, 1964) 260.

[27]Ibid., 263; Horn, *Army of Tennessee*, 55; Johnston, "Albert Sidney Johnston," 1: 544–45; *OR*, 3: 413–15.

[28]Hughes, *Old Reliable*, 81–82.

[29]*OR*, 4: 484.

[30]Roland, *Albert Sidney Johnston*, 271; *OR*, 4: 531.

[31]T. C. Hindman to F. A. Shoup, 14 November 1861, in Military Service Record of Thomas C. Hindman, NARA; *OR*, 4: 481–82, 485, 489, 491, 507, 548–49.

[32]T. C. Hindman to D. G. White, 31 October 1861, in Military Service Record of Thomas C. Hindman, NARA.

[33]Ibid.   [34]*OR*, 7: 2–4.

[35]Ibid.   [36]Ibid.   [37]Ibid.

[38]Nashville *Union and American*, n.d., quoted in the *True Democrat*, 5 December 1861.

[39]*OR*, 7: 443–44.   [40]Ibid., 7: 758–59; 52, pt. 2: 238.

[41]Ibid., 7: 760–61.   [42]Ibid.

[43]Ibid., 7: 19–20.   [44]Ibid.

[45]Ibid., 7: 16–21.   [46]Ibid., 4: 548–49; Duke, *Reminiscences*, 59.

[47]*OR*, 7: 507.   [48]Ibid., 4: 555.

[49] *OR*, 7: 498, 544, 780, 792–93, 844–45, 933–36; T. C. Hindman to D. G. White, 2 January 1862, in Military Service Record of Thomas C. Hindman, NARA; Program for "SHYNNEDYGGE MILITAIRE," in the J. P. Wilson Papers, Robert W. Woodruff Library, Emory University (Emory), Atlanta, Georgia.

[50]*OR*, 7: 79–82, 105–10.

[51]Ibid.

[52]Horn, *Army of Tennessee*, 69; Roland, *Albert Sidney Johnston*, 281–82; *OR*, 7: 79–82, 105–10; "Sketch of General Felix K. Zollicoffer," *Southern Bivouac* 2:11 (July 1884): 492–93. The first report indicating that Zollicoffer had been killed came in a telegram from Hindman who was "commanding" Johnston's "advance" position. See *OR*, 7: 844–45.

[53]Horn, *Army of Tennessee*, 69–70; *OR*, 7: 79–86.

[54]*OR*, 7: 124–25, 159–60; Lew Wallace, "The Capture of Fort Donelson," in *Battles and Leaders*, 1:398–429; Roland, *Albert Sidney Johnston*, 286; Horn, *Army of Tennessee*, 74–75.

[55]*OR*, 52, pt. 2: 265.

[56]Ibid., 7: 610–11, 615; New Orleans (LA) *Daily Picayune*, 16 February 1862.

[57]Calvin L. Collier, *First In-Last Out The Capitol Guards, Ark. Brigade* (Little Rock, AR: Pioneer Press, 1961) 21.

[58]Ed Porter Thompson, *History of the Orphan Brigade* (Louisville, Kentucky: Lewis N. Thompson, 1898) 79; New Orleans (LA) *Daily Picayune*, 2 March 1862.

[59]New Orleans (LA)*Daily Picayune*, 27 February: 7 March 1862.

[60]*OR*, 10, pt. 1: 385.

[61]Ibid., 10, pt. 1: 382–84.

[62]Ibid., 10, pt. 1: 392–95.

[63]Ibid.   [64]Ibid., 10, pt. 2: 387.

[65]Hughes, *Old Reliable*, 102; *OR*, 10, pt. 1: 567.

[66]*OR*, 10, pt. 1: 385–86,463–64, 567; Roland, *Albert Sidney Johnston*, 318–19.

[67]Hughes, *Old Reliable*, 103–104; Thomas Jordan, "The Battle of Shiloh," *Southern Historical Society Papers* 35 (January-December 1907): 205.

[68]Johnston, "Albert Sidney Johnston at Shiloh," 1: 556–57.

[69]Ibid., 1:556; John W. Coons, comp., *Indiana at Shiloh* (n.p.: Indiana Shiloh National Park Commission, 1904) 282–83.

[70]*OR*, 10, pt. 1: 330–31; Roland, *Albert Sidney Johnston*, 328.

[71]Vincent J. Esposito, chief ed., *The West Point Atlas of American Wars*, 2 vols. (New York: Frederick Praeger Publishers, 1959) 1: 31–38.

[72]*OR*, 10, pt. 1: 377, 382.

[73]Ibid., 10, pt. 1: 204–205, 580–84; Stanley, ed., *Autobiography*, 190–92; Johnston, "Albert Sidney Johnston At Shiloh," 1: 563.

[74]Johnston, "Albert Sidney Johnston At Shiloh," 1:559; George Withe Baylor, "With Gen. A. S. Johnston At Shiloh," *Confederate Veteran*, 5:12 (December 1897): 610; *OR*, 10, pt. 1: 465–67; *True Democrat*, 24 April 1862.

[75]*OR*, 10, pt. 1: 573–76, 577–80; M. F. Force, *From Fort Henry to Corinth* (New York: Charles Scribner's Sons, 1898) 144.

[76]*OR*, 10, pt. 1: 574; James Staley to Editor, 21 May 1893, *Confederate Veteran* 1:6 (June 1893): 172; New Orleans *Daily Delta*, 19 April 1862; Stevenson, *Thirteen Months in the Rebel Army*, 117; T. C. Hindman to Thomas Jordan, 24 April 1862, in Military Service Record of Thomas C. Hindman, NARA.

[77]S. A. M. Wood, Report of the Battle of Shiloh, 21 May 1862, in Thomas C. Hindman Papers, NARA.

[78]Roland, *Albert Sidney Johnston*, 338; Sam. R. Watkins, *"Co. Aytch,"* *Maury Grays, First Tennessee Regiment; or, A Side Show of the Big Show*, 2nd ed. (Chattanooga, TN.: Times Printing Company, 1900) 33–34.

[79]*OR*, 10, pt. 1: 386–87, 391; T. C. Hindman to Thomas Jordan, 24 April 1862, in T. C. Hindman Service Record, NARA.

[80]Coons, comp., *Indiana at Shiloh*, 213; *OR*, 10, pt. 1: 467.

[81]Coons, comp., *Indiana at Shiloh*, 283; *OR*, 10, pt. 1: 108–11, 248–54, 386–92.

[82]Stanley, ed., *Autobiography*, 189–97.

[83]*OR*, 10, pt. 1: 100–108, 395–96, 391; Hughes, *Old Reliable*, 111.

[84]Baylor, "With Gen. A. S. Johnston At Shiloh," 1: 610.

[85]Stevenson, *Thirteen Months in the Rebel Army*, 79.

[86]Ibid.

[87]*OR*, 10, pt. 1: 389–90, 466, 569.

Notes to Chapter 6

[1]T. C. Hindman to Thomas Jordan, 24 April 1862, in Military Service Record of T. C. Hindman, NARA; T. C. Hindman to General Beauregard, 18 April 1862, Thomas C. Hindman Papers, in Frederick M. Dearborn Collection, The Houghton Library, Harvard University, Cambridge, Massachusetts; Washington *Telegraph*, 16 April 1862.

[2]*The War of the Rebellion: Official Records of the Union and Confederate Armies*, 128 vols. (Washington D. C.: Government Printing Office, 1880–1902) 1st ser., 52, pt. 2: 303 (hereafter *OR*).

[3]Ibid., 10, pt. 2: 510.

[4]Leo E. Huff, "The Martial Law Controversy in Arkansas, 1861–1865: A Case History of Internal Confederate Conflict," *Arkansas Historical Quarterly* 37:2 (Summer 1978): 149–50.

[5]*OR*, 13: 827–28.

[6]Thomas L. Snead, "The Conquest of Arkansas," in *Battles and Leaders of the Civil War*, ed. R. U. Johnson and C. C. Buell (New York: Thomas Yoseloff, 1888) 3:443–44.

[7]*True Democrat*, 29 May 1862.

[8]Ibid.; Huff, "The Martial Law Controversy," 151–52; Harrell, "Arkansas," 10:97.

[9]*True Democrat*, 22 May 1862.

[10]Ibid.

[11]*OR*, 13: 933–34; Harrell, "Arkansas," 10:99–100; *True Democrat*, May 8, 1862; Bobby L. Roberts, "Thomas C. Hindman and the Trans-Mississippi District," *AHQ* 32:4 (Winter 1973): 298–99.

[12]Extract of Western Department General Orders No. 60, 27 May 1862, in Thomas C. Hindman Papers, NARA; *OR*, 13: 28, 828–29, 831–32.

[13]T. C. Hindman to George W. Brett, 21 May 1862 in Military Service Record of T. C. Hindman, NARA.

[14]Wakelyn, ed., *Biographical Dictionary of The Confederacy* (Westport, Conn.: Greenwood Press, 1977) 384.

[15]*Report of Major General Hindman, Of His Operations In The Trans-Mississippi District* (Richmond: R. M. Smith, Public Printer, 1864) 6.

[16]*True Democrat*, 20, 27 March; 1, 15 May 1862; Washington *Telegraph*, 26 March; 21 May 1862; John Q. Anderson, ed., *Campaigning with Parsons' Texas Cavalry Brigade, CSA: The War Journals and Letters of the Four Orr Brothers, 12th Texas Cavalry Regiment* (Hillsboro, Texas: Hill Jr. College Press, 1967) 41; *OR*, 10, pt. 2: 559; *Report of Major General Hindman, The Trans-Mississippi District*, 6.

[17]*True Democrat*, 5 June 1862; *Arkansas State Gazette*, 7 June 1862; Washington *Telegraph*, 11 June 1862; John N. Edwards, *Shelby And His Men: Or The War In The West* (Cincinnati: Miami Printing and Publishing Co., 1867) 64; John C. Wright, *Memoirs of Colonel John C. Wright* (n. p.: A. L. Scallion, 1982) 71.

[18]Edwards, *Shelby and his Men*, 186–89; New York *Daily Tribune*, 15 August 1862.

[19]Edwards, *Shelby and his Men*, 188–89; New York *Daily Tribune*, 26 August 1862.

[20]Edwards, *Shelby and his Men*, 189–90.

[21]*True Democrat*, 5 June 1862; *Arkansas State Gazette*, 7 June 1862; Washington *Telegraph*, 11 June 1862.

[22]Thomas, *Arkansas in War and Reconstruction*, 357; *True Democrat*, 20 June 1861; 8 May 1862; *Daily State Journal*, 5, 8, 17, 19 December 1861; John

W. Brown, Diary, 9, 25 December 1861; 7 January; 14, 18 May 1862, AHC; *Report of Major General Hindman, The Trans-Mississippi District*, 7.

[23]*True Democrat*, 5 June 1862; *Arkansas State Gazette*, 7 June 1862; Washington *Telegraph*, 11 June 1862. On 29 November 1861, Colonel Solon Borland, Commander of Confederate Forces in Upper Arkansas had proclaimed an embargo in an attempt to halt speculation and extortion in his area, but his order was unpopular and was quickly revoked by both Governor Rector and the Confederate War Department. *True Democrat*, 12, 26 December 1861; Pocahontas *Herald*, n.d., quoted in the *Daily State Journal*, 11 January 1862; *Daily State Journal*, 23 January 1862; Washington *Telegraph*, 22 January 1862.

[24]*True Democrat*, 5 June; 3 July 1862; *Arkansas State Gazette*, 7 June 1862; Washington *Telegraph*, 11 June 1862.

[25]*Arkansas State Gazette*, 7 June 1862; Washington *Telegraph*, 11 June 1862; *True Democrat*, 5 June 1862.

[26]*Arkansas State Gazette*, 14 June 1862; *True Democrat*, 19 June; 10 July; 6 August 1862; Washington *Telegraph*, 18 June 1862.

[27]*Report of Major General Hindman, Trans-Mississippi District*, 10; *OR*, 13: 833.

[28]*Arkansas State Gazette*, 14 June 1862.

[29]Ibid.; Washington *Telegraph*, 18 June 1862; *Report of Major General Hindman, Trans-Mississippi District*, 11.

[30]*Report of Major General Hindman, Trans-Mississippi District*, 8.

[31]Edwards, *Shelby and his Men*, 187–88; Wright, *Memoirs*, 72; *Report of Major General Hindman, Trans-Mississippi District*, 9; *Arkansas State Gazette*, 16 August 1862; Washington *Telegraph*, 2 July 1862; John W. Brown, Diary, 6 July 1862, AHC; Robert L. Kerby, *Kirby Smith's Confederacy: The Trans-Mississippi South, 1863–1865* (New York: Columbia University Press, 1972) 32.

[32]*Report of Major General Hindman, Trans-Mississippi District*, 9; *Arkansas State Gazette*, 7 June 1862; Albert Burton Moore, *Conscription and Conflict in the Confederacy* (New York: Macmillan Company, 1924) 33.

[33]Fort Smith (AR) *Tri-Weekly Bulletin*, 24 June 1862; *True Democrat*, 6 August 1862.

[34]Washington *Telegraph*, 23 April 1862; Moore, *Conscription And Conflict*, 123–24, 137.

[35]Wright, *Memoirs*, 74–75.

[36]*Report of Major General Hindman, Trans-Mississippi District*, 17; Wright, *Memoirs*, 78; James I. Robertson, Jr., *General A. P. Hill: The Story of a Confederate Warrior* (New York: Random House, 1987) 170–232.

[37]*Arkansas State Gazette*, 14 June 1862; Moore, *Conscription And Conflict*, 129.

[38]*Arkansas State Gazette*, 19 July 1862.

[39]*Report of Major General Hindman, Trans-Mississippi District*, 11, Anne J. Bailey, "Henry McCullough's Texans and the Defense of Arkansas in 1862," *AHQ* 46:1 (Spring 1987): 48- 51; *OR*, 13: 855, 934.

[40]*OR*, 13: 936; Walter Lee Brown, "Albert Pike, 1809–1891" (Ph.D. dissertation, University of Texas, 1955) 683–85.

[41]*OR*, 13: 936–43; William E. Woodruff, *With the Light Guns in 61–65: Reminiscences of Eleven Arkansas, Missouri, and Texas Light Batteries in the Civil War* (Little Rock: Central Printing Company, 1903) 71–73.

[42]*OR*, 13: 934, 947; Brown, "Albert Pike," 686–87.

[43]*OR*, 13: 856–57.

[44]Ibid., 13: 857–58; T. C. Hindman to Braxton Bragg, 7 July 1862, in Military Service Record of T. C. Hindman, NARA; *Report of Major General Hindman, Trans-Mississippi District*, 19–20; *Albert Pike's Letter Addressed to Major-General Holmes*, (Little Rock: J. D. Butler, Print., 1862); Albert Pike, *Charges and Specifications Preferred August 23, 1862, by Brigadier General Albert Pike, Against Major Gen. Thos. C. Hindman* (Richmond: Smith, Bailey & Co., Printers, 1863); Brown, "Albert Pike," 695–710.

[45]*Report of Major General Hindman, Trans-Mississippi District, 21.* See also, Kenny A. Franks, *Stand Watie and the Agony of the Cherokee Nation* (Memphis: Memphis State University Press, 1979) 130–31.

[46]*Report of Major General Hindman, Trans-Mississippi District*, 21–22; Wilfred Knight, *Red Fox Stand Watie and the Confederate Indian Nations during the Civil War Years in Indian Territory* (Glendale, California: The Arthur H. Clark Company, 1988) 111–32.

[47]Washington *Telegraph*, 21 May 1862; *True Democrat*, 22 May, 3 July 1862; *OR*, 13: 835; *Official Records Of The Union And Confederate Navies In The War Of The Rebellion*, 31 vols. (Washington: Government Printing Office, 1884–1927) 1st ser., 23: 186–87. Hereafter cited as *ORN*. All volumes cited, unless otherwise indicated, are Series 1.

[48]*ORN*, 23: 186–87; *True Democrat*, 6 August 1862.

[49]*True Democrat*, 22 May 1862; *Report of Major General Hindman, Trans-Mississippi District*, 10–11; Charles D. Field, *Three Years in the Saddle From 1861–1865: Memoirs of Charles D. Field* (n.p., n.d.) 16.

[50]*OR*, 2nd ser., 4: 524–25, 568–69, 572–74, 609, 749–50; *True Democrat*, 10 July 1862.

[51]Edwin C. Bearss, "The White River Expedition June 10- July 15, 1862," *AHQ* 21:4 (Winter 1962): 305; *ORN*, 23: 160.

[52]*Report of Major General Hindman, Trans-Mississippi District*, 12.

[53]Ibid.

[54]*Arkansas State Gazette*, 28 June 1862; *Report of Major General Hindman, Trans-Mississippi District*, 12; Bearss, "The White River Expedition," 316.

[55]*Arkansas State Gazette*, 28 June 1862; Edwards, *Shelby and His Men*, 65; *ORN*, 23: 166, 197, 200, 202.

[56]*ORN*, 23: 202; Harrell, "Arkansas," 10: 110.

[57]*ORN*, 23: 196, 201, 204–205; Edwards, *Shelby And His Men*, 67.

[58]*ORN*, 23: 171–90.

[59]*OR*, 13: 107–12, 119; Bearss, "The White River Expedition," 350–58;

[60]*Report of Major General Hindman, Trans-Mississippi District*, 15–16; Field, *Three Years in the Saddle*, 16–19;
St. Louis *Democrat*, 12 July 1862, reprinted in the New York *Daily Tribune*, 18 July 1862.

[61]*Report of Major General Hindman, Trans-Mississippi District*, 16; New York *Daily Tribune*, 17 July; 6, 21 August 1862; Mrs. T. J. Gaughan, ed., *Letters of a Confederate Surgeon, 1861–1865* (Camden, Arkansas: Hurley Co., Inc., 1960) 114.

[62]Bearss, "White River Expedition," 358–61.

[63]*ORN*, 23: 176, 181, 186, 193; *OR*, 13: 119.

[64]*Arkansas State Gazette*, 28 June 1862; Washington *Telegraph*, 2 July 1862.

[65]*ORN*, 23: 185–86.

[66]*Report of Major General Hindman, Trans-Mississippi District*, 17–18; *True Democrat*, 3 July 1862; Huff, "The Martial Law Controversy," 154. In May of 1862, Colonel Horace Randall declared martial law in Harrison County, Texas, and in June General P. O. Hebert extended it to the entire state. Thus, in the Trans-Mississippi West, the concept was not limited to Arkansas. Marshall *Texas Republican*, 24 May, 28 June 1862.

[67]*True Democrat*, 3 July 1862.

[68]*OR*, 13: 856; Brown, "Albert Pike," 689; John W. Brown, Diary, 18 July 1862, AHC; *Message of Gov. Henry M. Rector To The General Assembly Of The State Of Arkansas; Delivered Nov'r, 1862* (Little Rock, 1862) 5, 7–9. Even though Rector condemned martial law, in the same address he in effect justified it by his assessment of conditions in Arkansas when General Hindman assumed command of the Trans-Mississippi District.

[69]John W. Brown, Diary, 18 July 1862, AHC; Snead, "The Conquest of Arkansas," 3:445; *OR*, 13: 855. Although Hindman had been relieved by Holmes, in September several members of the Confederate House of Representatives continued to condemn his methods. On 1 September they demanded that President Davis explain under what "authority or instruction . . . said commanding general took such actions." *Journal Of The Congress Of The Confederate States Of America, 1861–1865*, 7 vols. (Senate Doc. No. 234, 58 Cong., 2 sess.) 5:331.

Less than three months later, the Arkansas House of Representatives lambasted Hindman and Roane (but not Holmes) for "illegal and oppressive military orders." *Arkansas Patriot*, n.d. as quoted in the Washington *Telegraph*, 3 December 1862.

[70]J. C. Wright, "Major General T. C. Hindman," Collected by Omer R. Weaver in Individual File of Thomas C. Hindman Materials, AHC; Hindman to Cooper, 9 June 1862, in Thomas C. Hindman Papers, NARA.

[71]Snead, "The Conquest of Arkansas," 3: 445–46; Huff, "The Martial Law Controversy," 167; Kerby, *Kirby Smith's Confederacy*, 32.

[72]Stephen B. Oates, *Confederate Cavalry West of the River* (Austin, TX: University of Texas Press, 1961) 30–31, 42, 51.

[73]Harrell, "Arkansas," 10:125–26.

[74]T. C. Hindman to the New York *News*, 25 June 1866, reprinted in the *Arkansas State Gazette*, 3, 6 August 1866; Huff, "The Martial Law Controversy," 166; Wright, *Memoirs*, 76; Edwards, *Shelby and his Men*, 188.

Notes to Chapter 7

[1]William J. Crowley, *Tennessee Cavalry in the Missouri Cavalry Major Henry Ewing, C.S.A., of the St. Louis Times* (Columbia, MO: Kelly Press, Inc., 1978) 66; F. R. Earle to Amanda Buchanan, 17 April 1863, in Robert E. Waterman and Thomas Rothrock, eds., "The Earle-Buchanan Letters of 1861–1876," *Arkansas Historical Quarterly* 33:2 (Summer 1974): 131; T. H. Holmes to Samuel Cooper, 17 August 1862 and T. H. Holmes to Jefferson Davis, 28 August 1862, both in Military Documents, 1862–1865 relating to the Civil War in Arkansas (microfilm copy of selected documents in the Theophilus Hunter Holmes Papers in the Duke University Library on deposit in the University of Arkansas Library (UAL). Responding to Holmes's failure to lift martial law, Judge Brown claimed that Arkansans were "slaves" whose "liberties are lost." John W. Brown, Diary, 5 September 1862, AHC.

[2]Robert L. Kerby, *Kirby Smith's Confederacy: The Trans-Mississippi South, 1863-1865* (New York: Columbia University Press, 1972) 34; Snead, "The Conquest of Arkansas," *Battles and Leaders of the Civil War*, ed. R. U. Johnson and C. C. Buell (New York: Thomas Yoseloff, 1888) 3:446; Stephen B. Oates, *Confederate Cavalry West Of The River* (Austin, TX: University of Texas Press, 1961) 41–42; Richard S. Brownlee, *Gray Ghosts of the Confederacy: Guerilla Warfare in the West, 1861-1865* (Baton Rouge, LA: Louisiana State University, 1958) 77–79.

[3]John N. Edwards, *Shelby and His Men: or, The War in the West*

(Cincinnati, OH: Miami Printing and Publishing Co., 1867) 80–82; Jon L. Wakelyn, ed., *Biographical Dictionary of the Confederacy* (Westport, CN: Greenwood Press, 1977) 381–82.

⁴Edwards, *Shelby and His Men*, 69, 72–73.

⁵*The War of the Rebellion: Official Records of the Union and Confederate Armies* (Washington D. C.: Government Printing Office, 1880-1902) 13: 236, 238–39 (hereafter *OR*); Oates, *Confederate Cavalry West Of The River*, 39–41; John C. Moore, "Missouri," in *Confederate Military History* 9:98–99; Leslie Anders, "Fighting the Ghosts at Lone Jack," *Missouri Historical Review* 29 (April 1985): 332–56.

⁶*OR*, 13: 235–36; Oates, *Confederate Cavalry West Of The River*, 39–40; Moore, "Missouri," 9:98–99.

⁷Oates, *Confederate Cavalry West Of The River*, 40–41.

⁸*OR*, 9: 731; 13: 46–47, 731; Snead, "The Conquest of Arkansas," 3:446–47.

⁹*OR*, 13: 18; Edwards, *Shelby and His Men*, 90.

¹⁰*OR*, 13: 13, 16–17; Snead, "The Conquest of Arkansas," 3:446–47.

¹¹*OR*, 13: 286–88, 301; Knight, *Red Fox*, 126–30; Edwards, *Shelby and His Men*, 87–89; Elmo Ingenthron, *Borderland Rebellion A History of the Civil War on the Missouri-Arkansas Border* (Branson, Missouri: Ozark Mountaineer, 1980) 227–33.

¹²*OR*, 13: 331–35.

¹³Ibid., 334–35; Wiley Britton, *Memoirs of the Rebellion on the Border, 1863* (Chicago: Cushing, Thomas & Co.,1882) 34.

¹⁴*OR*, 13: 883–84.

¹⁵Wakelyn, ed., *Biographical Dictionary of the Confederacy*, 310–11, 384.

¹⁶*OR*, 13: 47–48; John K. Hulston and James W. Goodrich," John Trousdale Coffee: Lawyer, Politician, Confederate," *Missouri Historical Review* 77:3 (April 1983): 285.

¹⁷Snead, "The Conquest of Arkansas," 3:447.

¹⁸Ibid., 448–49; Stephen B. Oates, "The Prairie Grove Campaign, 1862," *AHQ* 19:2 (Summer 1960): 121.

¹⁹Fort Smith (AR) *Tri-Weekly Bulletin*, 16 October 1862; *Arkansas Patriot*, 20 November 1862.

²⁰*OR*, 22, pt.1: 897–98; 17, pt.2: 783–84.

²¹Oates, "The Prairie Grove Campaign," 122; Henry F. Hartsell, "The Battle of Cane Hill, Arkansas, November 28, 1862," in *Civil War Battles in the West*, ed. LeRoy H. Fisher,
(Manhattan, Kansas: Sunflower University Press, 1981) 53.

²²*Arkansas State Gazette*, 31 July 1839; *OR*, 22, pt.1: 139.

[23] Stephen B. Oates, "The Cavalry Fight at Cane Hill," *AHQ* 20:1 (Spring 1961): 66–67

[24] *OR*, 22, pt.1: 43–46.

[25] Ibid., 55–59; Edwards, *Shelby and his Men*, 95 Hartsell, "The Battle of Cane Hill," 54–56.

[26] Edwards, *Shelby and His Men*, 100.

[27] *OR*, 22, pt.1: 41–46; Edwards, *Shelby and His Men*, 103.

[28] *OR*, 22, pt.1: 41–43; Edwards, *Shelby and His Men*, 111

[29] *OR*, 22, pt.1: 83. Wiley Britton of the Sixth Kansas Cavalry believed that this "bombastic" address found in the pockets of "most of the Confederate dead and wounded" "may have had some effect" during the battle. According to him, some of the Southerners taken prisoner "had very exaggerated notions about the alleged outrages committed by our troops, particularly the Kansas division." Wiley Britton, *The Civil War On The Border*, 2 vols. (New York: G. P. Putnam's Sons, 1899) 1:432; Britton, *Memoirs*, 43.

[30] *OR*, 22, pt.1: 83.

[31] Ibid., 22, pt.1: 138–39; Samuel Jones, "The Battle of Prairie Grove, December 7, 1862," *Southern Bivouac* 1:4 (September 1885): 207.

[32] *OR*, 22, pt.1: 139; Daniel O'Flaherty, *General Jo Shelby: Undefeated Rebel* (Chapel Hill: University of North Carolina Press, 1954) 147–48; Ival L. Gregory, "The Battle of Prairie Grove, Arkansas, December 7, 1862," in *Civil War Battles in the West*, 66.

[33] *OR* 22, pt.1: 805.

[34] Robert R. Logan, "Addresses at Dedication of Prairie Grove Battlefield Monument, December 7, 1956," *AHQ* 16:3 (Autumn 1957): 260, 264; *OR*, 22, pt.1: 139–40.

[35] Alwyn Barr, "Confederate Artillery in Arkansas," *AHQ* 22:3 (Fall 1963): 253–54; Edwards, *Shelby and his Men*, 111;
O'Flaherty, *Jo Shelby*, 148.

[36] *OR*, 22, pt.1: 72, 102–103, 140, 812–13; Logan, "Addresses," 260, 264; William Ward Orme to my dear wife, 9–10 December 1862, in William Ward Orme Papers, photocopies of letters in the Illinois State Historical Society on deposit in UAL.

[37] *OR*, 22, pt.1: 140; Jones, "The Battle of Prairie Grove," 205.

[38] Edwards, *Shelby and his Men*, 115.

[39] Ibid., 115–16; *OR*, 22, pt.1: 140.

[40] Edwards, *Shelby and his Men*, 115; *OR*, 22, pt.1: 140; Jones, "The Battle of Prairie Grove," 207.

[41] Edwards, *Shelby and his Men*, 116; C. Barney, *Recollections of Field Service with the Twelfth Iowa Infantry Volunteers; or What I saw in the Army* .

. . (Davenport, Iowa: *Gazette* Job Rooms, 1865) 118–19; Howard N. Monnett, ed., "A Yankee Cavalryman Views the Battle of Prairie Grove," *AHQ* 21:4 (Winter 1962): 295.

[42] *OR*, 22, pt.1: 102–103; Oates, "The Prairie Grove Campaign," 130.

[43] *OR*, 22, pt.1: 103, 147, 150; Oates, "The Prairie Grove Campaign," 130.

[44] *True Democrat*, 31 December 1862; *OR*, 22, pt.1: 141–44.

[45] *OR*, 22, pt.1: 141–42; O'Flaherty, *Jo Shelby*, 157.

[46] Chicago *Journal*, n. d., reprinted in *Rebellion Record: A Diary of American Events*, ed. Frank Moore (New York: G. P. Putnam, 1863) 6:75; William Elsey Connelley, *The Life of Preston B. Plumb, 1837–1891* (Chicago: Browne & Howell Company, 1913) 122.

[47] Jeremy H. Wilder, "The Thirty-Seventh Illinois at Prairie Grove," *AHQ* 49:1 (Spring 1990): 8, 12–13; *Missouri Democrat*, n. d., reprinted in *Rebellion Record*, 74–75; Barney, *Recollections*, 122–23; Monnett, ed., "A Yankee Cavalryman Views the Battle of Prairie Grove," 247.

[48] *OR*, 22, pt.1: 142; Barney, *Recollections*, 123, 136; Connelley, *The Life of Preston Plumb*, 122.

[49] Edwards, *Shelby and His Men*, 119–20.

[50] *OR*, 22, pt.1: 142; Gregory, "The Battle of Prairie Grove," 69.

[51] Edwards, *Shelby and His Men*, 125–27; *OR*, 22, pt.1: 84, 142.

[52] Edwards, *Shelby and His Men*, 127.

[53] Monnett, ed., "A Yankee Cavalryman Views The Battle of Prairie Grove," 301; Edwards, *Shelby and His Men*, 125–26.

[54] *OR*, 22, pt.1: 143–44.

[55] Ibid., 76, 107; Wright, *Memoirs*, 101.

[56] Barney, *Recollections*, 129–30.

[57] *OR* 22, pt.1: 820–21.

[58] Logan, "Addresses," 259, 266.

[59] *OR*, 22, pt.1: 167–70, 172; Memphis *Daily Bulletin*, 6 January 1863; *Arkansas Patriot*, 8 January 1863; Thomas E. Wright, ed., "The Capture of Van Buren, Arkansas, During the Civil War from the Diary of a Union Horse Soldier, *AHQ* 38:1 (Spring 1979): 83–87.

[60] Edwards, *Shelby and His Men*, 130; Memphis *Daily Appeal*, 4 March 1863; Snead, "The Conquest of Arkansas," 3: 450; *OR*, 22, pt.1: 171–73; 22, pt.2: 23–24, 27–28, 34; John Truss to My Dear Lady, 3 January 1863, in Johnette Highsmith Ray, ed., "Civil War Letters From Parson's Texas Cavalry Brigade," *Southwestern Historical Quarterly (SWQ)* 2 (October 1965): 219.

[61] William J. Oliphant, "Arkansas Post," *Southern Bivouac* 1:11 (April 1886): 736–39; Snead, "The Conquest of Arkansas," 3:451–53; Memphis *Daily Appeal*, 4 March 1863; Huff, "Confederate Arkansas," 126–28.

[62]Memphis *Daily Appeal*, 4 March 1863.

[63]*OR*, 22, pt.1: 194–201; Oates, *Confederate Cavalry West Of The River*, 113–20; Paul M. Robinett, "Marmaduke's Expedition Into Missouri: The Battles of Springfield and Hartville, January, 1863," *Missouri Historical Review*, 58:2 (January 1964): 151–73.

[64]Oates, *Confederate Cavalry West of the River*, 51.

[65]Washington *Telegraph*, 3 December 1862; *Arkansas Patriot*, 20 November 1862; *Message of Gov. Henry M. Rector To The General Assembly . . . Nov'r, 1862* (Little Rock, 1862) 7; Jefferson Davis to Hon. A. Garland, 28 March 1863, and Jefferson Davis to Senators and Representatives from Arkansas, 30 March 1863, both in *Jefferson Davis, Constitutionalist*, 5:457–63; *OR*, 22, pt.2: 780.

[66]*OR*, 22, pt.2: 784–88.

[67]*True Democrat*, 11, 18 March 1863; Junius N. Bragg to Josephine Goddard, 12 March 1863, Gaughan, ed., *Letters of a Confederate Surgeon*, 122–23.

[68]Elijah P. Petty to My Dear Daughter, 15 March 1863, in *Journey To Pleasant Hill: The Civil War Letters of Captain Elijah P. Petty, Walker's Texas Division, C. S. A.* (San Antonio, Texas: University of Texas Institute of Texan Cultures, 1982) 149–50.

[69]Elizabeth Pack to T. C. Hindman, 15 December 1862, in Thomas C. Hindman Collection, Phillips County Museum.

[70]"Address To The Troops Of Hindman's Division," in Military Documents, 1862–1865, (microfilm) UAL.

[71]R. C. Newton to Robert W. Johnson, 12 March 1863, in the J. P. Wilson Papers, Emory; Huff, "The Martial Law Controversy," 162–63; Proceedings of the First Confederate Congress," (Third Session) in *Southern Historical Society Papers*, 44–52 (Richmond, Virginia: Southern Historical Society, 1923–1959) 49:142–43; *Arkansas Patriot*, 23 May 1863.

[72]*Arkansas Patriot*, 12, 19 February; 5, 14, 28 March; 4, 18 April; 20 June 1863.

[73]*Arkansas State Gazette*, 13 June 1863.

[74]LON to the editor of Jackson *Mississippian* reprinted in the Memphis *Daily Appeal* (Atlanta, Georgia), 24 June 1863.

[75]Huff, "The Martial Law Controversy," 166–67; "A MISSOURI SOLDIER" to the editor of the *True Democrat*, 22 April 1863; Charles W. Adams to J. P. Wilson, 27 June 1863, J. P. Wilson Papers, Emory.

Notes to Chapter 8

[1]*The War of the Rebellion: Official Records of the Union and Confederate Armies*, 128 vols. (Washington D.C.: Government Printing Office) 6: 553–56.

[2]Ibid.   [3]Ibid., 22, pt. 2: 895–96.

[4]Ibid., 30, pt. 4: 495.

[5]Thomas Lawrence Connelly, *Autumn of Glory: The Army of Tennessee, 1862–1865* (Baton Rouge: Louisiana State University Press, 1971) 139; William M. Lamers, *The Edge of Glory: A Biography of General William S. Rosecrans, U. S. A.* (New York: Harcourt, Brace & World, Inc., 1961) 292.

[6]*OR*, 23, pt. 2: 791–92, 800, 823, 836, 868.

[7]Ibid., 30, pt. 5: 538, 540–41, 547, 695; 29, pt. 2: 924.

[8]Connelly, *Autumn of Glory,* 154–55; Glenn Tucker, *Chickmauga: Bloody Battle in the West* (Indianapolis: Bobbs-Merrill, 1961; Reprint, Dayton, Ohio: Morningside House, 1984) 33, 78.

[9]Daniel H. Hill, "Chickamauga—The Great Battle Of The West," in *Battles and Leaders,* 3:639–40, 644, 646.

[10]U. S. Grant, *Personal Memoirs of U. S. Grant,* 2 vols. (New York: Charles L. Webster & Company, 1885) 2:86–87.

[11]Connelly, *Autumn of Glory,* 75–76.

[12]Army of Tennessee, Special Orders No. 216 in Thomas C. Hindman Papers, NARA; *OR*, 30, pt. 4: 495; Kate Cumming, *Kate: The Journal of A Confederate Nurse,* ed. Richard Barksdale Harwell, (Baton Rouge: Louisiana State University Press, 1959) 125.

[13]*OR*, 30, pt. 3: 479, 481.

[14]*OR*, 30, pt. 3: 485–86; Hill, "Chickamauga," 3: 642.

[15]*OR*, 30, pt. 2: 28, 298–99. All correspondence relating to the incident in McLemore's Cove is available in the Hindman Papers (NARA) and in the *OR*. For convenience, we have cited the *OR*.

[16]*OR*, 30, pt. 2: 28, 137–38, 292–93, 300. Although he made no mention of sickness, on 15 October Cleburne stated that the gaps were in fact obstructed on the morning of the tenth and that it would have required several hours to clear them. P. R. Cleburne to D. H. Hill, 15 October 1863, in Daniel Harvey Hill Papers, Virginia State Library and Archives (VSLA), Richmond, Virginia.

[17]*OR*, 30, pt. 2: 28, 293, 297–300.

[18]Ibid., 28, 293–300.

[19]Connelly, *Autumn of Glory,* 178–79; *OR*, 30, pt. 2: 301.

[20]*OR*, 30, pt. 2: 294.

[21]Ibid., 294, 301–302.

[22]Connelly, *Autumn of Glory,* 181–82; *OR,* 30, pt. 2: 29.

[23]*OR,* 30, pt. 2: 29, 294–95.

[24]*OR,* 30, pt. 2: 296; S. B. Buckner to T. C. Hindman, 16 September 1863, Simon Bolivar Buckner Papers, Huntington Library, San Marino, California.

[25]*OR,* 30, pt. 2: 296; Bromfield Ridley, *Battles and Sketches of the Army of Tennessee* (Mexico, MO: Missouri Printing and Publishing Company, 1906; Reprint, Dayton, OH: Morningside Bookshop, 1978) 205–206.

[26]*OR,* 30, pt. 2: 296–97.

[27]Connelly, *Autumn of Glory,* 177, 184–85.

[28]R. Lockwood Turner, ed., *A Carolinian Goes to War: The Civil War Narrative of Arthur Middleton Manigault* (Columbia: University of South Carolina Press, 1983) 93–94; William B. Bate to Braxton Bragg, 29 September 1867, Braxton Bragg Papers, Western Reserve Historical Society (WRHS), Cleveland, Ohio.

[29]*OR,* 30, pt. 2: 530–31; Connelly, *Autumn of Glory,* 186.

[30]*OR,* 30, pt. 2: 44–45, 49.

[31]Connelly, *Autumn of Glory,* 193–94.

[32]*OR,* 30, pt. 2: 31.

[33]Ibid., 239–40, 254, 356–57; Ridley, *Battles and Sketches,* 209; George B. Guild, *A Brief Narrative of the Fourth Tennessee Regiment: Wheeler's Corp, Army of Tennessee* (Nashville, TN: n.p., 1913) 24; Turner, ed., *A Carolinian Goes to War,* 96; Horn, *Army of Tennessee,* 257.

[34]Hill, "Chickamauga," 3:649, 652; Ridley, *Battles and Sketches,* 209, 218–219; William M. Heartsill, *Fourteen Hundred and 91 Days in the Confederate Army,* ed., Bell I. Wiley, 2nd ed. (Jackson, TN.: McCowat-Mercer Press, 1954) 151; Richmond *Daily Dispatch,* 28 September 1863.

[35]Ridley, *Battles and Sketches,* 209, 218–19; Hill, "Chickamauga," 3:650–51.

[36]Ridley, *Battles and Sketches,* 221; Heartsill, *Fourteen Hundred and 91 Days,* 153; Richmond (VA) *Daily Dispatch,* 28 September 1863.

[37]Hill, "Chickamauga," 3:652; William M. Polk, *Leonidas Polk Bishop and General,* new ed., 2 vols. (New York: Longmans, Green, and Co., 1915) 2:255; Ridley, *Battles and Sketches,* 222; *OR,* 30, pt. 2: 286–87.

[38]Ridley, *Battles and Sketches,* 223; Hill, "Chickamauga," 3:653.

[39]Ridley, *Battles and Sketches,* 222–23; Turner, ed., *A Carolinian Goes to War,* 97.

[40]Ridley, *Battles and Sketches,* 223; *OR,* 30, pt. 1: 634–35; Hill, "Chickamauga," 3:657.

[41]Ridley, *Battles and Sketches,* 224; *OR,* 30, pt. 2: 303.

[42]*OR,* 30, pt. 1: 499–501, 580; George Binford to Cousin Bob, 11 October

1863, George Binford Letters, Virginia Historical Society, Richmond, Virginia.

[43]George Binford to Cousin Bob, 11 October 1863; *OR*, 30, pt. 2: 303–304; Memphis *Daily Appeal* (Atlanta, GA), 9 October 1863.

[44]Lamers, *The Edge of Glory*, 352–54.

[45]Ridley, *Battles and Sketches*, 225; *OR*, 30, pt. 1: 248–56; Hill, "Chickamauga," 3:659–61.

[46]Memphis *Daily Appeal* (Atlanta), 23 September 1863; *OR*, 30, pt. 2: 305.

[47]Richmond *Daily Dispatch*, 28 September 1863; Turner, ed., *A Carolinian Goes to* War, 106; *OR*, 30, pt. 2: 305.

[48]*OR*, 30, pt. 2: 289; 30, pt. 1: 253–54; G. Moxley Sorrell, *Recollections of a Confederate Staff Officer*, ed., Bell I. Wiley. (Jackson, TN.: McCowat-Mercer Press, 1958) 186.

[49]James Longstreet, *From Manassas to Appomattox*, ed. James I. Robertson, Jr., (Bloomington, IN: Indiana University Press, 1960) 456; Heartsill, *Fourteen Hundred and 91 Days*, 154; Sorrell, *Recollections*, 187.

[50]Richmond *Daily Dispatch*, 28 September; 2 October 1863; Guild, *A Brief Narrative*, 31; Heartsill, *Fourteen Hundred and 91 Days*, 160.

[51]Horn, *Army of Tennessee*; Longstreet, *From Manassas To Appomattox*, 458–60; Casualty Report of Hindman's Division in J. P. Wilson Papers, Emory.

[52]*OR*, 30, pt. 2: 34–37; Sorrell, *Recollections*, 187; Guild, *A Brief Narrative*, 33; Richmond *Daily Dispatch*, 28 September 1863.

[53]*OR*, 30, pt. 2: 54–55; Army of Tennessee, Special Order No. 249 in Thomas C. Hindman Papers, NARA. For Bragg's condemnation of Breckinridge after the Battle of Murfreesboro, see the Memphis *Daily Appeal* (Jackson, MS), 3 April 1863 and *OR*, 20: 663–72.

[54]T. C. Hindman to J. P. Wilson, 7 October 1863, in J. P. Wilson Papers, Emory.

[55]Ibid.

[56]T. C. Hindman to J. P. Wilson, 8 November 1863, in J. P. Wilson Papers, Emory. Hindman's report and accompanying exhibits are in *OR*, 30, pt. 2: 296–302.

[57]Polk, *Leonidas Polk*, 2:298.

[58]*OR*, 20: 684; Longstreet, *From Manassas To Appomattox*, 465.

[59]Polk, *Leonidas Polk*, 2:308–13; Longstreet, *Manassas To Appomattox*, 464–65; Hill, "Chickamauga," 3:662.

[60]*OR*, 30, pt. 2: 65–66.

[61]Howill Hinds to Jefferson Davis, 11 October 1863, in *Jefferson Davis, Constitutionalist*, 6:59–60.

[62]Washington *Telegraph*, 11 November 1863.

[63]Jefferson Davis to Braxton Bragg, 30 September; 3 October 1863 and the Charleston (SC) *Daily Courier,* 10 October 1863, all in *Jefferson Davis, Constitutionalist,* 6:53–58; Richmond (VA) *Daily Dispatch,* 8, 15 October 1863; J. Cutler Andrews, *The South Reports The Civil War* (Princeton, New Jersey: Princeton University Press, 1970) 358; Sorrell, *Recollections,* 191–92.

[64]*OR,* 30, pt. 2: 309–12; T. C. Hindman to J. P. Wilson, 2 December 1863, in J. P. Wilson Papers, Emory.

[65]T. C. Hindman to J. P. Wilson, 2 December 1863, in J. P. Wilson Papers, Emory.

[66]Jefferson Davis to Braxton Bragg, 29 October 1863, in *Jefferson Davis, Constitutionalist,* 6:69–71; Richard M. McMurry, *John Bell Hood and the War for Southern Independence* (Lexington: University Press of Kentucky, 1982) 88–89.

Notes to Chapter 9

[1]Joseph E. Johnston, "Opposing Sherman's Advance To Atlanta," in *Battles and Leaders of the Civil War,* ed. R. U. Johnson and C. C. Buell (New York: Thomas Yoseloff, 1888) 4:260–61; Sam. R. Watkins, *"Co. Aytch," Maury Grays, First Tennessee Regiment; or, A Side Show of the Big Show,* 2nd ed. (Chattanooga, TN: Times Printing Co., 1900) 106–107.

[2]*Culloden,* A "Suggestion," Memphis *Daily Appeal* (Atlanta, GA), 3 December 1863. On 10 April 1865, while recuperating in San Antonio, Hindman wrote to a friend in Austin that Southern states must act quickly to implement the recently passed law permitting the use of black soldiers. He also stated that he had sent an open letter to the Memphis *Daily Appeal* advocating the arming and enlisting of slaves prior to the proposal offered by Cleburne. He believed that had authorities in Richmond not turned a deaf ear to the idea of arming slaves when it was suggested by the generals of the Army of Tennessee, "Georgia and the Carolinas could not have been overrun, Virginia and Tennessee might have been recovered, the unfortunate Missouri expedition successful, and the enemy driven to the east portion of Arkansas, instead of holding three-fourths and threatening the remainder" of the South as it did in April 1865. "Letter from Gen. Hindman," 10 April 1865, printed in the Austin *Texas State Gazette,* 3 May 1865.

[3]Memphis *Daily Appeal* (Atlanta), 3 December 1863.
[4]Ibid.   [5]Ibid.
[6]Ibid.   [7]Ibid.
[8]*The War of the Rebellion: Official Records of the Union and Confederate*

Armies, 128 vols. (Washington D. C.: Government Printing Office, 1888–1902) 4th ser. 1: 482, 529; Thomas Robson Hay, "The South And The Arming Of The Slaves," *Mississippi Valley Historical Review*, 6:1 (June 1919): 36–38. A number of people had suggested using free blacks in the army, a concept endorsed by the Alabama and Tennessee legislatures and the governor of Louisiana. The Alabama legislature also proposed putting slaves to work in foundries, workshops, and on railroads to free soldiers for duty in the field. C. M. Hubbard to John Letcher [Governor of Virginia], 26 April 1861, in *OR*, 51, pt. 2: 47; Joint Resolution of the Alabama Legislature, 29 August 1863, in *OR*, 4th ser. 2: 767; Orders No. 426 of the Louisiana Adjutant and Inspector General, 24 March 1862, in *OR*, 4th ser. 1: 1020.

[9]Memphis *Daily Appeal* (Atlanta), 4 January 1864; and in the "Proceedings of the First Confederate Congress," (Fourth Session) in *Southern Historical Society Papers*, 50:141–42.

[10]Ibid.   [11]Ibid.

[12]Memphis *Daily Appeal* (Atlanta), 5 January 1864.

[13]Ibid.

[14]Irving Buck, *Cleburne and his Command*, ed. Thomas Robson Hay (Jackson, TN.: McCowat-Mercer Press, 1959) 21.

[15]Irving A. Buck, "Negroes In Our Army," in *Southern Historical Society Papers*, ed. R. A. Brock (Richmond: Southern Historical Society, 1903) 31:215–16; W. H. T. Walker to Braxton Bragg, 8 March 1864, Braxton Bragg Papers, WRHS, Wirt Armistead Cate, ed., *Two Soldiers The Campaign Diaries Of Thomas J. Key, C.S.A. December 7, 1863–May 17, 1865 And Robert J. Campbell, U.S.A. January 1, 1864–July 21, 1864* (Chapel Hill: University of North Carolina Press, 1938) 16–18. See also, Barbara C. Ruby, "General Patrick Cleburne's Proposal To Arm Southern Slaves," *Arkansas Historical Quarterly* 30:3 (Autumn 1971): 193–212.

[16]*OR*, 52, pt. 2: 586–92.

[17]Ibid.

[18]Buck, "Negroes In Our Army," 217; Cate, ed., *Two Soldiers*, 19.

[19]Buck, "Negroes In Our Army," 216; James Cooper Nisbet, *4 Years on the Firing Line*, ed. Bell Wiley (Jackson, TN.: McCowat-Mercer Press, 1963) 172–73; *OR*, 52, pt. 2: 598–99.

[20]Buck, "Negroes in our Army," 216; *OR*, 52, pt. 2: 608–609.

[21]Buck, "Negroes in our Army," 217; W. H. T. Walker to Braxton Bragg, 8 March 1864, Braxton Bragg Papers, WRHS; *OR*, 52, pt. 2: 593–94; 32, pt. 2: 537.

[22]*OR*, 52, pt. 2: 606–607.

[23]T. C. Hindman to Jefferson Davis, 16 January 1864, in Thomas C. Hind-

man Papers, HL.

[24]Ibid.   [25]Ibid.

[26]T. C. Hindman to J. P. Wilson, 2 December 1863, J. P. Wilson Papers, Emory; General Orders No. 9, Hindman's Corps, Thomas C. Hindman Papers, NARA; Jefferson Davis to T. C. Hindman, 26 January 1864, in *Jefferson Davis, Constitutionalist,* 6:161.

[27]Memphis *Daily Appeal* (Atlanta), 16 January 1864.

[28]T. C. Hindman to S. Cooper, 28 February 1864, in Thomas C. Hindman Service Record, NARA.

[29]T. C. Hindman to J. P. Wilson, 13 March 1864, in J. P. Wilson Papers, Emory. In December 1863 when rumors began circulating in Richmond that Davis had nominated Hindman for lieutenant general, Arkansas Congressman Thomas B. Hanley, an outspoken critic of the general, predicted that it was "certain" the "Senate will not confirm this nomination." Thomas B. Hanley to Harris Flanagin [Governor of Arkansas], 19 December 1863, in the Kie Oldham Collection, AHC.

[30]T. C. Hindman to S. Cooper, 28 February 1864, in Thomas C. Hindman Service Record, NARA; T. C. Hindman to J. P. Wilson, 3 April 1864, in J. P. Wilson Papers, Emory; *OR,* 52, pt. 2: 642–43, 646–47.

[31]Joseph T. Derry, "Georgia," in *Confederate Military History,* 6:299; William T. Sherman, "The Grand Strategy of the Last Year of the War," in *Battles and Leaders,* 4:252; Philip Secrist, "Resaca: For Sherman a Moment of Truth," *Atlanta Historical Journal* 22:2 (Spring 1978): 10, 15.

[32]Richard M. McMurry, "Resaca: 'A Heap of Hard Fiten,'" *Civil War Times Illustrated* 9:7 (November 1970): 44.

[33]Watkins, *"Co. Aytch,"* 127; Secrist, "Resaca," 17–18; Jacob D. Cox, *Atlanta* (New York: Charles Scribner's Sons, 1898) 44.

[34]Johnston, "Opposing Sherman's Advance to Atlanta," 4: 265; *OR,* 38, pt. 3: 615–16; McMurry, "Resaca," 12.

[35]McMurry, "Resaca," 44.

[36]Johnston, "Opposing Sherman's Advance to Atlanta," 4: 266; Ridley, *Battles and Sketches,* 300; Derry, "Georgia," 6: 305.

[37]Johnston, "Opposing Sherman's Advance to Atlanta," 4:266–67.

[38]James Barnes, *The Eighty-sixth Regiment Indiana Volunteer Infantry: A Narrative of its Services in the Civil War of 1861–1865,* (Crawfordville, IN: Journal Co., Printers, 1895) 345; Secrist, "Resaca," 38; McMurry, "Resaca," 48.

[39]Johnston, "Opposing Sherman's Advance to Atlanta," 4:269; *OR,* 38, pt. 3: 616; Horn, *Army Of Tennessee,* 330.

[40]Johnston, "Opposing Sherman's Advance to Atlanta," 4:269; *OR,* 38, pt. 3: 616; 38, pt. 1: 193–95.

[41]Johnston, "Opposing Sherman's Advance to Atlanta," 4:270; Memphis

Daily Appeal (Atlanta), 29 June 1864.

[42]*OR,* 38, pt. 3: 617.

[43]Johnston, "Opposing Sherman's Advance to Atlanta," 4:271–272; *OR,* 38, pt. 2: 14–15; 38, pt. 1: 68; Richard M. McMurry, "The Affair at Kolb's Farm," *Civil War Times Illustrated* 7:8 (December 1968): 22–23.

[44]"Hindman's Reply To Hood," *Confederate Veteran,* 8:2 (February 1900): 69.

[45]Watkins, "*Co. Aytch,*" 136–37.

[46]Richard M. McMurry, "Kennesaw Mountain," *Civil War Times Illustrated,* 8:9 (January 1970): 25; Watkins, "*Co. Aytch,*" 137–38.

[47]*OR,* 38, pt. 1: 69; Atlanta (GA) *Southern Confederacy,* 6 July 1864; Macon (GA) *Telegraph,* 7 July 1864; Chattanooga *Rebel* (Griffin, GA), 9 July 1864; Richmond (VA) *Daily Dispatch,* 12 July 1864; Harrell, "Arkansas," 10:293.

Notes to Chapter 10

[1]T. C. Hindman, Memo, 18 November 1864, Thomas C. Hindman Papers, NARA; T. C. Hindman to James A. Seddon, 10 July 1864, Letters Received by the Confederate Secretary of War, 1861–1865, NARA; *The War of the Rebellion: Official Records of the Union and Confederate Armies,* 128 vols. (Washington D. C.: Government Printing Office, 1888–1902) 41, pt. 2: 1031–32; 47, pt. 2: 1042.

[2]*OR,* 41, pt. 2: 1031–32; Hindman, Memo, 18 November 1864.

[3]T. C. Hindman to Dr. S. H. Stout, 24 July 1864, Thomas C. Hindman Papers, HL; Hindman, Memo, 18 November 1864.

[4]Hindman, Memo, 18 November 1864.

[5]Ibid., Memphis (TN) *Bulletin,* 24 November 1864, reprinted in the Little Rock (AR) *National Democrat,* 3 December 1864; *OR,* 41, pt. 4: 998; 41, pt. 3: 1008.

[6]Joseph Howard Parks, *General Edmund Kirby Smith, C. S. A.* (Baton Rouge: Louisiana State University Press, 1954) 432–55; Kerby, *Kirby Smith's Confederacy,* 388–89.

[7]John N. Edwards, *Shelby's Expedition to Mexico, an Unwritten Leaf of the War* (Kansas City, MO: Kansas City Times Steam Book and Job Printing House, 1872; Reprint, Austin: The Steck Company, 1964) 16; Austin (TX) *Weekly State Gazette,* 5 April 1865.

[8]W. B. Knox, et al. to Maj. Gen. Thomas C. Hindman, C. S. A., 23 January 1865, Thomas C. Hindman Collection,

Phillips County Museum.

[9]*National Democrat,* 7 May; 3 December 1864.

[10]Atlanta *Southern Confederacy* (Macon, GA), 27 January 1865; Richmond (VA) *Dispatch,* 20 February 1865; New York *Times,* 21 March 1865; Little Rock (AR) *Unconditional Union,* 30 March 1865; Louisville (KY), *Journal,* n.d., reprinted in the *National Democrat,* 22 April 1865; Memphis (TN) *Bulletin,* 24 November 1864, reprinted in the *National Democrat,* 3 December 1864.

[11]New Orleans (LA) *Picayune,* 17 May 1865.

[12]Parks, *Edmund Kirby Smith,* 456–57.

[13]Ibid., 458–62; Austin *Weekly State Gazette,* 29 March; 10 May 1865.

[14]Austin (TX) *Weekly State Gazette,* 3 May 1865.

[15]Galveston (TX) *Daily News,* 23 May 1865.

[16]Ibid.

[17]Parks, *Edmund Kirby Smith,* 470–78; Shreveport (LA) *South-Western,* 7 June 1865; *OR,* 48, pt. 2: 767.

[18]Biscoe Hindman, "Thomas Carmichael Hindman," 102; J. E. Barkley to T. C. Hindman, 19 May 1865, Mrs. Samuel Wassell Collection, AHC.

[19]Metamoras (Mexico), *Daily Ranchero,* 9–10, 23 June 1865; Eaton, *Jefferson Davis,* 260–61; Jonathan Truman Dorris, *Pardon and Amnesty under Lincoln and Johnson: The Restoration of the Confederates to their Rights and Privileges, 1861–1868* (Chapel Hill, University of North Carolina Press, 1953) 119–20, 244–77; Indictment of Thomas C. Hindman, 24 May 1865, United States District Court for the Eastern District of Ark., vol. D, Case O, 388; Parks, *Edmund Kirby Smith,* 481.

[20]Parks, *Edmund Kirby Smith,* 480–81.

[21]Edwards, *Shelby's Expedition to Mexico,* 16–17.

[22]Metamoras *Daily Ranchero,* 30 June 1865; Ted R. Worley, ed., "A Letter Written by General Thomas C. Hindman in Mexico," *AHQ* 15:4 (Winter 1956): 365–66; Alexander Watkins Terrell, *From Texas to Mexico and the Court of Maximillian in 1865* (Dallas: the Book Club of Texas, 1933) 25.

[23]Terrell, *From Texas to Mexico,* 9–11.

[24]Edwards, *Shelby and his Men,* 546–40; Sam Box, "End of the War—Exiles in Mexico," *Confederate Veteran* 11:3 (March 1903): 122. Box remembered the flag ceremony occurring on 1 July instead of 4 July as Edwards recorded.

[25]Worley, ed., "A Letter . . . by General Hindman," 366–67.

[26]Ibid.

[27]Ibid., 367; Biscoe Hindman, "Thomas Carmichael Hindman," 102.

[28]Andrew Rolle, *The Lost Cause, The Confederate Exodus to Mexico* (Norman, OK: University of Oklahoma Press, 1965) 21–22.

[29]Ibid., 22–23.

[30]Gene Smith, *Maximillian and Carlota: A Tale of Romance and Tragedy* (New York: William Morrow and Company, Inc., 1973) 198.

[31]Edwards, *Shelby's Expedition to Mexico,* 99–100.

[32]Alfred Jackson Hanna and Kathryn Abbey Hanna, *NapoleonIII and Mexico: American Triumph over Monarchy* (Chapel Hill: University of North Carolina Press, 1971) 224–25; J. Fred Rippy, *The United States and Mexico* (New York: Alfred A. Knopf, 1926) 248–49; George D. Harmon, "Confederate Migrations to Mexico," *Lehigh University Publications* 12:2 (February 1938): 464.

[33]Sarah Dorsey, ed., *Recollections of Henry Watkins Allen, Brigadier-General Confederate States Army, Ex-Governor of Louisiana* (New York: M. Doolady, 1866) 329; Terrell, *From Texas to Mexico,* 18, 21–23.

[34]Terrell, *From Texas to Mexico,* 23; Edwards, *Shelby's Expedition to Mexico,* 41–42.

[35]Edwards, *Shelby's Expedition to Mexico,* 24–25, 42.

[36]Terrell, *From Texas to Mexico,* 21.

[37]Ibid., 23, 29.

[38]San Antonio *Herald,* n.d., reprinted in the Galveston *Daily News,* 27 August 1865; T. C. Hindman to "My very dear friend," 21 August 1865, Mrs. Samuel Wassell Collection, AHC.

[39]T. C. Hindman to "My very dear friend," 21 August 1865.

[40]Ibid.

[41]*Mexican Times* (Mexico City), 23 September 1865; Galveston (TX) *Daily News,* 30 August 1865.

[42]Rolle, *The Lost Cause,* 86–87.   [43]Ibid., 90–91.

[44]Biscoe Hindman, "Thomas Carmichael Hindman," 102; Gertrude Mills to W. J. Lemke, 28 May 1956, Walter J. Lemke Papers, UAL; W. J. Lemke, "The Hindman Family Portraits," *AHQ* 14:2 (Summer 1955): 106. The Hindmans spelled their daughter's name Blanche Carlotta.

[45]Nash, *Biographical Sketches,* 216; Terrell, *From Texasto Mexico,* 40–41.

[46]U. S. Congress, House of Representatives, *Executive Documents,* 39 Cong., 2 sess., (Serial 1294), 12:503.

[47]House of Representatives, *Executive Documents,* 39 Cong., 2 sess., (Serial 1294, No. 76), 12:502; Galveston *Daily News,* 30 August 1865; *Mexican Times,* 14 October 1865; Carl Coke Rister, "Carlota, A Confederate Colony in Mexico," *Journal of Southern History* 11:1 (February 1945): 47.

[48]*Mexican Times,* 3 March 1866; Edwards, *Shelby's Expedition to Mexico,* 96.

[49]Galveston *Daily News,* 6 May 1866; Edwards, *Shelby's Expedition to Mexico,* 97; "Captain Cameron N. Biscoe," *Confederate Veteran* 33:10 (October 1925): 385.

[50]Rolle, *The Lost Cause,* 92–94.

[51]Ibid., 95; House of Representatives, *Executive Documents,* 39 Cong., 2 sess. (Serial 1294, No. 76), 12:512; Rister, "Carlota," 46.

[52]Rolle, *The Lost Cause,* 91, 115–16; Petersburg (VA) *Index,* n. d., reprinted in the Galveston *Daily News,* 3 August 1866; Rister, "Carlota," 47–48; T. C. Hindman to "My very dear friend," 21 August 1865.

[53]Galveston *Daily News,* 6 May 1866.

[54]*Mexican Times,* 23 September 1865; San Antonio *Herald,* n. d., reprinted in Galveston *Daily News,* 23 September 1865; Metamoras *Daily Ranchero,* 31 August 1865; New York *Herald,* 29 December 1865.

[55]*Mexican Times* 26 May; 9, 23, 30 June 1866; Tom Russell, "Adventures of a Cordova Colonist," *Southern Magazine,* 11 (August 1872): 90–102, 11 (September 1872): 155–66.

[56]New York *Herald,* 19 April 1866; T. C. Hindman to Mollie Hindman, 7 May 1866, Thomas C. Hindman Collection, Phillips County Museum; Biscoe Hindman, "Thomas Carmichael Hindman," 102.

[57]Galveston *Daily News,* 27 July 1866.

[58]Ibid., *Mexican Times,* 11 November 1865; 3, 17 February 1866; Ramon Eduardo Ruiz, ed., *An American in Maximillian's Mexico, 1865–1866: The Diaries of William Marshall Anderson* (San Marino, CA: The Huntington Library, 1959) 27.

[59]Harmon, "Confederate Migrations to Mexico," 480; Rolle, *The Lost Cause,* 180–81; Edwards, *Shelby's Expedition to Mexico,* 120; New York *Herald,* 8 June 1866.

[60]T. C. Hindman to the New York *Daily News,* 25 June 1866, reprinted in the *Arkansas State Gazette,* 3, 6 August 1866.

[61]Brownsville (TX) *Daily Ranchero,* 31 October 1866.

[62]T. C. Hindman to S. H. Tucker, 6 November 1866, Records of the War Department, The Adjutant General's Office, Amnesty Papers, Record Group No. 94, NARA.

[63]Charleston (SC) *Daily Courier,* 15 March 1867.

[64]*Arkansas State Gazette,* 16 April 1867; Edwards, *Shelby's Expedition to Mexico,* 123, 137–38.

Notes to Chapter 11

[1]United States Congress, House of Representatives, *Executive Documents,* 39 Cong., 1 sess. (Serial 1263, No. 99), 1–3; 39 Cong., 2 sess. (Serial 1289, No.

31), 22–24; 39 Cong., 2 sess. (Serial 1293, No. 116), 79–85.

[2] Arkansas, *Reports of Cases at Law and in Equity Argued and Determined in the Supreme Court of Arkansas*, 24:165–77; *Arkansas State Gazette*, 14, 28 July; 11 August 1866; Batesville (AR) *North Arkansas Times*, 30 June 1866.

[3] *Arkansas State Gazette*, 1 September 1866; Arkansas, *Biennial Report of the Secretary of State* (1907–1908), 146–48.

[4] Arkansas, *Acts* (1866–1867)90–96, 171–72, 185,195–96,307–308, 319, 519.

[5] United States Congress, *Acts and Resolutions*, 39 Cong., 2 Sess., 60; Van Buren (AR) *Press*, 19 April 1867.

[6] John C. Palmer to Isaac Murphy, 26 November 1866, and Isaac Murphy to Andrew Johnson, 7 December 1866, both in the Presidential Papers of Andrew Johnson, Library of Congress.

[7] Mary Hindman to Andrew Johnson, 28 November 1866, and James H. O'Connor to Andrew Johnson, 28 November 1866, both in Amnesty Papers, NARA. An account of O'Connor's marriage to Laura Biscoe is in the Shreveport (LA) *Southwestern*, 29 July 1863.

[8] *Arkansas State Gazette*, 19 May; 17 September 1867.

[9] Ibid., 16 April 1867; James D. Richardson, ed., *A Compilation of the Messages and Papers of the Presidents, 1789–1897*, 53 Cong., 2 sess., House Miscellaneous Doc. No. 210 (Washington D. C.: Government Printing Office, 1907) 6: 552; United States, *Constitution*, Amend. XIV.

[10] Helena *Clarion*, 23 May 1867, reprinted in the *Arkansas State Gazette*, 4 June 1867.

[11] Helena *Clarion*, 23 May 1867, reprinted in the *Arkansas State Gazette*, 4 June 1867; *Arkansas State Gazette*, 23 July 1867.

[12] *Arkansas State Gazette*, 11 June 1867; Little Rock *Daily Republican*, 11 June 1867.

[13] *Arkansas State Gazette*, 11 June 1867.

[14] *Daily Republican*, 1, 16 July 1867.

[15] *Arkansas State Gazette*, 23 July 1867.

[16] Ibid.　　[17] Ibid.

[18] New York *Times*, 15 July 1867.

[19] Memphis *Daily Appeal*, 11 July 1867.

[20] Batesville *North Arkansas Times*, 19 October 1867; Van Buren *Press*, 13 December 1867.

[21] *Arkansas State Gazette*, 26 November 1867; Thomas S. Staples, *Reconstruction in Arkansas, 1862–1874* (New York: Columbia University, 1923) 177.

[22] Staples, *Reconstruction in Arkansas*, 241–42. Arkansas, Constitution (1868), Art. 8, Sec 5.

[23]Batesville *North Arkansas Times,* 1 February 1868; *Daily Republican,* 3 February 1868; James M. Hanks, Diary, 27 February 1868, quoted in Bobby L. Roberts, "Thomas Carmichael Hindman: Secessionist and Confederate General" (M. A. thesis, University of Arkansas, 1972) 158.

[24]Staples, *Reconstruction in Arkansas,* 253; *Daily Republican,* 13–14, 18, 25, 27 February 1868.

[25]*Daily Republican,* 16, 25–27 March 1868; House of Representatives, *Executive Documents,* 40 Cong., 2 sess. (Serial 1343, No. 278) 30, 32–33, 39–40.

[26]House of Representatives, *Executive Documents,* 40 Cong., 2 sess. (Serial 1343, No. 278) 4, 28–29. *Daily Republican,* 8 April 1868.

[27]*Arkansas State Gazette,* 5 April 1868; Helena *Clarion,* n.d., reprinted in the Memphis *Daily Avalanche,* 24 March 1868.

[28]*Arkansas State Gazette,* 12 April 1868; Memphis *Daily Avalanche,* 16 April 1868.

[29]United States vs. Thomas C. Hindman, vol. E, April 1867–October 1869, Cases 22, 225–26, United States District Court, Eastern District of Arkansas, Little Rock; *Arkansas State Gazette,* 14 April 1868.

[30]Dorris, *Pardon and Amnesty under Lincoln and Johnson,* 354–55.

[31]*Arkansas State Gazette,* 1 September 1868.

[32]Ibid.

[33]Batesville *North Arkansas Times,* 26 September 1868.

[34]*Daily Republican,* 1, 12 September 1868.

[35]*Arkansas State Gazette,* 14, 20 August 1868; Helena *Clarion,* n. d., reprinted in the *Arkansas State Gazette,* 19 August 1868.

Notes to Chapter 12

[1]*Arkansas State Gazette,* 29 September 1868; *Daily Republican,* 21, 30 April 1873.

[2]Charles Edward Nash, *Biographical Sketches of Gen. Pat Cleburne and Gen. T. C. Hindman Together with Humorous Anecdotes and Reminiscences of the Late Civil War* (Little Rock, AR: Tunnah & Pittard, Printers 1895; repr., Dayton, OH: Morningside Bookshop, 1977) 218; *Arkansas State Gazette,* 29 September 1868; Biscoe Hindman, "Thomas Carmichael Hindman," 103.

[3]Nash, *Biographical Sketches,* 218; Biscoe Hindman, "Thomas Carmichael Hindman," 103.

[4]Nash, *Biographical Sketches,* 218; Biscoe Hindman, "Thomas Carmichael Hindman," 103; Funeral Program of General Thomas C. Hindman, Thomas C.

Hindman Collection, Phillips County Museum.

[5]*Arkansas State Gazette,* 29 September 1868; *White River Journal,* n. d., reprinted in the *Daily Republican,* 2 October 1868.

[6]"Hindman's Grave," by E., Memphis *Avalanche,* n. d., reprinted in the *Arkansas State Gazette,* 28 October 1868.

[7]*Arkansas State Gazette,* 29 September 1868; *Arkansas State Gazette,* 25 October 1868; Helena (AR) *Clarion,* n. d., reprinted in the Van Buren (AR) *Press,* 16 October 1868; Memphis *Appeal,* n. d., reprinted in the *Arkansas State Gazette,* 4 October 1868.

[8]Van Buren *Press,* 9 October 1868.

[9]*Daily Republican,* 9 October 1868; Helena *Southern Shield,* n. d., reprinted in the *Daily Republican,* 17 October 1868.

[10]*Arkansas State Gazette* 20 October 1868. Clayton's proclamation first appeared in the *Daily Republican,* 17 October 1868. Memphis *Avalanche,* 3 November 1868, reprinted in the *Arkansas State Gazette,* 21 November 1868.

[11]Van Buren *Press,* 9 October 1868.

[12]*Arkansas State Gazette,* 1 December 1868. Writing in 1915, Powell Clayton repeated the Cameron Biscoe story and asserted that personal interviews with Helena residents supported it. Powell Clayton, *The Aftermath of the Civil War in Arkansas* (New York: The Neale Publishing Company, 1915) 94–96.

[13]*Arkansas State Gazette,* 23, 25 March 1869; 9 June 1870; 18 December 1966.

[14]*Daily Republican,* 8 July 1870; Helena *Monitor,* n. d., reprinted in the *Arkansas State Gazette,* 17 August 1870.

[15]Memphis *Daily Appeal,* 16 April 1873. Receiving advance notice of the contents of the mysterious letters, the *Daily Republican* announced that they demonstrated that politics had nothing to do the case and that the killing was caused by Hindman's "*amour . . .* with a lady in Georgia or Helena." *Daily Republican,* 4 April 1873. The *Gazette* also indicated that the letters suggested the killers desired to "avenge the ruin of a young lady by Hindman." *Arkansas State Gazette,* 15 April 1873.

[16]Memphis *Daily Appeal,* 20 April 1873.

[17]Ibid., 16, 20, 28 April 1873.   [18]Ibid., 20 April; 4 May 1873.

[19]Ibid., 24 April 1873; D. A. Linthicum to Dr. John H. Erskine, 21 April 1873, reprinted in the Memphis *Daily Appeal,* 23 April 1873; Sallie Puckett to D. A. Linthicum, 26 April 1873, and M. B. Hindman to Dr. R. A. Price, 29 April 1873, both reprinted in the Memphis *Daily Appeal,* 7 May 1873.

[20]Helena *Clarion,* n. d., reprinted in the *Arkansas State Gazette,* 19 September 1873; Helena *World,* n. d., reprinted in the *Arkansas State Gazette,* 5 February 1874.

[21]*Arkansas State Gazette,* 18 December 1966; Biscoe Hindman, "Thomas Carmichael Hindman," 103.

[22]Helena *World,* n. d., reprinted in the *Arkansas State Gazette,* 26 May 1885.

[23]Helena *Clarion,* n. d., reprinted in *Arkansas State Gazette,* 30 March 1870; *Arkansas State Gazette,* 26 May 1892.

Notes to Epilogue

[1]*The National Cyclopedia of American Biography,* 1967 ed., s. v. "Biscoe Hindman," 24:360; Memphis *Daily Appeal,* 28 April 1873.

[2]*Arkansas State Gazette,* 8 July; 24 August 1876; Phillips County Probate Record Book 5, 1874–1880, (Case 5–91), 304–305, AHC

[3]Phillips County, Abstract and Index of Deeds, 1857–1869, Book 2, 320, AHC; N. R. Book 2, 67, AHC; United States, Manuscript Census, Phillips County, Arkansas, 143.

[4]*Arkansas State Gazette,* 24 February 1877.

[5]Phillips County, Probate Records, 45:40, 114–16, Phillips County Courthouse.

[6]*Arkansas State Gazette,* 31 July 1879; *The National Cyclopedia of American Biography,* 24:360

[7]*The National Cyclopedia of American Biography,* 24:360; *Confederate Veteran,* 8:5 (May 1900): 205; Unidentified newspaper clipping from the scrapbook of Mrs. H. P. Coolidge, Maple Hill Cemetery Association, Helena, Arkansas.

[8]*Arkansas State Gazette,* 8 May 1885; New York *Times,* 2 November 1934; Hall, *Those Who Came Before Us,* 119–20; W. J. Lemke, "The Hindman Family Portraits," 106.

[9]Phillips County Circuit Court Record in Chancery, Book L, 103, 256–57, 361, 406, Phillips County Courthouse, Helena, Arkansas; *Arkansas State Gazette,* 19 January 1890.

[10]Unidentified newspaper clipping from the scrapbook of Mrs. H. P. Coolidge, Maple Hill Cemetery Association; "A Patriotic Bequest," *Confederate Veteran,* 40:9–10 (September–October 1932): 365; Pine Bluff (AR) *Daily Graphic,* 2 November 1934.

[11]Gertrude Mills to W. J. Lemke, 28 May 1956, W. J. Lemke Papers, UAL; Mrs. M. B. Pilcher, "U. D. C. Day at Monteagle," *Confederate Veteran* 15:8 (August 1907): 377; "Daughters of the Confederacy at Monteagle," *Confederate Veteran* 16:9 (September 1908): 474.

[12]Jefferson Davis to M. T. Sanders, 3 June 1887, reprinted in Hallum, *Biographical and Pictorial History of Arkansas*, 372–73.

INDEX